Scottish History

Scottish History

The Power of the Past

Edited by Edward J. Cowan and Richard J. Finlay

Edinburgh University Press

© Editorial matter and information
Edward J. Cowan and Richard J. Finlay, 2002
© The chapters their various authors, 2002

Edinburgh University Press Ltd
22 George Square, Edinburgh

Typeset in 11pt Ehrhardt
by Hewer Text Ltd, Edinburgh, and
printed and bound in Great Britain by
Antony Rowe Ltd, Chippenham, Wilts

A CIP record for this book is available from the British Library

ISBN 0 7486 1419 2 (hardback)
ISBN 0 7486 1420 6 (paperback)

Contents

3M SelfCheck™ System

Customer name: O'Keefe, Angela M

Title: Scottish history : the power of the past /
edited by Edward J. Cowan and Richard J.
Finlay.
ID: 30114011229914
Due: 13-02-18

Total items: 1
16/02/2018 21:01
Overdue: 0

Thank you for using the
3M SelfCheck™ System.

Contributors

David Allan
Lecturer in Scottish History, Department of Scottish History, University of St Andrews

Steve Boardman
Lecturer in Scottish History, Department of Scottish History, University of Edinburgh

Dauvit Broun
Senior Lecturer in Scottish History, Department of History, University of Glasgow

Edward J. Cowan
Professor of Scottish History, Department of History, University of Glasgow

Richard J. Finlay
Senior Lecturer in History, Department of History, University of Strathclyde

Colin Kidd
Reader in Scottish History, Department of History, University of Glasgow

Michael Lynch
Professor of Scottish History, Department of Scottish History, University of Edinburgh

David McCrone
Professor of Sociology, Department of Sociology, University of Edinburgh

Catriona M. M. Macdonald
Senior Lecturer in History, School of Social Sciences, Caledonian University

Roger A. Mason
Reader in Scottish History, Department of Scottish History, University of Strathclyde

Murray G. H. Pittock
Professor of English Literature, Department of English Studies, University of Strathclyde

Fiona Watson
Director of the Centre for Environmental History and Policy, University of Stirling

Introduction

Edward J. Cowan and Richard J. Finlay

W hen T. S. Eliot famously wrote of time present and time past as existing in time future, he failed to mention the equally intriguing conundrum of the present in the past, the way in which we approach history by reading our own contemporaneous values, obsessions and concerns into it. Too often, in what we flatter ourselves is the era of the post-modern, the past is pejoratively made present, or as others might say, relevant. Agathon wrote that 'even God cannot change the past' but historians alter it on a daily basis, though the presumption is based, it is to be hoped, upon frailty rather than any sense of numinous competitiveness. The central theme of this book is twofold: the investigation of the power of the past to confer legitimacy upon present thought or action, and to explore the ways in which previous generations rewrote, manufactured and manipulated history to suit their own present contingencies and preoccupations. Historians at all times, whether subconsciously or otherwise, to a greater or lesser extent, always create the past in their own image to the point that we can learn much about the attitudes of successive societies by examining how certain icons change over time. For example, the William Wallace commemorated in the Abbey Craig monument at Stirling bore very little relationship to the individual who was butchered at Smithfield. The historical Mary Queen of Scots is barely recognisable in a recent study of the Marian cult.[1] The Scot confronting the increasingly numerous studies on the Scottish Enlightenment of the eighteenth century often has the uneasy feeling of visiting confusingly alien territory.

[1] Jayne Elizabeth Lewis, *Mary Queen of Scots: Romance and Nation* (London and New York, 1998).

History has always been with us but as an academic discipline it is, historically speaking, a fairly recent phenomenon. For most of history, history as we now understand it did not exist, or rather, what was available was known to comparatively few since society at large depended mainly upon the oral, as opposed to the written, medium. The Enlightenment inspired the movement to reconstruct the past on the basis of the known facts and evidence. Scots were at the forefront of this process, which was one of rediscovery rather than of innovation, for its practitioners were inspired by the historians of the classical world.

During this period men such as Adam Smith and Adam Ferguson, to name but two, investigated conjectural history, which was broadly concerned with how humanity had reached its present state. In the absence of evidence for societies which existed in what would now be categorised as prehistory, writers relied upon conjecture, drawing upon comparative history or anthropology, which informed their concentration, not to say fixation, upon 'manners'.[2] Just as such an approach can be traced back to the 'Father of History', himself – Herodotus – so the Greeks also inspired an interest in political or narrative history, empirically rooted, as practised by such luminaries as David Hume and William Robertson. Ever since such enlightenment, which had been anticipated by sixteenth-century Scottish historians steeped in the classics,[3] the best history has combined the two primary senses of the Greek word 'history', namely enquiry and story. However, so far as eighteenth-century writers were concerned the former sense, the conjectural, was concerned with more distant times, and the story, the empirical, with more recent. As Gilbert Stuart put it in 1782:

> When we trace the connection between the present and the
> past and mark the openings of a scene in which we ourselves
> bear a part, a period of greater interest appears, and historical
> studies come home to mankind.

---

[2] H. M. Hopfl, 'From Savage to Scotsman: Conjectural History in the Scottish Enlightenment', *Journal of British Studies*, 17 (1978), 19–40. For some further discussion of these matters see Edward J. Cowan, 'The Invention of Celtic Scotland', in Edward J. Cowan and R. Andrew McDonald (eds), *Alba: Celtic Scotland in the Medieval Era* (East Linton, 2000), 13–18.

[3] Edward J. Cowan, 'The Discovery of the Gàidhealtachd in Sixteenth-Century Scotland', *Transactions of the Gaelic Society of Inverness*, lx, 1997–8 (2000), 259–84.

Until that era of self-involvement, he thought, people should read history as scholars but thereafter as citizens.[4]

Citizens, however, could be monarchical or republican, right or left in sympathy, so conditioning their views of the past. Subjectivity, always present, had now explicitly raised its ugly head. David Hume had considered the perusal of history 'a calm entertainment' but thought it would be no entertainment at all 'did not our hearts beat with correspondent movements to those which are described by the historian'.[5] That was precisely the trouble. How could one ensure that all heartbeats were in sync? Manifestly they were not, a circumstance which led to Hume and Robertson fallaciously agreeing that medieval history was largely a waste of time, a view not entirely unknown in present-day Scotland. But at the beginning of the twenty-first century we exist in a climate in which history equates with the defunct, in which historical amnesia is commended, and relentless harping upon the 'new' implies the irrelevance of the old. Or so politicians, apparently intent upon tearing up the past in order to control the future, would have us believe. This despite or because of the fact that a powerful sense of the historical has been essential to the survival of the Scottish nation.

If the methodology of history was firmly established on the basis of empiricism, its use and purpose have ever since been subject to a great many points of view. The past has been variably used as a pointer to the future, a means of moral instruction, a source of storytelling, a badge of identity, a legitimiser of the present, a source of tradition, a harbinger of superiority or grievance and a font of entertainment; it has been whatever its makers wanted it to be. It is this dichotomy of a methodology which is largely in keeping with the social sciences based on empiricism and a usage dictated by the predominantly subjective qualities of the humanities that makes the study of the past so intriguing. In recent years, however, the bedrock of empiricism has come under sustained attack from the citadel of post-modernism.

Put simply, it is claimed that the limits of empiricism are shaped by the fact that the selection of evidence is not an objective exercise, but one conditioned by human concerns, needs and assumptions. In other words, we decide on the basis of what is important to us what was

---

[4] Gilbert Stuart, *Critical Observations Concerning the Scottish Historians Hume, Stuart, and Robertson: Including an Idea of the Reign of Mary Queen of Scots, as a Portion of History etc* (London, 1782), 5.

[5] David Hume, *Enquiry Concerning the Principles of Morals*, 4 vols (London, 1751), iv, 2.

4 EDWARD J. COWAN AND RICHARD J. FINLAY

fundamental in the past and so a truly objective reading of history is not possible. History is a text which can be read in all sorts of different ways, none of which, it is claimed, has any special merit or intrinsic value over the other. Furthermore, the ways in which we look at things are subject to ideological, gender, social and cultural contamination. We do not observe in a neutral way, although we may flatter ourselves that we do so. The reality is that we all have our moral, social, gendered, ideological and political preconceptions which inevitably colour our judgement even when we try to be non-judgemental. Every historian has these, for want of a better word, prejudices, and all history is therefore suspect. It is always easier, apparently, to detect such flaws in the writings of earlier historians while blissfully ignoring our own. Our ability to deconstruct such prejudices helps us to understand better the context of the times in which history was written, but it should also alert us to the fact that just as previous historians have had their baggage, so, it follows, we must have ours.

The ways in which post-modernism has affected recent historical studies can be seen in the growth of subjects such as gender, sexuality, popular culture, the subordinate classes in general and indigenous peoples, famously distinguished as 'the people without history'. History is no longer about the winners and rulers. As society has become more pluralistic and democratic, so has its history. Women, minorities, the oppressed and the everyday have all, most belatedly, been accorded historical worth. All of which takes us back to empiricism.

One of the ways in which it is claimed that our understanding has been slanted or ideologically predisposed towards certain topics has been the nature of the historical record. If, as Sherlock Holmes argued, we proceed from the facts and nothing but the facts, then we have a problem in that the evidence bequeathed to us in the form of historical documents must contain those very same prejudices and assumptions that we have already mentioned. They can be deconstructed and the bias exposed, but the issue extends to the nature of the documentation itself. Society collects evidence as defined by the assumptions and biases of the powerful: topics which we find historically important or interesting today may not be catered for in the documentary collections of the past. It would be like trying to construct day-to-day life in Britain from the Cabinet memoranda of Tony Blair's government in 700 years' time. It is the clash between the expectations of the present and the realities of what is knowable in the past that presents historians with the post-modern conundrum. Can we really know what happened in history and are our readings of history simply texts which can be read in a multiplicity of ways? Do we any longer believe in historical truth?

There are advantages and disadvantages with this sceptical approach. Historians are well aware that meanings change through time and that each age has its own ideological and cultural assumptions. To quote Gilbert Stuart again:

> The enlarging experience of men is ever altering their manners: the present still improves on the past: and those customs and attachments which one age adopts, and pursues with pleasure, the next renounces, and avoids as oppressive and grievous. Constant alone in the changes they exhibit, men are ever furnishing the materials of those motley pictures which compose their history.[6]

Historians are also well aware of the pitfalls of using documentary evidence and though most would not classify themselves as post-modernists, they have for long been happily deconstructing material, all too conscious that what is not stated in a document may be just as crucial as what actually appears. Again, historians have long known that seeking out the silent voices in history requires an imaginative inter-rogation of the sources, or, as our American colleagues are wont to express it, a massaging of the evidence. Such interpretations can lead to radically different or novel conclusions and, the cynic might assert, have proved the life-blood of the profession, keeping historians in business. However, despite the animadversions of post-modernists, the demand-ing discipline of academic history aspires to integrity and scrupulousness that will enlighten and entertain present and future generations while honouring those of the past.

In the heyday of the great nineteenth-century German empiricist Leopold von Ranke it was believed that history involved nothing more than the accumulation of facts. In the minds of many then the bottle labelled 'Scotch' would one day be filled up, placed on the shelf and decanted as required: there would be nothing left to discover. Only in the last fifty years has Scottish historiography begun to emerge from the Rankean shade. When Hume Brown produced his influential three-volume *History of Scotland* in 1900 he began his 'traceable sequence of cause and effect' with Agricola but felt no need to elucidate his

---

[6] Gilbert Stuart, *An Historical Dissertation Concerning the Antiquity of the English Constitution* (London, 1770), 111.

philosophy of history, simply describing what he had evidence for, with a supposed 'objectivity' that remained the bane of Scottish historical investigation until well into the second half of the twentieth century. Diversity of opinion has, of course, greatly enriched the study of history world-wide, but the wheel has now come full circle, if revolving on a somewhat errant path.

Post-modernists agree that historical research requires evidence but point out that the latter is, by definition, incomplete and that, furthermore, the only possibility of knowing what actually happened is through personal experience (and perhaps not even then). One might counter that although most readers of this book hopefully will not have been tortured, they will have sufficient empathy and knowledge to dread the experience. This is one of the problems of post-modernism: it can offer new ways of thinking but can easily degenerate into a *reductio ad absurdam* situation in which nobody can know anything. A further problem lies in the notion that all views are equally efficacious, a validation of ignorance that confers the same intrinsical worth upon *Eastenders* as the works of Shakespeare. All readings can be contested, right enough, but it is hard to imagine a murderer, say, successfully appealing his conviction on the grounds that truth is an intellectual construct. This kind of argument does not work in the real world where we have to make value judgements based on the available evidence. That no method of historical investigation is perfect is no argument against striving to get as near as possible to a sense of what happened in the past and for doing so within an open and intellectually rigorous frame of reference.

This book has been informed by the debate about post-modernism,[7] but as may by now be imagined is not an endorsement of it. It is an examination of the ways in which history has been used in the past, and how it has been constantly reshaped and moulded to suit the needs of the present. In other words, it is a study of living history and of the way it affects the contemporary societies that sustain that history. While our generation is arguably subject to the same pressures as others, it may be easier to be objective about past societies than our own because the particular axes that were being ground then no longer have the same resonance. Rather than offering a historiographical study, this book aims to show the evolution of historical understanding in Scotland by

---

[7] For a stimulating discussion of post-modernism in a Scottish context see Catriona M. M. Macdonald, *The Radical Thread: Political Change in Scotland. Paisley Politics, 1885–1924* (East Linton, 2000), 2–13.

examining how past societies contemplated, exploited and were inspired by their own history. In other words, the historical relativism of the book is divorced from the present in that we attempt to see history from its own past perspectives, observing the flux of Scottish history in its own fluid terms, rather than simply picking out the 'bits' that seem important, or relevant, to us now. The approach shows that the purposes history has served in the past were often very different from our own. It offers insights into the concerns of previous generations and sheds light on their own understanding of themselves and their past. Finally, it demonstrates that the evolution of the understanding of Scottish history – as opposed to the development of Scottish historiography *per se*[8] – was far more complex than our Olympian twenty-first-century perspective might suggest. To understand this process it is necessary to examine the Scottish historical wheels within historical wheels.

The three contributions on medieval Scotland illustrate the remarkable, and perhaps to some surprising, degree to which the Scots manipulated their history, particularly during the crisis which plunged the country into the Wars of Independence. Dauvit Broun, who has recently done so much to unsettle widely held assumptions about medieval Scottish historiography, scrutinises the role of the unfortunate Picts, who were as much of an embarrassment to medieval historians as they have proved a 'problem' to their modern successors. When Scots were content to trace their origins to Ireland the Picts were useful as the objects of conquest, but by the later thirteenth century they had to be integrated into the proto-history of Scotland, a feat ultimately accomplished by John of Fordun using materials assembled a century before he wrote. Fiona Watson, who, like the fourteenth-century chronicler Fordun, has recently spearheaded a search for Scotland,[9] investigates the reputation of king John I showing how his defamation at the hands of English chroniclers was matched by their Scottish counterparts busily orchestrating the epiphany of Robert Bruce. Indeed, as Bruce's stature grew in the course of the nineteenth century that of Balliol suffered further traducement, though currently Dr Watson detects something of role reversal. Steve Boardman investigates the ways in which late

[8] The subject of Scottish historiography has been somewhat ignored of late. Two worthy exceptions which take very different approaches are Ian Donnachie and Christopher Whatley (eds), *The Manufacture of Scottish History* (Edinburgh, 1992) and William Ferguson, *The Identity of the Scottish Nation: An Historic Quest* (Edinburgh, 1998). See also '*Writing Scotland's History': Proceedings of the 1996 Edinburgh Conference. Scottish Historical Review*, 71 (April 1997).

[9] Gordon Menzies (ed.), *In Search of Scotland* (Edinburgh, 2001).

medieval Scottish chroniclers accommodated the *Brut* legends and the stories of Arthur. Both represented English imperialist propaganda and were, potentially at least, virulently anti-Scottish. But Scottish chroniclers confidently assimilated such material while with equal certitude they cannily traced the royal line of Scotland through St Margaret to the kingship of Edward the Confessor.

Michael Lynch once again radically questions certain well-entrenched assumptions deeply rooted in Scottish historical writing. In order to take Scottish historiography in exciting new directions it is necessary to break some long-existing moulds and that of the Reformation is indisputably worthy of the sledgehammer. Thanks to the exertions of Professor Lynch the target becomes smaller with each hammer-blow. Roger Mason looks at how in the sixteenth century a new historiography was developed embracing Gaelicism (hitherto distinguished as 'Highland barbarism'), Scotland's ancient constitution and novel ideas about early Scottish Christianity. Ted Cowan explores the covenanting tradition with particular reference to the 'Killing Times', a period which proved equally productive of mythologisation and antiquarian flytings. David Allan indicates the wonderful potential for inventiveness in the seventeenth-century manufacture of family history, something of a craze during the period. As he shows, the obsession was only in part a reflection of family pride for an equally important contributory factor was aristocratic neurosis. Colin Kidd offers an adventure in navel-gazing which metamorphoses into a scrutiny of ideas about the Picts over some three hundred years. He amply demonstrates that Pictomania has claimed many victims not only in Scotland but in modern Ulster. A rather different, though comparable, mania has driven the supporters of the Jacobite cult as described by Murray Pittock. Posterity has invented a bewildering array of uses for the Jacobites ranging from the inspirational to the downright bizarre.

Richard Finlay notes the curious absence of work on the monarchy by Scottish historians, as opposed to the shoals of books on the Jacobites. He clearly demonstrates the intimate relationship between the cult of Victoria and that in which the queen projected herself as the true heiress of the Scottish monarchy. Catriona Macdonald, while indicating the poverty of historicism, tenders an eloquent plea against the neglect of women in the Scottish Radical Tradition, neatly illustrating the dangers of reinvented, reconstructed history to suit modern sensitivities and expectations. Her somewhat unsettling conclusions are that women were ignored and marginalised, rather like the hapless Queen Caroline, in the course of the Victorian era and that their situation was not spectacularly improved for much of the following century either. David McCrone provides a sociologist's perspective on the endless dialogue between the past and the present, borrowing from the Parti Québécois the evocative title, 'Tomorrow's Ancestors'. It is of interest that the great sixteenth-century Scottish historian and thinker George Buchanan believed that the purpose of history was 'to restore us to our own ancestors and our own ancestors to us', but, though he lived in a post-classical era, he was spared the doubts of his post-modern descendants.

Throughout the centuries the tasks and goals of historians have not been all that dissimilar. The past has always had the power to inspire or disillusion but above all, honestly investigated, it fosters humility and understanding. Yesterday's ancestors inform us who hope in some small way to perform a similar service for those of tomorrow.

The editors are grateful to their distinguished contributors as they are to John Davey of Edinburgh University Press for his patience and encouragement.

CHAPTER I

The Picts' Place in the Kingship's Past Before John of Fordun

Dauvit Broun

W e are accustomed in modern scholarship to regard the Picts as part of Scotland's history, even if there is disagreement about what part should be attributed to them. Isabel Henderson, the most distinguished scholar of Pictish studies of her generation, has remarked that 'if we Scots like to think of ourselves as something distinct from an Irish colony then it is the spirit of tribes who went to make up the Picts that we must invoke'.[1] It may seem obvious, therefore, that any vision of Scotland as an anciently distinct and independent entity would naturally seek to give prominence to the Picts.

This is not, however, what is found in the earliest extant documents in which the kingdom's claim to an ancient freedom was proclaimed. The most prominent among these is the magnificently confident and cogent defence of Scotland's independence written by the Scottish procurators at the papal curia in 1301, led by Baldred Bisset. This text, known as Bisset's *Processus* or 'Pleading', was written in response to the case put to the papacy by Edward I to justify his overlordship over Scotland, in which Edward famously resorted to a somewhat partial account of the legend of Britain's primeval division among the sons of Brutus, including Albanactus, eponym of Albany (i.e. Scotland).[2] Alongside this

---

[1] I. Henderson, 'The problem of the Picts', in Gordon Menzies (ed.), *Who are the Scots?* (London, 1977), 51–65, at 65.

[2] The text survives in a dossier of documents attached to the so-called *Gesta Annalia*: on this dossier, see most recently Dauvit Broun, 'A New Look at *Gesta Annalia* Attributed to John of Fordun', in Barbara E. Crawford (ed.), *Church, Chronicle and Learning in Medieval and Early Renaissance Scotland* (Edinburgh, 1999), 9–30. The documents in the dossier were inserted piecemeal by Walter Bower into his *Scotichronicon*. Bisset's *Processus* can, therefore, be most /over

should be considered the text (or, rather, two closely related texts) known misleadingly to posterity as the 'Instructions'. These were once regarded (improbably) as versions of a single text in which the Scottish government relayed detailed instructions to its procurators at the Curia. They have now, however, been identified by Donald Watt as the Scottish procurators' initial responses to the English case, providing much of the raw material for the cogent eloquence of Bisset's 'Pleading'.[3] Watt has suggested therefore that these should properly be referred to as the 'Objections'. The significance of the 'Objections' is that it enables us to glimpse the Scottish procurators at work as they fashioned a case for Scottish independence that would be announced in the most important legal and political forum in Latin Christendom.

Because Edward I had brought the ancient past into play, the Scottish procurators were bound to articulate an opposite view of origins and early history which would justify Scotland's independence. On the face of it it might be expected that in both the 'Objections' and the 'Pleading' the

cont'd   readily consulted (with translation) in *Scotichronicon by Walter Bower in Latin and English*, vi (books xi and xii), ed. Norman F. Shead, Wendy B. Stevenson and D. E. R. Watt (Aberdeen, 1991) (hereafter *Chron. Bower* (Watt), vi), 168–89. A slightly different version is found in the dossier associated with Fordun's *Chronica*: see *Chron. Bower* (Watt), vi, 279–80. For the text of Edward I's letter to Pope Boniface VIII (7 May 1301), see *Anglo-Scottish Relations 1174–1328: Some Selected Documents*, ed. and trans. E. L. G. Stones (London, 1965), 96–109 (no. 30), esp. 97–8. For the background to this exchange, see G. W. S. Barrow, *Robert Bruce and the Community of the Realm of Scotland*, 3rd edn (Edinburgh, 1988), 115–19. The use of history by Edward I and the Scottish procurators at the Curia has been discussed in R. James Goldstein, *The Matter of Scotland: Historical Narrative in Medieval Scotland* (Lincoln, NE, 1993), 57–78, and in E. L. G. Stones, 'The Appeal to History in Anglo-Scottish Relations between 1291 and 1401: Part i', *Archives*, ix (1969), 11–21.

[3] *Chron. Bower* (Watt), vi, 134–69 (for text with translation), and 260–1 (for discussion; see also R. James Goldstein, 'The Scottish Mission to Boniface VIII in 1301: A Reconsideration of the Context of the *Instructiones* and *Processus*', *SHR*, lxx (1991), 1–15. The text in *Scotichronicon* is in places significantly different from the copy found in the dossier attached to *Gesta Annalia*; see *Chron. Bower* (Watt), vi, 262–3, where it is suggested that each represents a different draft, so that 'there never was a single original text' (for an example of one difference between the two versions, see Dauvit Broun, 'The Birth of Scottish History', *SHR*, lxxvi (1997) 4–22, at 16 n. 51). The two versions are laid out together in W. F. Skene, *Chronicles of the Picts, Chronicles of the Scots* (Edinburgh, 1867) [hereafter Skene, *Chron. Picts and Scots*], 232–71, although only one witness is used for the version in the dossier attached to *Gesta Annalia*, which has obvious drawbacks (see for instance *Chron. Bower* (Watt), vi, 276, note referring to pp. 161–3, ll.1–14).

Scottish procurators would have employed the Pictish past as unblushingly as Edward had used the British past, regardless of the subsequent conquests (real or imagined) of Picts by Scots and Britons by English. But this was not what the procurators decided apon. In the 'Objections' they argued that 'the most ancient people of the Scots' eventually arrived first in Argyll, which they claimed was named by a combination of the names 'Erc' and 'Gaedel', the son and husband of the eponymous Scota daughter of Pharoah.[4] This Erc is otherwise unheard of, and was presumably meant to be Erc father of Fergus, the earliest Scottish king who appeared in the king-lists[5] – the only 'Erc' accorded a significant role in Scottish historiography. The procurators announced that the Scots from Argyll then conquered Albany, so that the 'memory of its British people was banished, and the new name of Scotland with its people took the place of the same Albany'.[6] Only then are we introduced to the Picts, described as incomers with whom the Scots divided their country and made an alliance against the Britons.

In this account, then, the Picts, far from playing a central role, were something of a distraction. But this was only a draft. When this passage was rewritten in Bisset's 'Pleading' the Picts were summarily tidied up into a streamlined sequence of invasions. The Britons, we are told, were dispatched by the Picts, but the Picts were then overthrown by the Scots, led by no less a person than the eponymous Scota, who for the first time was portrayed as arriving in Scotland.[7] From ancient times, according to this, the Scots had possession of Scotland, without any sharing with the Picts, and long before the English arrived in Britain. It seems that the procurators had initially been unsure of what to do with the Picts, and that their final decision was guided by their determination that nothing was to be allowed to complicate the clarity of their case for the Scots' primordial claim to freedom. Their final version of Scottish history was to get the Scots on stage as swiftly and decisively as possible, and to minimise any association with anyone else, the Picts included.

---

[4] *Chron. Bower* (Watt), vi, 142 (text), 143 (trans.); Skene, *Chron. Picts and Scots*, 241–2.

[5] That is, in king-lists which were not combined with origin-legend material, where occasionally Fergus son of Ferchar replaced Fergus son of Erc as 'first king'; Dauvit Broun, *The Irish Identity of the Kingdom of the Scots in the Twelfth and Thirteenth Centuries* (Woodbridge, 1999), 104–5.

[6] *Chron. Bower* (Watt), vi, 142 (and n. *e*): *exulauit . . . memoria Britonum gentis sue, in eiusdem locum Albanie successit nomen nouum Scotis* [read *Scotie*] *cum gente sua*. Skene, *Chron. Picts and Scots*, 241 (text in bottom half), has the same, except ends *nouum nomen Scocie cum sua gente*.

[7] *Chron. Bower* (Watt), vi, 182; Broun, *Irish Identity*, 120.

Much the same strategy was later deployed in the Declaration of Arbroath, in which a sequence of conquests concluded with the Scots' destruction of the Picts.[8] The extra touch here was that it was claimed that a succession of 113 Scottish kings had reigned without the intrusion of any foreigner. It is clear that this impressive figure was arrived at only by the inclusion of Pictish kings in the tally.[9]

The Picts, then, were an inconvenience to Scottish lawyers and politicians alike in their efforts to project a pure and potent image of an ancient Scottish kingdom. Indeed, wherever the Picts appeared in these texts there was a desire to diminish their role and eventually write them out altogether. This is plain in the treatment of another dimension of the case prepared by Scottish procurators at the Curia in 1301: their claim that the Scots were Christian centuries before the English. In one version of the 'Objections' the procurators referred to the foundation-legend of St Andrews in which a King Hungus in the fourth century established a church there after winning a victory over the English due to St Andrew's intervention.[10] The procurators evidently made use (either directly or indirectly) of 'version B' of the foundation-legend, which was written sometime between 1144 and 1152.[11] It was made clear in the legend that Hungus was a Pictish king, and that it was the Picts who had won the famous victory with St Andrew's help. If the procurators were keen to distinguish Scots from Picts, then this story could be of no relevance as evidence for the early conversion of the Scots. In the 'Objections', therefore, they adopted the simple expedient of tacking on the Scots; the famous victory was therefore won by an army of 'Scots and Picts'. In the other extant version of the 'Objections', the battle was not mentioned; instead, it was stated less dramatically that the relics of St Andrew had miraculously been brought to Scotland at the time when 'Drust or Hurgust' ruled the Picts and Erc son of Eochaid, brother of 'Eugenius', ruled the Scots.[12] This was simply another

---

[8] Sir James Ferguson (ed.), *The Declaration of Arbroath* (Edinburgh, 1970), 9.
[9] Broun, 'The Birth of Scottish History', 13.
[10] *Chron. Bower* (Watt), vi, 148 (text), 149 (trans.).
[11] The edition in Skene, *Chron. Picts and Scots*, 183–93, will soon be superseded by a new edition of this text (with, for the first time, a translation) which is being prepared by Dr Simon Taylor of the St Andrews Scottish Studies Institute, University of St Andrews. For a date of 1144–53 see G. W. S. Barrow, *The Kingdom of the Scots* (London, 1973), 222 and n. 57 (although the appearance of Earl Henry without mention of his death could point to sometime in or earlier than 1152).
[12] Skene, *Chron. Picts and Scots*, 248 (the version in the dossier attached to *Gesta Annalia*). This passage is discussed further in Broun, 'The Birth of Scottish History', 15–20.

way of presenting the legend as something which concerned Scots as much
as Picts. In Bisset's 'Pleading', however, it will be recalled that such a
partnership between Scots and Picts was rejected, and a clean-cut sequence
of Picts followed by Scots was envisaged. To the credit of Bisset and his
team, they did not take the rewriting of the St Andrews foundation-legend
one step further and turn it into a story about the Scots alone. Instead they
jettisoned it completely, relying instead on some other source from which it
was calculated that no fewer than thirty-six Catholic kings of Scots had
reigned before the conversion of the English.[13] There was, however, one
attempt later in the fourteenth century to remove the Picts from the St
Andrews' foundation-legend; this was by a scribe in St Andrews itself who,
when he copied out the legend, began to substitute 'Scots' for 'Picts'. He
soon abandoned the effort, though, with the result that, after the afore-
mentioned victory over the English gained with St Andrew's help, the Picts
inexplicably appear instead of the Scots![14]

It may come as no surprise that lawyers and politicians took a robust
approach to the past. They were not engaged in writing history as such,
and their forays into distant times were as brief as they were bold. It is
one thing to put together a sentence or two in which the Picts are
propelled back in time by a millennium, or insist that Pictish kings were
actually Scots, or potentially remove nearly ninety generations from the
royal genealogy by claiming that Erc was son of Scota and Gaedel; it is
another thing to present such radical ideas within a detailed exposition
which will carry conviction. Nevertheless, a narrative of the Scottish
kingship which would have achieved the desired effect of emphasising

[13] See further Broun, 'The Birth of Scottish History', 21–2.

[14] Wolfenbüttel, Herzog August Bibliothek, Cod. Guelf. Helmstadiensis 1108, fos.
32v–35r (one of a group of manuscripts in that archive which were taken by
Marcus Wagner in 1553 from St Andrews priory and other Scottish monasteries:
*Copiale Prioratus Sanctiandree: The Letter-book of James Haldenstone Prior of St
Andrews (1418–1443)*, ed. James H. Baxter (Oxford, 1930), xiii–xxxi). On the
first occasion when 'Picts' are mentioned in the text (the beginning of the second
paragraph in Skene's edition: *Tunc temporis Hungus filius Forso magnus rex
Pictorum* . . .) the scribe wrote *Scotorum* above *Pictorum*; he then wrote 'Scots'
rather than 'Picts' on the next four occasions, but retained 'Picts' from the end
of the account of the victory of Hungus over the English (the end of the second
paragraph in Skene's edition). None of this is noted in Skene's edition (or in the
selection of variants listed in Marjorie Anderson, 'St Andrews before Alexander
I', in G. W. S. Barrow (ed.), *The Scottish Tradition: Essays in Honour of Ronald
Gordon Cant* (Edinburgh, 1974), 1–13, at 11–13), but is made clear in Taylor's
forthcoming edition. I am grateful to Dr Simon Taylor for allowing me to refer
to his edition.

the significance of the Scots at the expense of the Picts is not incon-
ceivable. The potential for this may be glimpsed in an extended poetic
treatment of Scottish history from origins to the present which was
written at approximately the same time as Bisset and his team were at
work (it can be dated to some time between Edward I's taking of the
Stone of Scone in 1296 and Robert I's seizure of the throne in 1306).[15]
Priority of settlement over the Picts was not simply asserted here, but
was given some sort of explanation to make it square with the disagree-
able fact that the Pictish king-list which was then available was very
much longer (in every respect) than that of the Scots before their alleged
annihilation of the Picts. It was stated in the poem that the Scots had
arrived in Scotland 265 years before the Picts, but that the Scots did not
have kings until very much later.[16] This was as bold as it was disin-
genuous, especially as the information about this pre-Pictish settlement
of Scots originated in a king-list – the same king-list that yielded the
Declaration of Arbroath's figure of 113 kings in unbroken succession.
We will meet this king-list (known to scholarship as β) in due course.

Why did Scottish writers and thinkers who obviously identified with
the cause of Scottish independence wish to downgrade the role of the
Picts in their history? The answer lies in another feature which they all
share. The poem written some time from 1296 to 1306, Bisset and his
team in 1301, and the Declaration of Arbroath in 1320 are the earliest
extant texts in which Scotland is portrayed as homeland of the Scots.[17]
Hitherto it appears that Ireland, rather than Scotland, was regarded as
the Scottish homeland.[18] Each of these texts attempted different ways of
promoting Scotland as the homeland. It was claimed that the Scots took
their name from *Scotia* when they first arrived from Ireland; or that the
eponymous Scota came to Scotland herself (carrying with her the Stone
of Scone); or that the Scots arrived *en masse* in Scotland, omitting
Ireland altogether. All these were innovations. The Scots' total conquest

[15] This was the original version of the first poem in Bower's *Liber Extrauagans*: for
edition and translation see Dauvit Broun and A. B. Scott, '*Liber Extrauagans*', in
Chron. Bower (Watt), ix, 54–127, at 66–84 (the title *Poema Scotica* given in
brackets has no manuscript authority), and for the dating, see ibid., at 55–7,
where it is also suggested that the poem may be dated more precisely to Feb.
1304–Mar. 1306.
[16] Ibid., 68–71.
[17] Broun, *Irish Identity*, 119–21, 124, 198. Other less pronounced portrayals of
Scotland as homeland are noted, ibid., 121; none date from earlier than the reign
of King John (1292–1304).
[18] Ibid., esp. 78–81, 117–19, 129; see also 110.

of the Picts in ancient times, or the claim that they were the original settlers of Scotland, ahead of the Picts, can readily be explained as further dimensions of this quest for presenting Scotland as the Scottish homeland. The Picts were clearly an obstacle to this primeval proprietorial association of Scots with Scotland.

The urge to compose Scottish history along these lines during the Wars of Independence is striking; it would not have needed the creative genius of Geoffrey of Monmouth to put together a cogent account of the kingdom's history from ancient beginnings which would have given substance to these claims. But no such narrative was written. When we turn to the earliest extant full-scale history of the Scots, John of Fordun's *Chronicle of the Scottish People* (written some time between 1371 and 1387), a rather different approach to the Picts is apparent.[19] Here the Picts and Scots arrive at approximately the same time.[20] The notion that the earliest kings of Scots pre-dated the Picts by a couple of centuries is mentioned, but is neatly accommodated with the idea that these peoples arrived in Scotland more or less simultaneously. The way this is achieved is by picking up on a reference in a regnal list to the first Pictish king as a judge;[21] this is elaborated by stating that, to begin with, the Picts did not have kings but judges, so that Scottish kings may have pre-dated Pictish *kings* but the Scots did not necessarily pre-date the arrival of the Pictish *people*. (Fordun, it should be explained, stated that there were at least forty Scottish kings before Fergus son of Erc, the earliest Scottish king mentioned in the king-lists.)[22] Fordun, moreover,

---

[19] *Johannis de Fordun Chronica Gentis Scotorum*, ed. W. F. Skene, Historians of Scotland vol. i (Edinburgh, 1871) (referred to hereafter as *Chron. Fordun*, i); *John of Fordun's Chronicle of the Scottish Nation*, trans. Felix J. H. Skene, ed. W. F. Skene, Historians of Scotland, vol. iv (Edinburgh, 1872) (hereafter *Chron. Fordun*, ii). Bower's copy of Fordun (in *Chron. Bower* (Watt), i–iii) may be the best witness of Fordun's work; see Broun, *Irish Identity*, 28–31. For a full discussion of the dating of Fordun's chronicle, see Broun, 'A New Look at *Gesta Annalia*'.

[20] For this and what follows, see *Chron. Fordun*, i, 25–9; ii, 25–7, 29–30; *Chron. Bower* (Watt), i, 68–75, 84–7. Some of this has been edited afresh in Broun, *Irish Identity*, 56–60.

[21] Cruithne (the first king) *clemens iudex accepit monarchiam*; M. O. Anderson, *Kings and Kingship in Early Scotland*, 2nd edn (Edinburgh, 1980), 265, 271; see also 279. See also *Chron. Fordun*, i, 152; *Chron. Bower* (Watt), ii, 298.

[22] *Chron. Fordun*, i, 88; ii, 79 (forty-five, rather than forty kings); *Chron. Bower* (Watt), ii, 6 (where the manuscript's *xl videlicet* is mistakenly reported as *xlv*: the mistake is easy to make if looking only at the microfilm). Bower may be the best witness for Fordun's chonicle; see Broun, *Irish Identity*, 28–31.

described the earliest Picts and Scots as intermarrying and intermingling, and (after the Scots had been banished from their midst by the Picts and occupied their own territory in the west) they formed a defensive alliance which kept them at peace (we are told) for five hundred years. The next half millennium saw various wars and alliances, including the expulsion of the Scots altogether for just over forty years. This brief period when the Picts alone held sway in Scotland coincided with the arrival of St Andrew's relics, which, it will be recalled, originally concerned the Picts alone.[23] It will also be recalled that unconvincing attempts were made to intrude the Scots into this important event in Scotland's past. In Fordun, however, St Andrew's relics are not associated with the conversion of the Scots. Moreover, the exile of the Scots would have accounted for their absence from the story, making it easier to leave the Picts centre stage and thus use the original legend without doing violence to it. The Scots soon return under Fergus son of Erc; and eventually the Picts are wiped out by the Scots led by Cinaed mac Ailpín.

In this lengthy exposition of Scoto-Pictish relations Fordun certainly shows more interest in the Scots than the Picts. The narrative after Fergus son of Erc, for instance, is focused on the reign of each Scottish king; Pictish kings, in contrast, are simply listed in a section ruminating on the annihilation of the Picts by Cinaed mac Ailpín. A chapter is devoted to the conversion of the Scots to Christianity in AD 203, but we are never told precisely how the Picts became Christian. What is clearly lacking in Fordun's account, however, is a compelling vision of Scotland as homeland of the Scots. This is all the more apparent in book I of Fordun's history, in which the history of the Scots up to their arrival in Scotland is tackled. Here Fordun evidently repeated a synthesis of different origin-legend accounts in which Ireland was emphatically identified as the Scottish homeland, something that Fordun has allowed to stand without comment.[24] Fordun's history has often been regarded as a work inspired by the struggle for independence against the English.[25] There are, indeed, dramatic passages where Scottish freedom

[23] The five hundred years of peace and its breakdown are described in book II (the figure of five hundred years of peace is stated in *Chron. Fordun*, i, 67; ii, 59; *Chron. Bower* (Watt), i, 264–5), which finishes with the expulsion of the Scots and the arrival of St Andrew's relics; book III begins with the return of the Scots, and book IV begins with the annihilation of the Picts.

[24] Broun, *Irish Identity*, 33–132.

[25] See most recently Bruce Webster, *Medieval Scotland: The Making of an Identity* (Basingstoke, 1997), 100.

is vividly proclaimed.[26] And there are other sections where a more academic and argumentative approach is deployed to the same end.[27] The narrative as a whole, however, seems rather conservative, both in its apparently uncritical repetition of material and in its failure to promote a vision of Scotland as the Scottish homeland. There can be little doubt that Fordun's chronicle would have been a disappointment to Baldred Bisset and his contemporaries. This is an important point to which I will return.

Viewed in this light, Fordun's chronicle is something of a puzzle. The puzzle may be appreciated more acutely if Fordun and the texts discussed so far are placed in a wider context by examining briefly how the Picts were dealt with by Scottish writers on the history of their kingship in the period before the 1290s. In this way a pattern of development emerges into which Bisset and his contemporaries, and also Fordun, may be seen to fit.

I have argued elsewhere that the kingship's authenticating antiquity in the twelfth and thirteenth centuries was chiefly portrayed as Irish, although not to the exclusion of other possibilities, notably through Margaret's English royal ancestors.[28] The potential of the Picts, however, was utilised only rather belatedly. The main text on the Picts which was available for use in writing on the kingship's past was the Pictish king-list. Two recensions survive; we can follow Molly Miller in referring to them as *Series Longior* and *Series Brevior*, that is, the 'Longer List' and the 'Shorter List'.[29] The 'Shorter List' was not, in fact, particularly short. It consisted of about sixty kings whose combined reign-lengths gave a total of more than 1,200 years. It would have been of particular relevance for a number of important churches (Abernethy, Dunkeld, and St Andrews) which were said in the text to have been founded by Pictish kings. It survives only in a group of Scottish king-lists (Marjorie Anderson's X-group), whose archetype is

[26] For example, the letter to Julius Caesar, *Chron. Fordun*, i, 47–8; ii, 44–5; *Chron. Bower* (Watt), i, 200–3.
[27] For example, the discussion of whether 'Britain' included Scotland, *Chron. Fordun*, i, 35–8; ii, 30–4; *Chron. Bower* (Watt), i, 168–77.
[28] Broun, *Irish Identity*, esp. 165–96.
[29] Molly Miller, 'Matriliny by Treaty: The Pictish Foundation-Legend', in D. Whitelock et al. (eds), *Ireland in Early Mediaeval Europe: Studies in Memory of Kathleen Hughes* (Cambridge, 1982), 133–61, at 159–61. Key manuscript-copies of these lists have been edited in Anderson, *Kings and Kingship*, 245–9 (*SL1*), 261–3 (a MS of *SL2*), and 265–6, 271–3, 279–81, 286–7 (MSS of *SB*).

known to scholarship as ξ. We will return to this later. The Longer List, for its part, consisted of more than one hundred kings. All complete surviving copies of *Series Longior* include an account of the foundation-legend of Abernethy. The archetype was probably created during the reign of Custantin mac Cinaeda (862–76), and was almost certainly transmitted through Abernethy in the second half of the eleventh century.[30] It was known to at least one scholar in Scotland in the early years of the thirteenth century.[31] There is one recension of the Longer List in which the succession of Pictish kings is taken without a break beyond Cinaed mac Ailpín to a king of Alba (Mael Coluim Cenn Mór, 1058–93). That particular list, the archetype of *Series Longior* 2, is likely to have been written as part of a scholarly assemblage of texts relating to the early history of Britain, rather than as a separate entity on its own.[32] Its bald presentation of a Scottish king as successor of Pictish kings may therefore have been inspired by the

[30] The core of *SL* gives names using what has been identified as Pictish orthography, but material has been added at the beginning deploying Gaelic orthography; Gaelic orthography is also used for names from Cinaed mac Ailpín. Custantin mac Cinaeda is preceded by 'and', suggesting that the list once terminated with him. (On all this see Anderson, *Kings and Kingship*, 78–9, 90, 101–2.) A *prima facie* case can be made, therefore, that the material at the beginning of *SL* which makes it the 'longer list' was added at the same occasion as the list was continued to Custantin mac Cinaeda (presumably during his reign). That the list once terminated with Custantin would account for figures for the total number of Pictish kings 'from Cathluan to Custantin' in Irish texts (see most recently Broun, *Irish Identity*, 168–9). All complete witnesses of *SL* include the Abernethy foundation-legend (and no other), which points firmly to some connection with Abernethy.

[31] The author of the compilation of historical pieces in the 'Poppleton MS', datable from 1202 to 1214: see below, n. 36.

[32] It is found at the end of one recension of *Lebor Bretnach*, a Gaelic translation and rewriting, probably in the mid-eleventh century, of the "Nennian" Recension of *Historia Brittonum* (which was itself probably not much older). Until recently the continuation of the Pictish king-list has been regarded as the work of an Irish historian (see, for example, Broun, *Irish Identity*, 168–9). Thomas Owen Clancy, however, has recently shown that *Lebor Bretnach* was written in Scotland: T. O. Clancy, 'Scotland, the "Nennian" Recension of the *Historia Brittonum*, and the *Lebor Bretnach*', in *Kings, Clerics and Chronicles in Scotland, 500–1297: Essays in Honour of Marjorie Ogilvie Anderson on the Occasion of her Ninetieth Birthday* (Dublin, 2000), 87–107. His line of argument makes it likely that the Pictish list was originally attached to *Lebor Bretnach* (as well as, probably, the summary of Bede's *Historia Ecclesiastica* which follows the Pictish list). I am grateful to Dr Clancy for giving me access to his work on this in advance of publication.

emphasis on Britain in the text or texts with which it was originally associated.

No other attempt to identify a reigning Scottish king as a direct successor of Pictish kings can be identified until the reign of Alexander II (1214–49). Many king-lists made no notable claim to antiquity for the kingdom. They began either with Mael Coluim Cenn Mór and St Margaret (who both died in 1093),[33] or more commonly with Cinaed mac Ailpín (who died in 858).[34] A special effort was made on one occasion during William I's reign (1165–1214) to construct a list beginning with Fergus son of Erc, first king in the Dál Riata regnal list, in which William's ancestry could be traced back to Fergus.[35] There was also the so-called 'Poppleton compilation' of Scottish historical pieces, datable to between 1202 and 1214, which included this list from Fergus son of Erc and also the Longer Pictish king-list.[36] In the compilation the reigning king, William I, appeared as the final king in the list beginning with Fergus son of Erc; it seems that William was regarded more as a direct successor of Fergus than as a successor of Pictish kings.

Then, in the reign of Alexander II (1214–49), the 'Shorter' Pictish list was incorporated into the list which began with Fergus son of Erc to create ξ, the archetype of Anderson's X-group of lists.[37] In this text the Scottish kings from Fergus to Alpin, father of Cinaed destroyer of the Picts, were recognised as ruling an area corresponding generally with Argyll, west of Drumalban, while the Picts ruled to the east of

---

[33] Inserted fo. 13 in the Chronicle of Melrose (1198–1214); see Anderson, *Kings and Kingship*, 75, and D. Broun, 'Contemporary perspectives on the succession of Alexander II: the evidence of king-lists', forthcoming.

[34] Broun, *Irish Identity*, 137–46, 155–60.

[35] Ibid., 146–53.

[36] Edited in Anderson, *Kings and Kingship*, 240–60. At 68 she suggested a date of between 1165 and 1184 for the original compilation, but a cogent case has been made for dating it to 1202x14: Miller, 'Matriliny by Treaty', esp. 138; D. Broun, 'The Seven Kingdoms in *De situ Albanie*: A Record of Pictish Political Geography or Imaginary Map of Ancient Alba?', in Edward J. Cowan and R. Andrew McDonald (eds), *Alba: Celtic Scotland in the Middle Ages* (East Linton, 2000), 24–42, at 26–7. Roger of Poppleton was the name of the person who, *c.* 1360, commissioned the manuscript in which the collection uniquely survives: see Julia C. Crick, *The Historia Regum Britannie of Geoffrey of Monmouth*, iii, *Summary Catalogue of the Manuscripts* (Cambridge, 1989), 256–61.

[37] For the X-group see Anderson, *Kings and Kingship*, 52–67 (edition of witnesses 264–92); Broun, *Irish Identity*, 133–7.

Drumalban.[38] The kings from Fergus to Alpin and the Pictish kings were not, however, arranged in parallel columns; a simple lay-out was used, with the kings from Fergus to Alpin given first followed by the Picts and then by Cinaed mac Ailpín and his successors.[39] It would not take too much ingenuity to misread or reinterpret this as a single series, rather than two parallel successions united from Cinaed mac Ailpín onwards. Such a reinterpretation duly occurred: the archetype of this 'reinterpreted' text, which may be as late as the 1290s, has been dubbed β.[40] As noted already, it was β which ultimately furnished the unbroken succession of more than a hundred kings in the Declaration of Arbroath, and the Scottish settlement more than 265 years before the Picts in the poem written some time from 1296 to 1306. This list was not, however, taken directly from ξ. The material in ξ had earlier been brought together with two accounts of Scottish origins to form a text which can be traced in Fordun's chronicle and elsewhere. The archetype of this origin-legend-plus-king-list text has been dubbed α.[41] It was the king-list in this text which was reinterpreted as a single succession by the author of β.

The use of the Pictish past in ξ, therefore, was something of a novelty

---

[38] Lists D, E, F, I include a statement of the bounds of the kingdom ruled by Fergus mac Eirc. List I reads *ultra Drumalban usque Stuagmuner et usque Inscegall* (Anderson, *Kings and Kingship*, 281), and lists D and F similarly (ibid., 264, 270): it has become distorted in lists K and N (ibid., 286, 290) and adapted in list E (ibid., 253). *Stuagmuner* is not immediately identifiable (see ibid., 270 n. 54), but if the minims are reanalysed, it can be read *Stuaginnuer*, i.e. *Túag Inbir*, the mouth of the River Bann, the western border of Dál Riata in Ireland (*túag*, 'inlet of the sea', also appears as *stúag*: see *DIL* Concise edn, *s.v. túag*[1]). (For *Túag Inbir*, see Edmund Hogan, *Onomasticon Goedelicum* (Dublin, 1910), 648.) In List E this has been replaced by *ad mare Hibernie* (probably by the author of η). It was almost certainly present in ρ, and may thus have been inherited from the exemplar of its Dál Riata king-list which terminated with Fergus mac Echdach (d. 781). It was understood in ξ and α that kings of Picts and kings of Dál Riata were contemporaries (see Broun, *Irish Identity*, 107–9), in which case the Picts would have been located *citra Drumalban*, on the east side of Drumalban.

[39] The Pictish list, however, precedes the Dál Riata list in List I: there is a formal possibility that this was also the arrangement in ξ (Broun, 'The Birth of Scottish History', 12 n. 36). The exemplar of List I, however, was written by someone who made a number of innovations to the text of ξ (Anderson, *Kings and Kingship*, 62–3; Broun, *Irish Identity*, 136).

[40] Broun, *Irish Identity*, 133–7, 106–9, 198–200.

[41] The extant text nearest to this in form was incorporated by Sir Thomas Grey into his *Scalacronica* (written in the 1360s), which is in French: Broun, *Irish Identity*, 84–95, 109.

in the early thirteenth century; there is no evidence that David I and his grandsons, Mael Coluim and William, were ever explicitly presented as the successors of Pictish kings. The author of ξ may have been trying to say something new about the kingdom, giving more emphasis to the king as *rex Scocie* by presenting Alexander II as successor of earlier kingships which between them ruled an area corresponding to Scotland north of the Forth and Clyde – what might be described as 'greater Scotland' as this was generally understood at least until the early thirteenth century.[42] This greater territorial emphasis can also be seen when, in the account of events in 1216 given in the Chronicle of Melrose, 'Scotland' was used for the kingdom as a whole for the first time in the chronicle.[43] This, indeed, is the first extant occasion when someone writing within the kingdom's bounds used 'Scotland' in this way; hitherto there was significant ambiguity about what 'Scotland' signified territorially.[44] The kingdom was becoming a single country in the minds of (some) of its inhabitants, rather than a realm comprising a number of countries of which 'Scotland' was only one (albeit the core country). Although the author of ξ may have had an older idea of 'Scotland' in his mind, he apparently shared this heightened sense of the kingdom as a country.[45]

The Melrose chroniclers during Alexander II's reign may have considered themselves to be part of Scotland, but they did not yet regard themselves as Scots (and may not have done so until as late as 1285–91).[46] It is not so surprising, therefore, that no historian yet portrayed Scotland as the homeland of the Scots. For example, the vision of Ireland as the Scottish homeland was vividly expressed in a reworking of the origin-legend material in α (which I have dubbed the 'Éber' account).[47] Bisset's 'Pleading' (1301), the poem of 1296x1306,

[42] D. Broun, 'Defining Scotland and the Scots before the Wars of Independence', in Dauvit Broun, Richard J. Finlay, and Michael Lynch (eds), *Image and Identity: The Making and Re-making of Scotland through the Ages* (Edinburgh, 1998), 4–17, at 6.

[43] Ibid., n.3.

[44] Ibid., 6–7.

[45] Argyll and Pictland do not add up to Scotland, of course: the biggest gap is the kingdom of Dumbarton (later Strathclyde). Welsh king-lists, however, never seem to have existed (see D. N. Dumville, 'Kingship, Genealogies, and Regnal Lists', in P. H. Sawyer and I. N. Wood (eds), *Early Medieval Kingship* (Leeds, 1977), 72–104, at 96–7), so presumably no Strathclyde list (or the like) would have been available.

[46] Broun, 'Defining Scotland and the Scots', nn. 15, 24. These references to a wider sense of who were Scots relate to the mid-1260s, but cannot be shown to have been written earlier than 1285x91.

[47] Broun, *Irish Identity*, 74–7, 115–18.

and the Declaration of Arbroath (1320), can therefore be seen as standing at the end of a process in which a greater emphasis on the kingdom as a territory led to the portrayal of Scotland as homeland of the Scots. Before that final stage was reached there was apparently no difficulty in presenting the Picts as ruling part of Scotland alongside the earliest Scots. But as soon as the Scots ceased to be regarded as an Irish off-shoot, and Scotland itself was deemed to be their original homeland, there was no longer any room for sharing territory with the Picts. The only way the existence of Picts up to the ninth century was to be admitted was by asserting the prior settlement of Scotland by the Scots. The alternative was to project the Scottish conquest of the Picts back into the deepest past.

Before considering how Fordun fits into this scheme, it must be emphasised that the lineal development outlined above represents a progression from one innovation to the next. Each innovation would not, however, have heralded the complete abandonment of older versions of the kingdom's past. We should at least expect some overlap resulting from differences of opinion, if not simply time-lag. This is a particular problem when considering the date of β, whose distinguishing feature was the reinterpretation of the king-list as a single succession of more than one hundred kings. This change, at a stroke, tidied away the parallel Pictish and Scottish kingdoms. Implicitly the king-list in β related to a unitary kingdom over which the Scots explicitly had ruled first. Considered on its own this might perhaps be regarded as initially the unwitting creation of a careless copyist. Within a wider context, however, it appears more as an ingenious (if crude) attempt to express in terms of the past a new sense of Scotland as homeland of the Scots. Unfortunately the date-limits for this seminal work are no earlier than 1214 and no later than 1301. The only way to hone this down is to note that the first detectable instances of its being copied are in the reign of King John (1292–1304), while the latest example of the older arrangement, pioneered in ξ, being kept up-to-date is c.1290. I have suggested elsewhere, therefore, that 'the most likely period when β was written, or at least gained currency, would have been the 1290s'.[48] But a date for β itself in the 1280s, or even earlier, can hardly be ruled out.

Turning now to Fordun, a purely schematic view of where his history fits in would suggest quite clearly that it was before the vision of Scotland as homeland of the Scots, in various forms, became current in the reign of King John (1292–1304). The narrative of Scoto-Pictish

[48] Ibid., 198.

relations recounted by Fordun has, in fact, been carefully crafted so as to emphasis Scotland's territorial integrity. The initial union of Scots and Picts, through more or less simultaneous settlement, intermarriage and intermingling, dissolves only gradually, first into their separation into distinct peoples who share five hundred years of friendship, and then into five hundred years of intermittent warfare, until Scotland is again united when the Scots finally destroy the Picts. What we read in Fordun's chronicle as far as the beginning of book IV, then, is a narrative created by weaving together the history of the Scots and the history of Scotland. It has not been written as if the histories of Scotland and the Scots are indistinguishable. It is this, then, which differentiates Fordun from what seems to have been the norm in much smaller scale attempts in King John's reign to write the kingdom's past.

Fordun's chronicle, then, looks at first sight like a fully developed statement of an idea first expressed historiographically by the author of king-list ξ. It appears, moreover, that the radical departure of β was known and deftly integrated within the chronicle's vision of primeval Scoto-Pictish harmony. How are we to explain this? We know that Fordun lived in the 1370s and 1380s, not the 1270s and 1280s. Is it that Fordun, the first person to attempt a full-scale Scottish history, considered that the more ambitious vision of Bisset's 'Pleading' and the Declaration of Arbroath could not be sustained from the material he had to work with? Or did Fordun simply disagree with this view?

The most surprising explanation, however, would be that in Fordun's chronicle we are, indeed, reading a story which took shape in the 1270s and 1280s. On its own the treatment of the Picts in Fordun is hardly enough to support such a proposition. There are other indications, though, that Fordun inherited the narrative structure of his chronicle from a work which was written about a century earlier. These have been discussed in detail elsewhere, and will only be summarised here.

The most important evidence is the material known as *Gesta Annalia* which follows Fordun's chronicle in some of the manuscripts of his work. *Gesta Annalia* has been regarded as Fordun's drafts for book V, the incomplete book VI, and a projected book VII of his chronicle. There is little doubt, however, that *Gesta Annalia* was not written by Fordun.[49] It is, in fact, part of a history of Scottish kings finishing in 1285 which has been interpolated or otherwise enhanced sometime after 1320 by someone with a particular interest in the Wars of Independence, who has also added a dossier of documents relating to this issue; this

[49] Broun, 'A new look at *Gesta Annalia*'.

chronicle-plus-dossier has subsequently been updated by a rather disjointed account of events from 1285 to 1363 taken from a history of sorts written in or near St Andrews. There is internal evidence which suggests that the material finishing in 1285 ceased to be written some-time between 9 February and mid–April 1285. It was evidently once part of a larger work in six books, of which almost all the first four books and some of the fifth are missing. It cannot be assumed, on present knowledge, however, that this full-scale treatment of Scottish history, largely lost, was necessarily written in the early 1280s, but it is likely at least that it was in existence by then. It appears that Fordun used *Gesta Annalia* as a source after the addition of the dossier of documents. He would therefore have seen this larger work. In fact, nearly all book V (after Chapter 9) and the incomplete book VI of his chronicle have been taken by him from *Gesta Annalia* and Aelred's eulogy of David I which came to be attached to the dossier of documents. He has reorganised this material and changed the wording slightly, but the narrative substance is largely the same. There is a *prima facie* case, then, that the rest of his chronicle represents a similar treatment of the lost books of the substantial historical work likely to have been in existence by 1285 at the latest.

This can be supported by some detail. There are a number of places where *Gesta Annalia* shows knowledge of key elements in the narrative structure of Fordun's chronicle – Eochaid 'Rothay', leader of the first Scottish settlers in the Hebrides; Eochaid's great-grandfather Simón Brecc; Fergus son of Ferchar, first king of Scots in Scotland; the idea that Fergus' father was also called Feredach; and Éber Scot, whose description as the 'first Scot' is presumably a reference to his role as leader of the first Scots to settle in Ireland. All of this can be found in Fordun's chronicle; many of these details, moreover, are distinctive innovations.[50]

This is not all. There is one place where we can definitely catch a glimpse of what Fordun himself thought about the Picts' role in the kingship's past. In *Gesta Annalia*, during an account of Scone's founda-tion as an Augustinian priory, we are told that Scone was 'where ancient kings, from Cruithne first king of Picts, established the seat of the kingdom of Alba'.[51] When Fordun took this account of Scone's founda-

---

[50] Broun, 'The Origin of the Stone of Scone as a National Icon', in T. O. Clancy et al. (eds), *The Stone of Scone* (Edinburgh, forthcoming).

[51] *ubi antiqui reges, Cruthne primo Pictorum rege, sedem regni Albanie constituerant*; *Chron. Fordun*, i, 430.

tion in book V of his chronicle he rephrased this passage: Scone, he said, was the place 'where kings from ancient times, both Picts and Scots, established the chief seat of the kingdom'.[52] The Scots have been intruded in a way reminiscent of how the Scottish procurators at the Curia in 1301 contemplated muscling the Scots into the account of St Andrews' foundation. Fordun's statement, moreover, is inconsistent with the idea that the Scottish and Pictish kingdoms were territorially distinct (remembering that the Picts did not have kings, according to the chronicle, until after the Scots had separated from the Picts and established a succession of kings from Fergus son of Ferchar). In contrast, the statement in *Gesta Annalia* that Scone was established as chief seat of the kingdom by the first king of the Picts is entirely consistent with the chronicle's narrative. This would not be the only occasion in which statements definitely made by Fordun are out of kilter with basic features of the chronicle's narrative. A glaring instance is during the account of David I's genealogy, which Fordun acquired from Walter Wardlaw, bishop of Glasgow, where an ancestor of Simón Brecc is identified as the first Scot to settle the Hebrides, despite the fact that (according to the chronicle) Simón Brecc's ancestors were meant to be still in Spain in anticipation of Simón's taking of Ireland.[53]

When we read Fordun's chronicle, then, we must take very seriously the possibility that the narrative (but not necessarily each and every word) was written no later than 1285. To be more certain about this would require a thorough investigation of how *Gesta Annalia* was composed. This cannot properly be undertaken without a new edition of the text and the publication of a key source, the historical materials associated with the Life of Margaret which survive uniquely in a Dunfermline manuscript recently identified in Madrid.[54] Some explanation, moreover, can be given to why this 'proto-*Chronica*' apparently attracted little attention until John of Fordun rescued it from possible oblivion. I have argued elsewhere that Bisset and his team at the Curia in 1301 knew of this lost history.[55] They did not, however, base their case on it, presumably because it did not meet their expectations of what early Scottish history should look like. If Bisset's vision of Scotland as the Scottish homeland was typical during the Wars of Independence,

---

[52] *quo reges antiquitus tam Scoti quam Picti sedem regni primam constituerunt*; Chron. Fordun, i, 227; ii, 208; *Chron. Bower* (Watt), iii, 106–7.

[53] Broun, *Irish Identity*, 73, for discussion.

[54] *Chron. Bower* (Watt), iii, xvii–xviii; Broun, *Irish Identity*, 196.

[55] Broun, 'The Birth of Scottish History', 15–21.

then the apparent neglect of this great work would not be so surprising. Why, then, did Fordun give it new life? And why did Bower, whose patriotic zeal burns throughout so much of his own prose, make Fordun's chronicle the foundation of his own *magnum opus*? The real issue here, I suspect, is the extent to which the first great narrative of a kingdom's past, furnishing it with a continuous account of its history deep into early times, dictated the way that a kingdom's history was told thereafter.

This paper was given to the Scottish History Research Seminar, Edinburgh University, 4 November 1999. I am grateful to Dr Steve Boardman for the invitation to give the paper, and to those present for discussion. Its scope is much more limited than the paper that was originally delivered as part of the Glasgow–Strathclyde seminar series. I would also like to thank Dr Nerys Ann Jones for her unfailing support and encouragement.

CHAPTER 2

The Demonisation of King John

Fiona Watson

A t first glance, King John Balliol, the man on the Scottish throne at the beginning of the wars between Scotland and England in 1296, seems a poor historiographical subject, for the simple reason that one generally assumes that history is unanimous in its opinion of him: he was useless. Indeed, his general hopelessness has been so taken for granted that there has not yet been a coherent study of the man and his kingship, though histories of the period as a whole cannot avoid his reign en route to the far more satisfactory prospect of an analysis of that of King Robert Bruce. Such a situation is revealing in itself: it is accepted that Balliol is an irrelevancy, an interruption to the main story; even in recent historiographical times, when historians are trained to assume nothing, it has still been supposed that this 700-year-old presumption of in-competence in an overwhelming body of historical material must be more or less right.

But suspicions are growing. To some extent, this is a product of increasing scepticism about the reputation of Robert Bruce, which historians in the last thirty years, but particularly in the last ten, have finally begun to discuss seriously, though this has tended to be in huddled corners of conferences rather than in print.[1] The admission of the possibility that the mighty propaganda machine which explicitly

---

[1] With the exception of Michael Penman's article on the de Soules conspiracy and an article by Grant Simpson, who has certainly always questioned the perceived wisdom on the Balliol family up to the point when John became king. M. Penman, 'A fell coniuracioun agayn Robert the douchty king': the Soules conspiracy of 1318–1320, in *Innes Review*, vol. 1, no.1 (1999), 25–57; G. Stell, 'The Balliol Family and the Great Cause of 1291–2', in K. Stringer (ed.), *Essays on the Scottish Nobility* (Edinburgh, 1985), 150–5.

defended the honour, rightful royal claim and sovereign status of Scotland's hero-king might have had a profound effect on the writing of the history of Bruce's reign is now finding a more general acceptance, even if the implications of this have not yet been fully explored; it therefore follows that the period prior to Bruce's seizure of the throne in 1306 has been at least as affected by the need for the usurper king to explain away the tawdry events of his early career and how he came to be on the throne at all.

But this chapter is emphatically not about Robert Bruce, though his family certainly features. If one looks at how King John has been written about from his own times until now, the first thing that one notices is that though there is certainly a veneer of uniformity of opinion about him, this breaks down fairly quickly in the detail given for specific events. There can be little doubt that, for the Scottish chroniclers writing in the first 150 years or so after 1296, there was a party line to be explicitly toed – the Bruce claim was the best one and Balliol should not have been king because of that, and also because of his weak character; however, the writers' own information or opinion often cannot seem to help but contradict that line in specific points. Of course, as time passes, what has been written previously becomes accepted fact and later writers merely repeat it, though, as will be obvious from the rest of this book, no-one tells the story in exactly the same way and these differences – the slightly varying interpretations and emphases – reveal the particular outlook of a writer and his age.[2]

I would, however, claim that King John is a more difficult subject than usual to analyse in this way, for the simple reason, mentioned above, that it is usually done against the yardstick of what the current writer (i.e. me) believes to have happened. The lack of any coherent assessment of King John's reign for its own sake is thus a considerable handicap in judging what motivated the earliest chroniclers in particular to write what they did if this differed from actual events. This is most crucial in relation to the assertion – made first by contemporary English chroniclers – that King John was stripped of his executive power by the Scottish nobility and reduced to an imprisoned figurehead. Indeed, it was the English chronicler Rishanger who provided John with one of his epithets denoting intrinsic weakness, describing him as a lamb among wolves. This issue will be discussed in more detail below, but it is important to note that I myself am reasonably convinced that John was

[2] All the historians discussed in this particular article, with the obvious exception of myself, have been male.

not removed from power, or, at least, that what happened in a parliament of 1295 was not as described by the English chroniclers. Unfortunately it is as yet rather harder to produce a good theory as to why they should assert such a thing if it was not true; however, the more important point is that this image of an emasculated king, at the mercy of his nobility, is crucial to our perception of Balliol.

One of the great difficulties for the writing of Scottish history is the general lack of contemporary evidence from Scotland itself. Up till very recently it was, in fact, assumed that the first Scottish commentator on the period was John Barbour, who wrote his great eulogy on Robert Bruce and James Douglas some fifty to sixty years after the events described – in other words, at least two generations later. However, the recent work of Dauvit Broun has shown that later chroniclers, including the extremely influential John of Fordun, appear to have copied into their own work extracts from earlier lost sources. We should remember, of course, that plagiarism – the transference of more-or-less verbatim text from another source to your own work without acknowledgement – is now regarded with complete horror, but in earlier periods it was accepted as normal procedure, a part of the historical process. The modern historian must therefore appreciate the degree of layering in terms of authorship which typifies medieval chronicles and which can reveal a hidden history that the official line was designed to obscure. Specifically, in relation to King John, this might mean that contradictions in the text were perhaps a result of the author having copied from, or being influenced by, earlier lost writers who maintained a pro-Balliol, or politically neutral, bias that has been otherwise expunged from the historical record by the Bruces and their successors, the Stewarts.

Nevertheless, the history of this period is unusually dependent for its early historiography on English sources. These chroniclers – Langtoft, Lanercost, *Flores Historiarum*, Rishanger,[3] for example – are reasonably consistent in their descriptions of the important event mentioned above: in 1295 King John was replaced by a Council of Twelve who negotiated

---

[3] *The Chronicle of Pierre de* Langtoft, ed. T. Wright, Rolls Series (London, 1866); *Chronicon de Lanercost, 1201–1346*, ed. J. Stevenson (Maitland Club, 1839); *Flores Historiarum*, ed. H. R. Luard, Rolls Series (London, 1890); *Willelmi Rishanger, Chronica et Annales*, ed. H. T. Riley, Rolls Series (London, 1865); on *Flores Historiarum* originally compiled by Mathew Paris; see Antonia Gransden, *Historical Writing in England c.550–c.1307* (London, 1974), 357 note and 377 note.

a treaty with England's greatest enemy, France. However, they are by no means completely in agreement as to the details. Langtoft and *Flores*, for example, state that the twelve were responsible for the negotiation of the treaty with France, not the government of Scotland, although *Flores* does say explicitly that government was taken out of John's hands. In fact, the Scottish deputation consisted of only four members: the bishops of St Andrews and Dunkeld, Sir John Soules and Sir Ingram d'Umfraville. However, there can be little doubt that the parliament held at Stirling in July 1295 to set the negotiations with France in motion was very concerned to ensure that this move, which was tantamount to a declaration of war on England, was supported by a wider constituency. Thus the twelve could be seen as those Scottish notables who signed the final treaty,[4] which was also, most unusually, attested by representatives of the leading burghs who would certainly suffer in a war situation. It does not automatically follow, however, that this unusual consultation was a reflection of the king's own incapacity; it merely made prudent good sense.

That these English chroniclers often note that the Council of Twelve was modelled on French practice is surely also significant. The English would not have rated the Scots as much of an enemy – they were perhaps only marginally more significant than the Welsh; but the French were a different matter. Langtoft, for example, sees this quite straightforwardly as a conspiracy 'to destroy England from Tweed to Kent' in a joint Franco-Scottish venture, something that would have been laughable if the Scots were on their own. It is also important to note, as Professor Barrow certainly does,[5] that the removal of a monarch from active power was something the Scots had never done before; but the English certainly had, the last time being only forty years previously, and they seriously considered such a move against Edward I only two years later. Perhaps the Scottish nobility were finally catching up with the restrictive tendencies exhibited by their peers elsewhere in Europe; or perhaps the English commentators were trying to make sense – given the vague and disquieting rumours coming out of Scotland in the months leading up to the outbreak of war – of a situation wherein a man who was essentially one of their own, Sir John Balliol of Barnard Castle, was seen, from their point of view, to be biting the hand that had placed him on the throne. The real enemy, for the English chroniclers, was the Scottish nobility, portrayed as an almost anarchic body of impudent ingrates

[4] See Barrow, *Robert Bruce*, 3rd edn (Edinburgh, 1988), 65.
[5] Ibid., 64.

(Langtoft calls them 'mad'!); but the result of this divorce of responsibility, wherein the 'dishonest councillors' got the blame, has had the
effect of presenting King John as fundamentally weak and ineffectual.

Well, was he? It is not within the remit of this discussion to answer
that question in relation to the historical Balliol, but rather to examine
how subsequent Scottish writers have dealt with this issue in particular,
and King John's character and actions as a whole. Nevertheless, it
should be noted that it has taken seven hundred years for this question to
be specifically asked.

Though John Barbour and John of Fordun are the first identifiable
Scottish authors to write about the wars with England, the Scots – or at
least, those in government employ – had been busy rewriting their
history long before the 1360s and 1370s. King Robert certainly had to
work hard to explain not only to the people of Scotland how he had come
to be on the throne, but to other European leaders as well. In 1309 he
and his advisers found it politic to have the top clergy of Scotland write
to the pope, who was known to be inviting the great and the good of
Europe to a meeting at Vienne. Unfortunately, King Robert had not yet
received his invitation and there was a gnawing suspicion that King
John, who had been given some degree of papal support for his
restoration as king of Scots at the beginning of the decade and was
currently resident on his family lands in Picardy, might well have got
one instead. To tackle this eventuality head on, a parliament at St
Andrews in March 1309 agreed to the first of many pro-Bruce versions
of what had happened from 1291 onwards: this so-called Declaration of
the Clergy provides us with 'a clear enunciation of the belief that Balliol
had been made king of Scotland by Edward I *de facto* in defiance of a
universal belief among the Scottish people that Robert Bruce had a
better title', together with 'the earliest appearance of the powerful myth
that John Balliol was merely an English puppet'.[6] So, we have already
noted the accusation made by English sources that King John was a
Scottish puppet; now we have the Scottish corollary – that Balliol was
subject to *English* control – together with the first reworking of the Great
Cause[7] in Bruce's favour.

But King John should perhaps have counted himself lucky that he got
a mention in the 1309 Declaration, because he had been completely
written out of official Scottish history by the time of the more famous

---

[6] Ibid., 184.

[7] The process whereby a new king was chosen after the death of Alexander III
and his heir, the Maid of Norway.

Declaration of 1320. In the intervening period it had suited Bruce to ignore his predecessor altogether, in order to portray himself as the true and actual heir of Alexander III (a view of himself he often liked to employ in official documentation).[8] There was a specific need in 1309 to deny Balliol's credentials as king, but subsequently it was better to ignore him. In 1321 the Scots again tackled the issue of the Great Cause, which the Bruces had lost, but this time without reference to the actual winner: the issue was solely that King Edward had intruded himself as Lord Superior to try the issue, but his judgement was 'null since he was not a true judge'. Again, as with both declarations, the 'whole people' supposedly unanimously gave the crown to Bruce as the rightful king.[9]

Of course, most of this was outright propaganda. In the first place, if the Scottish political community had been able to vote directly for a king at the time of the Great Cause then Balliol would undoubtedly have won, not least because he was supported by the most dominant political faction of the time, the Comyns. Second, if any of the candidates had shown himself overwhelmingly willing to acquiesce in anything Edward I wanted in order to be king, it was Robert Bruce the Competitor; in fact Balliol tried hard not to swear homage and fealty to Edward, having recognised that, given that he was generally regarded as the best claimant, this would severely handicap his authority as king.[10] On the other hand, one could accept, from a Scottish point of view, the argument presented in 1321, that Edward I had no right to judge the issue as Lord Paramount of Scotland.

Even Barbour, who perhaps did more than anyone to define the hero-king in the minds of the Scottish people, recognised that the Great Cause was viewed by contemporaries through the eyes of two fundamentally opposed camps, Bruce and Balliol; in other words, he does not follow the government arguments presented in the documents mentioned above, presumably for the simple reason that he did not have access to them. Indeed, as we shall see below, the kind of historical research that we take for granted today, revolving round the examination of archive material, was not applied with regularity to Scottish history (as elsewhere) until the nineteenth century. Thus the only sources

---

[8] See, for example, *The Acts of Robert I*, ed. A. A. M. Duncan (Edinburgh, 1986), 48.

[9] Extract from an account of Anglo-Scottish relations, submitted by the Scots to the pope in 1321; E. L. G. Stones, *Anglo-Scottish Relations, 1174–1328* (Edinburgh, 1970), 38.

[10] See A. A. M. Duncan, 'The Process of Norham, 1291', in P. R. Coss and S. D. Lloyd (eds), *Thirteenth Century England V* (Woodbridge, 1995), 220.

accessed by earlier historians were the writings of others, and Barbour, who above all wanted to tell a good story, was no exception. But even he is not immune to some inherent contradictions with regard to Balliol when he says:

> He was king for only a short time, and by great cunning and guile, for little or no reason, he was taken and arrested, and then degraded of his honour and dignity. Whether that was right or wrong, God knows, for he is omnipotent.[11]

To some extent Barbour's ambivalence here could be explained by his strong monarchism; the lack of a king had got Scotland into the mess of the wars with England in the first place, and removing a king, even one like Balliol, was an abhorrent idea, especially since this deposition was done by Edward I alone, not the Scottish nobility. We must at least consider the possibility that Barbour is echoing a more widespread sympathy for Balliol which had survived, if only at the back of people's minds, throughout the fourteenth century. If he was merely reflecting a distaste for king unmaking, then he surely would not have said that this was done 'for little or no reason', given that the Bruce line would certainly have it that there was plenty reason.

John of Fordun's *Chronica de Gentis Scottorum* (Chronicles of the Scottish People), which were brought to completion by the author's death *c*.1385, is the earliest straightforward narrative account of the wars and was regarded as something of a definitive work to be incorporated into later writings (though Fordun himself also included earlier works). As a chronicler, rather than a storyteller with a moral purpose, he differs from Barbour in the greater overall detail he brings to his work, descriptions of events which soon became standard throughout the Middle Ages and beyond. But quite emphatically and remarkably we find that Fordun, like Barbour and all subsequent medieval Scottish chroniclers, makes no mention of any deposition taking place in 1295. However, he obviously knew something of what the English chroniclers had said, since he transposes the episode to a later period to make the twelve become the guardians of Scotland appointed *after* Balliol had been deprived of the throne by Edward I and Scotland had been taken under direct English rule.[12]

---

[11] John Barbour, *The Bruce*, ed. A. A. M. Duncan (Edinburgh, 1997), 54.

[12] *John of Fordun's Chronicle of the Scottish Nation*, trans. Felix J. H. Skene, ed. W. F. Skene Historians of Scotland, vol. iv (Edinburgh, 1872) (hereafter *Chron. Fordun*, ii), 321.

Instead of power being wrested from the unfortunate John by his bellicose nobility, Fordun provides a rather different picture of the build-up to war, in which Balliol comes across as far more pro-active and even patriotic. Having been summoned to the English parliament to answer for legal decisions taken by him in Scotland and deliberately humiliated by Edward, King John returned home and immediately called his own parliament, where he laid forth his grievances. As a result of the advice given to him there, he then sent a renunciation of his homage to Edward 'as wrung from him by force and fear',[13] an action which all must have known was likely to lead to war. The French alliance is not mentioned by Fordun, though later writers embellish this same tale with details of the treaty.

We should not be surprised. In the first place, these early Scottish monastic writers, whose secluded way of life was profoundly affected by war, were usually extremely concerned with the issue of national unity and the presentation of a concerted front against the English enemy; indeed, they were often scathing about the Scottish nobility, as a result of their perception that the latter too often put their own internal differences ahead of the common weal.[14] Overall, they liked kings as the means of maintaining internal stability, and, as indicated above, they were unlikely to overtly condone getting rid of one, however necessary John's departure was for King Robert Bruce and his successors, the Stewarts.

But, again, we must entertain the possibility that the Scottish writers did not include the English story for the simple reason that it formed no part of the collective memory of the period. It is significant that the direct and deliberate Bruce propaganda makes no mention of Balliol's expulsion from power in 1295, surely an event that would have given added credence to any view that King John had come to power against the wishes of the majority of the Scottish nobility. The idea that King John was moved to action himself also conforms to much of the evidence emerging from his reign which sheds some light on the king's character, including, as mentioned above, his attempt to avoid paying homage and fealty in the first place. As we shall see, descriptions of Balliol contained in the works of later writers also accord with this impression, even when direct comments on his character never fail to be unflattering.

[13] *Chron. Fordun*, ii, 316.

[14] Barbour certainly did not mince his words, describing the nobility's inability to choose a king from among themselves in the following manner: 'Oh, blind folk, sunk in stupidity, if you had really considered the danger that threatened you, you would not have acted in that way.' Barbour, *The Bruce*, 50.

Fordun also provides the first mention of a most illuminating episode following on from John's decision to defy King Edward. In Scottish accounts a considerable amount of time tends to be spent on the Great Cause, for the simple reason that the post-1306 official view needed to ensure that the Bruce claim (and hence the right of their Stewart successors to sit on the throne) was regarded as the rightful one from the very beginning. English chroniclers, on the other hand, were not terribly interested in the Great Cause, except in order to prove King Edward's right as Lord Paramount of Scotland. In the Scottish versions, the line was generally taken that the legal advice given to Edward backed up the Competitor's claim, but Bishop Anthony Bek of Durham pointed out that Bruce was far too upstanding a man to be manipulated as king of Scots and so the crown should only be given to him if he would accept the English king as overlord. Bruce, of course, refused to 'reduce [the kingdom] to thraldom', but Balliol, 'after having quickly deliberated with his council, which had been quite bought over',[15] agreed to the terms.

Once again, the actual evidence indicates that such an interpretation was later Bruce propaganda, pure and simple. Nevertheless, Scottish writers like Fordun did not end the story there, noting that once Balliol had sent his *diffidatio*[16] to Edward, the latter contacted Bruce, apologised for having got the original judgement wrong and promised to remove King John and appoint the Competitor in his place. From our point of view, this seems a high-risk assertion indeed – it is almost impossible not to see Bruce as a traitor to Scotland, a man who would stop at nothing to get to the throne (perhaps a reasonable assessment); indeed, the whole point of Edward's about-turn was allegedly to persuade Bruce 'to write a letter himself to his friends dwelling in Scotland and advise them to surrender and deliver up to him all castles and fortified strongholds'.

How utterly treacherous, we observe! But we must remember that even these monastic writers, who were in the advance guard at the time in terms of holding up as desirable an overriding loyalty to the abstract concept of the kingdom, were still influenced by the mainstream medieval belief in fundamental loyalty lying with the much more powerful leader, usually the king. In other words, Bruce's actions were

---

[15] *Chron. Fordun*, ii, 309.
[16] The technical term given to the renunciation by a vassal of his homage and fealty to his lord, which was acceptable only as a result of a gross dereliction by the lord of his responsibilities or, as in this case, a forced oath.

seen as necessary, and excusable, in order to bring him (or at least, his grandson) to his rightful place on the throne; only then, once Scotland had its legitimate leader in place, could liberation be achieved. This is, of course, a backwards reading of history, but the point is that it worked and, indeed, had become the very touchstone of Scottish independence by the time that Fordun and the others were writing. These same chroniclers do provide us with evidence of the kind of impersonal patriotism (and by that, I mean associated with the state, rather than an individual leader) that we are forever looking to the wars between Scotland and England to exemplify but which can be more usually found in the modern period. But they were by no means completely convinced that this was always right, and just because later writers, who had inherited a different mindset, chose to miss out this most bewildering assertion does not mean that it was not true; we certainly know that the Bruces did indeed fight with Edward I in 1296 against Balliol and the Scottish army. Indeed, just because it seems so inexplicable to us, this episode is surely an extremely significant exemplar of contemporary beliefs: the rights of a lord, whether to an estate or, as in this case, a kingdom, and the rights of other nobles to support him in his just cause had been the *modus operandi* of medieval society for centuries; the overriding rights of the kingdom – or, in reality, its people – to continue to exist and operate in one particular way was still a comparatively novel idea.

Scottish historians continued in a similar vein for the next hundred years or so. Andrew of Wyntoun, who finished his chronicle around 1426, also presents a picture of an assertive king whose patience finally snapped in 1295: 'But John the Balliol in no wise would make him [Edward I] fealty, nor service, Nor at his call would ever appear, Nor bow to him in any manner.' Yet, despite the above, he is still happy to accord King John his most famous epithet: 'Tome-Tabart'.[17] Walter Bower, writing in the 1430s and 1440s, says that Balliol 'strove to the best of his manly ability for a remedy to be applied by all means against the wickedness of the aforesaid king [Edward]',[18] though again he has nothing good to say about the king when drawn to make a direct comment on him. Nevertheless, as with Fordun, if we choose to look

---

[17] Andrew of Wyntoun, *The Orygynale Cronykil of Scotland (Chron. Wyntoun)*, ed. David Laing, 3 vols (Edinburgh, 1872) vol. 3 odd pagination, 325–6, 329, 338–9, 337.

[18] A. B. Scott and D. E. R. Watt (eds), *Scotichronicon by Walter Bower in Latin and English* (Aberdeen, 1996) (hereafter *Chron. Bower* (Watt)), vol. vi, 43.

behind the obvious rhetoric, Wyntoun and Bower's description of events actually places the Scottish nobility firmly behind their king, who consequently appears, at times at least, authoritative and in control.

Obviously, we should not give uncritical acceptance to this inter-pretation of Balliol's reign; Scottish writers had reason enough to present a picture of concerted action against the imperialist English from the word go even if that sometimes stood awkwardly with the details of the official pro-Bruce line. However, Fordun and Wyntoun were not alone in presenting King John in this more pro-active light, however partially; it is therefore quite possible, if one looks, to see two distinct interpretations of the reign – one positive and the other negative – existing side by side within the same medieval Scottish chronicles. Indeed, their authors were profoundly aware of the fact that this issue revolved more around politics than patriotism. As Fordun says expli-citly, and this seems to me to put the finger on exactly the crux of the matter:

> And even as afterwards, while King Robert de Bruce was
> making war, all Balliol's followers were looked upon with
> mistrust in the king's wars, so also in this Balliol's wars, the
> aforesaid bishop and earls [Robert of Glasgow and Atholl and
> Mar, who were the alleged recipients of Bruce's letters in
> 1296], with all the abettors of Bruce's party, were generally
> considered traitors to their king and country.[19]

The 'patriotic' tag, as it has been and always will be in war, becomes the prerogative of the victor; in this war the Bruce faction ultimately got to write up the history, but there is enough remaining from that written or remembered from before 1306 to make it clear that King John had operated a similar policy towards his enemies in Scotland. After all, this was a king who had managed to force the young earl of Carrick (the future Robert I) to swear homage and fealty to him, having confiscated the earldom in the meantime.[20]

For at least 150 years after the outbreak of the wars with England, the continuing struggle between the two countries ensured that the chroni-clers – every one a cleric – concentrated on presenting internal division as just as much of a moral judgement on the nation as the evils of the

[19] *Chron. Fordun*, ii, 319.
[20] *Acts of the Parliaments of Scotland (APS)*, ed. T. Thomson and C. Innes, 12 vols (Edinburgh, 1814), vol. 1, 448.

imperialist neighbour. Imprecations against those who persevered with their peacetime alignments despite the external threat – a quite natural mode of behaviour for the nobility of the time, not to mention subsequently – have continued as a theme right up to the present. However, another moral issue was gaining prominence within Scottish society in the latter half of the fifteenth century and this soon found its way into interpretations of the nation's past.

The first chronicler to noticeably deviate from what had become a very consistent line, or at least embellish it, was the author of the *Book of Pluscardine*, begun in 1478 and completed eighteen years later. Though he based his work on Fordun and then Bower's continuation, the opportunity is taken, in relation to the reaction to Edward's increasing pressure on the Scots, for a more complex analysis of why they had been right to go back on the oath of homage and allegiance sworn by their king: the three estates had not been consulted on this issue and therefore John had had no right to swear it in the first place. The discussion of the part played by the coronation oath[21] and the role of a king as a public, not a private, person shows a clear knowledge and understanding of the debates surrounding the deposition of a monarch that had been current in England since early in the reign of Edward II.[22]

It has been argued recently[23] that Scotland had been in the forefront of contemporary European thought and practice regarding the contractual relationship between king and people. This is based on the passage in the Declaration of Arbroath of 1320 that states that King Robert would be removed from power if he ever handed Scotland over to the English *and* on the fact that the Scots had previously taken such a step with King John in 1295. Medieval political theory was quite able to countenance the removal of a useless (*inutile*) king under the same conditions as would apply to government during a royal minority; this certainly happened in Scotland in the later fourteenth century, when Robert II and Robert III were both replaced, in terms of their executive power, with lieutenants (or guardians) from within the royal family. Both were technically useless because of old age or illness, but this was not the same as a king who allegedly would not do what his political community wished him to do (in John's case, go to war with England).

---

[21] Though John was not, in fact, crowned but inaugurated; Scottish kings only gained the right to a coronation in 1328.

[22] *Liber Pluscardensis*, ed. F. J. H. Skene, 2 vols (Edinburgh, 1877), vol. ii, 141–2.

[23] E. J. Cowan, 'Identity, Freedom and the Declaration of Arbroath', in D. Broun, R. J. Finlay and M. Lynch (eds), *Image and Identity: The Making and Remaking of Scotland through the Ages* (Edinburgh, 1998), 51–3.

Now, whatever the current view might be about whether or not King John was actually deprived of power in 1295, it should be clear from the above discussion that the collective memory up until *Pluscardine* maintained that this had not happened; so far as the Scots were aware, they had never, unlike the English, had to deal with a king who was physically and mentally capable but failing in his duty, as defined by his political community in parliament, to maintain the kingdom's best interests.

But the Scots in the later fifteenth century were being faced with just such a situation, although when the monk from *Pluscardine* began his history, the issue had not yet been resolved. Nevertheless the current king, James III, was the first Scottish monarch to be deprived of power in this way, first in 1482 and then, leading to his death, in 1488. What is interesting, in relation to the argument about whether or not this had happened to John, is the fact that the author of the *Book of Pluscardine*, though he is surely reacting to the contemporary situation when he underlines the duty of a king to uphold the public good, does not mention the potential precedent of the removal of the king in 1295. This would have been the ideal moment to draw attention to such a thing, but instead he remains content merely to point out that John and the Scots were within their rights to withdraw homage and fealty from Edward of England because the initial oath had been sworn without the consent of parliament.

This legal justification regarding homage – part of a much wider and longer-term debate regarding whether ultimate sovereignty lay with king or parliament – found its way into succeeding authors, including Hector Boece's *History and Croniklis of Scotland*. But overall it is remarkable how the basic story, as laid down by Fordun, remained the same, including the continuing assertion that Bruce had tried to woo his own supporters away from Balliol's side in 1296.

So when did writers begin to accept the early English chroniclers' version of events? Sir Walter Scott, in his nineteenth-century *Tales of a Grandfather*, still follows the basic medieval Scottish account, stating that King John was about to hand over a number of Scottish castles to Edward, as a symbol of his continuing vassalage, 'but the people murmured against this base compliance and Balliol himself, pereceiving that it was Edward's intention gradually to destroy his power, was stung at once with shame and fear'.[24] However, by the end of the century,

---

[24] Sir Walter Scott, *Tales of a Grandfather*, abridged by Elsie M. Lang (London, 1925), 44.

when Scottish writers had begun to gain far more access to the original evidence for the period (held predominantly at that time in the Tower of London), together with a growing fashion for original research, including the systematic analysis of other chronicle sources, we finally see King John begin to lose his position. Patrick Tytler, whose *History of Scotland* was published from 1841 to 1850, agrees with the English chroniclers that Balliol's English friends were expelled from the court and the king himself was made captive. John retains some residual sympathy, in the sense that the primary blame is placed on the factious nobility, most particularly the Comyns, who are allegedly responsible for the king's imprisonment.[25] The Comyns, of course, came in for even more direct propaganda from Robert Bruce, who had killed the head of the family in 1306, than even Balliol, but that is a different story (and again one that has only recently begun to be tackled).

John Hill Burton, in his *History of Scotland* (1852–70), spends a lot of time analysing the events in question. The issue of an overriding sense of national identity, which fundamentally underpinned the development of the modern nation-state and the expansion of empire, is supremely important. He does not blame the Competitors for swearing homage and fealty to Edward I – no, as Normans, outsiders, 'a class of aliens', they could not help themselves for they were men 'unburdened by nationality or other serious creeds', and, therefore, it is clearly implied, morally inferior. Hill Burton, and others of his time, was responsible for taking the medieval concept of the community of the realm and identifying it in the modern period with the middle classes, who now challenged the age-old supremacy of the nobility in government and in determining prevailing ideologies. The community of the realm, which in the medieval period comprised precisely these so-called 'alien' aristocrats and the rest of the higher nobility, had now become that even vaguer entity, 'the people', 'nourished in independence and national pride, who must be bent or broken'.[26]

Carrying on a major theme developed by the medieval chroniclers, Hill Burton is even more cutting – as we would expect from someone who was inherently anti-noble – about the role of all the protagonists in the fight for the kingship:

---

[25] Patrick F. Tytler, *History of Scotland*, 9 vols (Edinburgh, 1828–43, 1892 edn, 4 vols), vol. 1, 41–2.

[26] John Hill Burton, *History of Scotland*, 3rd edn, 8 vols (Edinburgh, 1876), vol. 1, 124–5; 152.

The name of Bruce became eminently popular in Scotland, and it became something more than a fashion to say and to think everything good of it. There are, in fact, two great elements of disturbance of the truth in the history of this period: the one arises out of the national quarrel, in which English and Scots writers each took the part of his country; the other comes of the division at home between the two parties – Bruce's and Baliol's. Bruce's party have the last word in the dispute, and far the stronger part in it, since their hero and his country were victorious together before the Scots chroniclers began their work.[27]

There is much in the above that contemporary historians could agree with. The only difference now is that we are beginning to work more systematically through the implications of this state of affairs.

For, yet again, the author has some positive things to say about Balliol. Having studied the original documents, Hill Burton was aware of the kinds of arguments used by the future king in support of his claim during the Great Cause, being moved to say that 'here the tone of Balliol's pleading has in it a touch of dignity as supporting some remnant of separate sovereignty for Scotland, while the others seek to remove the last shred of it'. But that does not stop him, typically, from accepting the perceived wisdom – begun six hundred years earlier by the English chroniclers – that: 'He does not seem to have been a man of much ability – indeed he is liberally termed a fool by friends as well as foes – but his position was one in which courage and ability might only have made mischief.'[28] Damned by faint praise, indeed.

Hill Burton's work was also hugely influential, with passages finding their way into, for example, A. F. Murison's *Sir William Wallace*, published in 1898. However, Murison added a further layer to the Balliol mythology with his assertion that 'The preference of Balliol, after an ostentatiously elaborate process of legal formality, not only wore the aspect of a profound homage to law, but also placed on the throne of Scotland the candidate that would be most plastic in his hands.'[29] It is ironic that, at the very moment when access to the original documents had entered the historical process, the mythology was now so firmly established that even the overtly obsequious actions of Bruce the

---

[27] Hill Burton, *History*, vol. 1, 122–3 n. 1.
[28] Hill Burton, *History*, vol. 1, 150–2, including n. 1.
[29] A. F. Murison, *Sir William Wallace* (London, 1898), 9.

Competitor were overlooked in terms of judgements on Balliol. In addition, these nineteenth-century writers had also decided to erase from their record any mention of the Bruces' actions in 1296, presumably because deliberately siding with Edward I in order to gain the crown was far too problematic for modern sensibilities inured to the ideal of impartial patriotism. Even if Hill Burton could tar the Bruces with the same brush as the rest of the nobility, the prevailing tendency was to ignore or directly refute any dubious tendencies which might be imputed to the hero-king or his family.

Finally to take Balliol's historiography right up to date, it is important to note, in the first place, the superficial consistency of the myth that has sprung up about him. This seems to me primarily a result of the fact that no-one has had reason to be interested in King John for his own sake: he really has been in the way in terms of the writing of history since his throne was taken over by Robert Bruce in 1306.

It is also the case that, while the myth itself remains relatively static, the uses to which it is put certainly reflect contemporary concerns. This is just as true today. Scottish historians have, in the last four decades or so, fought an increasingly convincing battle against the traditional picture of Scottish history as profoundly dark, bloody and backward, especially in comparison to English constitutional history. As part of that process, it has been tempting to look at this period of the past as indicative of an advanced constitutional awareness, with the Scots putting forward some of the earliest nationalist sentiments in European history, and also some of the earliest notions of contractual kingship.[30] It is likely, though time has still to tell, that we have gone too far; certainly my own view is that there is no consistent discussion in the Scottish chroniclers (as opposed to official government propaganda) of the implications of a king making a decision against the will of the community of the realm in relation to the Wars of Independence until the *Book of Pluscardine*.

But what seems to me to be the most interesting facet of the whole sorry tale of King John is the fact that Scottish historians from the fourteenth century onwards, forced initially by contemporary political circumstances to indicate the inevitability and righteousness of a Bruce succession, are nevertheless manoeuvred into contradiction by an awareness of an alternative history of patriotism and moral righteousness

[30] See F. Watson, 'The Enigmatic Lion', and E. J. Cowan 'Identity, Freedom and the Declaration of Arbroath', in Broun, Finlay and Lynch (eds), *Image and Identity*.

which surely reverberates from the time of Balliol and the pre-Bruce leadership. Thus, despite the imprecations against internal dissent made explicit from the beginning, the history of the wars with England has in fact been profoundly shaped by the very same political divisions that beset the protagonists at the time. The lesson for those of us trying to escape such historiographical chains relates to far more than the thirteenth century: there is no Truth in history; it just depends where you stand. On the other hand, accepting, and presenting, all positions as equal (subject to corroborating evidence – I would not condone denying the Holocaust, for example) brings us closer to understanding the pressures on contemporaries to make sense of a world which, just like our own, presented a range of right and wrong options from which to choose. The recycling of history only comes about when we feel inclined to judge the particular options chosen, usually by the standards of our own time. Future generations of historians will, of course, be eternally grateful for such judgements, since they provide considerable insight, not necessarily into the original events, but into the belief systems of those describing them. Unfortunately, the very act of putting pen to paper locks the next writer into the same unbreakable chain of history. Perhaps, then, we should have a little more sympathy for John Barbour's veiled comment that, 'Whether that was right or wrong, God knows, for he is omnipotent.'

CHAPTER 3

Late Medieval Scotland and the Matter of Britain

Steve Boardman

L ate medieval Scotland saw the production of a series of chronicles that sought to trace the story of the Scottish kingdom and people from their earliest origins. John of Fordun's *Chronica Gentis Scottorum* (1371–87), Andrew of Wyntoun's *Original Chronicle* (1408–1424) and Walter Bower's *Scotichronicon* (1441–7) all attempted to provide a coherent and unified historical narrative that explained and illustrated the emergence and development of the Scots as a distinct people under its own sovereign rulers from biblical times onwards.[1] At the heart of these accounts was the story of Scottish kingship and the royal dynasty that stood for and symbolised the *Gens Scottorum*. The chronicles established ancient precedents for the political status and territorial integrity of the late fourteenth- and fifteenth-century kingdom as a fully independent monarchy, and gloried in the way in which that standing had been won and maintained against a series of internal and external enemies and threats.

Historians have tended to see the production of these late medieval chronicles as part of a 'war of historiography' and propaganda that ran alongside and contributed to the less cerebral conflicts of the Wars of Independence.[2] Fordun's work, in particular, has been characterised as

---

[1] For dates see Dauvit Broun, *The Irish Identity of the Kingdom of the Scots* (Woodbridge, 1999), 96 (Wyntoun); Dauvit Broun, 'A New Look at *Gesta Annalia* Attributed to John of Fordun', in Barbara E. Crawford (ed.), *Church, Chronicle and Learning in Medieval and Early Renaissance Scotland* (Edinburgh, 1999), 9–30, at 20 (Fordun).

[2] M. Drexler, 'Fluid Prejudice: Scottish Origin Myths in the Later Middle Ages', in J. Rosenthal and C. Richmond (eds), *People, Politics and Community in the Later Middle Ages* (Gloucester and New York, 1987), 60–77; *|over*

a direct response to the English crown's deployment of the mythical history of the ancient British kingdom to justify its claims to superiority over the entire island of Britain. The appearance of Fordun's *Chronica Gentis Scottorum* is also held to have introduced a view of the kingdom's past that was swiftly established as the orthodox and dominant tradition in Scotland. Fordun's Latin chronicle was certainly incorporated, and to an extent modified and expanded, by Walter Bower, abbot of Inchcolm in the production of his mammoth work, the *Scotichronicon* (also in Latin), in the 1440s. Thereafter, most chronicles of the second half of the fifteenth century and the early sixteenth century relied heavily on the narrative framework provided by Fordun/Bower as the basis for their discussion of the history of the Scottish kingdom.[3] By the mid-fifteenth century Fordun's vision of the origins of the Scottish royal line in the eponymous Egyptian princess Scota, and the subsequent history of the dynasty and race descended from her, was to be found also in short vernacular histories. Incidental and off-hand references to the story of Scota in the sixteenth century suggest that by then it was a widely understood tale, accepted by many Scots as an explanation of the origins of their ancient race and the emergence of the independent kingdom which bore her name and, of course, particularly relevant in the refutation of English political pretensions.[4]

The elegance and economy of the argument linking the development of this dominant late medieval chronicle tradition to the demands of war and diplomacy has been rather ruffled by recent research which has modified the notion that the narrative found in the late medieval chronicles was inspired directly and simply by the need to counter the ambitions and propaganda of English kings in the period after 1291.

---

cont'd   R. J. Goldstein, *The Matter of Scotland: Historical Narrative in Medieval Scotland* (Lincoln and London, 1993); William Ferguson, *The Identity of the Scottish Nation* (Edinburgh, 1998), 12–16 and ch. 3; R. A. Mason, 'Scotching the *Brut*: Politics, History and National Myth in Sixteenth-Century Britain', in R. A. Mason (ed.), *Scotland and England, 1286–1815* (Edinburgh, 1987), 60–84. For an earlier perspective on the development of these myths, see E. J. Cowan, 'Myth and Identity in Early Medieval Scotland', *Scottish Historical Review* [*SHR*], lxiii (1984), 111–35.

[3]   See S. Mapstone, 'The *Scotichronicon*'s First Readers', in Barbara M. Crawford (ed.), *Church, Chronicle and Learning in Medieval and Early Renaissance Scotland* (Edinburgh, 1999), 31–56, for a fascinating sketch of the popularity of the Scotichronicon and the way in which various manuscript copies of the work were circulated, amended and recast.

[4]   Drexler, 'Fluid Prejudice', 60–2; 66–70; e g. 'The Ring of the Roy Robert', *Maitland Folio MS*, Scottish Texts Society [STS], 1917–27, ii, 127–33.

Dauvit Broun's dissection of the sources for Fordun's *Chronica* suggests that many of the key elements of Fordun's work, including the Scota origin legend, were derived from thirteenth-century chronicles which themselves synthesised earlier origin legends and king-lists in an attempt to provide an all-embracing and coherent account of the origin, development and recent history of the Scottish kingdom.[5] In this thirteenth-century context, as Broun has shown, the real significance of the Scota legend was not as a response to the *Brut* myth, but in the establishment of an account of Scottish origins which gradually but decisively broke with a historical scheme which had previously regarded Scottish kingship and the Scots as offshoots of Irish society and culture. Moreover, it can be argued that the Fordun/Bower tradition did not achieve an immediate or easy monopoly over the ways medieval Scots interpreted and thought about the past. Other literary and historical traditions remained potent and vibrant. Explanations of topographical features, the histories of individual aristocratic lineages, burghs or churches, often drew on accounts that were, at first sight, incompatible with, or unrelated to, the story of the Scottish kingdom as it was envisaged by the clerical chroniclers of the fourteenth and fifteenth centuries. In particular, although the developing 'national' history of late medieval Scotland has been characterised as emerging, in some senses, in opposition to the 'matter of Britain', the *Brut* histories and Arthurian romances inspired, directly or indirectly, by Geoffrey of Monmouth's twelfth-century *Historia Regum Brittaniae*, continued to exert an influence on the way Scots perceived the past.

It is probably fair to say that the systematic hostility of Scottish medieval chroniclers to the 'matter of Britain' has been overemphasised. Andrew of Wyntoun, in particular, made extensive use of Geoffrey of Monmouth's *Historia Regum Brittaniae*, and the *Brut* histories, with no recourse to the icy critique of Geoffrey's historical worth typical of Fordun.[6] Wyntoun's casual cross-referencing to a version of the *Brut*

---

[5] Broun, *Irish Identity*.

[6] A point made some time ago. See especially Flora Alexander, 'Late Medieval Scottish Attitudes to the Figure of King Arthur: A Reassessment', *Anglia*, 93 (1975), 17–34; Robert Huntington Fletcher, *The Arthurian Material in the Chronicles*, revised by Roger Sherman Loomis (New York, 1966), 242; M. Drexler, 'Fluid Prejudice', 66–8. Indeed, Fordun himself was quite happy to use Geoffrey as an 'authority' in areas where his narrative did not contradict Fordun's historical scheme. Curiously, Wyntoun seems to have misread one of the few direct comments made by Geoffrey in connection with Scotland. Monmouth's description of the Scottish towns founded by Ebraucus, /over

and to an account of the deeds of King Arthur by one 'Huchown of the Awle Ryale' makes clear that he at least valued these works and expected them to be familiar and available, in the vernacular, to his intended audience.[7]

A further testimony to the enduring popularity and influence of 'British' themes was the appearance of the all-conquering Arthur in the local histories and legends of the late medieval kingdom.[8] The 'matter of Britain' may have had at its core a historical perspective that was, from the Scottish viewpoint, flawed or unpalatable, but it had spawned a huge vernacular literature that helped to define and reflect the interests, physical, emotional and spiritual, of the chivalric classes across much of western Europe.[9] Fordun and Bower, the purveyors of serious, chronologically coherent, and scholarly history in Latin may well have been hard pressed to compete with the cosmopolitan glamour of the *Brut*. Scota and Gaythelos, and the long line of early medieval Scottish kings descended from them, may have provided an intellectual counterweight to the *Brut* legends, but for members of the armigerous class in Scotland the literary heroes of the 'British' past seem to have retained a deeper

cont'd   the descendant of Locrine, included Edinburgh, Dumbarton (Alt Cluit) and Melrose. Wyntoun conflates these names and treats them all as synonyms for Edinburgh. *Chron. Wyntoun* (Laing), i, 153. 'He byggit Edynburgh wythy alle, And gert thaim Allynclowde it calle/ The Maydyn Castell, in sum plas/The Sorowful (Hill) it callyd was.'

[7] Which version of the *Brut* Wyntoun was familiar with is wholly unclear. See Andrew Galloway 'Writing History in England', in David Wallace (ed.), *The Cambridge History of Medieval English Literature* (Cambridge, 1999), 255–83, at 266–74, for the complexity and variety of the *Brut* tradition. *Chron. Wyntoun* (Laing), ii, 10, where Wyntoun abandons a detailed description of the fate of the British kings because 'The Brwte tellys opynly: Thare-for I lewe now that story', *Chron. Wyntoun* (Laing), i, 292–3 (on Emperor Claudius) 'The Brute tellys it sa oppynly, That I wyll lat it now ga by' and 12, where he makes a pointed defence of Hugh's general 'suthfastnes', 'And men off gud dyscretyowne/Suld excuse, and love Huchowne/That cunnand wes in literature'. The rest of Hugh's works cited by Wyntoun all seem to pursue Arthurian themes, the Adventure of Gawain, the Gest of Arthur (perhaps the same as his Gest Hystoryalle) and the 'Pystyll off Swete Swsane'. In general Wyntoun seems to have accorded the Monmouth tradition far greater respect and to have included elements that would have been unacceptable to Fordun e.g. *Chron. Wyntoun* (Laing), i, 126 (talking of Brutus), 'That *this* land fra geawndys (giants) wan, and eftyr hym wes callyd Brytan', and i, 149, 'The next Chapitere folowand/ Schall tell qwhen Brwtus wan this land.'

[8] See R. S. Loomis, 'Scotland and the Arthurian Legend', *PSAS* (1955–56), 1–21; Mason, 'Scotching the Brut', n. 85.

[9] See, Julia C. Crick, *The Historia Regum Brittannie of Geoffrey of Monmouth*, vol. iv: *Dissemination and Reception in the Later Middle Ages* (Cambridge, 1991).

emotional resonance and a more immediate relevance to their ambitions and lives as members of a cosmopolitan martial elite.

At around the same time as John of Fordun worked on his long history of the descendants of Scota, Robert II (1371–90), the first Stewart king of Scotland, commissioned John Barbour, the author of the *Bruce*, to produce a genealogical history of the king's ancestors. Barbour's work has not survived, but the vague outline of some sections of the history/genealogy can be reconstructed through references to it in other works.[10] It would seem that the study included, or was based around, a genealogy that traced Robert II's ancestors back through and beyond the line of British kings descended from Brutus to the mythical Sir Dardane, lord of Frigia. Wyntoun's other references to Barbour seem to confirm that the latter's work essentially followed the genealogical scheme laid out in the *Brut*.[11] The supposed genealogy of the kings of Britain was widely known, but it remains unclear how precisely Barbour might have linked Robert II's historical ancestors to this scheme.[12] MacDiarmid advanced the argument that Barbour simply claimed a generic 'British' descent for the Stewarts as a family descended from the refugees who fled Britain with the last of their kings, Cadwallader, and which, after a long exile in Brittany, returned to the island via the Welsh borderlands. As MacDiarmid points out, no extant

---

[10] The chief witnesses to the structure of the lost work are the chroniclers Andrew of Wyntoun and Walter Bower, both of whom had access to the history/genealogy and commented on it. From Wyntoun we learn that Barbour made a 'proper genealogy' from 'Sere Dardane, lord de Fryga', the son of the Assyrian king 'Nynus' to 'Robert oure Secownd kyng, that Scotland had in governyng'; *Chron. Wyntoun* (Laing), i, 76. Wyntoun also informs his audience that pagan stories 'That is bot fabyll or fantys' suggested 'That Jupyter gat on Electra,/Sere Dardane lorde off Fregya'. The chronicler was hardly consistent in applying this distinction, since he later described Sir Dardane as the son of Saturn. On another occasion Wyntoun referred his readers to Barbour's 'tretise' if they wished to learn more of Brutus' lineage: *Chron. Wyntoun* (Laing), i, 153 'Off Bruttus lyneage quha wyll here/He luke the Tretis off Barbere/Mad in tyll a Genealogy/Rycht wele, and mare perfytly/Than I can on ony wys/Wytht all my wyt to yowe dewys.'

[11] *Chron. Wyntoun* (Laing), i, 97–8 (Book 2, Chapter 9). In a discussion of the origins of the Irish Wyntoun reveals that Barbour agreed with the account given 'be the Brwte' concerning the British king 'Gurgwnt-Badruk'.

[12] For contrasting views see Barbour, *Bruce*, Matthew P. McDiarmid and James A. C. Stevenson (eds), 3 vols (STS, 1980–5), i, 18 and R. J. Lyall, 'The lost literature of Medieval Scotland', in J. D. McClure and M. G. Spiller *Bryght Lanternis: Essays on the Language and Literature of Medieval and Renaissance Scotland* (Aberdeen, 1989), 33–47, 39.

Scottish source gives an indication of how the generations between the
exile of Cadwallader, the last of Monmouth's British kings, and 'Fleance
de Warenne', the supposed progenitor of the Stewart family, might have
been filled.[13] This silence might argue against the identification of
Fleance, first explicitly made by Hector Boece and his vernacular
translators early in the sixteenth century, as the exiled son of the ill-
starred Banquho, driven from Scotland by the machinations of Mac-
Beth. If the Stewarts' genealogy had included the figure of Banquho,
active in eleventh-century Scotland, then neither Wyntoun nor Bower,
both of whom had seen Barbour's work, felt moved to mention it in their
treatment of MacBeth's life. However, the whole point of a genealogy
was to provide a direct unbroken line of descent, through named
individuals, that linked a contemporary figure to his illustrious forbears.
Even if the tale of Banquho has to be treated circumspectly, other
aspects of the story as it appears in early sixteenth-century sources may
be worth considering. Fleance's exile is said to have resulted in a
surreptitious liasion with a daughter of a prince of Wales that eventually
cost Fleance his life. Despite Fleance's death, his son by the princess,
Walter, grew to manhood in Wales before returning to his paternal
homeland.[14] That Barbour presented Walter, the Stewarts' ancestor, as
coming to Scotland from Wales is undoubted; if the suggestion of a
marriage into a native Welsh royal line also originated in Barbour's work
then the 'missing' section of the Stewarts' genealogy, linking the
historical family with Monmouth's British kings, could well have traced
the lineage of Fleance's supposed bride.[15] A genealogy produced for

---

[13] The latest British king known to feature in Barbour's work was in fact
'Gurgwnt-Badruk'.

[14] *The Chronicles of Scotland, Compiled by Hector Boece, Translated into Scots by
John Bellenden, 1531* ed. Edith. C. Batho and H. Winifred Husbands (STS,
1941), ii, 154–6.

[15] *Chron. Bower* (Watt), ix, 46–9. Bower notes that 'Barbour asserts that the
Stewarts (le Stewartis) came from Wales, and had their origin in "Fleance de
Warenne", Hary's *Wallace* (STS), i, 2, 126–8 (notes). Outlining the career of one
of William Wallace's ancestors, Hary notes that he was alive at the time when
Walter Stewart 'her of Waillis fra Warayn socht. Quha likes til haif mar
knowledge in that part, Go reid the rycht lyne of the first Stewart.' In Barbour's
tale then Walter, son of Fleance, arrived in Scotland from Wales. This certainly
tallies with Bellenden's account. Moreover, Bellenden also incorporates the only
other known elements of Barbour's treatment of the early Stewarts in Scotland,
i.e. Walter fitz Flaald's campaign against Galloway and his son's involvement in
the first crusade. The chronological problems detected by Bower in Barbour's
genealogy at this point seem to have arisen from Barbour's conflation,   /over

Roger Mortimer, the English earl of March, at almost exactly the same time as Barbour worked on the Stewarts' descent, followed precisely this scheme, with the marriage of one of Mortimer's ancestors to a native Welsh dynasty providing a perfect opportunity to map out the descent of the earl through the female line back to Cadwallader.[16]

Barbour's 'Fleance' seems to be one and the same with the undoubtedly historical Flaald fitz Alan, whose grandson, Walter fitz Alan (d. 1177), arrived in Scotland during the reign of David I (1124–53).[17] Little is known of Flaald's life beyond the facts that he was the son of Alan the Steward of the bishop of Dol in Brittany and that he was active in the Anglo-Welsh border area, appearing at the dedication of Monmouth Priory in 1101–2.[18] There is nothing in the documentary record to either support or disprove the notion that Flaald married into a native Welsh family.[19]

At any rate, it is clear that while Fordun was producing his hostile assessment of Geoffrey of Monmouth and the *Brut*, the newly established Scottish royal dynasty was loudly proclaiming its Trojan origins. Moreover, Barbour seems to have had no knowledge of (or at any rate no

cont'd deliberate or otherwise, of tales relating to Flaald's brother Alan, Flaald's son (also Alan) and Flaald's great-grandson (Alan fitz Walter), who was active in Scotland around the turn of the thirteenth century. As Bower points out, the claim that the last of these men, Alan fitz Walter, took part in the first crusade (1097–8) is simply impossible. Yet Barbour's tale was not a complete invention, for ancestors of the Stewart line had indeed participated in the first great expedition to the Holy Land. Flaald's brother, Alan, and the father-in-law of Alan fitz Flaald, Arnulf de Hesdin, had both taken the cross. The important reality of 'proto-Stewart' involvement in the crusade was thus preserved in Barbour's account although transferred to a later Alan. see M. Chibnall (ed.), *Orderic Vitalis: The Ecclesiastical History* v, 58–9; P. J. Riley-Smith, *The first crusaders* (Cambridge, 1997), 83, 92–3; *Chronica monasterii de Hida juxta Wintoniam* (ed. E. Edwards, Rolls Series, 45, London, 1866), 301–2. The chronological problems were addressed in Bellenden by moving forward Walter's arrival in Scotland to the reign of Malcolm III (perhaps suggesting that this interpretation came through Bower's asides rather than direct from a copy of Barbour's work?).

[16] *The Chronicle of Adam Usk, 1377–1421*, ed. and trans. by C. Given-Wilson (Oxford, 1997), 40–3. Although in this case the marriage of Mortimer's ancestor to a daughter of Llywelyn ab Iorwerth (d. 1240s) is historically verifiable.

[17] G. W. S. Barrow, *The Anglo-Norman Era in Scottish History* (Oxford, 1980), 64–70.

[18] J. H. Round, *Studies in Peerage and Family History* (London, 1901), 120.

[19] See A. J. Roderick, 'Marriage and Politics in Wales, 1066–1282', *Welsh History Review*, 4 (1968–9), 1–20 for intermarriage between native Welsh families and 'Marcher' lords.

time for) two of the critical arguments advanced by Fordun to limit the appeal and applicability of Monmouth's work to the Scots. In the *Chronica Gentis Scottorum* Fordun contended that the British kingdom, even at its greatest extent, had never embraced the territory north of the Forth. In addition, Fordun also managed to hint that Arthur was illegitimate, a usurper of the kingship that by rights belonged to his nephew Modred. In Barbour's *Bruce*, however, Kildrummy castle in Mar was casually identified as 'Snawdoun', i.e. the supposed site of Arthur's fortress city of Snowdon.[20] The placement of Snowdon in Aberdeenshire suggests that some of Fordun's contemporaries simply did not heed his argument as to the northern boundary of the British kingdom lying on the Forth. Similarly, the suggestion in *Chronica Gentis Scottorum* that Arthur was illegitimate and that the throne rightfully belonged to Modred does not seem to have held sway for the author of the *Bruce*. In the *Bruce* Barbour mentions Arthur only once, in a digression on treachery, where he sets out how, despite Arthur's 'gret valour' and his numerous triumphs, he was slain by 'Modreyt his syster son' through 'tresoune and throu wikkitnes, The Broite beris tharoff wytnes'.[21] On this point, then, Barbour hardly conformed to what has been outlined as a distinctively Scottish attitude on Arthurian matters that regarded Modred as the rightful king.[22]

Overall, Barbour's work suggests a largely uncritical acceptance of the *Brut* and Arthurian legend. In this, Barbour presumably reflected the views of his principal patrons, the Stewarts. Barbour's genealogy of the family may have incorporated material that had been deployed and developed by the Stewart family in their capacity as great regional magnates in the south-west of Scotland and the Firth of Clyde from the twelfth century onwards.[23] The circumstances and timing of Stewart settlement in this region may well have encouraged a fascination with things Arthurian and British.[24] The arrival of Walter fitz Alan in Scotland was swiftly followed by the appearance of Geoffrey of

---

[20] John Barbour, *The Bruce*, ed. A. A. M. Duncan (Edinburgh, 1997), Book 4, l. 181.

[21] *Bruce* (Duncan), Book 1, ll. 549–60.

[22] Fletcher, *Arthurian Material*, 242. For further discussion of 'positive' portrayals of Arthur in late medieval Scottish literary works, see Alexander, 'Scottish Attitudes to the figure of King Arthur,' 17–34.

[23] Barrow, *Anglo-Norman Era*, 64–70.

[24] Loomis, 'Scotland and the Arthurian Legend', 5–6, 9, 13, for an argument that Stewarts, as a family of Breton descent, may have played a significant role in promoting Arthurian and British material in the reign of David I.

Monmouth's hugely influential history of the kings of Britain. Walter's lord, David I, and his immediate successors seem to have enthusiastically embraced the political and cultural symbolism of a restored British kingship wielding authority across a unified island.[25] The attractions of this twelfth-century Frankish courtly, aristocratic culture may have been intensified for the Stewarts by the nature of the lordships they acquired in Scotland. As Barrow has noted, the Cumbric-speaking society that had once predominated in south-western Scotland seems to have left few tangible influences in the late medieval kingdom.[26] Yet, the notion that the Stewarts represented the return of a 'British' dynasty may have made the settlement of Renfrew, Strathgryfe and Kyle seem rather more like a restoration of lost rights than the acquisition of new territory through unbridled aristocratic power and royal favour. The sense of a British past, whether generated by the popularity of Monmouth's work and the literary evocation of Arthurian heroes or, as seems less likely, by an awareness of a genuine Brittonic history, certainly still resonated in the south-west of Scotland in the later Middle Ages. The hilltop fortresses of Stirling and Dumbarton, in particular, were hung about with a mist of British associations. The burgh seal of Stirling as recorded in 1296, for example, depicted two groups of armed men on the bridge over the Forth with the curious legend 'Here stand the Britons, saved by their arms; here stand the Scots, saved by the cross'.[27] If the 1296 seal points to a local conviction that Stirling had been a centre of British power, then by 1365 this had become an explicit identification of the burgh with the Arthurian city-fortress of Snowdon. In that year, King David II proudly informed Jean Froissart, during the latter's visit to Scotland, that Stirling castle was the site of Snawdon (Smandon), where King Arthur had held court.[28] In 1421 another visitor to Stirling, the Burgundian Gilbert de

[25] See Cowan, 'Myth and Identity', 132–5; D. D. R. Owen, *William the Lion, 1143–1214* (East Linton, 1997), chs 6, 7 and conclusion.

[26] G. W. S. Barrow, 'Scotland and Wales in the Middle Ages', *Welsh Historical Review*, 10 (1981), 302–19, at 303–5.

[27] Stevenson and Wood, *Scottish Seals*, i, 80. The seal was known and commented on by the chronicler Walter Bower in the 1440s; see *Chron. Bower* (Watt), iv, 473–5; vi, 355–7.

[28] See Roger Sherman Loomis, 'From Segontium to Sinadon – The Legends of a *Cité Gaste*', *Speculum*, 22 (1947), 520–33 for an explanation of how the Roman fort of Segontium at the base of Snowdon came to be transformed into the literary home of Arthur; Froissart, *Oeuvres*, ed. Kervyn de Lettenhove (Brussels 1867), ii, 313; Philippe Contamine, 'Froissart and Scotland', in G. Simpson (ed.), *Scotland and the Low Countries, 1124–1994* (East Linton, 1989), 55.

Lannoy, noted that Stirling was a 'tres fort chastel assis sur une roch que fist le roy Artus, comme on dist'.[29] The promotion of Stirling as an Arthurian site by the Scottish crown continued through the fifteenth century with the emergence of a Stirling-based 'Snawdun Herald' before 1431, while in the 1470s the English commentator William of Worcester was informed by a visiting Scot that 'King Arthur kept the Round Table in Stirling Castle, otherwise called Snowdonwest castle.'[30] Stirling's claims were accommodated in the narrative provided by Fordun and Bower. Bower, in commenting on the burgh seal, noted that Stirling had, of old, stood on the boundary between Scotia and Britain, thereby reconciling the local belief in Stirling's British past with Fordun's insistence that the northern limit of the historical British kingdom had been the Forth.[31]

Even the view of Fordun's narrative as an unequivocal rejection of the 'British' past may not be entirely accurate. There seems to have been an attempt by the chronicler, or more likely the sources on which he drew, to allow the Scottish royal dynasty a prestigious Brittonic ancestry without accepting the overall narrative of British history as supplied by Geoffrey. The crucial figure in this was the British duke Fulgentius. Fulgentius appears under a variety of names in different versions of Monmouth's tale, where he is briefly noted as the leader of the Britons who defeated and killed the Roman Emperor Severus, who had vainly tried to contain the British threat by constructing a wall 'between Deira and Albany'.[32] In Fordun, however, Fulgentius emerges as a much more important figure, whose descendants reappear at regular intervals, distinguished in political terms by their close co-operation with the Scots. All this, as the most recent editors of Bower's *Scotichronicon* have pointed out, makes it likely that the account of

---

[29] *Oeuvre de Ghillebert de Lannoy, voyageur, diplomate et moraliste* (Louvain, 1878), 168.
[30] *Calendar of Documents relating to Scotland*, iv, no. 1067; Loomis, 'Segontium', 532; William Worcestre, *Itineraries*, ed. John. H. Harvey (Oxford, 1969), 6–7. Stirling was similarly styled 'Snawdoun', and praised for its 'Chapell royall, Park, and tabyll rounde' in Sir David Lindsay's *Complaynt of the Papingo* (1530). *The Works of Sir David Lindsay of the Mount, 1490–1555* ed. Douglas Hamer, 4 vols (STS, 1931), i, 75. For other Scottish sites that attracted Arthurian legends see R. S. Loomis, 'Scotland and the Arthurian Legend', 1–2; Contamine, 'Froissart and Scotland', 55; Froissart, *Oeuvres*, ii, 264.
[31] *Chron. Bower* (ed. Watt), iv, 473–5; v, 355–7.
[32] *The Historia Regum Britannie of Geoffrey of Monmouth*, 1, ed. Neil Wright (Cambridge, 1985), 47–8 (Fulgentius appears under the name Sulgenius).

Fulgentius found in Fordun/Bower was derived from a modified text of Monmouth's work.[33] Collecting the references to Fulgentius and his descendants we learn that he was 'the consul or duke of the Britons of Albany . . . who was descended from the lineage of their ancient kings'. Facing the advance of Severus, 'he hurried off into Scotland, and entered upon a firm agreement of perpetual peace with the king of Scots and the Picts and of eternal fellowship with their nations, leaving behind his two sons as hostages'. Severus constructed a wall (evidently thought by Fordun to be the Antonine Wall) to keep Fulgentius and his allies at bay, but eventually the British leader laid siege to York and killed his opponent.[34] After Fulgentius' own death we hear of his grandson Gothorius (a son of the duke's daughter) who fought to keep 'the dominions of the late Duke Fulgentius on the bank of the river Humber' from Roman occupation 'with the help of the Scots during the course of many years'. Another descendant of Fulgentius appears later in the Fordun narrative, Grim the Briton, whose daughter was supposedly married to the Scots' king Fergus mac Erc. After Fergus' death Grim was appointed as regent and guardian of the kingdom for his young grandson Eochaid, because he was 'outstanding in military matters and was also descended from the family of their own ancient kings'. After Eochaid came of age, he and his grandfather attacked and destroyed the Roman defences running from the Forth to the Clyde (the Antonine Wall), the ruins of which were, according to Fordun, thereafter known as Grim's Dyke (Grimisdik).[35] One of Eochaid's aims in this expedition was said to be the recovery of lands to the north of Humber (*ad boream Humbri*) belonging to himself, 'and formerly to Fulgentius'.[36]

[33] *Chron. Bower* (Watt), i, 378.

[34] *Chron. Bower* (Watt), i, 251–7. Geoffrey is explicitly quoted (256–7) by Bower as the source of this part of the account.

[35] *Chron. Fordun*, i, 91; *Chron. Bower* (Watt), ii, 15. A more likely explanation of the name, which Fordun claimed was used by the inhabitants of the region in his own day, may be that it was a common name in England for such ancient structures and reflected a belief that Odin (Grim) had been responsible for their construction; see *The Concise Oxford Dictionary of English Place-Names*, ed. Eilart Ekwall, 4th edn (Oxford, 1960), at p. 205. I am grateful to my colleague Alex Woolf for this observation.

[36] *Chron. Bower* (Watt), i, 269; ii, 13, 14–15, 29. 'Grim the war leader and chief counsellor of King Eochaid, after performing the office of guardian for nineteen years, during which time he both ruled the kingdom nobly and even more nobly restored it to its original condition, died an old man of a natural death.'

Whether the various snippets relating to Fulgentius and his descendants ever formed a continuous coherent narrative before they surfaced in Fordun's *Chronica* is wholly unclear. The portrayal of a lineage descended from the British royal line, consistently allied to the Scots, and eventually joined to the Scots royal house by the marriage of Grim's daughter to Fergus mac Erc, the founding figure of the kingdom, hints at an attempt to give the Scots dynasty a direct link to the British past without validating Geoffrey's vision of the threefold division of the island between the sons of Brutus. Moreover, the notion that the Scottish kings had a claim to Fulgentius' patrimony north of the Humber suggests strongly an attempt to find a historical justification for the assertion of the Scottish dynasty's rights in Northumbria during the late twelfth century.[37]

The final invocation of duke Fulgentius in Bower's chronicle is also intriguing. Describing the bestowal of ducal rank in 1398 on Robert III's son, David (as duke of Rothesay), and the king's brother Robert, earl of Fife and Menteith (as duke of Albany), Bower comments that there had been no record of anyone bearing the title duke since the death of Fulgentius. Is it possible that Robert, earl of Fife, was himself conscious of the precedent and deliberately chose to associate his lordship with that of Fulgentius by assuming the title Albany, in memory of the 'duke of the Britons of Albany'?[38] At the time of his adoption of the title, Robert's political and territorial interests were centred in areas where references to a British hero might be expected to elicit a positive response. From 1373 Robert, already earl of Menteith, had been custodian of Stirling castle, Arthur's Snowdon. From Stirling and Menteith, Robert's influence had flowed west into the Lennox and Argyll, perhaps the Scottish region richest in supposed Arthurian sites (at least partly generated by a physical landscape that incorporated Roman remains such as the Antonine Wall) and families that claimed

---

[37] Other significant figures were claimed as representatives of Fulgentius' line in the Fordun/Bower history, most notably Loth, Lord of Lothian, the husband of Arthur's sister Anna and the father of Gawain and Modred. *Chron. Fordun*, i, 109. Bower adds that Loth and Anna also had a daughter, Thaney, the mother of St Kentigern, the chief saint, of course, of the diocese of Glasgow. *Chron. Bower* (Watt), ii, 65.

[38] *Chron. Bower* (Watt), viii, 13. Alternatively the assumption of the title Albany has been explained as a piece of Gaelic revivalism. See J. W. M. Bannerman, *Studies in the History of Dalriada* (Edinburgh, 1974), 118–19; Steve Boardman, *The Early Stewart Kings: Robert II and Robert III 1371–1406* (East Linton, 1996), 207–8.

real or imagined Brittonic descent.[39] Another major fortress that fell within Robert's sphere of influence was Dumbarton castle, like Stirling occupying an ancient and precipitous hilltop location, and apparently identified in 1367 as 'Castrum Arthuri'.[40]

In the second half of the fourteenth century then, Robert II, his son Robert, duke of Albany, and, we may presume, the rest of the extended royal family, seem to have had few ideological problems with the literary legacy of the *Brut*, British kingship and Arthur. Despite the way in which the *Brut* myth had been, and continued to be, used to underpin the claims of the English crown to superiority over the Scottish realm, the early Stewart kings saw no need to abandon or forget their family's prestigious descent.[41] Nor was the acceptance of the authority and relevance of the matter of Britain confined to the royal house, for the two most important writers in the Scots vernacular in the late fourteenth and early fifteenth centuries, Barbour and Wyntoun, clearly viewed Arthurian and 'British' material in a positive light. Much, however, may turn on context and audience. The Stewart genealogy, despite the royal status of the family after 1371, was essentially concerned with tracing the ancestry of a single baronial lineage. Similarly, the proliferation of 'Arthurian' sites did not necessarily point to an automatic recognition of the reliability of Galfridian history in other situations. Crucially, the historical framework provided by Geoffrey never seems to have been adopted as the sole and sufficient explanation of the origins and early history of the monarchy or kingdom as it was in thirteenth- and fouteenth-century England. Arguments from silence are never wholly compelling, but it may be significant that, as yet, none of the numerous extant medieval reworkings of the *Historia Regum Brittaniae* or the French and English prose *Bruts* are known to have been

---

[39] Most obviously the Campbells, for whom see W. D. H. Sellar, 'The Earliest Campbells – Norman, Briton or Gael?', *Scottish Studies*, 18 (1973), 109–22. Sellar also points out the regular appearance of Arthur as a Christian name in the Campbell kindred and in other Lennox/Argyll families. In fact, the name was common in and around the Firth of Clyde in the twelfth and thirteen centuries (and often in areas of Stewart influence) e.g. *c*.1200 Arthur Ardrossan of that Ilk, W. Fraser, *Memorials of the Montgomeries*, 18–19; Arthur of Dunoon, apparently custodian of Dunoon castle for the Stewarts.

[40] See Loomis, 'Segontium to Sinadon', 532.

[41] In 1400 Henry IV would deploy the Brutus legend again, to justify his invasion of Scotland in that year and his demand for Robert III's homage. E. L. G. Stones, 'The Appeal to History in Anglo-Scottish Relations between 1291–1401', *Archives*, ix (1969), 11–21, 80–3.

of Scottish provenance and to have presented the late medieval Scottish monarchy as a seamless continuation of the line of Brutus and Albanactus.[42] The simplest explanation for the apparent reluctance of the Scots to embrace the notion of a British origin for the late medieval kingdom surely lies not in the demands of warfare and propaganda from the 1290s onwards, but in the fact that there was already a well-established account of the origins of the kingdom and race that Geoffrey was simply unable to displace. Indeed, throughout the late medieval period Anglo-Scottish conflict *was* one of the contexts in which the Scots were happy to deploy 'British' material and themes. Regardless of the *Brut*'s particular association with the imperial ambitions of the English crown, the notion of the triumphant reclamation of political authority over the entire island of Britain by the 'heirs of the Britons', was very much a double-edged weapon which might also be turned against the English monarchy.[43] Far from accepting an 'English' interpretation of the mythic history of Britain, Barbour's Stewart genealogy, drawing on the established traditions of the family, may well have been a bold and threatening statement of the history and destiny of the new dynasty. Robert II, as much as any English king, could portray himself as the heir to the legacy of the Britons, and could ponder on the deep and dark prophecies which promised the resurrection of the power of the Britons in league with the Scots, and the ruination of those who had usurped their hegemony over Britain's broad acres.

An aggressive awareness of the Scottish dynasty's place in the history of the entire island was reflected in the persistent cultivation within the northern kingdom of another historical tradition closely allied to the

---

[42] One bizarre late fourteenth-century attempt to lay out the 'genealogia' of Scots kings from Brutus through Albanactus travels via a sequence of British, Pictish and Gaelic royal names to end in a jumbled series of Malcolms, Edwards, Alexanders, Williams, Davids and Johns. It is clearly of English or Anglo-Welsh origin; see Wigmore Abbey Chronicle, MS 224, f10r–11r, University of Chicago. Diana B. Tyson, 'Handlist of manuscripts containing the French prose *Brut* chronicle', *Scriptorium*, 48 (1994), 333–44, mentions two MSS that include the descendants of Queen Margaret of Scotland. One of these, Royal Library MS 75 A 2/2, The Hague, is concerned only with illustrating the marriage of Margaret's daughter to Henry I. The other, in the College of Arms, remains to be investigated.

[43] See J. C. Crick, 'The British Past and the Welsh Future: Gerald of Wales, Geoffrey of Monmouth and Arthur of Britain', in *Celtica*, 23 (1999), 60–75, for the way in which twelfth-century Anglo-Norman writers could view Monmouth's work as an implicit threat to the English kingdom.

Brut and British material. It was common for manuscripts of the *Brut* composed in England to be accompanied by genealogies of the English royal line and/or histories of the English kingdom. In a sense the *Brut* and the Anglo-Saxon genealogies and histories formed a unified story that together explained the emergence of the medieval English kingdom. Despite the emphasis of Fordun and Bower on the Gaelic antecedents of the Scottish royal house, the influence of this 'English' material on Scottish historical writing, including Fordun and Bower themselves, remained profound.

The pivotal figure that made the history of the English royal house relevant to late medieval Scots was, of course, Queen Margaret, the wife of Malcolm III. There was a number of factors that ensured that Margaret would attain an early prominence in both Scottish and English historical writing. A considerable part of the narrative of Fordun, Bower and Wyntoun as it related to Margaret was ultimately derived from Turgot's description of the queen's life, or Ailred of Rievaulx's *Genealogia Regum Anglorum*.[44] The production of contemporary or near contemporary works that displayed a profound interest in the Scottish queen was, at least partly, stimulated by Margaret's position as a descendant of the English royal house, for Margaret and her children could be portrayed as representing the legitimate line of the English royal dynasty displaced by the conquest of 1066. This notion was acceptable to both the English and Scottish royal dynasties of the early twelfth century, for both could claim to embody Margaret's bloodline. While David I was obviously Margaret's son, English accounts, such as Ailred's *Vita Beati Eduardi Regis et Confessoris*, focused on the marriage of Margaret's daughter Matilda to Henry I and suggested that through the match the ancient English royal line had been re-established.[45] The evocation of Matilda and Henry's marriage as an act that restored Angevin kingship to its Anglo-Saxon and indeed British roots was later to be found in Wyntoun's chronicle. Here, Matilda's marriage to Henry was presented as a means of regenerating the tree of English kingship because the royal bride was a bearer of Saxon as well as Scottish blood. The couple's offspring

---

[44] See Broun, *Irish Identity*, 196; J. P. Migne (ed.), *Patrologiae cursus completesseries Latina*, CXCV. Cols 711–38.

[45] H. R. Luard (ed.), *Lives of Edward the Confessor*, Rolls Series 3 (London, 1858), 286–7; See also *Orderic Vitalis*, v, 298–301. In the context of the politics of twelfth-century Scotland the concentration on the heirs of Malcolm and Margaret was surely also designed to exclude dynastic rivals from collateral branches of the Scottish royal house.

would thus revive the line of English kingship that had been established by Locrine, son of Brutus 'that wan thir landis . . . fra gyandis',
and thereafter ruled the kingdom for 2,000 years without interruption
until 'Harrauld, William Bastard and William Reid'.[46] The presentation of the story of English kingship as one that embraced the history of
the early British kings and the royal Saxon dynasty in a seamless unity
was fairly typical.

The descendants of Malcolm and Margaret that sat on the Scottish
throne also, of course, possessed that mix of Scots and Saxon blood that
made Matilda such a beguiling figure for the Angevins. From an early
stage the dual descent of the Scottish royal house allowed the Scots to
champion the right of their kings as heirs to the English throne usurped
by William I in 1066.[47] It is likely that twelfth-century Scottish kings,
with their extensive political and territorial interests in Cumbria and
Northumbria and, perhaps, in the reign of David I a more than passing
interest in the competition for the English throne itself, were enthusiastic promoters of this view of their own dynasty. While these
arguments were most obviously deployed in periods of outright Anglo-Scottish hostility, the notion of a unified Saxon/Scots royal house
also seems to have generated visions of a more amicable settlement
between the two kingdoms and peoples that would effectively have
embraced the entire island of Britain. An enigmatic elaboration of this
theme is to be found in Fordun's unfinished book VI, in an introduction
to a discussion of the Scottish king's English ancestors. Addressed
directly to the 'King of the Scots', the passage relates how the royal lines

---

[46] In this episode an ancient English knight, who had served as Steward in King
Edward's household before the conquest, explained how the union made clear
the terms of a riddle that had been posed to him in those pre-conquest days as
to the future of the English kingdom. The riddle concerned a tree that was sawn
down and removed from its roots, but would later be reattached and bear leaves
and fruit once more. This was clearly a reference back to the *Vita Edwardi*.
Chron. Wyntoun (Laing), ii, 168–73; *Chron. Wyntoun* (Amours), iv, 358–67.

[47] *Orderic Vitalis*, v, 93. An account of a supposed plot of 1137, discovered by
Bishop Nigel of Ely, to slaughter all Normans and give the crown to the king of
Scots. See also Adam of Dryburgh writing in the 1180, J. P. Migne (ed.),
Patrologiae cursus completesseries Latina, CXCVIII. Cols 609–792, at 722–3. The
theme also figured strongly in Scottish historical arguments presented during
negotiations of 1321 between representatives of Robert I and Edward II, where
it was openly stated that the right to govern in England rested with the Scottish
dynasty descended from Margaret. P. A. Linehan, 'A fourteenth-century history
of Anglo-Scottish relations in a Spanish manuscript', *Bulletin of the Institute of
Historical Research*, xlviii (1975), 106–22, at 116–17.

of Scotland and England 'combine and meet in you' and exhorts the monarch to rejoice because 'you are descended from glorious roots that have been joined together'. Moreover, 'these two royal lines, for whom the size of the island was formerly insufficient for living in peace and harmony, are now joined together as one and are at peace in the person of one ruler'. The king was enjoined to 'maintain the traditions of the brilliant fighting force of a victorious fighting island, that is of the Scots and the English'.[48]

The entrenched and institutionalised anglophobia that seems to have become part of the mental make-up of the Scottish elites in the fourteenth and fifteenth centuries made pious hopes of unity and harmony essentially redundant.[49] Nevertheless, Scottish works from this period also deployed the imagery of dynastic union and the joint occupation of a shared island home, Britain, although there was normally a rather more bellicose subtext. A Latin poem on the battle of Otterburn (1388), for example, opens with a conventional lament for the bloodshed and destruction between 'two warlike kingdoms' and then observes 'The island home of the British (*Insula Britonum*) contains two most excellent kingdoms, from which is banished every benefit of peace by the craft of the devil.'[50] Another product of border lordship patronage, the sabre-rattling mid-fifteenth century 'Buke of the Howlat' included an optimistic portrayal of the Scottish king:

---

[48] *Chron. Bower* (Watt), iii, 307; *Chron. Fordun*, i, 387. It is unclear whether the passage is meant to address a particular king and time. If so then there are obvious questions to be answered as to which Scottish king could be meant. One possibility is that Fordun may be adapting a passage relating to the reign of David I. A more intriguing explanation would see the passage as a commentary on Fordun's own time, and the attempts by David II to have a son of Edward III accepted as his heir. This would require the 'one ruler' to be a future hope, rather than, as the passage suggests, a delivered reality.

[49] For a recent study emphasising the animosity that was woven into, and sustained, Anglo-Scottish border warfare, see Alastair J. Macdonald, *Border Bloodshed: Scotland and England at War, 1369–1403* (East Linton, 2000), esp. Chs. 5 and 6.

[50] *Chron. Bower* (Watt), viii, 421. It seems that the poet here is suggesting that the Scots and English together made up the 'British' who inhabited the island, although the possibility that it was a deliberately antiquarian phrase to indicate that the island had belonged to the unified British people of an earlier age should not be discounted.

> 'Quhilk sall be lord and ledar
> Our braid Brettane all quhar'
> As Sanct Margaretis air'[51]

Here, clearly, the picture of a Britain (re)unified by the military/dynastic victory of the Scots was a bald threat to the English crown. That individual Scots noblemen in the fourteenth and fifteenth centuries could continue to think in 'pan British' terms is suggested by the reputed tomb inscription of George Dunbar, earl of March. The most able Scottish military commander of his generation, Dunbar's sepulchre is said to have described the resting warrior as 'Erll George the Brytane', kinsman to the kings of Scotland, England and Denmark.[52] It may or may not be coincidental that the Otterburn poem, the Buke of the Howlat and Dunbar's tomb were all associated with aristocrats who were active in Anglo-Scottish warfare and diplomacy.[53] The notion of the unification of the two 'British' kingdoms, peaceful or otherwise, had long been reduced to a vague aspiration for the powerful English monarchy let alone the warleaders of fourteenth- and fifteenth-century Scotland. Yet there was little indication in these snippets of a retreat behind the historiographical barriers erected by Fordun.

Aside from the importance of Queen Margaret in Anglo-Scottish relations, the figure of the saintly Saxon monarch also had a profound effect on the way the Scots regarded their own dynasty and kingdom. Queen Margaret's pre-eminence in Scottish historiography was heightened by the successful mid-thirteenth-century campaign for her canonisation. The subsequent development of a specifically 'royal'

---

[51] 'The Buke of the Howlat', in Priscilla Bawcutt and Felicity Riddy (eds), *Longer Scottish Poems*, vol. 1 (1375–1650) (Edinburgh, 1987), 60. A similar sentiment was expressed by the deeply anglophobic Blind Hary in the 1470s, when he wrote of his hope for the day that one of Margaret's heirs would reclaim the stone of destiny. *Vita Nobilissimi Defensoris Scotie Wilelmi Wallace Militis* (STS, 1968), i, 5.

[52] *Chron. Bower* (Watt), viii, 201. If genuine the epitaph may have been developed to reflect George's evident pride in his descent from both the English and Scottish royal lines. Like Scottish kings, then, George was aware of a dual ancestry that spanned the Anglo-Scottish border. George's long career as a political exile in England from 1401 onwards would obviously have heightened his sense of operating beyond the confines of either realm.

[53] That chivalric honour and prestige could also be thought of, and won, in a 'British' context may be suggested by the throwaway description of Sir John Swinton, killed at the battle of Humbleton in 1402, as 'the most worthy knight in arms in the whole of Britain'. *Chron. Bower* (Watt), viii, 47.

devotion focused on St Margaret saw Dunfermline Abbey emerge as a 'cult centre of Scottish kingship'.[54] Moreover, as Broun has noted, from the mid-thirteenth century onwards Scots chroniclers increasingly focused on Malcolm III and St Margaret as 'dynastic founders' rather than Cinaed Mac Alpin.[55] This theme was developed in a number of late medieval works where the marriage of Malcolm and Margaret was seen as producing a 'new' dynastic line. Wyntoun, in particular, suggested that the reign of Malcolm III saw the institution of what was, in effect, a fresh Scottish royal house. The chronicler observed that none of the kings he had outlined in the descent 'from Adam through the Irishry' had left lineal descendants and that it was from the marriage of Malcolm and Margaret that all subsequent Scottish kings descended.[56] Thus, Wyntoun could describe late fourteenth-century rulers in terms of the number of generations they were removed from Margaret. In a tribute to the character of Robert, duke of Albany (d. 1420), for example, Wyntoun introduced the duke as

> The tenth person he wes begat
> In lineale descent fra Sanct Margrat:
> Of that roout the kynd flewoure,
> As flouris havand that sawoure,

---

[54] *Bruce* (Duncan), 756; Broun, *Irish Identity*, 196, n. 5. Already established, in the eleventh century, as a significant royal sepulchre, Margaret's canonisation seems to have reconfirmed the attractiveness of the abbey for royal burials. As Duncan points out, Alexander III, his first wife, Robert I and his queen, Elizabeth, were all buried in Dunfermline, while David II was born there. Despite the implication that, thereafter, the royal lineage showed less affection for the abbey as a burial site, there remained some significant connections, particularly for Scottish queens. David II and his second wife, Queen Margaret Drummond, evidently planned to be buried at Dunfermline before their acrimonious divorce in 1368. *The Exchequer Rolls of Scotland (ER)* ed. J. Stuart et al. (Edinburgh, 1878–1908), ii, 300, 348. Robert II's queen, Euphemia, *was* buried there; see *Chron. Bower* (Watt), ix, 137. Robert III's wife, Annabella Drummond, was also buried in the abbey and may well have deliberately chosen Dunfermline as the location for the birth of her third son James (the future James I) in 1394. *Chron. Bower* (Watt), viii, 37. The wearing of St Margaret's shirt (kept at Dunfermline) by Scottish queens at the birth of their children is well attested, and explains why so many royal births occurred there. The practice was still in place in the fifteenth century with St Margaret's shirt used at the births of James III (1451) and James V. *ER*, v, 447, 512. I am grateful to Dr Michael Penman for this last reference.

[55] Broun, *Irish Identity*, 195–7.

[56] *Chron. Wyntoun* (Laing), ii, 142.

He had, and held, and all tyme grew,
Ay blossoming in bownté new.[57]

Walter Bower's account of Queen Margaret's miraculous intervention in
the battle of Largs in 1263 reveals his view that Scotland's royal dynasty
properly consisted of Margaret's divinely blessed heirs. Bower recounts
that as Haakon IV Haakonson's war-fleet overran Bute and Arran a strange
vision appeared to Sir John Wemyss, who lay incapacitated and apparently
terminally ill, in far-off Fife. Suddenly transported in a feverish dream to
the doorway of the church in Dunfermline, Wemyss was confronted by the
sight of St Margaret leading her husband and three of her sons to war
against the Norse. Margaret explained to Sir John 'I am hurrying to defend
our country at Largs, for you must know that *I received this kingdom from
God, granted in trust to me and our heirs for ever.*'[58] Moved by this mystical
encounter, Wemyss set out for Dunfermline, where his tearful supplication
before St Margaret's shrine brought about a marvellous restoration of his
health, a recovery which coincided exactly with the arrival of the joyful
news that the Scots had defeated the Norwegian king at Largs. In Bower's
account we see intertwined St Margaret's effectiveness as an intercessory
saint and a focus for popular devotion, and her role as the progenitor and
defender of the royal dynasty and the kingdom given to them by God.

For Bower and others, therefore, the descendants of Malcolm and
Margaret were quite properly distinguished from previous Scottish
monarchs by reason of their 'membership of a gens or a renowned
genus', through which they shared 'in a collection of gifts and powers
transmitted by blood'.[59] Margaret's saintly bloodline could, of course,

---

[57] *Chron. Wyntoun* (Laing), iii, 101. The sense of renewal of the line descended
from St Margaret in each new generation of the royal family, and the notion of a
real and direct link to the family founder, was presumably encouraged by the use
of Margaret's birthing shirt. The protection of the saintly queen was extended to
her descendants from the moment of their arrival in the world of men; see note
54. Unfortunately, Wyntoun's calculation of the intervening generations seems to
have been slightly faulty, as he also described Albany's father, Robert II, as the
tenth person in lineal descent from Malcolm III, *Chron. Wyntoun* (Laing), ii,
142. A similar idea appears in the potted history of Anglo-Scottish relations
produced in 1321. Here Robert I is described as the seventh Scottish king
descended from St Margaret. Linehan, 'Spanish Manuscript', 116.

[58] *Chron. Bower* (Watt), v, 337–9. In the fourteenth and fifteenth centuries St
Margaret continued to function as an intercessory saint with a pilgrimage centre
in Dunfermline, and to play a crucial symbolic role as an effective founding
figure for the royal dynasty. *Chron. Bower* (Watt), vii, 98–9.

[59] André Vauchez, *Sainthood in the later Middle Ages* (Cambridge, 1997), 178–83.

be traced back further to her Saxon kinsmen, most notably Edward the Confessor. There is thus little surprise in the interest displayed by late medieval Scots in Edward the Confessor and the English dynasty of which he was a part.[60] Scottish royal genealogies of the fifteenth century, both literary and pictorial, tended to show the joining of two great royal lines, Scots and Saxon, in the marriage of Malcolm and Margaret.[61] The representation of the Scottish royal arms accompanying a genealogy of the kings of Scotland and England to 1449 in the Corpus Christi Manuscript of Bower's *Scotichronicon*, for example, shows the Scottish lion rampant impaled with the supposed arms of Edward the Confessor. The Confessor's arms, presumably representing Margaret's bloodline, also appear on the heraldic ceiling of St Machar's cathedral, dating from around 1520, where they occupy the second place, behind those of the then Scottish king (James V), in a series depicting the arms of the secular nobility of Scotland.[62]

Despite the location of the emergence of a new and sanctified royal line late in the eleventh century, the 'Margaretsons' were not divorced from the ancient history of their kingdom. Just as the

---

[60] It is also intriguing to note how the development of the Margaret cult and the re-establishment of her church at Dunfermline as a royal sepulchre coincided with a renewed interest in Henry III's England with the cult of Edward the Confessor and the emergence of his church at Westminster as a burial place for English monarchs. Paul Binski, *Westminster Abbey and the Plantagenets: Kingship and the Representation of Power, 1200–1400* (Yale, 1995), Ch. 2 (The Cult of St Edward). Indeed, the interest of the Scottish royal house in Edward's cult pre-dated, or was at least contemporaneous with, that of Henry III. From around 1225, William the Lion's English widow, Queen Ermengarde (Beaumont), was involved in the preparations for the foundation of a new abbey dedicated to St Edward at Balmerino in Fife. In this enterprise she was supported by her son Alexander II (by this stage the brother-in-law of Henry III). Ian B. Cowan and David E. Easson (eds), *Medieval Religious Houses: Scotland* 2nd edn (London, 1976), 72–3. Ermengarde was the granddaughter of Constance, an illegitimate daughter of Henry I. The elevation of Edward and the canonisation of Margaret, then, may have been part of a wider movement supported by both the Scottish and English dynasties in the thirteenth century. Both families regarded themselves as heirs to the Saxon royal line, and a shared outlook on the value of their mutual saintly ancestors may well have been encouraged by intermarriage between the two dynasties during the twelfth and early thirteenth centuries.

[61] Broun, *Irish Identity*, 195–6.

[62] *Chron. Bower* (Watt), ix, 164 (Fig. 7b); D. McRoberts, 'The Heraldic Ceiling of St Machar's Cathedral Aberdeen', *Friends of St Machar's Cathedral Occasional Papers* No. 2 (1976).

Angevin monarchy grafted its story on to Saxon and British roots, the unbroken tradition of Scottish kingship and the long line of Gaelic rulers that had created and defended the kingdom against all-comers, Britons, Picts, Danes, Norwegians and, of course, the English, provided sure historical and intellectual foundations that would not be willingly abandoned.[63] Nevertheless, the fact that the living legacy of Scottish kingship could be seen as originating in the marriage of Malcolm and Margaret, in their union of Scots and saintly Saxon blood, may have been important in a number of ways.[64] It may have been especially significant for the English-speaking lowland aristocracy of the medieval kingdom. Many of the dominant aristocratic families of late medieval Scotland were the descendants of the native aristocracy of Lothian, an area forcibly annexed by Gaelic-speaking Scots kings in the eleventh century, or of twelfth-century and thirteenth-century incomers of English, French and Flemish extraction.[65] The founders of these families had obviously played no direct part in the struggles of the ancient Gaelic kingdom. Queen Margaret's marriage to Malcolm III, how-ever, could be used to suggest that these lineages had arrived in Scotland at a crucial, indeed formative, point in the kingdom's history. There was simply no need to seek any earlier validation. In the late Middle Ages, lowland lineage histories seem to have made no real attempt to extend family origins beyond the eleventh century

[63] R. A. Mason, 'Scotching the *Brut*', 63–5.

[64] *Chron. Wyntoun* (Laing), ii, 167; *Chron. Wyntoun* (Amours), iv, 354–5. 'The Saxonys and the Scottys blude/In natyownys twa before than yhud/Bot the barnetyme off that get,/That Malcolme had off Saynt Margret,/Togyddyr drw full unyowne/To pas syne in successyowne'. See also the newly edited *Liber Extravagans* in *Chron. Bower* (Watt), ix, 73, 91 and notes (p. 124).

[65] The exact status of the lands controlled by the Scottish crown south of the Forth was unresolved for much of the period between the eleventh and early thirteenth centuries. In 1202x14, for example, the Forth could still be regarded as the boundary between the kingdoms of Scotland and England. D. Broun, 'The Seven Kingdoms in *De Situ Albanie*: A Record of Pictish political Geography or imaginary Map of ancient *Alba*', in E. J. Cowan and R. Andrew McDonald (eds), *Alba: Celtic Scotland in the Medieval Era* (East Linton, 2000), 24–42, at 38–9. The English or continental origins of a number of Scottish families, such as the Lindsays, Grahams and Comyns, were well known and, in the case of the Sir David Lindsay, first earl Crawford, became the subject of a purportedly witty exchange between English and Scottish knights during a tournament at Smithfield in 1390. *Chron. Bower* (Watt), viii, 15–17, *Chron. Wyntoun* (Laing), ii, 321.

and the reign of Malcolm III.[66] By the early sixteenth century, a large group of families claimed either to have some direct association with Margaret and her immediate family's arrival in Scotland, to have accompanied Malcolm III on his expedition from England to recover his kingdom from the 'usurper' MacBeth, or to have been forced to flee to the northern kingdom by William I as a result of their continued support for the rights of members of the Old English royal house.[67] Since their arrival in the eleventh century implied loyalty and service to the late medieval royal dynasty from the moment of its inception, it is no surprise that this type of origin came to be regarded as especially prestigious. By the fifteenth century, even families with reputable and far older genealogical

---

[66] The contrast with the genealogies, histories and poetry produced by the learned orders of Gaelic Scotland is striking. For many, the Fordun/Bower tradition was almost wholly irrelevant in terms of providing a historical scheme into which their family history could be fitted and their power and status in their own society derived and explained. The Gaelic-speaking aristocracy of the Hebrides and much of the west and central Highlands retained their direct acquaintance with Irish historiography. MS 1467, a collection of family genealogies largely composed around 1400, illustrates that the principal concern of the compiler was to place the families involved into a direct relationship with established figures in the Gaelic historiographical tradition. M. D. W. MacGregor, 'A Political History of the MacGregors before 1571' (unpublished Ph.D. thesis), Edinburgh, 1989, Appendix 13: The Dating and Composition of MS 1467, 414–20.

[67] Earlier accounts allowed this elaboration by commenting, in a very general way, on the flight of oppressed English nobles to Scotland in the face of William the Conqueror's aggression. Malcolm III 'gert procure thame rycht welle/In all thare lykyn ilka delle'. *Chron.Wyntoun* (Laing), ii, 159. By the sixteenth century families in Berwickshire and Lothian seem almost uniformly to have located the foundation of their fortunes in the region in this period. The Swinton origin-legend recorded in the sixteenth century, for example, suggests that 'Edulf of Swinton gave valuable service to Malcolm Canmore in his struggle for the recovery of the Scottish throne.' The sixteenth-century account of the Setons also claimed that 'their surnam came home with King Malcolme Canmoir forth of Ingland'. John Bellenden could assert that before Malcolm III's reign there had been no surnames in Scotland, but that his territorial settlement in favour of the men who had supported him against MacBeth gave rise to a whole series of families adopting the name of the estates they had been given. Thus, Bellenden explained the origins of the Gordons, Calders, Lokarts, Lauders, Wawanes, Libertons, Meldrums, Shaws, Learmonths, Cargills, Rattrays, Dundases, Cockburns, Abercrombies, Myretons, Menzies and Leslies. *The Chronicles of Scotland compiled by Hector Boece*, translated into Scots by John Bellenden 1531, 2 vols (STS, 1938–41), ii, 168–9.

traditions attempted to fix their origins in Scotland to this period.[68]

The elaboration of myths outlining the attachment of English families to the cause of Malcolm III and his Saxon queen helped to explain, in a positive way, the fact of a large population of English descent and speech, loyal to a monarchy that traced its origins to a distant Gaelic past. Moreover, the emergence of an understanding that the 'Margaretsons' represented a mix of 'Scots and Saxon' blood may well have both reflected, and contributed to, the successful absorption of different cultural and linguistic groups into a single polity.

As Robin Frame and Rees Davies have emphasised, the story of the eleventh and twelfth centuries, often characterised as an age of Francophone aristocratic expansion, was just as notable for the expansion of an English-speaking peasantry and burgess class into Wales, Ireland and Scotland.[69] In Wales and Ireland this aristocratic, burghal and peasant expansion could form communities, the so-called 'Englisheries' of Wales and Ireland, that retained, developed and cultivated a sense of legal, cultural and linguistic separateness from their neighbours and that remained politically tied to the English crown. In the thirteenth century the English monarchy was able to deploy notions of its leadership of a reconstituted English-speaking nation to express and advance its political agenda in these areas.

In Scotland, the sense that those of English speech and descent formed a distinct group with a natural attachment to the affairs,

---

[68] Including the Campbells and the Drummonds. It is probably not coincidental that these adaptations were advanced at a point when these families began to play a more prominent and direct role in royal government. The Drummonds claimed descent from a Hungarian who accompanied Margaret to Scotland. Other families who asserted that they were in that category included the Lothian families of Crichton and Borthwick. 'Five names . . . came out of Hungary with Agatha and her Children, to wit, Crichton, Maule, Borthwick, Giffard and Fotheringham, who at first all got lands in Lothian, and settled there.' William Stewart, *Buik of the Chroniclis of Scotland: A Metrical Version of the History of Hector Boece*, ed. W. B. Turnbull 3 vols (London, 1858), vol. 1, 664–5. In the early fifteenth century the Crichtons and Borthwicks were prominent royal officeholders. The close relationship between these families and the crown in the early fifteenth century was demonstrated in 1430, at the knighting of James I's infant sons, when the heirs of Crichton and Borthwick were also knighted. It may have been that descent from the members of St Margaret's household was seen to be particularly apt for families who were part of the crown's regional lordship in Lothian.

[69] R. R. Davies, *The First English Empire: Power and Identities in the British Isles, 1093–1343* (Oxford, 2000); R. R. Davies, 'In Praise of British History', in R. R. Davies (ed.), *The British Isles, 1100–1500*, 9–26.

concerns and interests of the English nation as embodied in the kingship of England never seems to have been allowed to develop. In Wales and Ireland distinctive identities were sharpened by a clash between rival, well-defined and mutually exclusive visions of the past. In Scotland, twelfth-century monarchs seem to have been adept at juggling the well-established history of the kingdom and the Scots in Gaelic historiography with the vision of a 'British' past revitalised by Geoffrey of Monmouth and an awareness of the 'English' roots of the dynasty to which they belonged. In the course of the thirteenth century more and more emphasis seems to have been placed on this final element. It would be tempting, although speculative, to link the thirteenth-century presentation of Margaret and Malcolm as dynastic founders with the contemporary reassertion of the ancient English roots of the southern kingdom, the renewed interest in Edward the Confessor, and the emergence of the site of the Confessor's tomb at Westminster as the chief burial place for English monarchs.[70] The thirteenth-century 'rediscovery' and reassertion of the importance of the English past was a phenomenon with implications well beyond the political and territorial boundaries of the English kingdom.

Overall, then, it is difficult to see a comprehensive, popular and uniform Scots rejection of the 'Matter of Britain' taking shape in the late medieval kingdom. The straight line drawn between the pleadings of Scots clerics at the papacy in the first decade of the fourteenth century, the Declaration of Arbroath, Fordun's *Chronica*, and Bower's *Scotichronicon* rather obscures the fact that works in the Scots vernacular intended for a secular audience continued to revel in Arthurian and British themes. Moreover, the suggestion that the Fordun/Bower tradition arose from, and had a special role to play in, the justification and sustenance of the Scots' position in conflict with England also has problems. As we have seen, the bellicose ambitions of the Scottish crown and kingdom in Anglo-Scottish warfare could be easily expressed, and probably most often were, in terms that drew on a 'British' frame of reference in the form of Merlinic prophecies or the rights of the dynasty as the true heirs to the throne of England. The one area in which British material was not rehearsed and entertained was in the laying out of the history of Scottish kingship. Any debate over the applicability of Geoffrey's saga to the northern kingdom in this regard must have been decided long before the opening of the Wars of Independence. The prominence of Saint Margaret in late medieval accounts of the royal

[70] D. A. Carpenter, *The Reign of Henry III* (London, 1996), Chs 14, 20, 21.

dynasty and kingdom seems crucial. The royal house descended from Margaret was clearly regarded as, in some senses, a 'new' or transformed dynasty. Moreover, Margaret's English descent opened up an obvious route for the Scots to claim for their own royal line an unbroken connection to Brutus and the ancient British monarchy. Yet, this opportunity was not exploited, and the Fulgentius material fossilised in Fordun's chronicle gives the only hint of an accommodation with the notion of a Brittonic legacy to Scottish kingship. In the end, Fulgentius and Margaret were both absorbed into a narrative that remained fundamentally rooted in the kingdom's Gaelic past, a story that was too powerful and entrenched to be subverted even by the seductive voice of Geoffrey of Monmouth.

The author is grateful to Dr Dauvit Broun, Dr Roger Mason, Professor Geoffrey Barrow and Dr Sally Mapstone for their helpful comments on earlier drafts of this chapter.

CHAPTER 4

In Search of the
Scottish Reformation

Michael Lynch

T he standing of the Scottish Reformation has undergone considerable change in the course of the past generation. As late as its
quatercentenary in 1960, the professor of Church History in the
University of Glasgow was still able to claim with confidence that
the Reformation had produced a church which was a 'national symbol'
and that 'one may doubt whether there could be a Scotland without it'.[1]
In the Scottish diaspora, in places such as small-town Canada or New
Zealand, where John Knox and Andrew Melville churches, replicating
faithfully stages of the schisms and reunions within the nineteenth-
century church, this is probably still the prevailing view. One of the
most influential works ever to come out of that diaspora claimed that:

> Scotland and Presbyterianism seem to have been made for each
> other. Even to this day, when the old dogmatisms have
> softened and sometimes all but evaporated, a thoroughbred
> Scots who for one reason or another is not a Presbyterian tends
> to feel somewhat ill at ease about it, even a little embarrassed,
> almost as might an American who preferred cricket to baseball
> or an Englishman who liked Cervantes better than
> Shakespeare.[2]

Within Scotland itself, however, such moral certainties now seem
outdated. An article by a conservative columnist in *The Scotsman*,

---

[1] J. M. Reid, *Kirk and Nation* (Glasgow, 1960), 173.
[2] Geddes MacGregor, *Scotland: An Intimate Portrait* (Boston, MA, 1990), 78;
originally published as *Scotland forever Home* (New York, 1985).

during the meeting of the General Assembly in May 1999, argued that the 'Church of Scotland may still be the established national church but it is no longer the church of the nation.' The fact that the General Assembly then met in another place, supplanted by the new Scottish parliament, which is what now represents the Scottish nation, exaggerated still further the dislocation of the two of the key elements of Scottish identity – a Protestant church for a Protestant people. The same piece pointed to a severe drop in attendance over the past generation: the Church of Scotland had been losing members 'almost as fast as the Scottish Conservative and Unionist Party has lost voters'. Although it had 680,000 communicant members, 'only 17 per cent of Scotland's adult population are now members of the Kirk'.[3] In a country where prayers in the new parliament were allocated on a proportional basis to the various faiths of the people it represents, where stands now the long enduring twin ideas that the Reformation of 1560 was one of the central facts of Scottish history and that Protestantism has been the historic backbone of the nation?

It is not the case that everywhere in an increasingly secular age the Reformation has lost ground as a symbol of the nation. The Netherlands still has an official Protestant historiography of its past, cast in the form of a heroic struggle for independence and freedom. The visual propaganda of the age still evokes powerful images. It is made up of two basic elements: images such as the Antwerp Fury of 1576 still underpin the notion of a heroic past, based on the escape from foreign oppression. And the biblical analogies afforded by events like the raising of the siege of Leiden in 1574, acting out the parable of God's people, nourished by loaves and fishes, help sustain the idea of the divine deliverance of a Protestant nation from oppression.[4] The irony is that there are more Catholics than Protestants in the present-day Netherlands. Here, however, is a nation which still clings to the congenial religious parts of its past and has continued to embellish an iconography of national identity over the course of the last century.

In Scotland, by contrast, the Reformation is no longer a usable past. Outside of the zealots, most Scots and certainly most contemporary Scots politicians, of all parties, can see little point in the arcane religious

[3] Allan Massie, 'Alternative Parliament that Shaped the Nation', *The Scotsman*, 11 May 1999.
[4] 'The Spanish Fury in Antwerp, 1576' (anon.) and 'Distributing herrings and white bread following the liberation of Leiden, 1574' (Otto van Heen), reproduced in K. Bussmann and H. Schilling (eds), *1648: War and Peace in Europe* (Munster, 1998), 27–8.

struggles and debates of the Reformation. Notions of oppression and a release from the 'thralldom of strangers' now seem remote. Even Scottish nationalism has lost the distinctly Protestant tinge that it possessed as late as the 1970s. Just as Protestant historians of the nineteenth century preferred to pass over the Middle Ages to find Protestants before their time, whether in the culdees or Columba, so twenty-first-century Scots, looking for moral certainties to help reconstruct a new national identity, passed over the confusions of the Reformation period, which as well as underlining Scotland's distinctiveness also set Scot against Scot and turned Scotland away from Europe towards a Protestant-beleaguered isle. Wallace and the Wars of Independence or, for some, Fletcher of Saltoun and federal parliaments are more meaningful icons to be plucked from the past to use in the present. Scotland's alternative parliament, the General Assembly, is an alternative no more. The only *aficiandos* of John Knox are historians of ideas, zealots or his occasional biographers. Debates over former fundamental issues such as the role of superintendents in the post-Reformation church are now the harmless eccentricity of a handful of academics.

Has a balanced view of that Reformation yet been arrived at? In August 1998, a controversy was manufactured in a Sunday newspaper over a set of official support materials provided for secondary schools on Mary Queen of Scots and the Scottish Reformation. A right-wing Catholic columnist, with some support from Catholic schoolteachers, took strong objection to schools being 'fed Protestant myths' and saw the support pack as a 'slur on Catholicism'. In fact, the pack had relatively little to say about the pre-Reformation church, but what there was fell well short of acceptable standards of historical analysis.[5] The subsequent correspondence, from rival religious viewpoints, exchanged views and traded errors but much of it had one thing in common: an inherent assumption that this history *belonged* to someone, as the intellectual property of one or other of the denominational churches.

There is an irony here. Although the Scottish Reformation is no longer a powerful myth, it has largely been abandoned to those for whom it still *matters*. The situation brings to mind a common visual metaphor

---

[5] *Scotland on Sunday*, 6 and 13 September 1998; *Mary, Queen of Scots and the Scottish Reformation, 1540s–1587* (Higher Still History Support Materials, August 1998), 11, 12, 39–40, 43, 93. One extract read: 'Although it was carefully organised and very wealthy, few people wanted to join the church for religious reasons. Most of those who did become churchmen were attracted simply by the church's wealth.'

of the sixteenth century, the weighbeam: on it, all the accumulated dregs of papistry, including the pope's triple crown, are outweighed by the pure, simple truth of the Gospel. An alternative, in later images and one probably more congenial in Scotland, is that the counterweight was Calvin's *Institutes*, sometimes also with a sword.[6] The Reformation is perhaps the most difficult period in Scottish history for professional historians to act out their accustomed role, of challenging received establishment views. In other areas of Scotland's past, recent historians have consciously taken on the role of the awkward squad; they have been prominent as critics of William Wallace assembly-line histories and the output of Templar websites; they revel as exposers of half-truths peddled by politicians and journalists; and they enjoy their work as deconstructionists, whether of British identity or Highland folk myths. By contrast, even at an academic level, Reformation history is still too often the preserve of historians who are religionists, having a personal investment in what they are researching. Where else in Scottish history would crude ideological determinism – such as an argument based on the force of 'the simple truth of the Gospel' – be allowed to operate? Are there many other areas where historians would be permitted to claim proprietary rights to a topic or to dismiss historical findings on the grounds that they were either a 'slur on Catholicism' or offensive to modern-day Protestants? Are heirs of nineteenth-century landowners or now, for that matter, the descendants of cleared crofters afforded such moral high ground?

As a result, many myths of the Scottish Reformation, while they no longer enjoy a high profile, remain largely unchallenged. One of the most influential and perceptive studies of the Reformation is Euan Cameron's *The European Reformation*. It reflects a historio-graphy which, over the past twenty-five years, has been revisionist, challenging and provocative. When it reaches Scotland, such ques-tions are conspicuous by their absence.[7] There is instead a traditional mixture of ecclesiastical history and politics, reflecting the agenda established by Gordon Donaldson but also utilised by his presbyter-ian opponents:

The preoccupation of any historian of the Scottish Reformation must be, as the preoccupation of contemporaries was, with

---

[6] Reproduced in *De Kracht van het Geloof: De Kerk en de Europese Samenleving* (Wording van Europa: Hilversum, 1992), 89.
[7] E. Cameron, *The European Reformation* (Oxford, 1991), 385–8.

church order, with systems of administration, with organisation and even with finance.[8]

When decoded, what this meant was history according to contemporary *divines*. Such history will be at its most revealing in analysing the progress and internal politics of the post-Reformation church as an institution. It will touch on but not fully explain a reformation of religion since it largely relies on evidence of a clergy-driven movement, which is often in the form of fairly raw data of the provision of ministers or readers to parishes. And it will scarcely reach the subject of a reformation of manners. The stranglehold of such institutional history, in which the main concern of many of the practitioners is to defend their corner, helps to explain how conservative the process of questioning the Reformation century has been in Scotland.

Judged from elsewhere in Reformation studies, the possibility of four basic, interacting patterns needs to be postulated.

1. a rapid reformation from below?
2. a rapid reformation from above?
3. a slow reformation from below?
4. a slow reformation from above?[9]

It has been argued that England experienced a combination of the third and fourth of these patterns: a slow reformation from both above and below.[10] In Scotland, the equation is likely to be different, not least because its Reformation, by most comparisons, came so late. But if it is accepted that the Reformation in Scotland was, as in England, a two-speed phenomenon, the most plausible combination is that it took the form of a rapid reformation from above and a slow reformation from above.[11] The former might have a timeframe of *c*.1557–60, from the time of the First Bond of the Lords of the Congregation to the Reformation parliament or the convention of nobility which considered the First Book of Discipline late in 1560. Alternatively, it might be seen as operating from *c*.1557–67, and the relaunching of the Reformation after the deposing of Mary, Queen

---

[8] G. Donaldson, *The Scottish Reformation* (Cambridge, 1960), 1–2.

[9] Cameron, *European Reformation*, 239–40, 300–4, 396–400, 411–16.

[10] C. Haigh, 'The Recent Historiography of the English Reformation', *Historical Journal*, xxv (1982), 995–1007: R. Hutton, *The Rise and Fall of Merry England: The Ritual Year, 1400–1700* (Oxford, 1994), 73–4, 107–10.

[11] This is discussed more fully in my 'A Reformation from Above or Below? The Scottish Example' (forthcoming).

of Scots.[12] Whatever the precise timeframe, there can be little doubt that the elite remained firmly in control: the excesses of the 'rascal multitude' were held in check after the initial outbreak of popular iconoclasm at Perth in May 1560; and the lairds who flooded to the Reformation parliament in unprecedented numbers in August 1560 came as a demonstration orchestrated by the nobility[13] rather than as part of an attempt to claim for themselves a greater influence in the new Protestant commonweal. If there was a 'novel appeal . . . to a public opinion',[14] seen in documents such as the 'Beggars' Summons', it was almost invariably the case of the elite resorting to populist propaganda rather than a genuine demand from the lower orders.

The slow reformation from above[15] has a different agenda, looking for genuine and widespread conversion rather than mere conformity to Protestantism and, as such, it needs a much longer timespan, extending over three or four generations after 1560, except perhaps in those areas such as Kyle and Angus where there had been significant growth of a Protestant movement for a generation or more before 1560. The key element lay in discipline. It operated through the agencies of the newly established church courts, run at local level by the existing elites, which complemented the expanding authority in this period of the baron court or town council. In the Highlands, where few kirk sessions appeared before the second quarter of the seventeenth century,[16] a variant of the same phenomenon appeared: there, the progress of the Protestantism depended on the more informal authority of clan chiefs, kindred and the learned orders.[17] In both

[12] *Booke of the Universal Kirk: Acts and Proceedings of the General Assembly of the Church of Scotland [BUK]*, ed. T. Thomson, Bannatyne Club, 3 vols (Edinburgh, 1839–45), i, 94–5, 106–07, 121.

[13] M. D. Young (ed.), *The Parliaments of Scotland: Burgh and Shire Commissioners*, 2 vols (Edinburgh, 1993), ii, 809–11.

[14] G. Donaldson, *Scotland: James V to James VII* (Edinburgh, 1965), 102.

[15] This is discussed in M. F. Graham, *The Uses of Reform: 'Godly Discipline' and Popular Behavior in Scotland and Beyond, 1560–1610* (Leiden, 1996); and M. Lynch, 'Preaching to the Converted? Perspectives on the Scottish Reformation', in A. A. MacDonald, M. Lynch and I. B. Cowan (eds), *The Renaissance in Scotland: Studies in Literature, Religion, History and Culture offered to John Durkan* (Leiden, 1994), 301–43.

[16] Cf. J. Kirk, *Patterns of Reform: Continuity and Change in the Reformation Kirk* (Edinburgh, 1989), 305–33.

[17] J. Dawson, 'Clan, kin and kirk: The Campbells and the Scottish Reformation', in N. S. Amos, A. Pettegree and H. van Nierop (eds), *The Education of a Christian Society: Humanism and the Reformation in Britain and the Netherlands* (Aldershot, 1999), 211–42; D. S. Thomson, 'Gaelic Learned Orders and Literati in Medieval Scotland', *Scottish Studies*, xii (1968), 57–78.

cases, however, the spread of Protestantism depended on a top-down, *sustained* implementation of a reformation of manners, enforced by new or enhanced instruments of social discipline, as well as a mere reformation of religion.

The idea of a two-speed Reformation can cut through a series of contradictions or ambiguities in interpretation. In particular, it can contextualise the claims and counter-claims made by presbyterian and episcopalian historians that the Reformation was both 'radical' and 'moderate'. The orthodox case has been succinctly put:

> In worship, out went Latinity, sacerdotalism, altars and
> unleavened wafers, auricular confession, the cult of Mary and
> the saints, the celebration of holy days and feast days, prayers
> for the dead, belief in purgatory.

This is the basis for the argument that the hallmarks of the Reformation were 'radical and innovative'.[18] By contrast, the case that the Scottish Reformation was characterised by moderation rests, for the most part, on implied contrasts with England: in Scotland there was no Act of Uniformity, no Test Act (at least not until 1573) and no forced evacuations of the religious houses.[19] What, however, was never fully explained was *why* these did not happen, for it is clear they formed part of the reform programme for radicals like Knox, who felt a keen sense of betrayal as a result. When Lord James Stewart, former Augustinian prior of St Andrews as well as leader of the Lords of the Congregation, blocked Knox and other Protestant demonstrators from access to Queen Mary's first Catholic mass in August 1561, he was also blocking these radicals from the monastic precinct of his commendator half-brother.

A third influential historian is worth considering. David Hay Fleming in his book, *The Reformation in Scotland*, devoted two chapters to what he called the 'characteristics' of the Scottish Reformation. He began:

> If the Reformation in Scotland had to be characterized in one
> word, that word might be *thorough*. Its thoroughness was at
> once its chief characteristic and its glory.

In two following chapters, entitled 'Consequences', he went on to describe the destruction of manuscripts, books and buildings: 'It

---

[18] Kirk, *Patterns of Reform*, p. xvi.
[19] Donaldson, *Scottish Reformation*, 64, 69, 74–5, 176, 179.

may be frankly acknowledged that the Scottish Reformers heartily approved and encouraged the destruction of altars, images and service-books', although, he claimed, 'there was apparently much less of that in Scotland than in England, even proportionately.' His last line of defence of the stripping of the altars was:

> Lovers of art may have good cause to regret the loss of
> priceless treasures, but . . . when immortal souls are in the
> balance with works of art, no Christian can hesitate as to which
> should be preferred.[20]

There can be little doubt that Hay Fleming was a religionist, who shared a belief in the message of Protestant propaganda such as the weighbeam: the corruptions of papistry were, for him, swept aside by the force of the Gospel.

These three sets of propositions – radical and innovative; moderate; thorough – seem incompatible yet each has within it at least a half-truth. The Scottish Reformation began with a revolution, of sorts, but what followed was less a tidy story of steady consolidation than a series of contradictions and ambiguities which were largely provoked by the initial flurry of events in 1559. In the short term, that Reformation was violent as well as moderate. Hay Fleming's was the last work of any consequence, apart from occasional essays by Catholic historians,[21] either to attempt to justify or to describe in any fullness the widespread iconoclasm and image-breaking which so clearly marked the Scottish Reformation. Only two pre-Reformation altarpieces survive[22] and only two craft banners. One of the latter is the Fetternear Banner, the altar cloth of the Edinburgh fraternity of the Holy Blood, preserved in hiding in a remote location;[23] the other is the craft banner of St Bartholomew, patron saint of the glovers, which was at the mender's when the riot incited by John Knox swept through the parish church of St John in Perth in May 1559.[24] There

---

[20] D. Hay Fleming, *The Reformation in Scotland: Causes, Characteristics, Consequences* (London, 1910), 241–313, 314–428, at 241 (author's italics), 315.

[21] D. McRoberts, 'Material destruction caused by the Scottish Reformation', in D. McRoberts (ed.), *Essays on the Scottish Reformation, 1513–1625* (Glasgow, 1962), 415–62.

[22] T. S. Robertson, 'The Church of Fowlis Easter', *Trans. of Aberdeen Ecclesiological Society* (1888), 39–42.

[23] D. McRoberts, 'The Fetternear Banner', *Innes Review*, vii (1956), 69–86.

[24] D. McRoberts, 'A Sixteenth-Century Picture of St Bartholomew from Perth', *Innes Review*, x (1959), 281–6.

has instead been something of an embarrassed silence over the 'stripping of the altars'. Yet historians, to understand the complex loyalties and emotions which were at work in and after 1560, need to come to terms with the motivations and reactions of different sets of contemporaries involved in the cleansing of 'idolatry': they would have included convinced iconoclasts, mere looters, the urban mob, descendants of those whose family tombs were desecrated and the patrons (both individual and institutional) of looted altars, in which there had been considerable investment over the course of the previous century. Such patrons would have ranged from rural lairds or nobles to urban craftsmen.[25] The enforced auctions of ecclesiastical valuables and vestments organised by town councils in and shortly after 1560 were a calculated attempt both to exploit and to harness the force of radical Protestantism as part of a calculated effort to retain their authority amidst the Reformation crisis.[26]

There has also been a reluctance until recently to admit either the internal contradictions among the reformers or that the Reformation hit rough water in the mid-1560s, forcing further compromise and retrenchment. Yet 1565 and 1566, beginning with the Chaseabout Raid, the first failed Protestant noble coup, and ending in Queen Mary's 'triumph' at Stirling[27] after a second, unsuccessful rebellion, were by any measures *anni horribiles* for Knox and the radicals.[28] By then, there was a chorus of complaints from the General Assembly about the spread of the 'pollution' of the mass in various parts of the country, growing fears of an international Catholic conspiracy against 'the religion' and a growing, worrying dependence, for the radicals at least, of the new church on the patronage of a Catholic queen. The resort of Knox to a 'no surrender' defence of the purity of the new church, seen in both the Preface to Book IV of his *History* and his tract on Fasting, needs to be seen as a reflection of the problems faced by the Reformation rather than a measure of its success to that date.

The impact of the Reformation, what it did and did not do, has wider implications: it has cast something of a shadow over the history of the

---

[25] Seen, for example, in the illustration of the 'Iconoclastic Fury' (1566) in the Netherlands, reproduced in *De Kracht van het Geloof*, 90.

[26] Hay Fleming, *Reformation*, 319–22.

[27] M. Lynch, 'Queen Mary's Triumph: the Baptismal Celebrations at Stirling, December 1566', *SHR*, lxix (1990), 1–21.

[28] W. I. P. Hazlett, 'Playing God's card: Knox and Fasting, 1565–66', in R. A. Mason (ed.), *John Knox and the British Reformations* (Aldershot, 1998), 185–6.

century before 1560[29] and it has also forced rather too much of the history of the three-quarters of a century after 1560 into the straitjacket of an ecclesiastical history agenda. Both points are beginning to be recognised.

It has recently been complained, if only as an aside, that the cultural history of late medieval Scotland has suffered as a 'result of a Protestant-dominated historiography which had no wish to recognise the richness of the material and literary culture which the Reformation destroyed, or to admit the reformers' collusion in its destruction'.[30] The renewed interest in late medieval literature, music and philosophy has tended to be driven by subject specialists rather than historians. Yet it needs to be remembered that the cultural world we have lost – whether of Henryson, Carver or John Ireland and John Mair – would, in contemporaries' minds, have been inseparable from the religious world which was lost in or after 1560. There is an analogy to be made here with Jenny Wormald's trenchant complaint about the confusion in historians' minds over James VI and I: was he 'two kings or one'?[31] Much the same stricture could be applied to the century after 1450. Or is it too often seen as the century before 1560? Was this an age of cultural achievement or a period of spiritual decay? It is difficult to argue for both since many of the artefacts – the books of hours, the music of Carver and others, the collegiate churches, the cult of the Passion – were made for religious purposes. Most of the personnel were the same, whether we are thinking of philosophers (of the circle of John Mair or of a generation earlier), educationalists or other kinds of humanists. A good deal of the content of the Protestant reform programme when it was belatedly drawn together in the autumn of 1560 was the product of either the pre-Reformation generation or the generation before that.

Spiritual truth, divine providence and the glory of God were the motivation of makars, musicians and philosophers alike.[32] As a result, the reaction of conservative Protestants or Erasmians after 1560 was to try to preserve as much of the past as could be salvaged, in sharp contrast

---

[29] S. Boardman and M. Lynch, 'The State of Late Medieval and Early Modern Scottish History', in T. Brotherstone and D. Ditchburn (eds), *Freedom and Authority: Scotland c.1050–c.1650: Historical and Historiographical Essays Presented to Grant G. Simpson* (East Linton, 2000), 44–59.

[30] R. A. Mason, *Kingship and the Commonweal: Political Thought in Renaissance and Reformation Scotland* (East Linton, 1998), 105n.

[31] J. M. Wormald, 'James VI and I: two kings or one?', *History*, lxviii (1983), 187–209.

[32] A. Broadie, *The Shadow of Scotus: Philosophy and Faith in Pre-Reformation Scotland* (Edinburgh, 1995), 3–4.

to radical iconoclasts like Knox.[33] The result was a cultural diversity within Protestantism, which has as yet fully to be dissected. Which better represents its mainstream: the books of Knox's uncompromising *History* which can be dated to 1565–6 or the *Bannatyne Miscellany*, a collection of late medieval poetry, including largely orthodox religious lyrics, brought together about the same time by an Edinburgh scribe, who was at the centre of a circle of literary patronage?

Such an example of a close linkage with the past raises a fundamental question. It is by now widely accepted that, in most centuries of known Scottish history before modern times, continuities are liable to outweigh changes.[34] Is it possible to apply that dictum to the Reformation century, in which change seems so obvious and demonstrable? Or is it the great exception?

To illustrate this point, it is worth turning to another recent, populist treatment of the Scottish Reformation:

> By the end of the fifteenth century the church had become massively influential and hugely wealthy. But it was also bloated and corrupt, and it has started to sow the seeds of its own destruction . . . By 1500, many ordinary Scots had stopped going to church. They were fed up with its less reputable practices, such as the custom [of] . . . indulgences.[35]

The only evidence for this assertion is a single passage in a provincial council's report:

> The present convention, perceiving that the greatest neglect of the divine mysteries has prevailed among the subjects of the realm within these last few years, so that very few indeed out of the most populous parishes deign to be present at the sacrifice of the holy mass on Sundays . . . or to attend the preaching of God's word.[36]

---

[33] T. van Heijnsbergen, 'The Interaction between Literature and History in Queen Mary's Edinburgh: The Bannatyne Manuscript in its Prosopographical Context', in MacDonald et al., *Renaissance in Scotland*, 183–225.

[34] M. Lynch, *Scotland: A New History* (London, 1991), p. xvii.

[35] 'Waging War in Name of God', Millennium Life series on Scottish History, *Daily Record*, 3 April 1999.

[36] *Statutes of the Scottish Church, 1225–1559* (Scottish History Society [SHS], Edinburgh, 1907), 138–9.

But the report dates to 1552, half a century later. When scrutinised, what evidence there is points in a very different direction. 'Within these last few years' suggests that in 1500 attendance was not the problem which it would later become, probably some time during the disturbances of the 1540s.

There is here a problem of balance, which has a wider resonance. Is there in this passage and in other, more academic treatments an unspoken assumption that the Reformation produced dramatically improved attendance after 1560? The difficulty is lack of evidence. We simply cannot be sure. The only attempt to address this question came in a study of the Reformation in Angus and the Mearns, which used the data from 1560 onwards of plate collections in the small parish of Monifeith, near Dundee. Although an imperfect science, as its author readily admitted, these calculations seemed to show that attendance varied hugely; from week to week it averaged only 10 per cent of the potential congregation in the 1570s, with larger numbers being guaranteed only at what were the former great feast days of the old church, Easter and Christmas.[37] The result, it might be concluded, in this heartland of Protestantism, was a reformation of religion but not, a social historian of the Reformation might deduce, a reformation of manners.

This is not an isolated example. One of the central concerns of orthodox Catholic reformers, in Scotland as well as elsewhere, was irreverent behaviour in church and especially during holy communion:

> Ye vicaris, curatis, and uther priestis . . . thole nocht your
> parrochianiris to cum to this blysit sacrament misordourlie. But
> put tham in ordoure be your ministeris before the altare, and
> requyre tham to heir yow reid the afore wryttin exhortatioun,
> without noysse or din, and to sit styll swa in deuotiuon, with
> deuote hert and mynde, quhill thay be ordourlie seruit of the
> saide blyssit sacrament.[38]

The arrangements for communion after 1560, that it be celebrated four times a year in towns and twice a year in rural parishes, mirrored the concerns of the Genevan authorities that over-frequent celebration might risk public disorder. Even so, complaints by the General Assembly in 1617 seem to indicate that little had changed:

[37] F. D. Bardgett, *Scotland Reformed: The Reformation in Angus and the Mearns* (Edinburgh, 1989), 158–9.
[38] *Statutes of Scottish Church*, 190.

To remedy this irreverent behaviour of the vulgar sort in receiving the holy Communion, it is found meet by this assembly that the minister shall in the celebration give the elements out of his own hand to every one of the communicants saying when he gives the bread, 'Take, eat, this is the body of the Lord Jesus Christ, which was broken for you; do this in remembrance of him' . . . [At the end] the Minister . . . gravely exhort his people that they communicate reverently, and show a humble and religious behaviour in receiving the same.[39]

On a series of issues – including ineffective preaching and catechising the young as well as poor attendance and irreverent popular attitudes to communion and church services – it is not difficult to find parallels which show that both human nature and the problems of the churches were not greatly different in 1600 from what they had been in the 1550s.[40]

Would it not be reasonable to conclude, as historians of many other European reformations have done, in many cases over twenty years ago,[41] that the problems of faith, discipline and order were faced by all sixteenth-century churches, Catholic, Calvinist, Lutheran, and that none was particularly more successful in dealing with them than any other? If so, this conclusion might point to two other, general suggestions. Based on the evidence we have – as distinct from negative evidence or mere wish-fulfilment – it looks as if a reformation of manners was slow in arriving and there may well have been relatively little difference in the state of popular religion in 1500 and 1600. In turn, that may suggest that Scottish society, especially in rural areas, was throughout the Reformation century naturally resistant to change and more afflicted by popular unrest than has hitherto been assumed.

The difficulty in reaching the lower levels of Scottish society in this period because of the nature of the sources raises the question of what justification there is for talking, as some Protestant historians are fond of

---

[39] *BUK*, iii, 1141; Lynch, 'Preaching to the Converted', 332–3.

[40] For attendance, see *Statutes of the Scottish Church*, 138–9 (1552); *BUK*, ii, 716, 719 (Dumfries and Fife, 1588); for preaching, *Statutes*, 171–2 (1559); Alexander Hume, 'Ane Afolde Admonitioun to the Ministerie of Scotland' (1609), *Wodrow Misc.*, 569–90, at 588; for catechising the young, *Statutes*, 145 (1552); *BUK*, iii, 1126–7 (1616).

[41] G. Strauss, 'Success and Failure in the German Reformation', *Past and Present*, lxvii (1974).

doing, of a 'people's church' emerging after the Reformation?[42] Does that claim not assume that the church before the Reformation was somehow divorced from the people? But where, in turn, is the evidence for that assumption? What little work has been done, which has not been contradicted, has tended to emphasise the close-knit ties of priest, vicar or curate with his flock.[43] And a recent study of the Dominicans in the century before the Reformation showed that the order, like parish churches, was staffed by local men – sons, brothers or neighbours of the local congregation.[44] After the Reformation, because of the emphasis put by Protestant reformers on the need to raise the status of the parish clergy, through education and income, a distinction can be made: the new presbyters of the late sixteenth century were usually of a higher social standing and better education than the old priests and were, ironically, 'even further away from the origins of their parishioners'.[45] In that sense, the church of 1600 was less a people's church than that of 1500. But this trend was probably already under way before 1560 and it was certainly replicated in other European countries, both Catholic and Protestant, as confessional churches tried to professionalise and control their clergy more closely than before. What has been called 'the age of the catechism',[46] was also the age of the disciplinary tribunal, whether it took the form of the exercise and presbytery or the diocesan court.

If the church in post-Reformation Scotland was a church of the people, it might well be asked, which people? Here, there are specific examples for the noble or lairdly classes which suggest continuity across the Reformation century in patterns of religious piety and the motives which underpinned them. Consider two images. The first is Rosslyn Chapel, although it could be Crichton, Lincluden or a score or more of other rural churches upgraded to collegiate status in the century after 1450, a process linked to the emergence in the 1450s of a new class of landed power, the lords of parliament.[47] The second is Skelmorlie Aisle, at Irvine in Ayrshire, built by the Montgomery family in 1636, dubbed a

---

[42] See e.g. M. H. B. Sanderson, *Ayrshire and the Reformation: People and Change, 1490–1600* (East Linton, 1997), ch. 9: 'The People's Church after 1560'.

[43] D. McKay, 'Parish Life in Scotland, 1500–1560', in McRoberts (ed.), *Scottish Reformation*, 85–115.

[44] J. Foggie, 'The Dominicans in Scotland, 1450–1560' (University of Edinburgh Ph.D., 1998).

[45] Sanderson, *Ayrshire*, 133; see also Cameron, *European Reformation*, 390–96.

[46] J. Bossy, *Christianity in the West, 1400–1700* (Oxford, 1985), 119–20.

[47] I. B. Cowan and D. E. Easson (eds), *Medieval Religious Houses: Scotland*, 2nd edn (London, 1976), 213–30.

'Protestant equivalent of chantry chapels'[48] and one of the most prestigious of seventeenth-century, elaborate funerary monuments. The motives involved in these two examples are likely to have been much the same. Rosslyn was a pilgrimage church but also a burial vault and family chapel, designed to allow worship in private. Skelmorlie, like many other examples of the same period, was entered from outside the church by means of a separate doorway, above which was an elaborate armorial. Inside, the family tomb, built of marble and complete with painted ceiling, was no less impressive.[49] The resort of many post-Reformation nobles to family burial aisles, sepulchres and mausoleums circumvented the reformers' desire for public worship but it also continued in the tradition of the collegiate church, often intended as a *private* chapel. It also fed the desire of new *arrivistes* to devise for themselves a past and a lineage. Prayers for the dead and the belief in purgatory may have gone, as presbyterian historians insist, but the same underlying fears of death persisted. Such physical demonstrations of conspicuous piety as Crichton and Skelmorlie reflect those fears as well as a parallel desire for status and godliness. Seen in this light, it matters little if these pious investments were meant to achieve less time in the purgatory by means of the Catholic votive mass for the dead and the treasury of merits or to allow the founder and his family to elbow their way up the queue of the 144,000 Calvinists predestined for salvation.

The godly actions of lairds like Robert Campbell of Kinzeancleuch, who, because of his dissatisfaction with provision by local ministers, made a nightly scrutiny in the 1560s of his immediate family and servants and a weekly examination of his tenantry, have been used by sceptical historians to argue for the imperfection of pastoral care in a shire which had 100 per cent absentee clergy before 1560 and inadequate provision after 1560.[50] Viewed from a different perspective, it is likely that Campbell's initiative was merely a return to past practice, when the grant made by the papal Penitentiary of a licence to a family chaplain for a portable altar made private worship possible.[51] The wholesale de-

---

[48] J. Dunbar, 'The Post-Reformation Church in Scotland', in J. Blair and C. Pyrah (eds), *Church Archaeology: Research Directions for the Future* (CBA Research Report no. 104, 1996), 131.

[49] Dunbar, 'Post-Reformation Church', 131–2; D. Macgibbon and T. Ross, *The Castellated and Domestic Architecture of Scotland*, 5 vols (Edinburgh, 1887–92), v, 193–200

[50] Lynch, 'Preaching to the converted', 333.

[51] I am grateful to Dr Janet Foggie for the point regarding licences for portable altars, discovered by her in an exploration of Vatican Penitentiary records.

christianisation of the medieval nobility is a curious and implausible creation of modern historians. Late medieval religion has been caught in a vacuum, between the predominantly political interests of the recent generation of late medieval historians and the predetermined agenda of many post-Reformation ecclesiastical historians. Medieval historians have on the whole tended to know more and care much more about ecclesiastical politics – and particularly disputes over benefices and tussles for control of religious houses – than about religion.[52] The result is that post-Reformation godly nobles seem to be a new phenomenon[53] when the overwhelming likelihood is that they were continuing in an established vein amidst new circumstances.

The point is not an isolated one. The late medieval world which we have lost, or not yet reclaimed, will, once reclaimed, change the way we look at the Reformation itself. The faults of the old church are liable to be linked to the fault lines within the new church. And the strengths which the new church had are likely to be in the areas where the link with the past was best preserved.

Brief examples of each phenomenon must suffice. There was a certain amount of anti-clericalism evident in the 1530s and 1540s. It was not as conspicuous or as violent in Scotland as in England, yet it undoubtedly existed. Once the genie of popular anti-clericalism, however, was out of the bottle, it was difficult to put it back in. In 1560–61, the new Protestant regime in Edinburgh, brought to power by a coup from outside, was in a genuine quandary. On the one hand, it wanted to push ahead, in advance of national agenda, by throwing into exile clergy of the old church and flirting with the popular anti-clericalism which had exhibited itself in Edinburgh in the St Giles' Day riot of 1558. On the other hand, the new regime was also nervous of popular riot and clamped down hard, and probably too zealously, on craft disturbances; one of Knox's closest associates even fired a handgun into the crowd when the council was trapped in the tolbooth by a protesting crowd in the spring of 1561.[54] By 1600, it possible to argue that, with the new presbyters having their incomes restored to what benefice holders probably enjoyed in fourteenth century,[55] there was considerable anti-clerical feeling in some towns, such as Edinburgh and Perth.

[52] Boardman and Lynch, 'Scottish History', 52.
[53] K. Brown, 'In Search of the Godly Magistrate in Reformation Scotland', *Journal of Ecclesiastical History*, xl (1989), 553–81.
[54] Knox, *History*, i, 127–9, 358.
[55] A. Grant, *Independence and Nationhood: Scotland 1306–1469* (London, 1984), 96–7.

Anti-clericalism, it is likely, was as significant a phenomenon in 1600 as it was in 1500, even if it had different effects.

The ethos of the kirk session in Angus and the Mearns, it has been claimed, was the reflection of a deeply conservative lairdly culture.[56] In the sophisticated world of professions and merchants in the capital, an urban version of the same phenomenon was prominent soon after 1560. Edinburgh's lawyers formed an intelligentsia which 'had merged Christian or Erasmian humanism containing Lutheran elements with a native tradition of learning'.[57] They wanted to reform society without breaking the cultural values which underpinned it. Such men were hardly likely to be Knox-style moral bulldozers or converts with a simple mission. Their Protestantism conformed to their existing values, and high among those was a deeply conservative desire to preserve Scotland's cultural heritage. This was the cast of mind which produced, for the entry into the capital of Charles I in 1633, a parnassus with a contemporary version of the nine 'ancient worthies for learning', going back to Duns Scotus.[58] These are further examples of a top–down reformation.

Is it likely that, in such an environment, the uncompromising preacher would quickly produce results? Comparisons with missionaries in other centuries are seldom used by Reformation historians, despite the gaps in their own evidence. Yet historians of the fifth and sixth centuries, who have a keen appreciation of the problems of the laconic nature of the sources for early Christianity, have turned to the highly developed techniques of historians and social anthropologists of missionaries in the eighteenth and nineteenth centuries for guidance: the conclusion that conversion almost never happened overnight and that it took titanic and prolonged efforts by driven men and women over decades seems highly plausible.[59] Why should the sixteenth century be different? Why should the process of evangelisation and conversion – as distinct from mere conformity – have been easier with the Reformation, when many of the best established instruments to aid clergy trying to catechise their flocks had been jettisoned and were not yet effectively replaced? Statues of the saints, altarpieces, stained-glass windows, all of them the 'so-called bibles of the humble', were destroyed without much of an arsenal of ready-made replacements at hand. Cheap bibles were not available in Scotland before the 1630s or 1640s.[60] In such

---

[56] Bardgett, *Scotland Reformed*, 157.
[57] Van Heijnsbergen, 'Bannatyne Manuscript', 195–6, 214.
[58] M. Lynch, 'The Age of Renaissance and Reformation', in R. Mitchison, *Why Scottish History Matters*, 2nd edn (Edinburgh, 1997), 42–4.
[59] C. Thomas, 'The Origins of Insular Monasticism' (Rhind lectures, 1999).
[60] Lynch, 'Preaching to the Converted', 329–30.

circumstances, would it not be fair to suggest that any work which relies for evidence on the 'pure, simple truth of the Gospel' should mentally be recatalogued under 'tracts, catechetical, Protestant'?

Where analogies have been identified, linking the pre-Reformation world to that of post-Reformation culture, there has been a tendency to judge such linkages from the standpoint of the future rather than the past – a breach in the normal operation of the historical mind. The tracing of common threads linking the intellectual world of the pre-Reformation Renaissance and the circle of John Mair to the philosophical historians of the high Enlightenment demonstrated an important continuity of scholarship over more than two centuries. Yet to label it 'Calvinist humanism'[61] was akin to claiming that Home Rule was the preserve of a nationalist party, which was founded some fifty years after the idea emerged in the 1880s.

The creation of a forerunner is a natural temptation for the Reformation historian, anxious to detect the roots of the Protestant movement and its causation. All too often, however, it is an illusion. Much the same kind of intellectual forerunner was devised by Gordon Donaldson, when he tried to trace the origin and impact of the cult of the Passion. Citing three short passages from Arundel MS 285, one of the key documents of late medieval Passion poetry in Scotland, he detected a tension between the cult of the Passion and worship of the Virgin Mary: 'clerical eyebrows must have been raised', it was claimed, by such lines.[62] Yet this misunderstood the late medieval Catholic mind, in which there was no necessary conflict between the two cults. On the fringes of the Fetternear Banner, crafted for the Edinburgh merchant guild in the 1520s and showing the direct influence of the Flemish cult of the Holy Blood, are rosaries – the penitential exercise devoted to the Virgin Mary.[63] The cult of Mary as mother of Christ was also a favourite theme of the Dominicans, strange as it may seem to those who know them as frontline troops in the battle against heresy or as a recruiting ground for early Protestants. Again, the propaganda of later Protestant reformers was readily accepted as evidence, rather than as propaganda. As a result, continuities were mistaken for precursors.

The history of Scotland in the three-quarters of a century after 1560 has too often been presented in terms of an ecclesiastical history writ

---

[61] D. Allan, *Virtue, Learning and the Scottish Enlightenment: Ideas of Scholarship in Early Modern History* (Edinburgh, 1993).

[62] G. Donaldson, *Faith of the Scots* (London, 1990), 61–2.

[63] D. McRoberts, 'The Rosary in Scotland', *Innes Review*, xxiii (1972), 81–6.

large or as a road between the first reformation of 1560 and a second, in 1638. In both versions, the rival reformed traditions have sought to impose their own agendas. The decades of the 1580s, 1590s and later are bestrewn with the happenings dictated by these agendas. One need think only of the vocabulary of the period – the 'Negative Confession' of 1581, the 'Black Acts' of 1584, the 'Golden Act' of 1592 – to demonstrate that. Here, the distinction between what is merely happening and the more fundamental question of what was really going on[64] may again help cut a swathe of understanding through rival myths. To date, the 'what's going on' school has largely been composed of historians of ideas. They have often been concerned with an updated, more sophisticated version of Sidney Burrell's search for the origins of the covenanting tradition,[65] recently defined as 'an ongoing process of Scottish self-definition – and definition – which began with the Reformation of 1560 and was to culminate . . . in a second Reformation in the late 1630s and 1640s'.[66]

The difficulty here is twofold. One difficulty is the timespan involved – seventy or eighty years, amounting to two or three generations between 1560 and the undoubted change of gear which came some time in the 1630s. As a result, one may wonder whether such a search falls foul of the mistake of trying to explain historical processes before they bit. The second difficulty is that this approach tends to overlook the contrary developments which took place in between. The reasons are understandable: the long reign of James VI (1567–1625) still awaits analysis. In particular, what is often missed is the growth of state power: the new dimensions of authority available to the crown and its supporters (including the church) in the decisive second and third generations after 1560. State formation,[67] which has become one of the key components in early modern history, both extended and set limits on the process of a slow reformation from above.

Unpalatable as it may be to many, the Reformation in Scotland, like other late reformations in Protestant Europe, was essentially a top-down

---

[64] A. Grant, 'To the Medieval Foundations', *SHR*, lxxiii (1994), 5–6.

[65] S. A. Burrell, 'The Covenant Idea as Revolutionary Symbol: Scotland 1596–1637', *Church History*, xxvii (1958), 338–50.

[66] R. A. Mason (ed.), *Scots and Britons: Scottish Political Thought and the Union of 1603* (Cambridge, 1994), 4.

[67] S. G. Ellis and S. Barber (eds), *Conquest and Union: Fashioning a British State* (London, 1995); B. Bradshaw and J. Morrill (eds), *The British Problem, 1534–1707: State Formation in the Atlantic Archipelago* (London, 1996). See also J. Goodare and M. Lynch (eds), *The Reign of James VI* (East Linton, 1999), 11–12, 21, 23–4, 29–31.

phenomenon. A useful, widely recognised benchmark worth bearing in mind is that the later that reformations occurred in sixteenth-century Europe the more directed and authoritarian they were likely to be. That dictum can be applied both to local or civic reformations and, above all, to territorial monarchies.[68] Here is a different context in which to understand the remarkable fact that no-one holding major office lost it as a result of 1560 and very few town councils experienced a coup.[69] No prominent social group, it might be added, lost position or power. The path was prepared for the coming to power of a godly prince and for the laying down of what has notably been called the 'fitted carpet' of state power,[70] extending to the furthest parts of the realm; it gave a new level of protection to landowners as well as to the monarchy.

It could well be argued that the King's Confession of 1581 (only later dubbed 'Negative'), together with the actions of parliament in 1584 and 1592 (the so-called 'Black' and 'Golden' Acts) saw both a decisive move towards state formation and an attempt at a further reformation, this time under the control of the state. In this context, it is as well mentally to put to one side (until the breakdown of relations between king and kirk in 1596) the all too familiar figure of Andrew Melville as leader of an ecclesiastical protest movement, and to recall a different Melville, the confidante of James VI and court poet in the 1580s and early 1590s. Many of the initiatives taken to implement a second-stage reformation were those of this new state. The *Second Book of Discipline*, which was as principled and impractical as the *First* and was out of date by the time it was approved by the General Assembly in 1578, also occupies far too much of the centre stage of history in this period. The first attempt to make ownership of the Bible compulsory was not an initiative of the church but an act of parliament, in 1579.[71] And it needs to be remembered that the first National Covenant was an act of the state. In February 1581, the young godly prince had his whole court subscribe the King's Confession on their knees during a two-week celebration of the marriage of the daughter of the murdered earl of Moray and the obscure Stewart courtier later to be acclaimed as the bonnie earl of Moray. A month later, the Confession was read from pulpits, by royal

---

[68] K. von Greyerz, *The Late City Reformation in Germany: The Case of Colmar, 1522–1628* (Wiesbaden, 1980), 196–205; Cameron, *European Reformation*, 233–4, 246.

[69] G. Donaldson, *All the Queen's Men: Power and Politics in Mary Stewart's Scotland* (London, 1983), 51.

[70] J. Goodare, *State and Society in Early Modern Scotland* (Oxford, 1999), 286–311.

[71] *APS*, iii, 139, 211.

decree, which insisted it be subscribed throughout the realm.[72] In October of the same year, parliament passed a series of acts, confirming previous religious legislation since 1560, condemning adultery, blasphemy, pilgrimages and other 'superstitious rites', and acknowledging that every parish should have a pastor with a 'sufficient and ressonable stipend'.[73] This state-sponsored second reformation, run in the name of a godly prince, needs to be more fully acknowledged, even if it does not conveniently fit into notions about a divide between the 'two kingdoms', later to be visited on the period by presbyterian historians of the early seventeenth century. It had some successes, notably in the areas of augmentation of stipends and promotion of new levels of social discipline, but it was far from being a complete success. Yet it was only after the consensus between state and church broke down in 1596 that a clerical opposition party began to materialise in any clear-cut form.

One way to escape the myths of the post-Reformation period would be to substitute a different set of questions, about authority rather than ecclesiastical politics or religion as such. Here, the central figures would not be clerical leaders such as Andrew Melville or popular, mythological figures ranging from John the Commonweill to Jenny Geddes, but the godly magistrate, operating either in his baron court or local kirk session, and the professional minister, enjoying by the 1620s a new level of security and prosperity, as a pensioner of the state, largely protected from taxation. In terms of his social role, the minister was as much a *fonctionnaire* of the state, whether defined as at central or local level, as an instrument of the church. Is it sensible, amidst the complexities which enmeshed a Protestant church in a Protestant state, for historians to cling, Melvillian-style, to a theocratic notion of two separate kingdoms – the kingdom of God and that of the world? Or would it be more realistic to begin with the dilemmas of a state church obliged to operate in a new kind of state?[74]

Alternative sets of questions would be forced, too, about the social effects of the rise of Protestantism. Was the key instrument of evangelisation the Bible, which could bring a new and potentially subversive freedom of thought to its readers,[75] or the catechism and the communion

[72] M. Lynch, 'Court Ceremony and Ritual during the Personal Reign of James VI', in Goodare and Lynch (eds), *Reign of James VI*, 71–3; Calderwood, *History*, iii, 501–06; Melville, *Diary*, 87.

[73] *APS*, iii, 210–14.

[74] See Goodare, *State and Society*, 172–213.

[75] Donaldson, *All the Queen's Men*, 34, likened the appeal of the reform programme in 1559–60 to a modern 'theology of liberation'.

token, which brought new dimensions of social control? This opens up a more complex world than the one protected by conventional myths about the Reformation. Which was the real world? The answer, at times – as it is with this case – is that both were. Within that conundrum, there lies a more plausible answer to the roots of the social and religious tensions of the seventeenth century than responses driven by one or other of the standard myths of the Scottish Reformation.

CHAPTER 5

Civil Society and the Celts: Hector Boece, George Buchanan and the Ancient Scottish Past

Roger A. Mason

The purpose of this chapter is to explore certain aspects of Lowland attitudes to the Highlands, and more particularly the language, culture and history of the Gaels, as these developed in the sixteenth century. In a sense, this is a very straightforward, though hardly edifying, story. From the suppression of the Lordship of the Isles in 1493 through to the Statutes of Iona in 1609, one can trace increasing hostility and contempt among Scots-speaking Lowlanders for the manners and mores of their Gaelic-speaking compatriots – a hostility and contempt that by the close of the sixteenth century was commonly articulated in polarised terms as the difference between Lowland 'civility' and Highland 'barbarism'. Of course, this process of polarisation began long before 1493 and continued long after 1609, but it is not the intention here to try and explain in any detail why it occurred or even to comment more than indirectly on the roots and implications of the language in which it came to be couched.[1] As a preliminary, however, it is important to establish a broad interpretative framework within which these developments can be set.

Two interrelated perspectives offer themselves as obvious candidates

---

[1] There is a fine recent discussion of the background to many of the issues touched on here in J. Dawson, 'The Gaidhealtachd and the Emergence of the Scottish Highlands', in B. Bradshaw and P. Roberts (eds), *British Consciousness and Identity: The Making of Britain, 1533–1707* (Cambridge, 1998), 259–300. On the language of barbarism and civility, see A. H. Williamson, 'Scots, Indians and Empire: The Scottish Politics of Civilization, 1519–1609', *Past & Present*, cl (1996), 46–83. For a rather different approach see Edward J. Cowan, 'The Discovery of the Gaidhealtachd in Sixteenth-Century Scotland', *Transactions of the Gaelic Society of Inverness*, lx 1997–8 (2000), 259–84.

for explaining what, from a Lowland point of view, came to be identified as the 'Highland Problem'.[2] On the one hand, in the course of the long sixteenth century demographic and tenurial change saw a more dynamic and urbanised Lowland economy outstripping its Highland equivalent and underwriting the smug self-righteousness with which the inhabitants of the former came to regard those of the latter.[3] It was, for example, commercial motives that helped to shape James VI's perceptions of the Highlands and Islands as not just an untamed wilderness, but a kind of Gaelic Eldorado whose immense riches were there for the taking. On the other hand, however, while the significance of the Highlands and Islands as a potentially lucrative source of crown revenues should not be under-estimated, James' attitude to Gaeldom was also clearly inspired by the related need to bring the outlying reaches of the realm more firmly under direct royal control. Viewed from this essentially political perspective, the fashionable way of characterising what occurred in the Highlands in the sixteenth and seventeenth centuries is as part of a process of Scottish, and subsequently British, 'state-formation'. But the idea of 'state-formation' is something of a *portmanteau* concept whose usefulness is often handi-capped by the unwillingness of historians to define what it means with any great clarity. Perhaps its implications are so obvious that it needs no further explanation. Nevertheless, the sceptic may be forgiven for think-ing that it evokes a whig teleology that is at least potentially anachronistic and misleading.[4]

[2] Though only indirectly concerned with the period dealt with here, A. I. Macinnes, *Clanship, Commerce and the House of Stuart, 1603–1788* (East Linton, 1996), is the most effective attempt to combine the socio-economic and political perspectives detailed below.

[3] On the Highland economy, see generally I. D. Whyte, *Scotland Before the Industrial Revolution: An Economic and Social History, c.1050–c.1750* (London, 1995), 251–70; and for more detailed treatment, R. A. Dodgshon, *From Chiefs to Landlords: Social and Economic Change in the Western Highlands and Islands, c.1493–1820* (Edinburgh, 1998).

[4] These thoughts were drafted before confirmation appeared in the form of J. Goodare, *State and Society in Early Modern Scotland* (Oxford, 1999), where the Highlands are discussed (ch. 8) in the context of the emergence of an 'absolutist state' in the reign of James VI that, curiously, had little if any direct control over much of its territory. A less extreme version of the same 'statist' thesis can be found in M. Lynch, 'James VI and the "Highland Problem" ', in J. Goodare and M. Lynch (eds), *The Reign of James VI* (East Linton, 2000), 208–27. For a broader British perspective that adopts the same underlying dynamic, see B. Bradshaw and J. Morrill (eds), *The British Problem, c.1534–1707: State Formation in the Atlantic Archipelago* (London, 1996), and S. G. Ellis and S. Barber (eds), *Conquest and Union: Fashioning a British State, 1485–1725* (London, 1995).

Fundamentally, after all, what we are dealing with here is not a 'state' in anything like the modern sense of the term, but rather with a monarchy and with processes of monarchical consolidation and expansion. If what is meant by 'state-formation' is simply the imposition by the crown of its will and its law on outlying regions of the kingdom, then Scotland, like other early modern kingdoms, doubtless experienced a process of 'state-formation'. Contemporaries, however, would have characterised it differently. For not only was the word 'state' itself relatively unfamiliar in the sixteenth century, and only just beginning to take on its modern connotations,[5] but Scotland was no ordinary monarchy. On the contrary, it was an imperial monarchy – an empire in and of itself – and had been so described since the reign of James III. What this implied was not so much that the Scottish crown laid claim to dominions beyond the territorial bounds of the kingdom *per se* (though it could mean that), but rather that just as the Scottish crown recognised the superiority of no external jurisdiction, such as the pope, the emperor or the king of England, so it would brook no jurisdictional rival within the kingdom, be it a quasi-autonomous province such as the Lordship of the Isles, the franchise courts traditionally operated by the landed elite or the greatest of all jurisdictional franchises, that operated by the medieval Catholic church and subsequently reincarnated in the form of the presbyterian kirk.[6]

Imperial ideas and ideology are most often associated with the royal supremacy over the church. However, the civil-law doctrine that the king was emperor in his own kingdom (*rex in regno suo est imperator*) was profoundly important in temporal as well as ecclesiastical affairs, capable of underwriting absolutist notions of royal authority and a drive towards uniformity not only of law and jurisdiction, but also of beliefs, customs and manners. In Scotland before 1603 such uniformity under the king's law might be seen as more of an aspiration than a reality, though it would be interesting to speculate on what might have transpired had not that most imperially-minded of Scottish monarchs, James V, died when barely thirty years old. In any event, there is clearly a sense in which James VI can be construed as looking back to his grandfather's reign and

---

[5] Q. Skinner, *The Foundations of Modern Political Thought* (Cambridge, 1978), i, pp. ix–x; R. Tuck, *Philosophy and Government, 1572–1651* (Cambridge, 1993).

[6] R. A. Mason, 'This Realm of Scotland is an Empire? Imperial Ideas and Iconography in Early Renaissance Scotland', in B. Crawford (ed.), *Church, Chronicle and Learning in Medieval and Early Renaissance Scotland* (Edinburgh, 1999), 73–92; and R. A. Mason, *Kingship and the Commonweal: Political Thought in Renaissance and Reformation Scotland* (East Linton, 1998), 126–37.

reasserting the crown's imperial status in the aftermath of the multiple challenges to its authority thrown up by the mid-century Reformation and the brief reign and ultimate overthrow of his mother, Mary Queen of Scots. In terms of civil peace, order and stability, Lowland Scots had much to gain in the last two decades of the sixteenth century from heeding James' oft-repeated claim to be the ultimate source of authority within his kingdom – even if the Highlands still remained beyond the effective reach of royal government. After 1603, however, in a context where the king exercised imperial authority over a multiple monarchy, encompassing Britain and Ireland as well as dominions overseas, Lowland as well as Highland Scots began to experience the downside of the conformity demanded by an increasingly Anglo-British monarchy. If by the 1630s Lowlanders felt sufficiently alienated and marginalised to rise in open revolt against the Stuart dynasty, what of the Highlanders, the mainland equivalent of the native Irish, stigmatised even by their own countrymen as at best barbarians and at worst Catholic barbarians?[7]

All this may seem some way removed from the subject of this collection, the recycling of Scottish history and the way in which the past has been continually reshaped and rewritten to meet the needs of the present. Yet there is in fact a strong if paradoxical link between the consolidation of an essentially Lowland Scottish imperial monarchy, increasingly inclined to see Gaeldom as culturally alien and politically subversive, and the exploitation of a usable Scottish past.[8] For in the course of the sixteenth century, at one and the same time as Lowland disdain for the Gaels was developing apace, the history of Scotland was being rewritten in such a way as to give increasing prominence to the Gaelic origins of Scottish kingship, the Scottish kirk and Scottish civility itself. The key man in this process was the formidable George Buchanan, born near Killearn in 1506 and almost certainly himself a native Gaelic-speaker, whose magisterial *Rerum Scoticarum Historia* was first

---

[7] J. H. Ohlmeyer, ' "Civilizinge of those Rude Parts": Colonization within Britain and Ireland, 1580s–1640s', in N. Canny (ed.), *The Origins of Empire: The Oxford History of the British Empire I* (Oxford, 1998), 124–47; see also M. Lynch, 'National Identity in Ireland and Scotland, 1500–1640', in C. Bjorn, A. Grant and K. Stringer (eds), *Nations, Nationalism and Patriotism in the European Past* (Copenhagen, 1990), 109–36. For a broader perspective on the development of the idea of empire in early modern Britain, see D. Armitage, *The Ideological Origins of the British Empire* (Cambridge, 2000), esp. 24–60.

[8] For more on 'The Gaelic Dilemma in Early Modern Scottish Political Culture', see C. Kidd, *British Identities Before Nationalism: Ethnicity and Nationhood in the Atlantic World, 1600–1800* (Cambridge, 1999), ch. 6.

published at Edinburgh in 1582, the year of its author's death. Almost as significant was his distinguished predecessor, the Dundonian humanist, Hector Boece, first principal of the University of Aberdeen and author of the highly influential *Scotorum Historia*, published at Paris in 1527, from which Buchanan drew much of the raw material for his later version of Scotland's story. Together, and with remarkable success, these two Renaissance scholars effectively refashioned the account of Scottish history bequeathed to them by the medieval chroniclers in such a way as firmly to embed (or, perhaps more accurately, re-embed) the Scottish present in its Gaelic past. Three themes in particular feature prominently in their historical writings that are worth closer attention here: first, the idea of Gaelic 'primitivism' and their projection of the values and virtues of humanist civil society on to the vast canvas of Scottish prehistory; second, their understanding of Gaelic kingship and the idea of an 'ancient Scottish constitution'; and finally, their inter-pretation of the Celtic kirk and the critical redefinition of St Columba and the Culdees in proto-presbyterian terms to which Buchanan made a seminal contribution. In developing these themes, Buchanan in parti-cular not only provided the basis for mounting a powerful critique of imperial monarchy, whether in its Scottish or Anglo-British guise, but also contributed significantly to the apparently paradoxical way in which contemporary Scots regarded their Gaelic heritage and identity.

William Ferguson has recently, and rightly, drawn attention to the hugely influential role played by Livy's account of the early history of Rome in shaping Renaissance Scots' perceptions of their own remote past.[9] The early books of Livy's *Ab Urbe Condita* are more mythopeia than history, but they served the crucial function of allowing Livy to construct an image of pristine Roman virtue that acted as a benchmark against which to measure the deeds and conduct of all subsequent generations of Roman citizens. If Cicero's *De Officiis* provided Re-naissance humanists with a standard handbook of civic values, it was Livy who lent substance to the Ciceronian dictum that history was philosophy teaching by example. Hector Boece's *Scotorum Historia* was clearly written in this humanist spirit, as an extended treatise of moral philosophy, heavily influenced by the civic values of republican Rome as exemplified in the early books of Livy's history. Boece's predecessors in the field of Scottish historiography, notably John of Fordun in the 1380s and Walter Bower in the 1440s, had frequently appealed to the example

[9] W. Ferguson, *The Identity of the Scottish Nation: An Historic Quest* (Edinburgh, 1998), esp. 57–9.

of virtuous 'elders' as a model to be emulated by their Scots' descendants. In Boece's work, however, this is taken to much greater – some would say absurd – lengths.[10] For example, as is well known, Fordun and Bower, as well as systematising the myth of origins that traced the Scots' descent from the Greek prince Gathelus (or Gaythelos) and the eponymous Scota, daughter of Pharaoh, had also located the foundation of the Scottish kingdom by the legendary Fergus I in 330 BC. However, they had had virtually nothing to say about the forty-five kings who, they claimed, had reigned over Scotland between then and the succession of Fergus II in the early fifth century AD.[11] Boece, in contrast, had a very much fuller tale to tell, devoting six of the seventeen books of his chronicle to recounting in remarkable detail the deeds of forty kings (including the two Ferguses) who were now alleged, with a wealth of circumstantial detail, to have reigned over the Scottish kingdom during these first, formative, seven centuries of its existence.[12]

There is no need here to dwell on the thorny problem of Boece's sources for this extraordinary account of Scotland's remote prehistory.[13] Suffice it to say that, whether or not one sets any store by his claims to have uncovered chronicles unknown to his predecessors, it is safe to assume that he deliberately elaborated on them, à la Livy, imagining into existence a pristine Scottish civilisation against which the manners

---

[10] The best available analysis of Boece as a historian is N. Royan, 'The *Scotorum Historia* of Hector Boece: A Study' (D.Phil. Thesis, University of Oxford, 1996).

[11] On the development of these myths, see M. Drexler, 'Fluid Prejudice: Scottish Origin Myths in the Later Middle Ages', in J. Rosenthal and C. Richmond (eds), *People, Politics and Community in the Later Middle Ages* (Gloucester and New York, 1987), 60–77; Mason, *Kingship and the Commonweal*, 78–103.

[12] The *Scotorum Historiae a prima gentis origine libri XVII* was printed in Paris by Jodocus Badius, but bears no date of publication. The dedications to James V and Archbishop James Beaton are both dated Aberdeen 1526, apparently the source of the common error that the work was published in that year. However, a subsequent address to the nobility by Alexander Lyon, precentor of Moray, immediately preceding Book I of the history proper is dated 'Ex Parrhisiorum Academia celeberrima ad Idus Martias MDXXVII ad calculum Romanum'. Subsequent references to Boece, *Historia*, are to this 1527 edition; parallel references to Bellenden, *Chronicle*, are to the first edition of John Bellenden's Scots translation printed at Edinburgh in the 1530s (see below, note 20).

[13] Serious debate over Boece's sources has a long pedigree, beginning with Father Thomas Innes' *Critical Essay on the Ancient Inhabitants of the Northern Parts of Britain or Scotland* (1729). The fullest and most sympathetic discussion is in Royan, 'Boece's *Scotorum Historia*', 168–236, who thinks it unlikely that Boece simply invented works such as the chronicle he attributes to the shadowy figure of Veremundus.

and mores of all subsequent generations of Scots are constantly measured – and just as constantly found wanting.[14] There is a significant
'constitutional' dimension to this to which we must return shortly, but
for the moment two other aspects of Boece's account of Scotland's
ancient past are worth further comment. First, the pristine Scottish
virtue that Boece evokes is essentially martial and manly in character,
sustained through adherence to a physical discipline of Spartan auster-
ity. Thus the ancient Scots slept on hard boards with rocks for pillows
and ate only one frugal meal a day. Any relaxation of this masculine
discipline led to a soft effeminacy that weakened the Scots' capacity to
uphold and defend the commonweal and liberty of the realm.[15] It was
entirely characteristic of Boece that he interpreted the Anglo-Norman
innovations of the twelfth century in terms of the introduction to
Scotland of effete English manners that corrupted the traditional
discipline, and thus the civic virtue, that had sustained the kingdom
since its foundation. Thereafter, the Scots were more inclined to eat two
or even three times a day, dining on foreign delicacies rather than
homely bannocks, as well as adopting new titles of nobility and elaborate
foreign finery.[16] Of course, not all Scots were corrupted in this way, and
there remained those who upheld the ancient virtues and discipline in

[14] The comparison with Livy is all the more apt in that Boece tells us that John
Campbell, the king's treasurer, had tried to complete an earlier but unsuccessful
effort on the part of Aeneas Sylvius Piccolomini (later Pope Pius II) to travel to
Iona in search of some of the lost books of Livy's history, allegedly deposited
there for safekeeping by Fergus II following the fall of Rome to the Goths in
412. According to Boece, Campbell returned from Iona in 1525 bringing with
him five ancient books, which, though fragmentary and largely illegible, seemed
to the humanist Boece to read more like Sallust than Livy. Perhaps more
importantly, however, Campbell also brought back a work by Veremundus,
archdeacon of St Andrews, containing the history of Scotland from the beginning
to the time of Malcolm Canmore. This author, together with the 'most wise'
Bishop Elphinstone, Boece claims to follow in his own chronicle. However,
neither of these alleged sources has come down to us. See Boece, *Historia*, fo.
cxviiir–v, and the reference to his sources in the dedication to James V, *ibid.*, sig.
aiiiv; Bellenden, *Chronicle*, fos. lxxxiiv–lxxxiiir.
[15] This picture of primitive virtue is conveniently epitomised in the last chapter of
the 'Scotorum Regni Descriptio' that precedes the main body of the text, where
ancient Scottish manners are compared favourably to those of Boece's own day:
Boece, *Historia*, sig. cciv–cciiiiv ('Scotorum prisci & recentes mores'); Bellenden,
Chronicle, sig. Cviv–Diiir ('Ane prudent doctryne maid be the auctoure
concernyng baith the new maneris and the auld of Scottis').
[16] Boece, *Historia*, sigs. cciiiv–cciiiir, fo. cclxviir–v; Bellenden, *Chronicle*, sigs. Dii
r–v, fos. clxxixv–clxxxir.

the face of such temptations of the flesh. For Boece, indeed, as for Livy, the historical process was essentially cyclical rather than linear, a constant round of decay followed by regeneration, which saw successive generations of Scots either embracing or rejecting the civic virtues and values of their ancient forebears.[17]

It is worth emphasising, and this is the second aspect of Boece's account of the remote Scottish past that requires comment here, that these forebears were for Boece unequivocally Gaelic. Although six-teenth-century understanding of the Celtic peoples who inhabited early Britain and Ireland was distinctly limited (and the term Celtic itself had little contemporary currency), Scottish chroniclers had long been aware of the multilingual character of the Scottish kingdom. Thus Boece differentiates between the Scots-speaking Lowlanders, who had ac-quired the Saxon tongue through centuries of close association with England, and Highlanders whose language – 'Gatelic' – was named after Gathelus.[18] By the same token, Boece was well aware of the racial and linguistic affinity between the Gaels of Scotland and Ireland – the peoples described by classical Roman authors simply as *Scoti*. As a result, like Fordun and Bower before him, Boece had little hesitation in exploiting to the full the elasticity of the Latin term and appropriating all things Irish to Scottish use. As this suggests, however, whether or not his pillaging of Irish annals was a conscious deception, Boece was well aware that the Scots originated in Ireland, that the kingdom of Dalriada was Gaelic in language and culture, and, most importantly, that vestiges of that Gaelic civilisation – and thus of the discipline that animated the civic virtue of the ancient Scots – still survived in the Highlands and

[17] The theme is conveniently recapitulated in the lengthy speech that Boece attributes to Bishop Henry Wardlaw, addressing a parliament convened by James I, in the last book of the *Historia* (fos. ccclxiiir–ccclxivv; Bellenden, *Chronicle*, fos. ccxlvir–v). For further comment, see N. Royan, 'The Uses of Speech in Hector Boece's *Scotorum Historia*', in L. Houwen, A. MacDonald and S. Mapstone (eds), *A Palace in the Wild: Essays on Vernacular Culture and Humanism in Late-Medieval and Renaissance Scotland* (Louvain, 2000), 75–94, esp. 90–2.

[18] Boece, *Historia*, sigs. aaiiiir, cciiiv; Bellenden, *Chronicle*, sigs. Biv, Diir. It is noticeable that Boece does not account for the rise of English through an influx of English-speaking peoples to Scotland, but rather by the intercourse of Scots with their southern neighbours through which their original Gaelic tongue was lost. Nor are the origins of Gaelic from the Greek Gathelus explained in satisfactory terms; indeed, the matter is still further complicated by Boece's reference to the Scots' Egyptian inheritance and the now lost ability of the ancient Scots to write in hieroglyphs.

Islands of sixteenth-century Scotland.[19] It was, therefore, to the Gaelic west and north that Boece urged his contemporaries to look in order to recapture the pristine virtue of their forebears.

How much this Gaelicism actually appealed to Boece's readership is a matter of debate. However, the *Scotorum Historia* was almost immediately translated into Scots for King James V by John Bellenden – the translator also, and significantly, of the early books of Livy – and subsequently published by Thomas Davidson at Edinburgh in the mid-1530s.[20] The first vernacular history of Scotland to appear in print, its influence among Scots-speaking Lowlanders was immense, and clearly indicates that its blend of civic and chivalric idealism, if not necessarily its glorification of the Gaels, struck a powerful chord among contemporaries.[21] Certainly, it exerted far greater influence and appeal than the strikingly different vision of Scottish civilisation articulated by Boece's erstwhile colleague and friend, the scholastic theologian, John Mair, whose *Historia Maioris Britanniae tam Angliae quam Scotiae* had appeared in 1521, a few years before Boece's chronicle.[22] Mair's hostility to the Gaels is well known: building on some casual asides of Fordun and Bower, he was among the first to express in any detail the view of the

---

[19] This is evident in the 'Scotorum Regni Descriptio' as well as in the early books of the *Historia* proper.

[20] The manuscript copy presented to James V is now in the Pierpont Morgan Library, New York, but formed the basis of the Scottish Text Society's *The Chronicles of Scotland, compiled by Hector Boece, translated into Scots by John Bellenden*, ed. R. W. Chambers, E. C. Batho and H. W. Husbands (STS, 1938–41). A facsimile of Davidson's Edinburgh edition of *The Hystory and Croniklis of Scotland* was published as Hector Boethius, *Chronicle of Scotland* (Edinburgh, 1540?) in the English Experience series no. 851 (Amsterdam, 1977). The fullest discussion of the date of the vernacular Scots edition is in A. E. Sheppard, 'John Bellenden', printed as an appendix to the STS edition of the *Chronicles*, ii, 411–61, where it is concluded that 'the most probable date for Davidson's edition is 1533' (pp. 444–6). On Bellenden as a translator of Livy, see J. MacQueen, 'Aspects of Humanism in Sixteenth- and Seventeenth-Century Literature', in J. MacQueen (ed.), *Humanism in Renaissance Scotland* (Edinburgh, 1990), 10–31.

[21] A. H. Williamson, *Scottish National Consciousness in the Reign of James VI* (Edinburgh, 1979), 120, describes its publication as 'a major cultural event for contemporaries'. Its context and significance are explored more fully in Mason, *Kingship and the Commonweal*, 78–103.

[22] John Mair, *A History of Greater Britain as well England as Scotland*, ed. and trans. A. Constable (Scottish History Society, 1892). Boece and Mair had been students together in Paris in the 1490s, at the same college (Montaigu) as Erasmus. See *Hectoris Boetii Murthlacensium et Aberdonensium Episcoporum Vitae*, ed. and trans. J. Moir (Spalding Club, 1894), 88–9.

Highlanders as indolent, undisciplined and aggressive – in a word, 'barbaric' – as opposed to the more civilised and law-abiding Lowlanders.[23] Paradoxically, however, and it is a paradox that runs throughout the sixteenth century and well beyond, Mair was not prepared to ditch the legendary line of Dalriadic kings that 'proved' the autonomy as well as the antiquity of the Scottish kingdom. Although the first Scot to argue at any length the case for Anglo-Scottish union, his understanding of the commonality of language, law and custom that existed among Lowland Scots and English did not extend to arguing the case for a common ethnic identity, Germanic rather than Celtic, that would have wholly marginalised the Gaels within his vision of a united British kingdom.[24] Nevertheless, Scotland's Gaelic heritage is only saved from wholesale abandonment by Mair's desire to see Anglo-Scottish union as one based on parity of status and esteem. To achieve that end, and counter English claims to feudal superiority over the northern realm, Mair had little choice but to stick to the traditional totem of Scottish independence and maintain the historicity of the ancient line of Dalriadic kings, even if the elaborate tales told by Boece of their heroic defence of the kingdom's freedom were entirely unknown to him.[25]

Among the many celebrated scholars who were taught by Mair during his long career in Paris as well as Scotland was, of course, George Buchanan. However, just as Buchanan rejected Mair's scholastic method in favour of a more fashionable commitment to humanist grammar and rhetoric, so his understanding of the early history of Scotland has much less in common with his former teacher than it does with the humanist approach pioneered by Hector Boece. As much a devotée of Livy as Boece, Buchanan was also a considerable philologist with at the very least a working knowledge of Gaelic. On linguistic as well as commonsensical grounds, therefore, he ditched the legend of the Scots' descent from Gathelus and Scota, famously

[23] Mair, *History of Greater Britain*, 48–50.

[24] Interestingly, in the 1540s, another Scottish Unionist, James Henrisoun, did posit a common Anglo-Scottish racial identity, based on the dubious argument that even in the sixteenth century sufficient residues of aboriginal British (i.e. Welsh) blood still coursed through the veins of Scots and English to justify his belief that that they were a single people who ought to be ruled by a single monarch. Henrisoun, of course, repudiated Boece's Dalriadic kings in favour of the English claim to sovereignty over Scotland as legitimised by Geoffrey of Monmouth and the legendary 'Welsh' material of the Brut chronicles. See Mason, *Kingship and the Commonweal*, 253–6.

[25] For this interpretation of Mair's text, see Mason, *Kingship and the Commonweal*, 36–77.

pioneering instead the crucial distinction between P- and Q-Celts that allowed him correctly to identify the hitherto mysterious Picts as also of Celtic stock.[26] He did not, however, proceed from there to argue for any kind of pan-Gaelic identity. Rather, he went on to give a much compressed account of the reigns of the early (mythical) kings of Dalriada, reducing the half-dozen books which Boece had devoted to them to a single one. If this drastic compression suggests some scepticism on Buchanan's part, it need not lead us to conclude with Trevor-Roper that he continued to cling to Boece's ancient kings only because they provided critical support for the radical political theory he developed to justify the revolution against Mary Queen of Scots.[27] As has been argued elsewhere, Buchanan's motives for upholding the historicity of these kings were in fact much more complex than this allows. At the very least, like Boece and even Mair before him, he saw them as essential to demonstrating the original autonomy and continuing integrity of the Scottish kingdom.[28]

In addition, however, again like Boece, though in contrast to Mair, Buchanan saw among the primitive Gaels a pristine virtue against which to measure the successes and failures of their descendants. This is evident not just in the single book that Buchanan does devote to the early kings, but also in the 'Description of Scotland' that prefaces the main text of his *Historia Rerum Scoticarum*. For there, particularly in his account of the Western Isles, where he drew on but greatly embellished the contemporaneous description compiled by the archdeacon of the Isles, Donald Munro, there emerges a picture of a primitive if untutored virtue, untainted by luxury and corruption, that still upheld the ancient discipline of Scotland's remote Gaelic past.[29] As he wrote of the island of

---

[26] As Ferguson, *Identity of the Scottish Nation*, ch. 5 and *passim*, points out, Buchanan's insight was subsequently obscured and it is only in modern times (if even then) that his pioneering work has received the credit it deserves; cf. W. Ferguson, 'George Buchanan and the Picts', *Scottish Tradition*, xvi (1990–1), 18–32.

[27] H. R. Trevor-Roper, 'George Buchanan and the Ancient Scottish Constitution', *English Historical Review*, supplement 3 (1966).

[28] See R. A. Mason, 'Scotching the Brut: Politics, History and National Myth in Sixteenth-Century Britain', in R. A. Mason (ed.), *Scotland and England, 1286–1815* (Edinburgh, 1987), 60–84, at 73–4.

[29] See George Buchanan, *History of Scotland*, trans. J. Aikman (Glasgow, 1827), i, 1–63 (all references to the *History* are to this edition). Dean Donald Munro's 'Description of the Western Isles' was written *c.*1549, but not published until 1774; see R. W. Munro (ed.), *Monro's Western Isles of Scotland and Genealogies of the Clans, 1549* (Edinburgh, 1961). However, Buchanan must have known Monro personally as both served on various General Assemblies in the 1560s and in the *History*, i, 39, Buchanan refers to him warmly as 'a pious and diligent man'.

Rona, 'here alone in the universe, I imagine, are to be found a people who know no want, among whom every necessity of life abounds even to satiety. Unacquainted alike with luxury and avarice, they find in their ignorance of vice, that innocence and tranquillity of mind, which others search for in the discipline and precepts of wisdom.'[30] To be sure, Buchanan's admiration was tempered by his knowledge that their virtuous manners were less a matter of choice than a product of their impoverished environment. Nevertheless, and once again like Hector Boece, Buchanan looked west and north rather than south for the inspiration to fashion a civil Scotland. Ever the humanist, however, he sought to marry austere Gaelic virtue with the riches of Roman literature and culture, famously envisaging the 'gradual extinction of the ancient Scottish language' and its replacement by 'the softer and more harmonious tones of Latin. For if in this transmigration into another language, it is necessary to yield up one thing or other, let us pass from rusticity and barbarism, to culture and civilisation, and let our choice and judgment repair the infelicity of our birth'.[31]

At this point, in this Latinate Celtic twilight, it is time to leave the theme of Gaelic primitivism and turn instead to Scottish kingship and the idea of an 'ancient Scottish constitution'. It will be clear enough already that medieval Scots had invested heavily in the construction of a royal lineage deliberately designed to emphasise the high antiquity, and thus the autonomy, of the Scottish kingdom. As Dauvit Broun has recently shown, in the twelfth and thirteenth centuries, this involved a close and self-conscious identification of (and with) the Irish roots of an essentially Gaelic Scottish kingship.[32] Such enthusiasm for the Scots' Irish ancestry is much less evident in the later chroniclers of Lowlanders such as Fordun and Bower; nevertheless, both the origins' legend and the royal genealogy remained for them critical evidence of the kingdom's

---

[30] Buchanan, *History*, i, 55; cf. his description of the similarly abstemious Orkney islanders, where he concludes: 'whence it may be easily conjectured that the moderation I have mentioned has arisen not so much from reason, or reflection, as from penury; and that that necessity which produced it at first preserved it so long among them. As they became better acquainted with their neighbours, they became gradually corrupted by luxury, declined from their ancient discipline, and gave themselves up to enervating indulgencies. . . . But this degeneracy of manners is confined almost entirely to the great men and priests; among the common people many traces of pristine sobriety still remain' (ibid., i, 57).

[31] Ibid., i, 9.

[32] D. Broun, *The Irish Identity of the Kingdom of the Scots in the Twelfth and Thirteenth Centuries* (Woodbridge, 1999).

historic and continuing freedom from English overlordship. Although, as Steve Boardman suggests, late medieval Scottish Lowlanders were keener to tie in their family genealogies with Malcolm Canmore, and especially his Saxon wife, St Margaret, than to trace their descent to the Gaelic kings of Dalriada, the Scottish kingdom's independent status continued to be predicated on its Celtic ancestry.[33] Hector Boece's extravagant refurbishment of Scotland's early history, recounting in unprecedented detail the careers of the Dalriadic kings, undoubtedly served to revitalise the Gaelic dimension of Scotland's past history and present identity. At the same time, however, in showing how some thirteen of the first forty of Scotland's monarchs were resisted and deposed for their tyranny, Boece appears to have anticipated George Buchanan's understanding of the elective nature of Scottish kingship and the historic rights of the people to hold their rulers to account.

It is, however, well worth casting a critical eye over the commonly-held view that Boece was, as it were, arguing Buchanan's case *avant la lettre*. For example, two key assumptions that underlie this view need to be approached with some caution. First, there is no very clear evidence that Boece ever intended his account of Scotland's early and largely mythical kings to serve any 'constitutional' function at all.[34] To be sure, many of them did meet unsavoury ends at the hands of their subjects for their tyranny or depravity or, more usually, both. Nevertheless, and notwithstanding the recent arguments of J. H. Burns to the contrary, they read far more like the moral exemplars so beloved of humanists than constitutional precedents.[35] This

[33] See above, Chapter 3; cf. I. Campbell, 'A Romanesque Revival and the Early Renaissance in Scotland, *c.*1380–1513', *Journal of the Society of Architectural Historians*, liv (1995), 302–25, which reveals the highly self-conscious way in which late medieval Scottish clerics as well as the Stewart kings looked back to the reign of the Canmore dynasty as a 'golden age' that was worth reviving.

[34] The idea, originating with Father Thomas Innes in the eighteenth century and repeated by J. B. Black in the twentieth, that Boece was legitimising the 'deposition' of James III in 1488 has no evidence to sustain it; see J. B. Black, 'Boece's *Scotorum Historiae*', in *University of Aberdeen, Quatercentenary of the Death of Hector Boece, First Principal of the University* (Aberdeen, 1937), 30–53. However, the view that he was advocating resistance and tyrannicide is hardly dependent on this connection.

[35] J. H. Burns, *The True Law of Kingship: Concepts of Monarchy in Early Modern Scotland* (Oxford, 1996), 78–86, recognises the 'broadly moral purposes' that Boece had in mind, but argues that this is 'a political morality, a morality of government' and that 'the implication of his history is plainly that the nobles and people of Scotland had the right and had repeatedly demonstrated the power to call errant rulers to account and to punish their misdeeds' (p. 82). There is no doubt that Boece can be (and was) read in this way, but in my view it is less clear that this was how the author intended that his work should be interpreted.

view is partly based on the moralising tone of the chronicle as a whole, but also on the fact that Boece explicitly acknowledged that the 'tanistic' laws of succession that prevailed in early Scotland, by which the kingship might alternate between different branches of the royal lineage, and on which the idea of a Scottish elective monarchy was largely built, were altered in the tenth century in favour of a system of male primogeniture.[36] Under this new dispensation, the role of the community, and more especially the aristocracy, in restraining or deposing an errant monarch, survived (if it survived at all) only in a highly attenuated and ambiguous form. Although parliamentary or conciliar approval might be sought for a new king, there is little to suggest that the political community had the right to determine the succession by overriding the hereditary right of the ruling dynasty. To be sure, as Burns points out, Boece entangled himself in some serious difficulty by arguing the case for the legitimacy of John Balliol's kingship after he was awarded the crown in 1292 following Edward I's adjudication in the 'Great Cause'. Yet, arguably, that is simply testimony to Boece's desire to achieve the impossible feat of reconciling Balliol's legitimate succession by hereditary right with the subsequent but equally legitimate hereditary succession of Robert Bruce. Significantly, if not surprisingly, Bellenden's translation reverts to the erroneous but much more straight-forward account of the medieval chroniclers who insisted that Balliol was a

[36] There is no doubt that Boece believed that Fergus I was elected king of Scots (Boece, *Historia*, fos. viv–viir; Bellenden, *Chronicle*, fo. vir), or that the kingship was subsequently entailed in his family in a manner that encouraged alternating succession between different branches of the royal kin (Boece, *Historia*, fo. xv; Bellenden, *Chronicle*, fo. ixr). What is less commonly acknowledged, however, is Boece's subsequent account of the struggle for the crown on Fergus' death and his adverse comments on a law of succession that he evidently saw as harmful to the commonweal: 'multorum inde et regum et principum caedes, non sine magna reipublicae iactura sequutas' (Boece, *Historia*, fo. xiiir; Bellenden, *Chronicle*, fos. xv–xiv). Likewise, Boece appears to approve of the change in the law of succession to one of male primogeniture allegedly introduced by Kenneth III (*recte* Kenneth II) in the tenth century, attributing to the king a robust speech in defence of the change that Boece says nothing subsequently to undermine (Boece, *Historia*, fos. ccxxxviiiv–ccxlr; Bellenden, *Chronicle*, fos. clxir–clxiiir). For an interesting discussion of these speeches, however, arguing for a degree of ambivalence in Boece's attitude to the respective merits of elective and hereditary succession, see Royan, 'The Uses of Speech in Boece's *Scotorum Historia*', 83–6. On balance, however, it does not seem to me that Boece was a principled believer in either elective monarchy or the right of the nobility to resist tyrannical rule. In the dedication to James V, for example, he refers critically to nobles whose 'immoderata potentia' leads them to rise against the king (Boece, *Historia*, sig. Aiiiiv).

usurper imposed on the Scots by Edward I to the exclusion of Bruce's rightful claim.[37]

The second commonly-held assumption that underlies interpretations of Boece's chronicle, and on which some doubt may be cast, is that there existed in late medieval Scotland a tradition of radical political thought, stemming from the Declaration of Arbroath of 1320 and traceable through to the sixteenth-century writings of Mair, Buchanan and even Knox, to which Boece is also alleged to have adhered.[38] The evidence for such a tradition is so far from overwhelming as to raise the question of how and why it was identified in the first place. One might hazard a guess that it was actually a product of eighteenth- and nineteenth-century whig efforts to salvage something of value from the perceived anarchy of Scotland's otherwise eminently forgettable feudal past.[39] However, as we no longer believe that medieval Scotland was either unusually anarchic or best forgotten, so we need no longer console ourselves with the thought that it incubated modern democracy. What it did, of course, incubate was a feudal-baronial ideology – a form of aristocratic conciliarism – that encouraged the nobility to see themselves as the king's natural-born counsellors, as responsible as he was for ensuring the common good of the realm as a whole. It is certainly possible – indeed probable – that out of such an ideology there might emerge in times of crisis a more hardline constitutionalism that vested in the nobility the right to resist and restrain a monarch who ruled tyrannically. And the recent research of Roland Tanner and Michael Brown makes clear that *in extremis* the well-established right to counsel the king was in the fifteenth century supplemented by calls forcibly to resist and/or restrain him.[40] Yet what is

---

[37] Burns, *True Law of Kingship*, 87–9; on the development of 'Brucean ideology', designed to bear out the legitimacy of Robert I's succession by hereditary right, see R. J. Goldstein, *The Matter of Scotland: Historical Narrative in Medieval Scotland* (Lincoln, NE, and London, 1993).

[38] See, for example, M. P. McDiarmid, 'The Kingship of the Scots in their Writers', *Scottish Literary Journal*, vi (1979), 5–18, heavily criticised in R. A. Mason, 'Kingship, Tyranny and the Right to Resist in Fifteenth-Century Scotland', *Scottish Historical Review*, lxvi (1987), 125–51, reprinted in Mason, *Kingship and the Commonweal*, 8–35; however, for criticism of the view presented there, see the work cited in note 40 below.

[39] On this generally, see C. Kidd, *Subverting Scotland's Past: Scottish Whig Historians and the Creation of an Anglo-British Identity, 1689–c.1830* (Cambridge, 1993).

[40] R. J. Tanner, *The Late Medieval Scottish Parliament: Politics and the Three Estates, 1424–1488* (East Linton, 2001); M. Brown, ' "I have thus slain a tyrant": *The Dethe of the Kynge of Scotis* and the Right to Resist in Early Fifteenth-Century Scotland', *Innes Review*, xlvii (1996), 24–44.

striking about fifteenth-century Scottish political culture is that, despite the general availability of such ideas, the belief in the right to counsel was so rarely re-formulated in the more radically constitutionalist form of a 'contract' between king and people. The point is an important one in the present context, for whereas Boece's chronicle is certainly redolent of an ideology of aristocratic conciliarism, often made more pointed by being decked out in the language of classical republicanism, it is much less clear that it is vesting in the community in general or the nobility in particular the right forcibly to resist, restrain or kill a monarch whose rule threatens the 'commonweal' of the realm as a whole. On the contrary, as we have seen, Boece is at the very least ambivalent about the principles of elective monarchy on which the right to resist was generally founded and, arguably, deliberately distanced himself from their radical implications.

If there is still some lingering doubt over Hector Boece's precise attitude to the powers of the community in relation to the crown, the same can hardly be said of George Buchanan. Buchanan's radical political ideas, as expressed in the *Historia* but more particularly in his brief tract *De Iure Regni apud Scotos Dialogus* of 1579, are a rich and eclectic mix of Aristotelian natural law theory, the classical republicanism of Livy and Cicero, and perhaps a touch of Mair's ecclesiastical conciliarism.[41] It is important to recognise, however, that his theoretical arguments for popular sovereignty and the elective nature of monarchy are, if you will, free-standing: *pace* Trevor-Roper, the illustrations that Buchanan drew from Scotland's recent as well as remote history are precisely that – illustrations.[42] They provided Buchanan with an important source of *exempla*, but they are not the essential foundations of his political ideas. Nevertheless, Buchanan clearly did believe that the natural law principles on which his radical political theory was based were exemplified throughout the history of Scotland. As a result, in writing his *Historia*, he did what Boece had failed to do and made quite explicit the constitutional significance of the fate of those early mythical kings of Dalriada who had been restrained, deposed and killed by their subjects.[43] Moreover, and again in

---

[41] The various strands of thought in Buchanan's political philosophy are discussed more fully in the introduction to a forthcoming critical edition of the *De Iure Regni apud Scotos Dialogus*, ed. and trans. R. A. Mason and M. S. Smith.

[42] Trevor-Roper, 'Buchanan and the Ancient Constitution'; cf. Mason, 'Scotching the Brut', 73–4.

[43] Buchanan, *History*, i, 149–210 (Book IV covering the first forty kings from Fergus I to Fergus II), and 211–71 (Book V, which takes the story on to the reign of Kenneth MacAlpine).

contrast to Boece, he made quite explicit that the tenth-century change to the succession laws amounted to a deal between the monarchy and the aristocracy. According to Buchanan, hereditary succession by male primogeniture was granted in return for recognition, formalised in the contractual terms of the coronation oath, that the community retained the right to resist and depose a monarch who acted contrary to the common-weal of the realm.[44] Buchanan, however, went further still, and in a way that returns us to the main theme of this chapter. For he argued in both the *Historia* and the *De Iure Regni* that among the clans of the Highlands and particularly the Western Isles these practices were still in operation and that the clan chiefs – or *phylarchi* as he liked to call them – were still unquestionably elected by their clansmen and bound on pain of resistance to follow the advice of their councils.[45]

The question immediately arises whether this vision of the survival of pristine Gaelic 'constitutionalism' has any basis in reality? Does it point to a tradition of political thought and practice, known to Buchanan and possibly also to Boece, that would lend a much harder edge of legitimate resistance theory to the feudal-baronial conciliarism referred to earlier? As regards Boece, despite the Gaelic provenance of some of his key sources, this seems unlikely, as he quite explicitly says that the tenth-century change to the succession laws applied as much to the nobility as it did to the crown.[46] In other words, clan chiefs were to succeed by the principles of male primogeniture and not by election. In fact, although male primogeniture was increasingly the norm in the Highlands as it was in the Lowlands, there is some evidence that the kin-based Gaelic practice of tanistic succession did survive into the sixteenth century.[47]

---

[44] Such is the argument of Buchanan, *De Iure Regni apud Scotos Dialogus* (Edinburgh, 1579), 61–6; however, as Burns, *True Law of Kingship*, 218, points out, Buchanan retreats from this highly idealised position in the *History* (i, 306–13, 324–5), where the new law of succession is imposed by force rather than agreed as part of a bargain struck with the community.

[45] See Buchanan, *De Iure Regni*, 65: 'Scoti enim prisci ad nostram usque aetatem suos eligunt phylarchos, et electis consilium seniorum adhibent; cui consilio qui non parent, honore privantur'; and *History*, ii, 601–2.

[46] Boece, *Historia*, fo. ccxlr ('cunctis ex Scotorum gente in haereditatem succedentibus idem ius servato'); Bellenden, *Chronicle*, fo. clxiiv.

[47] See, for example, K. A. Steer and J. Bannerman, *Late Medieval Monumental Sculpture in the West Highlands* (Edinburgh, 1977), 100, 113, 132–3, 148. Cf. J. Bannerman, *The Beatons: A Medical Kindred in the Classical Gaelic Tradition* (Edinburgh, 1986), 86–7, for the survival of such practices among the Gaelic learned orders throughout the seventeenth century. I am grateful to Steve Boardman for bringing these references to my attention.

Likewise, it is clear that Lowland magnates as well as Highland chiefs held 'councils' of the leading men of their affinities. Generally of an informal nature, and leaving no written records, such meetings were nonetheless integral to the exercise of aristocratic power in the localities.[48] It is curious that Buchanan makes rather less than his source, Dean Munro, of the somewhat more formal fourteen-man Council of the Isles that had traditionally met at Finlaggan on Islay to advise the Lord of the Isles.[49] Yet, his belief that such councils might assume a 'constitutional' role in arbitrating in matters as critical as a disputed succession is plausible enough. In effect, Buchanan might be said not simply to have highlighted and idealised the conciliar dimension of the exercise of aristocratic power (whether in the Lowland or the Highlands), but also to have teased out and formalised the quasi-contractual basis on which it rested.

The third and last theme to be touched on here, the early history of Celtic Christianity and the Celtic kirk, is probably also the best known and most fully explored. William Ferguson, for example, has recently offered a useful survey of changing attitudes to St Columba and the Culdees that, although underestimating the signal importance of George Buchanan's reinterpretation of early Christianity in Scotland, serves to place his writings in the perspective of earlier accounts of Scottish ecclesiastical history.[50] Thus he rightly argues that the late medieval chroniclers, not least Fordun and Bower, went to considerable lengths to minimise, if not to eliminate altogether, the distinctive character of the Christian religious practices of the Scottish and Irish Gaels. Their reasons for doing so are not hard to find. Acutely conscious of the claims of York and Canterbury to ecclesiastical supremacy over Scotland, and desperately keen to assert the Scottish church's status as a 'special

---

[48] See J. Wormald, *Lords and Men in Scotland: Bonds of Manrent, 1442–1603* (Edinburgh, 1985), esp. 95–6. See also J. Wormald, ' "Princes" and the Regions in the Scottish Reformation', in N. Macdougall (ed.), *Church, Politics and Society: Scotland, 1408–1929* (Edinburgh, 1983), 65–84, for an analysis of the exercise of noble power which, while not explicitly concerned with local conciliarism, makes abundantly clear how constrained great nobles were by the need to accommodate the views of the leading men of their affinities.

[49] Compare Buchanan, *History*, i, 44, with Monro, *Western Isles*, 57. Buchanan merely says: 'Near to Isla, but smaller, is Round island, called also the island of Council, for there was a court in it, in which fourteen of the chief men sat daily for the administration of justice, and discussing the most important affairs of the country, whose strict equity and moderation secured peace, both at home and abroad, and plenty, the constant attendance on peace.'

[50] Ferguson, *Identity of the Scottish Nation*, ch. 6.

daughter' of the Roman see, it was imperative for them to demonstrate not only the antiquity and hence the autonomy of Scottish Christianity, but also its impeccable orthodoxy.

Chronologically, there were for Fordun and Bower two dates that emerged as critical for the early history of Christianity in Scotland. First, the year 203, in the pontificate of Victor I, when, they argued, the Scots first formally adopted the Catholic religion.[51] This is most likely an attempt to match the equivalent English tradition, originating with Nennius but popularised by Geoffrey of Monmouth, that the Britons were first converted in the late second century (the year 187 was settled on later) under King Lucius.[52] Fordun and Bower were unable to name the Scottish king responsible for Christianising his people, but predictably Hector Boece was better informed and identified him as Donald I.[53] The year 203, however, pales into relative insignificance when compared to the second date lighted upon as crucial to Scottish ecclesiastical history. For, according to Fordun and Bower, it was in the year 430 that 'Pope Celestine [I] sent St Palladius as the first bishop of Scotland'.[54] Palladius, so far as he is known to history at all, is known only as a native of southern Gaul who undertook missionary work among the *Scoti* of Ireland in the fifth century. But, as we have seen, it is wholly typical of Fordun and Bower, not to mention Boece, that they should exploit the ambiguous meaning of *Scoti* to appropriate Irish saints as well as Irish kings to Scottish use.[55] Significantly, however, for Fordun and Bower, Palladius was rather more than just a saint; he was also a bishop of the Roman Catholic church. The inference of this is fairly clear: fully a century and a half before St Augustine of Canterbury

---

[51] *Chron. Fordun*, ii, 57–8; *Chron. Bower*, i, 256–9.

[52] Geoffrey of Monmouth, *History of the Kings of Britain*, ed. and trans. L. Thorpe (Harmondsworth, 1966), 124–6.

[53] Boece, *Historia*, fo. lxxxixr; Bellenden, *Chronicle*, fo. lxiiir. Both Boece and Bellenden admit that the Britons received the faith before the Scots, but they add that, while the Britons frequently lapsed due to pagan persecution, the Scots had remained steadfast throughout their history and had never fallen prey to heresy.

[54] *Chron. Bower*, ii, 20–2. Bower goes on: 'Therefore it is fitting that the Scots should celebrate diligently the festivals and memorial days of the church, because he carefully taught both by his words and by his example the orthodox faith to their own race, that is the Scots, although they believed in Christ long before.' Cf. *Chron. Fordun*, ii, 85.

[55] There may be some justification for this in so far as it is possible that Palladius did extend his mission from Ireland to Scotland; see D. H. Farmer, *The Oxford Dictionary of Saints* (Oxford, 1978), 310–11.

undertook a similar papal mission to England in 597, Palladius had securely established in Scotland a form of Christianity that, in terms of both organisation and worship, was unquestionably orthodox.

Of course, having got Scottish ecclesiastical history off to such a start, it was incumbent on Fordun and Bower to ensure that its orthodoxy was maintained. One interesting consequence of this was that most of the Irish saints appropriated to Scottish use were repackaged as good Catholic bishops. Thus, for example, Kentigern, Baldred, Aidan, Finan and Colman are all said to be bishops operating in accordance with the episcopal system established by Palladius. Columba, interestingly enough, is an exception to this rule: both Fordun and Bower describe him as a monk and acknowledge that he was in fact Irish (though at least one late sixteenth-century Catholic writer did portray him as a Highland Scot).[56] Be that as it may, there was a further consequence of the approach adopted by Fordun and Bower to early Scottish ecclesiastical history: namely, that they inevitably ran into some difficulty dealing with the Venerable Bede's well-known and highly influential *History of the English Church and People*. Bede's eighth-century account of the dramatic clash over the dating of Easter between orthodox Roman Catholics and representatives of the Celtic church at the Synod of Whitby in 664 was a particularly knotty problem, but one that Fordun and Bower did not so much confront as ignore.[57] Instead, they edified their readers with an account of how English kings had originally been evangelised and baptised by Scottish bishops (in reality, Irish monks) only to experience the subsequent ingratitude and ill-will of southern clerics who refused to recognise the Scottish church as the founder of their own.[58]

---

[56] *Chron. Fordun*, ii, 103; *Chron. Bower*, ii, 68–71. Cf. *De antiquitate Christianae religionis apud Scotos* (Rome and Douai, 1598), ed. and trans. H. D. G. Law, in *SHS Miscellany II* (SHS, 1904), 115–32, where the supposed author, George Thomson, claims (p. 127) that Columba was a Scot 'born in a mountainous district of Scotland'.

[57] For Bede's account of the discussions at Whitby, which ends with the Irish clergy being convinced of the error of their ways, see *Ecclesiastical History of the English People*, ed. and trans. L. Sherley-Price and R. E. Latham (Harmondsworth, 1965), 186–92. Fordun and Bower only refer to the Synod in the most oblique terms, never mentioning it by name or discussing the dispute over the dating of Easter: see the editorial notes to *Chron. Bower*, ii, 245, 247.

[58] *Chron. Fordun*, ii, 117; *Chron. Bower*, ii, 118–35: 'Therefore, through the agency of these holy men the bishops Aidan, Finan and Colman, either personally or through others that they had consecrated themselves and given to the Angles to be their bishops and priests, together with other preachers and with the   *[over*

In the light of this, one final twist to the medieval chroniclers' reading of early Scottish ecclesiastical history becomes fairly predictable. That is, that neither Fordun nor Bower attach any real importance to the ancient monastic communities of Culdees or *Céli De* ('vassals of God'), which were later to emerge as crucial to Protestant accounts of early Scottish church history.[59] For in so far as these communities represented a survival or revival of a heterodox form of Celtic Christianity, they had no significant place in a Scottish kirk predicated on unwavering adherence to Rome from the time of Bishop Palladius through to the reign of Malcolm and St Margaret.[60]

Overall, the attitude of Fordun and Bower to the early ecclesiastical history of Scotland is best summed up in their account of the proceedings leading to the issuing in 1192 of the celebrated bull *Cum Universi*. By the terms of the bull, Pope Celestine III conferred on the Scottish church the status of a 'special daughter' (*filia specialis*) of the Roman see, thus effectively recognising the *Ecclesia Scoticana* as a separate province of the Catholic church, free of the jurisdiction of York or Canterbury. According to Bower, at a council held at Northampton in 1176, presided over by the archbishops of York and Canterbury, and attended by clergymen of both realms, 'a certain Scots cleric named Gilbert' became infuriated by what he saw as English attempts to subordinate the Scottish kirk to English jurisdiction. Gilbert then went on to denounce the assembled English prelates as not just arrogant, but thoroughly ungrateful:

> on top of all the wickedness you have perpetrated in your exercise of power, you are trying to suppress your own mother,

cont'd cooperation of the kings and the hierarchy of the Scots, four kingdoms, namely two of Northumbria, one of the Mercian Middle Angles and the middle part of the kingdom of the East Saxons almost up to the banks of the River Thames, were converted to Christ' (ibid., ii, 131). 'Throughout the time of the mission of the Scots in England there was unshaken peace and intercourse without contentious strife. Finally when the native-born clergy of the English had grown in number the increase was mainly due to the instruction of the Scots – instead of showing gratitude they began to be resentful of their saintly teachers and to find a great variety of opportunities for forcing them to return to Scotland' (ibid., ii, 133).

[59] Their references to the Culdees are few and far between and none is of any great consequence; see the general index to *Chron. Bower*, ix, 435, where half a dozen references are noted.

[60] In fact, Bower canonises Malcolm as well as Margaret (*Chron. Bower*, iii, 70) and also subsequently refers to David I as a saint (ibid., iv, 2–3).

namely the Scottish church, which has been from the outset
Catholic and free, not basing your action on any lawful reason,
but on the premise of your power. When you were wandering
through the trackless desert of paganism, this [the Scottish]
church set you up on the mare of faith, and led you back to
Christ . . . This church washed your kings and princes along
with their peoples in the waters of holy baptism . . . Likewise
it consecrated your bishops and priests, appointed and ordained
them. Moreover, over a period of thirty years or more it held
the primacy over all the area from the north bank of the River
Thames northward and the highest episcopal office, as Bede
bears witness.[61]

As Bede bears witness, indeed! Yet the idea that the ancient Scottish
Catholic church was the 'mother' of its English equivalent was, for
Fordun and Bower, a fittingly patriotic riposte to the imperialist
ambitions of York and Canterbury.

Such in brief was the account of early Christianity in Scotland
developed by the medieval chroniclers and bequeathed to their
sixteenth-century successors. It was not an account that Hector
Boece saw fit to challenge or to which he added much of substance.
However much he may have wished to highlight the Gaelic origins
and distinctiveness of Scottish kingship, the early Scottish kirk
remained for him impeccably orthodox on the lines laid down by
Fordun and Bower. To be sure, as an evangelical humanist and
friend of Erasmus, Boece is both more sympathetic to primitive
religious practices and highly critical of contemporary clerical corruption, which he contrasts with the virtue and piety of the saintly
religious of the past.[62] Yet, not only does Boece insist that the Scots
had remained free of heresy since their first conversion under Donald
I, but he follows Fordun and Bower in crediting Palladius with
establishing episcopacy in Scotland and has the irascible cleric
Gilbert delivering a similar, albeit much shorter, defence of the

[61] *Chron. Bower*, iv, 326–31; cf. *Chron. Fordun*, ii, 262–3.
[62] See, for example, Boece, *Historia*, fo. ccxcr–v, Bellenden, *Chronicle*, fos.
clxxxxv–clxxxxvir (comparing the manners of old and new kirkmen); and Boece,
Historia, fo. ccclvr, Bellenden, *Chronicle*, fo. ccxliv (a lament on clerical
corruption prompted by James I's love of learning and the foundation of St
Andrews University). For a more sympathetic view of the Culdees than is usual
in Fordun or Bower, see Boece, *Historia*, fo. xciiiir–v, Bellenden, *Chronicle*, fo.
lxviiv.

historic freedom of the *Ecclesia Scoticana*.[63] In effect, Boece may be construed as pursuing the same humanist agenda as his patron, Bishop William Elphinstone, whose researches for the *Aberdeen Breviary*, an attempt at fashioning a uniquely Scottish liturgy that was published in two hefty volumes in 1510, famously took him to the Western Isles in search of early Christian remains.[64] However, it was not so much the distinctiveness of Celtic Christianity that interested Elphinstone as its antiquity and Catholic orthodoxy. Tellingly, in the 1490s, shortly after St Andrews was elevated to archiepiscopal status, the then primate, the devious but scholarly William Scheves, set about reinvigorating the cult of St Palladius at Fordoun in the Mearns, building a new chapel to house the relics of Scotland's first Roman Catholic bishop.[65]

The chapel has not survived; and neither, needless to say, has very much of the historical interpretation that lent Palladius – 'the apostle of the Scots' – such significance in pre-Reformation Scotland.[66] There is perhaps no better example of how the Scottish past has been recycled and repackaged than the way in which Protestant reformers set about rewriting the early history of Christianity in Scotland in order to prove precisely what the medieval chroniclers had consistently sought to deny: namely, that Celtic Christianity, the faith of St Columba and the

---

[63] Boece, *Historia*, fos. lxxxixr (Donald I), cxxxiiv–cxxxiiir (Palladius 'Scotorum apostolus'), cclxxxiiv (Gilbert); Bellenden, *Chronicle*, fos. lxiiiir (Donald I); lxxxxiiir (Palladius); clxxxxir (Gilbert). Boece, however, is noticeably less strident in crediting Scots missionaries with evangelising England and does not claim that the Scots' kirk was the mother of the English – perhaps reflecting his greater respect for the authority of Bede?

[64] Boece, *Episcoporum Vitae*, 99–100. On the *Aberdeen Breviary*, see L. J. Macfarlane, *William Elphinstone and the Kingdom of Scotland, 1431–1514* (Aberdeen, 1985), 231–46.

[65] Campbell, 'A Romanesque Revival and the Early Renaissance in Scotland', 307, 310–11. Cf. Boece, *Historia*, fo. cxxxiiir; Bellenden, *Chronicle*, fo. lxxxxiiir, for an account of the silver reliquary in which St Palladius' remains were placed.

[66] It is worth noting that Palladius does not merit an entry (even under Celtic saints) in the recent N. M. de S. Cameron (ed.), *Dictionary of Scottish Church History and Theology* (Edinburgh, 1993) and is mentioned only incidentally in A. MacQuarrie, *The Saints of Scotland: Essays in Scottish Church History*, AD 450–1093 (Edinburgh, 1997). A sad decline in fortune for a saint described in the *Aberdeen Breviary* (under his feast day of 6 July) as well as by Boece as 'the apostle of the Scots'. However, as Professor J. H. Burns has kindly pointed out to me, the extraordinary Catholic polymath Thomas Dempster fought a characteristically spirited rearguard action on Palladius' behalf in his *Historia Ecclesiastica Gentis Scotorum* (Bologna, 1627), 515–19.

Culdees, was indeed different, distinctive and unique – Catholic but certainly not Roman Catholic. How this was achieved, and with what consequences, has been extensively treated by Colin Kidd and David Allan and need not be rehearsed here.[67] However, it is worth challenging William Ferguson's contention that George Buchanan played no significant role in this process of rewriting and Protestantising Scottish church history.[68] In fact, secular though Buchanan's mindset certainly was, his *Historia* said or implied quite enough about the proto-presbyterianism of the Culdaic communities to excite the keen interest of Andrew Melville. As has been shown elsewhere, Melville's own annotated copy of Buchanan's *Historia* demonstrates his wholehearted approval of Buchanan's attribution to the early Scottish kirk of a primitive presbyterian discipline from which it had subsequently and disastrously declined.[69] The pre-Palladian (and thus pre-episcopal) kirk was marked for Buchanan by its simplicity, piety and learning: 'for until that time [the mission of Palladius], the churches were governed by monks, without bishops, with less splendour indeed, and external pomp, but with much greater simplicity and holiness'.[70] It was passages such as these in Buchanan's *Historia* that would set the pattern for future historical interpretation among Scottish Protestants who viewed St Palladius as nothing less than an agent of the papal Antichrist.

The courtier Sir James Melville of Halhill recalled in his *Memoirs* telling James VI that 'the Kingis of Scotland wer never riche sen they left the hylandis to duell in the law landis, bot haue euer sen syn deminissit ther rentis'.[71] It was a view that clearly informed the king's own attitude to the commercial potential of the 'barbarian' regions of his kingdom, but one of which his former tutor would have sternly disapproved. As Arthur Williamson has shown, Buchanan was a severe

---

[67] Kidd, *Subverting Scotland's Past*, esp. ch. 4; D. Allan, *Virtue, Learning and the Scottish Enlightenment: Ideas of Scholarship in Early Modern History* (Edinburgh, 1993).

[68] Ferguson, *Identity of the Scottish Nation*, 106–7.

[69] Mason, *Kingship and the Commonweal*, 183–5. Melville's annotated copy of Buchanan's *Historia* is in St Andrews University Library: Buchanan Collection DA775.B8B82.

[70] Buchanan, *History*, i, 229–30. Buchanan believed the Culdees to have derived their piety and learning from disciples of John the Evangelist and that it was only the pernicious influence of papal emissaries like the 'ambitious monk' St Augustine, that had corrupted the purity of the Culdaic religion until 'scarcely a vestige of true piety remained' (ibid., i, 249–50).

[71] *Memoirs of His Own Life by Sir James Melville of Halhill, 1549–1593* (Bannatyne Club, 1827), 392.

and effective critic of both commerce and empire, viewing trade as the source of the luxury and corruption that sapped the civic virtue which was the only true defence against tyranny.[72] James VI's belief in the imperial nature of his authority was wholly, and deliberately, at odds with Buchanan's portrayal of Scotland's early Gaelic civilisation as founded on the austere moral principles of classical republicanism. Perhaps paradoxically, however, James was no more prepared to abandon the Dalriadic kings than any of his predecessors, glorying in his descent from Fergus I – carefully redefined as a king by conquest rather than by election – while expressing his extreme hostility to the language and culture of the Gaels.[73] To be sure, the paradox dissolves if the continuity with Scotland's Celtic past is seen in institutional rather than ethnic terms.[74] Yet, as the paradox dissolves, so the ironies multiply. On the one hand, for early modern Lowland Scots, preoccupied with asserting the historic independence of their realm, belief in the continuity of their ancient royal lineage clearly entailed no sense of community with the Gaelic world in which it originated. On the other hand, however, Highland Scots, caught in the seventeenth and eighteenth centuries between Lowland prejudice and the pressure exerted by an imperial British monarchy, sought to reassert the primacy of Gaelic civilisation by identifying ever more closely with the Stewart descendants of Fergus I and the Dalriadic line of kings. Ironically, if not surprisingly, just as Buchanan's whig-presbyterian politics were reviled by generations of episcopalians and Jacobites, so his Celticism was little appreciated in the Gaelic-speaking world of early modern Scotland.[75]

I am grateful to participants in the seminar for a helpful discussion of this paper when originally presented, and to J. H. Burns, Jane Dawson and Colin Kidd for commenting on a draft text. Errors and omissions are of course entirely my own responsibility.

---

[72] A. H. Williamson, 'George Buchanan, Civic Virtue and Commerce: European Imperialism and its Sixteenth-Century Critics', *Scottish Historical Review*, lxxv (1996), 20–37; see also the introduction to *George Buchanan: The Political Poetry*, ed. and trans. P. J. McGinnis and A. H. Williamson (SHS, 1995).

[73] Mason, *Kingship and the Commonweal*, 229–30; *King James VI and I, Political Writings*, ed. J. P. Sommerville (Cambridge, 1994), 24, 73.

[74] A theme explored more fully in Kidd, *British Identities Before Nationalism*, ch. 6.

[75] See, for example, Dawson, 'The Emergence of the Scottish Highlands', 293, for a telling instance of how Highlanders saw Buchanan as having betrayed both the Gaelic language and his own Gaelic roots.

CHAPTER 6

The Covenanting Tradition in Scottish History

Edward J. Cowan

> The Solemn League and Covenant
> Now brings a smile, now brings a tear.
> But sacred Freedom, too, was theirs;
> If thou'rt a slave, indulge thy sneer.
> Robert Burns

> Let us grapple with that grizzly
> monster, Covenanting Tradition.
> Mark Napier

Burns' sentimental if self-righteous puff on one of the covenants reflects a superficial reading of history while demonstrating the bard at half-cock, composing for the next drink. But as one who spent his life in the counties of Ayr and Dumfries he could not ignore their legacy or their lore while basically finding himself out of sympathy with both. He would have concurred with the judgement of Mark Napier, sheriff of Dumfries, on the monstrous nature of the covenanting tradition.

The National Covenant of February 1638 and The Solemn League and Covenant of October 1643, though imperfectly understood, have both proved capable of generating extreme responses for three and a half centuries. They have spawned a substantial, if surprisingly unhelpful, literature largely manufactured by worthy ministers more concerned with revelation than with history. Yet Scottish historians have been oddly reluctant to confront the essential ideas behind, and implicit in, the covenants themselves while also ignoring their lingering influence in subsequent generations. Furthermore they have singularly failed to investigate what might be termed the covenanting mythos, particularly that of the notorious 'Killing Times' of the 1680s which would eventually embody a corpus of Lowland tradition embracing heroism, atrocity and sacrifice, arguably the only such body of legend and tradition to rival that of the Jacobites or the Highland Clearances and, since equally rooted in orality rather than literacy, just as resistant to proof or disproof.

The covenants are unique to Scotland, structurally arising out of Scottish society. They are not to be written off in some modern faddish way, as the relics of long-forgotten religious controversy. Scottish adherents subscribed to the idea of the double covenant; they advocated a covenant to reform and safeguard the kirk as well as one for the protection and reformation of society. There was a covenant between God and his people and another between God, the king and his people, the one religious and the other constitutional. From at least the time of Andrew Melville the idea of the Two Kingdoms was central to Protestant Scottish political and religious thinking. The covenanting movement, from the 1630s, enjoyed brilliant intellectual leadership in Alexander Henderson and Archibald Johnston of Wariston.

The National Covenant fell into three parts. The first comprised the so-called Negative Confession of 1581, a total abjuration of popery initially subscribed by the household of the young James VI. The second part rehearsed a lengthy list of statutes which were deemed to safeguard the reformed church. The third section demanded the constant adherence of signatories to the reformed religion as well as the rejection of recent ecclesiastical innovations, but it also required a commitment to 'stand to the defence of our dreade Soveraigne, the king's Majesty, his Person and Authority, in the defence and preservation of the foresaid true Religion, Liberties and Lawes of the Kingdom'. The realisation of potential incompatibility in the defence of king and kirk was perhaps heralded in a clause of mutual defence which stated that the covenanters would in no way allow themselves 'to be divided or withdrawn by whatsoever suggestion, allurement, or terror from this blessed and loyall conjunction'. Had they been truly confident their sacred bond would have needed no such qualification.

What was truly remarkable was the phenomenon which has attracted surprisingly little critical comment, namely that the covenant was a physical document which people actually signed. To Protestants throughout Europe the covenant was hitherto largely an abstraction. God, who presumably had not been consulted as to whether he was willing to enter into a Scottish covenant, would, in his omniscience, have been perfectly well aware of who had joined the compact. Rather it was the civil dimension that was being addressed, a new era of contract and justification. The insistence upon signatures reflected a new sense of civic responsibility. The revolutionary situation in which they found themselves dictated that the Covenanters who wished to limit monarchical authority must make themselves visible, or, to put it another way, must take full responsibility for their own actions. In pursuit of their goals they drew inspiration from the sixteenth-century Dutch Revolt, which similarly combined religious and secular ends and which had, in turn, drawn upon the ideas of such Scottish luminaries as George Buchanan. Such synergy was of crucial importance, but it was the stress upon civic responsibility in opposition to the forces of Stewart tyranny which would remain the most inspirational aspect of the covenant in the shorter and longer terms.[1]

The Solemn (in the sense of sacred) League and Covenant was a religious covenant with England which sought the imposition of religious conformity upon the two kingdoms as dictated by Scottish covenanters, but it was also a civil league to provide military assistance for the parliamentarians against Charles I. This was a much more cynical affair, the negotiations for which were inordinately complicated and which are still quite obscure, but two points stand out. First Alexander Henderson forcefully argued that the covenant arose out of Scottish experience and therefore could not be imposed upon England; it was not possible in his view to export a revolution, though the *idea* was exportable. Second, after the execution of Charles I in 1649, even people like Samuel Rutherford recognised that the civil-league part of the agreement was now redundant.[2] That such a view was far from universal would be revealed in the unfolding of the covenanting drama throughout the years of savage persecution and yet to come. Those who suffered for their faith, though distinguished as deluded by their opponents, believed that once a pact had been drawn up with God it existed for eternity.

[1] See in general Edward J. Cowan, 'The Making of the National Covenant', in *The Scottish National Covenant in its British Context 1638–51* (Edinburgh, 1990), 68–89 and references. See also David Stevenson, *The Scottish Revolution 1637–44: The Triumph of the Covenanters* (Newton Abbott, 1973) and A. I. Macinnes, *Charles I and the Making of the Covenanting Movement 1625–41* (Edinburgh, 1991).

[2] Edward J. Cowan, 'The Solemn League and Covenant' in Roger A. Mason (ed.), *Scotland and England 1286–1815* (Edinburgh, 1987), 182–202 and references. An important study is John Coffey, *Politics, Religion and the British Revolutions: The Mind of Samuel Rutherford* (Cambridge, 1997).

In the minds of later generations – those of the late seventeenth century and beyond – Reformation and Revolution were part of the same organic whole. Many of the seeds which flourished in the 1680s had been planted in the early seventeenth century when radical ministers fled to Ireland and the Netherlands, and the first field conventicles (open-air services) were held in Scotland. Activists such as James Stewart, Alexander Shields, James Renwick and Richard Cameron, to name a few, self-consciously operated within a tradition stretching back to the first stirrings of Reformation, not only in Scotland, but in Europe at large. For a time the Bass Rock, Scotland's Alcatraz, truly represented a revolutionary cell. It has too often been assumed that the obsession with the covenants ended at the so-called Glorious Revolution, the crucial consequences of which were not only the Claim of Right, which enshrined many covenanting credenda, but also the outlawing of prelacy (1689), the total condemnation of popery and the establishment of presbyterian government as ratified in James VI's so-called 'Golden Act' of 1592. An important concomitant was the abolition of lay patronage, a goal towards which the reformers had been striving since the *First Book of Discipline*.[3]

Long-cherished ideas about the covenants certainly did not disappear. Part of the reason for the failure of the Darien Scheme was that men of covenanting sympathies practised a type of anarcho-syndicalism in the disorganisation of the voyages, different chairpersons being chosen almost every day. The lessons of the 1640s, when military commanders were paralysed, through having to refer to Edinburgh for decisions, were ignored, their effects compounded when committees and crews were separated by thousands of miles of ocean.[4] At the Union of 1707 many clearly considered a commitment to the covenants to equate with devotion to an independent Scotland. The worst fears of the devout were realised when the kirk became the subject of some of the first infringements of the Treaty of Union. The first, and only, violent agricultural protest in Scotland, that of the Galloway Levellers in the 1720s, was rooted in covenanting ideology. The Levellers actually drew up a covenant to resist enclosures.[5] Just as it has been shown that the idea of the covenant owed

---

[3] *Acts of the Parliament of Scotland [APS]*, ix, 104, 133–4, 196–7.

[4] See in general *The Darien Papers: Being a Selection of Original Letters and Official Documents Relating to the Establishment of a Colony at Darien by the Company of Scotland Trading to Africa and the Indies 1695–1700*, ed. J. H. Burton, Bannatyne Club (Edinburgh, 1849).

[5] J. Leopold, 'The Levellers' Revolt in Galloway in 1724', *Journal of the Scottish Labour History Society* 14 (1980).

something to the convention of banding from the Late Middle Ages, so the notion remained almost innate in Scottish thinking when any kind of communal or communitarian activity was planned or underway. This chapter will not investigate the central role of the covenants in the long drawn-out ecclesiastical controversies of the eighteenth and nineteenth centuries, not because they are unimportant or irrelevant, but because this has already been competently investigated elsewhere.[6]

John Howie in 1775 published an influential work, *The Scots Worthies*, in which political ideology was as important as religious inspiration. The book offered biographies of Reformation and covenanting heroes, arranged 'according to the time of their exit, and not of their birth'. The pages are soaked in the blood of the 'martyrs', but an appendix attempted to demonstrate that most of their torturers achieved ignominious and bloody ends, gloatingly detailed in *The Judgment and Justice of God Exemplified in a Brief Historical Account of the Wicked Lives and Miserable Deaths of some of the most Remarkable Apostates and Bloody Persecutors in Scotland, from the Reformation till after the Revolution*. Howie sanctimoniously ignored the possibility that those covenanters who were cut off in their prime could equally be seen as the objects of God's wrath, but his main concern was the backsliding which had taken place since the heady days of the covenants:

> Instead of our covenants, an unhallowed union is gone into
> with England, whereby our rights and privileges are infringed
> not a little, lordly patronage is also restored and practised, a
> toleration bill is granted, whereby almost every error, heresy,
> and delusion appears triumphant, prelacy is become
> fashionable, and of popery we are in as much danger as ever.

It was his considered view, borrowing from Ovid, 'that we live only in fable, and nothing remains of ancient Scotland but the name'.[7] At a

---

[6] See A. L. Drummond and J. Bulloch, *The Scottish Church 1688–1843: The Age of the Moderates* (Edinburgh, 1973) and *The Church in Victorian Scotland 1843–1874* (Edinburgh, 1975); Colin Kidd, *Subverting Scotland's Past: Scottish Whig Historians and the Creation of an Anglo-British Identity, 1689–c.1830* (Cambridge, 1993).

[7] John Howie of Lochgoin, *The Scots Worthies, Containing A Brief Historical Account of the Most Eminent Noblemen, Gentlemen, Ministers, and Others Who Testified or Suffered for the Cause of Reformation in Scotland, from the Beginning of the Sixteenth Century, to the Year 1688* (1775: Glasgow, 1845), xxx–xxxi, xxxv, 559–604.

popular level his book probably had a greater impact in the shorter term than all the works of Enlightenment philosophers put together.

Several commentators testify that in the eighteenth and early nineteenth centuries Scottish farmers, artisans and craftsmen busily read such authors as Samuel Rutherford and Alexander Shields. The holdings of libraries, organised by and for the non-elite, for example the Miners' Library at Leadhills, contain significant quantities of seventeenth-century theological works. What, we may wonder, did they make of such literature, those people who had but recently learned to read?

As has been indicated,[8] there was a close association in the last decade of the eighteenth century between the Seceders and the Society of the Friends of the People. Archibald Bruce, professor of divinity and minister of Whitburn wrote of how the Scottish aristocracy, had, for their own selfish ends, supported Reformation in 1560 and in 1638–43, but had, in 1794, abandoned the good old cause by supporting the Moderates and ecclesiastical patronage. 'The burden of the struggle for liberty and reform is now wholly devolved on the inferior and poorer sort of the people, with whom the former or higher class have now completely lost their credit and influence.' In this there were echoes, probably conscious and deliberate, of John Knox's *Address to the Commonalty of Scotland* (1559). In Bruce's view, one which was widely shared, the Scottish Reformation had been brought about by popular revolt. The rights and privileges secured by the covenanters had been lost but their mantle had descended to the political reformers of the 1790s; civil and religious liberty remained the two great branches of the same expanded tree. Both William Skirving and Thomas Muir, two of the political 'martyrs' created by contemporary treason trials, used similar analogues. Despite such promising examples, however, it has been concluded that so far as the majority of the political reformers of the 1790s was concerned, the ideas of the later covenanters were far too radical.

But the arguments continued in a sequence which was essentially historicist. The Chartists in the period 1838–48 would also invoke the covenant as had activists working towards the Reform Act of 1832. It informed the rhetoric of Keir Hardie and many other left-wingers. The

---

[8] John Brims, 'The Covenanting Tradition and Scottish Radicalism in the 1790s', in Terry Brotherstone (ed.), *Covenant, Charter and Party: Traditions of revolt and protest in modern Scottish History* (Aberdeen, 1981), 50–62. See also in the same volume V. G. Kiernan, 'A Banner with a Strange Device: The Later Covenanters', 25–49.

Home Rule movement coalesced around a covenant which secured some two million signatures, some of them bogus, in 1949. Reference to the idea has not been absent in the move towards devolution in recent decades. It has been invoked, seized upon as a source of inspiration, traduced, condemned, written about and fictionalised in virtually every generation since the movement supposedly ended in the late seventeenth century.

It has not been sufficiently recognised that a major transformation in Scottish historiography came about when the sufferings of the later covenanters were written up for the first time. Crucial in this development was Robert Wodrow, minister of Eastwood. Richard Finlay suggests that Wodrow attempted to portray the covenanting movement as 'civic constitutionalism', that his *History* was a clear attempt to reinvent the Scottish religious tradition into one more suited to a changed political and intellectual environment of the early eighteenth century.[9] In a sense, though, Wodrow did not manufacture such a tradition, which, after all, had been forcefully and frequently articulated during the previous century. Rather, he sought to ensure its survival.

Wodrow's *History of the Sufferings of the Church of Scotland*, published in 1721–2, opened with the aggressive assertion:

> It must appear strange to all disinterested persons who know
> any thing of Scottish affairs from the restoration to the
> revolution that there is a party among us who deny there was
> any persecution of presbyterians for conscience sake in that
> period and yet raise a terrible cry of severity and cruelties
> exercised upon the episcopal clergy at, and since, the happy
> revolution.

He regretted that he had not been in a position to produce his *History* thirty years earlier, 'when the particular instances of oppression and barbarity, now much forgotten, were recent and the witnesses alive'.[10] He claimed that some narratives had been prepared at the time, some of which he had seen, though others, he thought, may have been lost. In fact he had been anticipated. David Calderwood's *History* of the Church

---

[9] Richard J. Finlay, 'Keeping the Covenant: Scottish National Identity', in T. M. Devine and J. R. Young (eds), *Eighteenth-Century Scotland: New Perspectives* (East Linton, 1999), 124–5, following Kidd, *Subverting Scotland's Past* 68.

[10] Robert Wodrow, *The History of the Sufferings of the Church of Scotland*, 4 vols (Glasgow, 1823), i, xxxvii–xxxix.

of Scotland told the first part of the story. John Brown, minister of Wamphray, had published his *Apologetical Narration of the Particular Sufferings of the Faithful Ministers and Professors of the Church of Scotland Since August 1660* in 1665, though the sufferings he described were mild compared with what was to follow.

Much more significant was Daniel Defoe's *Memoirs of the Church of Scotland* (1717) which covenanting apologists eagerly embraced, blissfully ignoring another Defoe production *An Historical Account of the Bitter Sufferings . . . of the Episcopal Church in Scotland, under the Barbarous Usage and Bloody Persecution of the Presbyterian Church Government* (1707). The prolific pamphleteer really was 'all things to all men' but as a propagandist for union he took care to cultivate the clergy because he shrewdly detected that the covenanting faction posed the greatest threat to English plans. His 400-page book was written for an English audience which, like Robert Harley 'knew no more of Scotch business than of Japan', and which assumed that abjuration oaths equated with pro-Catholic, and Jacobite, sentiment. Defoe was intent upon demonstrating the fiercely anti-Catholic tenets of the Covenanters, with whose political philosophies he, as the author of the tract *The Original Power of the Collective Body* and of the poem *Jure Divino*, undoubtedly empathised. What he produced was a hotchpotch of bits and pieces, purporting to derive from personal interviews with participants, but in reality derived, in the main, from earlier pamphlets and pious anecdotage.[11] Wodrow believed he was providing a corrective to the propagandist who, he thought, did not understand his subject.

A central concern in Wodrow's work was the tension between tradition and record, the respective merits, or demerits, of orality and literacy. He was uneasily aware that some of his material would not admit of proof for the very good reason that, as unsupported tradition, it could not be corroborated. The Covenanters were in good company, for neither did Homer ever write anything down but his poetry 'passed up and down like a piece of a ballad song that people got by rote, till in the end, copies were taken on it from dictates by word of mouth'.

Robert Wodrow was something of a folklorist, if a somewhat uncritical one, as his obsession with portents, prodigies and the supernatural shows. But as a historian he felt compelled to take a scrupulous approach: 'I design that as little of this history as may be should lean

[11] Paula R. Backscheider, *Daniel Defoe: His Life* (Baltimore and London, 1989), 161–2, 203, 218–19, 242–5.

upon me: let every one see with his own eyes, and judge for himself, upon the very same evidence I have.' He once confided that he was such 'an unbeliever in historical facts' that he had to seek confirmation in original papers. Yet he admitted that the written and printed sources available to him were exceedingly biased. They cast the Covenanters in an extremely poor light and so he felt obliged to supply certain correctives, namely 'well-attested accounts' of the experiences of the sufferers themselves. The writing of history was difficult at any time – harder still 'to write accounts of times a man hath not personally known', with no threads to guide him, no existing histories upon which he might draw, 'especially when the times are full of heat, rents and divisions, and any accounts that remain are various, according as the several parties stood affected'.[12]

Mark Napier, the perfect example of the historian as polemicist, deplored 'the trash of vulgar tradition . . . the apocryphal rubbish of fanatical pathos', hotly disputing the axiom that 'a tradition cannot have been invented'. Having single-handedly canonised Montrose, he set about the resurrection of John Graham of Claverhouse in opposition to what he distinguished as two of History's most 'incorrigible calumniators', Thomas Babington Macaulay and Robert Wodrow. Napier characterised Macaulay as 'delighting to revel in all the criminative power of the English language . . . ferocious as a covenanting dominie in objurgations against the falling Stewarts'.

In one of his numerous essays Macaulay asserted that the government of Charles II had employed Maitland of Lauderdale 'to carry on the most atrocious system of misgovernment with which any nation was ever cursed; to extirpate Presbyterianism by fire and sword', utilising such methods as 'the drowning of women' and 'the frightful torture of the boot'. Napier sought to defend his hero, Claverhouse, demolishing Macaulay in the process, by traducing the trustworthiness of Wodrow and other covenanting writers in order, as he hoped, to discredit forever the Whig tradition in Scottish historiography. In his view 'fanatic' and 'Whig' were one and the same. He dismissed Wodrow's *History* as a 'most heterogeneous magazine of materials' from which the 'most valuable characteristics of History appear as if absolutely excluded'. He considered its author narrow-minded, of limited intellect, 'prone to the most senseless and illiterate superstitions, and somewhat deficient in the quality of conscientiousness'. Furthermore he was guilty of glossing iniquity, confounding truth, maligning the high-minded, and sanctify-

[12] Wodrow, *History*, i, xxxix–xlii.

ing the murderer. Wodrow had been too much persuaded by the advice of George Redpath, who counselled that in writing his *magnum opus* he should leave out 'what is merely circumstantial, excepting where it is necessary for illustrating the matter, or aggravating the crimes of our enemies'.[13]

Napier was just as guilty of some of the faults that he detected in others but he was no fool. His subjectivity, like Wodrow's, is often perversely delightful, his barbed style and loquaciousness frequently hilarious, but, despite some of his dafter notions – such as identifying extreme covenanters with the Fenians of his own day – many of his criticisms were sound. It is easy to understand Napier's frustration in surveying the covenanting literature of the later seventeenth century which would have the reader believe that 'among all the rebels of the west of Scotland' from 1679 to 1689 'there was not one single criminal'. On the other hand all members of the royal family, all statesmen, noblemen, military commanders and lairds were characterised as:

> men without pity or principle, without a spark of Christian feeling or natural humanity in their bosoms; and daily occupied, as a pleasant pastime, with slaughtering some harmless and saintly peasant, at his cottage door, or by the wayside, or in the arms of his wife . . . No rebel, however rampant, was ever deprived of his life, in battle, or under martial law, or by judicial sentence, that was not murdered, – that had not lived a saint and died a martyr. What a picture of Scotland!

His point was sound but he promptly squandered it by revealing his pernicious class-based agenda: 'During the the latter half of the seventeenth century, all the lowest in the land represented Heaven, all the most noble and exalted represented Hell!'[14] Herein, at the heart of the covenanting debate, reposes one of the central discourses which transcends both religion and politics; the arguments of Napier and his supporters were relentlessly elitist and anti-democratic.

He took particular exception to Macaulay's use of the phrase, 'the drowning of women', unleashing torrents of prose on this episode which

---

[13] Mark Napier, *Memorials and Letters Illustrative of the Life and Times of John Graham of Claverhouse, Viscount Dundee*, 3 vols (Edinburgh, 1862), i, 2, 145, 148, 155; ii, 43, 59.

[14] Napier, *Memorials of Dundee*, i, 108.

has become one of the great icons of the Killing Times, the notorious affair of the Wigtown Martyrs. To disprove the reality of the episode is by no means to imply that all of the atrocities endured by the covenanters never happened. Many of the people that Wodrow commemorates as martyrs did in fact perish. On the other hand some of the persecuted proved themselves to be even more blood-thirsty and murderous than their tormentors. As so often in history the effect is all in the telling.

Wodrow frequently descends from history to parable. The case of John Brown of Priesthill, a carrier in the parish of Muirkirk, is one such example. He was at home, on 1 May 1685, watched by his child and pregnant wife as he cast his peats, when Claverhouse and his dragoons appeared. Claverhouse ordered his instant death, although he was 'no way obnoxious to the Government, except for not hearing the Episcopal ministers', whereupon Brown fell to his knees and commenced prayer. So emotionally overcome were the dragoons that they refused to obey orders. Patrick Walker in his *Life of Peden* (1724) knew nothing of a mutiny; in his version six soldiers blew out Brown's brains. Claverhouse's own account matter-of-factly related that Brown refused to take the oath of abjuration or to swear that he would not rise in arms against the king; indeed 'he knew no king'. When ammunition and treasonable papers were found in his house 'I caused shoot him dead, which he suffered very unconcernedly'.[15] Wodrow has Claverhouse interrupt a rural idyll on May Day: it is a truism of atrocity propaganda that the more idyllic the setting, the more heinous the crime.

Charles II died on 6 February 1685 to be succeeded by his brother James. The Earl of Argyll launched his ill-favoured rebellion in support of Monmouth in late April, though it had been expected since November; both were executed in July. Since Argyll had anticipated covenanting support, springtime must have been filled with rumour and expectation despite the fiasco that transpired. Wodrow admitted that some denied that the executions, on 11 May 1685, of Margaret Wilson and Margaret McLachlan, or Lachlisone, ever took place. He claimed to base his account on information supplied by the late Mr Rowan, minister of Penninghame, the parish in which Margaret Wilson's family lived. Her parents were described as good episcopalians, admittedly a strange assertion for Wodrow. They lost much of their

[15] Napier, *Memorials of Dundee*, i, 140–8; iii, 457–9. See also Patrick Walker, *Six Saints of the Covenant* ed. D. Hay Fleming introduction by S. R. Crockett, 2 vols (London, 1901), i, 84–7; ii, 135–8.

wealth through being fined for the non-conformity of their three children, Margaret who was 18, Thomas 16 and Agnes 13. This all seems very odd, as are the statements that Gilbert Wilson had to suffer some hundred troops at a time quartered on his property, and that he was appearing almost weekly at the Wigtown court to answer for his children. Equally unlikely is the story of an informer who tried to persuade two teenage girls to drink the king's health.

The two girls, along with Margaret McLachlan, 63, who had refused the abjuration oath were tried on 13 April before the justiciary court. Wodrow's allegation that the three were indicted for being present at Bothwell Bridge and Aird's Moss is quite untenable since Agnes would then have been 7, and in any case she can be removed from the picture because the privy council explicitly restricted the required oaths to those aged 16 and over. Indeed the council was reluctant to question any women unless they had been 'active in a signal manner'. A petition submitted to the privy council in Edinburgh on McLachlan's behalf admits that she was justly condemned to die because she refused to disown the Apologetical Declaration (of 1684 which threatened all opposed to the covenants with death) and had declined abjuration.[16] However she now acknowledged that the said declaration was traitorous, tending to rebellion and sedition, and contrary to the word of God. She was now willing to abjure. The petition was signed by a notary because Margaret, aged about 70, could not write. It must be assumed that a similar plea was entered for Wilson because both women received a reprieve on 30 April.[17] The documented evidence, such as it is, suggests that, *pace* Wodrow, the executions never took place.

According to him, young Agnes was freed on payment of £100 sterling, an unrealistically enormous sum. In his version the other two were condemned to be tied to stakes between the high and low water mark, McLachlan being placed further out to encourage Wilson to recant, but to no avail. Instead the younger woman sang the 25th psalm and read from Romans while her sister in Christ expired. Margaret Wilson was held above the rising waters one last time, but she refused the opportunity to save herself and so perished.[18] This is an exceedingly famous case which is still capable of generating considerable heat and

---

[16] It is somewhat ironic that Defoe's *Memoirs* was written to support the withdrawal of the Oath of Abjuration, which was the cause of so many atrocities during the persecutions.

[17] *Records of the Privy Council* (RPC) 3rd Series vol. xi, 1685–6, 286, 33.

[18] Wodrow, *History*, iv, 246–9.

anger. It represents a classic example of the ongoing tensions between oral tradition and documented corroboration. To deny the executions is to be accused of entering into an establishment conspiracy to subvert the people's history, worse to devalue the female experience and contribution. Yet facts are chiels that winnae ding. The present investigation was, in part, motivated by the desire to demonstrate the value and validity of oral tradition in opposition to the insufferable snobbery and inflated rhetoric of Napier, and yet his elaborate arguments against the executions ever having taken place are convincing.

It is true that in 1684–5 the privy council decreed that any women found guilty of treason were to be drowned, but despite Macaulay's assertion that the government attempted to extirpate presbyterianism through such means, no-one ever suffered that fate. There is considerable evidence that women were prominent in the cause of the covenant. When men were away from home they were reportedly reluctant to be held responsible for religious activities in their absence, 'so mad are some of their wives'. Women were to the fore in demonstrations and in petitioning the privy council. As Napier never tired of reporting, only two women in the entire reigns of Charles II and James VII were ever executed for crimes against the state. Lord Fountainhall, who commented on the case of these women, hanged in 1681, was not convinced that people should pay the supreme penalty for opinion rather than action. He reported that some thought the women should be drowned 'privately', or secretly, in the Nor Loch, Edinburgh, in order to deprive them of the public forum of execution and thus the possible advancement of their cause. Both Fountainhall and Sir George Mackenzie of Tarbat were very interested in the subject of women and the law, for example in the context of witch persecution. If the Wigtown women had been executed they would undoubtedly have discussed what would have been a highly publicised case.

Napier questioned the authenticity of the Wigtown executions in his three-volume study of Claverhouse (1859–62). He replied to some of his critics in *The Case for the Crown in re the Wigtown Martyrs Proved to be Myths Versus Wodrow and Lord Macaulay, Patrick the Pedler and Principal Tulloch* (Edinburgh, 1863). The Rev. Archibald Stewart, minister of Glasserton, responded with *History Vindicated in the case of the Wigtown Martyrs, Margaret Lauchlison and Margaret Wilson drowned at Wigtown 11th May 1685 in answer to Mr Mark Napier's Case for the Crown* (1869), which enabled Napier to return to the fray in 1870 with *History Rescued in answer to History Vindicated*.

As Napier argued in his *Memorials of Dundee* the first seed of an idea which grew into a mighty tree was Alexander Shields' allusion in *A Hind Let Loose* (1687) to the circumstance that some women were hanged but 'some drowned tied to stakes within the sea-mark, to be devoured gradually with the growing waves, and some of them very young, some of an old age'. This legend seems to have derived from the legislation of 1684–5. An illustration, or frontispiece, shows two women tied to the same stake, but it also depicts a female being dismembered on a scaffold, something which, as Napier gleefully reports, never happened. However, in his *Short Memorial of Sufferings and Grievances* (1690), Shields does mention the women among those 'killed in cold blood, without trial, conviction, or any colour of law'. Margaret Lauchlan, upwards of 60 years, and Margaret Wilson, about 20, were 'illegally condemned, and most inhumanly drowned, at stakes within the sea-mark' at Wigtown.[19] A pamphlet, of 1691 repeats the names and ages stating that they were tied to a stake and left to the mercy of the tide, 'and this was done without any legal trial'. Napier became almost apoplectic at the rhetoric employed in these pamphlets but since Shields and his acolytes did not recognise Stewart government they deemed all of its actions illegal. The fact that the women were tried by a commission of justiciary was irrelevant so far as they were concerned. Napier argued that Shields, having mentioned the drownings in 1687, matched them to the trial of the two Margarets at Wigtown in April 1685. Dr Gilbert Rule, author of the 1691 pamphlet was so tentative as to render his information doubtful even to himself:

> The truth of matters of fact asserted in this treatise is not to be taken from me, but from those who are my informers. Few of them I pretend to personal knowledge of; therefore, not my veracity is pledged for them but that of others. If I have here asserted anything that I cannot bring creditable witnesses for, let me be blamed; but if they have deceived, or been deceived (which I hope shall not be found), I am not to answer for that.[20]

What is remarkable is that James Renwick's *Informatory Vindication* (1687) refers to Charles II 'drowning women, some very young, and

---

[19] Napier got this wrong in *Memoirs of Dundee*, iii, App. wherein he stated that Shields' pamphlet did not mention the two women, but he corrected the oversight in *Case for the Crown*, 84.

[20] Napier, *Case for the Crown*, 86.

some of exceeding old age' but he does not mention the Wigtown Martyrs; nor do at least three pamphlets published in 1688. The event is not noticed in covenanting correspondence of the period, though Michael Shields, brother of Alexander, also refers to the drowning of females in Charles II's reign. A pamphlet of 1714, *Popery Reviving*, admits that the Wigtown executions were 'ordinarily denied' by the Jacobite faction 'and said to be a calumny raised to asperse the late government'. This pamphlet was known to Wodrow, who, as noted, was also aware that many doubted whether the event had taken place, but he eschewed the pamphleteer's version of the drowning – an elaborate account of posts erected on the bank and long tethers so that the executioners could observe dry-shod while their victims were thrown into the estuary. Even Patrick Walker, 'the chapman of treason', admitted in 1727 that many denied the drowning of the Margarets 'to be a matter of fact'.[21] After 1691 there was no further mention of the pair, at least in print, until 1711 when, in response to the kirk's appeal, first issued in 1708, for information about the late sufferings, the Rev. Rowan of Penninghame produced the somewhat overblown version used by Wodrow. The kirk session at Kirkinner, however, knew of the fate of the elder Margaret but had no knowledge of the younger, and it took the minister and elders over a year to assemble even that much information. Wodrow bemoaned the lack of materials he had to work with in March 1711. Well over two years later he could still report that nothing had reached him concerning the sufferings; 'very few accounts came to my hands'.[22] Tradition, it would seem, was somewhat moribund, informants not exactly lining up to impart their lore. In 1717 Defoe's *Memoirs* told of two nameless women, one poor, the other a young maiden of about 16, who were both attached to the same stake, 'being also tormented almost to death with the cold, by standing in the water so long as till the tide was high enough to drown them'.

The longer Napier allowed the 'scribbling, nibbling and quibbling' to obsess him, the more vituperative his language became. *The Case for the*

---

[21] Napier, *History Rescued in Answer to History Vindicated*, lxvi, lxix–lxxi, cclii–iii, cclxiv–v, xxxi; Walker, *Six Saints*, i, 329–30. For the record, the case had nothing to do with Claverhouse, though his brother David was involved. According to Walker, the leading villain was Sir Robert Grierson of Lagg 'a great persecutor, a great swearer, a great whorer, blasphemer, drunkard, liar and cheat, and yet out of hell'. Walker uniquely alleges that a third woman was involved at Wigtown, Margaret Maxwell, who was sentenced to be scourged, 330.

[22] Napier, *Case for the Crown*, 88–105.

Crown is altogether more hysterical in tone than the *Memorials*. Covenanting martyrology has become a 'cancerous growth' upon Scottish History, Wodrow the author of 'a calumnious tissue of monstrous fables'. Napier broadly rehashed much of his earlier material but he had not convinced everyone on the merits of Bonnie Dundee. When the anniversary of the Sanquhar Declaration was celebrated in the Dumfriesshire town, in July 1860, a Colonel Shaw of Ayr expressed his loathing and contempt for Dundee: 'he could not dip his tongue in a cesspit vile and filthy enough to paint his character'. Incredibly, in 1861 a woman named Margaret Wilson swore to the authenticity of an obviously forged petition supposedly addressed to parliament against Grierson of Lagg over his part in the executions in 1685. Such developments were eagerly followed in, and commented on, by the press and its readership, as were the flytings in which the irrepressible Napier became involved.

Archibald Stewart, in his *History Vindicated*, was moved, in part, to challenge Napier because the latter had 'made some converts even in Galloway', to which the Graham apologist responded, 'if my little finger have been felt on the loins of Galloway, I am satisfied with its weight'. Stewart's *History Vindicated* invoked five 'witnesses': tradition, the evidence of old pamphlets, the memoirs of martyrdoms personally collected by Defoe, and, fourth, Stewart cited the testimony of ministers, presbyteries, kirk sessions and other witnesses and informants. Fifth was Margaret Wilson's tombstone in Wigtown churchyard, with the inscription, 'Within the sea ty'd to a stake/ She suffered for Christ Jesus sake'.

Napier was able to answer all of those points, among others. Perhaps the most controversial concerned the graves, still a touchy issue with many. Covenanting monuments represent Scotland's first war memorials even though the 'warriors of Christ' that they commemorate were civilians. Some cairns may well have been erected immediately after the killings and many still bear crude, sometimes barely literate, inscriptions – and very moving they are – but almost none are original. Most, if not all, have been replaced. In some cases it seems that the graves, and/or the memorials, were manufactured long after death. There is no evidence, for example, that Margaret Wilson's gravestone at Wigtown was in existence before 1730. Indeed, if she resided in Penninghame, why was she buried in Wigtown? It is a similar story with Margaret McLachlan, who came from Kirkinner. In other words, wondrously evocative though they are, the 'grey recumbent tombs of the dead in desert places' cannot be used as evidence of anything save the continuing appeal of the covenanting tradition.[23] The monument in Stirling, erected in the 1860s, depicts the Wilson sisters, omitting the senior Margaret, while the statue of Margaret Wilson at Knox College, Toronto, was deemed so beguiling that it eventually had to be removed in defence of student virtue. The 'new' monument to the Martyrs at Wigtown was dedicated as recently as 1938.[24]

Napier found precedent and parallels for reprieve of the condemned and for the transfer of prisoners to Edinburgh while their appeals were heard. He showed that the authorities were often surprisingly moderate in their treatment of the disaffected and that they were extremely reluctant to act against women especially, even though he himself believed that many 'proved the most determined and dangerous of fanatics, becoming absolutely unsexed when excited on the subject'. The question then arises of why the two Margarets were tried before fifteen jurors of the justiciary court in the first place. We may never know, but a list of the inhabitants of Kirkinner, supplied and certified by the minister Andrew Sympson in 1684, contains the entry, 'Margaret Lauchlison: Disorderly'.[25] This aged lady had a reputation and, perhaps having spoken out once too often, she just could not be ignored. The story of Gilbert Wilson's difficulties may have originated in some sort of father/daughter tension, possibly exacerbated by a display of religious mania on the part of young Margaret. Such is, of course, pure hypothesis, but it seems likely that both Margarets were pardoned, subsequently disappearing from the record.

Wodrow assembled his materials at a particularly significant historical juncture, the Union of 1707, when the church appeared under serious threat, both before and after the legislation of 1 May 1707. Dozens of covenanting pamphlets from the 1640s were reissued at this time. To many, safeguarding the covenants equated with the preservation of the

[23] On this vexed topic see Thorbjörn Campbell, *Standing Witnesses: A Guide to the Scottish Covenanters and their Memorials with a Historical Introduction* (Edinburgh, 1996). The classic work is J. H. Thomson, *The Martyr Graves of Scotland* (Edinburgh and London, n.d. *c*.1895).

[24] James Barr, *The Scottish Covenanters* (Glasgow, 1947), 168. In 1883 the Rev. Robert Riach composed 'The Wigtown Martyrs, a Collection of Poems' which included the type of effusion that we might nowadays associate with Irish republican sentimentalia: They speak of it in Scotland's homes,/Tis told in far-off lands,/How in the bloom of youth she died/Upon the Solway Sands. And how she kept her trust in God,/And how she scorned the foe,/ And how she lived and how she died,/ Two hundred years ago', 169.

[25] Napier, *History Rescued* cxcvi. Andrew Sympson was the author of *A Large Description of Galloway* (1684). RPC x 1684–5, 266.

integrity of the ancient kingdom of Scotland, an assertion of identity, a gesture much more profound and tenacious than ditties, evocative though they are, about 'a parcel o rogues' being 'bought and sold for English gold'. Wodrow kept a diary during and after the Union; he is an important authority on that event. His diligence in collecting traditions, by means of which he almost single-handedly provided, for the first time, a martyrology for the Church of Scotland, should be seen in the same light as James Watson's efforts to preserve vernacular Scottish poetry in his *Choice Collection* (1706) or Allan Ramsay's endeavours in *The Evergreen* (1724).

Old Mortality, published in November 1816, was Walter Scott's attempt to confront the Covenanters. It is important to note that it appeared in the year after Waterloo. The French wars had ended but already signs of distress were to be detected throughout central Scotland. The year 1816 was one of unemployment, returning soldiers and agricultural and industrial depression, all combined with some of the coldest and most miserable weather on record. It was certainly not a time to be courting radicals, not that Scott was remotely in any danger on that score. The novel centres on the covenanting victory at Drumclog in 1679 and the rout of the righteous three weeks later at Bothwell Bridge.

Old Mortality has been described as a study in revolution, a subject which Scott always found inherently distasteful. There is no doubt that he constructed a sort of 'paradigm of a revolutionary movement',[26] showing that the revolutionaries – the Covenanters – occupied a spectrum extending from those involved by accident and those who became entangled against their wishes, all the way to the totally committed, the power-hungry and the mad. The story, which allowed Scott to indulge in another of his tiresome 'I know not who wrote it' ploys, was phenomenally successful. The novel-buying public, after all, was in a celebratory mood; the worst excesses of the French Revolution and the dictatorship of Napoleon had been defeated. The book was particularly well received in England, clearly demonstrating that the most successful historical novels are those set in the least familiar historical periods.

Many Scots, however, deplored Scott's treatment of the Covenanters. Thomas McCrie wrote three lengthy reviews in *The Christian Instructor* (1817), later issued anonymously as *A Vindication of the Scottish Covenanters*. He was far from impressed:

---

[26] Edgar Johnson, *Sir Walter Scott: The Great Unknown*, 2 vols (London, 1970), i, 600.

We would advise those who write for public amusement to be
cautious in the choice of their subjects. Surely if the blood of
God's dear saints be precious in the sight of their Almighty
Redeemer, it is unsafe to make their general character, or even
their weaknesses, in the hour of trial, the subject of sport, or of
frivolous entertainment; lest, when His hand taketh hold on
judgment, and he ariseth to render vengeance to His adversaries,
and to make inquisition for blood, He remembers them.

McCrie, author of a famous biography of John Knox (1812), was a
minister of the Constitutional Associate Presbytery (later the Original
Secession). The critic had courted unpopularity among his fellow
worshippers by enthusiastically welcoming the Waverley novels and
his review of *Old Mortality* hints that he knew perfectly well who wrote
it. As a Borderer – he was born in Duns and preached for a time in Kelso
– McCrie empathised with much of Scott's existing output, but he
articulated the response of many who believed that the novel satirised
the covenanters while proving far too kind to their adversaries. He
accused Scott of violating both truth and probability. While admitting
that he enjoyed some of the descriptive passages which showed that the
author had 'the imagination and feeling of a poet', he deplored his
deficiencies 'in the judgment and discriminating task of a historian':

> What person of judgment and candour will condemn the
> Covenanters, or say that they acted otherwise than it became
> men of conscience, integrity, and spirit to act? Men who had
> been betrayed, insulted, harassed, pillaged, and treated in every
> way like beasts rather than reasonable creatures; and by whom?
> by a perfidious, profane, profligate junto of atheists and
> debauchees, who were not fit for governing even a colony of
> transported felons, aided by a set of churchmen the most
> despicable and worthless that ever disgraced the habit which
> they wore, or profaned the sacred function in which they
> impiously dared to officiate.[27]

Scott attempted to counter some of the foregoing criticisms by writing
an anonymous review of his own novel for the *Quarterly Review*, but,

[27] [Thomas McCrie], *A Vindication of the Scottish Covenanters: Consisting of A
Review of the First Series of the 'Tales of My Landlord'*, *Extracted from the
Christian Instructor for 1817* (Glasgow, 1824), 4, 33–4.

shrewd operator that he was, he no doubt also realised that there was money in controversial reviews, just as there was in the anonymity game, and he wanted to keep the hare running. It was to run a long time. In 1932 Principal Robert Rait contributed an influential chapter on 'Walter Scott and Thomas McCrie' to Herbert Grierson's *Sir Walter Scott Today*. More recently the same prey was tracked by Edgar Johnson, David Brown and James Anderson,[28] and it doubtless still has its coursers in certain quarters. Such discussions usually degenerate into arguments about whether McCrie or Scott had the 'better' or 'more correct' version of History, which, in the early nineteenth century, equated with something called 'Truth', and of course the dialectic ultimately dissipates in fields of utter sterility.

The trouble was, as George Gilfillan pointed out, that Scott was 'haunted with the idea of a cavalier; it seemed to him representative of a knight of chivalry';[29] thus he proved rather blind to the undoubted faults of John Graham of Claverhouse, 'Bluidy Clavers' to his enemies and 'Bonnie Dundee' to his admirers, though he was not actually raised to the peerage as Viscount Dundee until November 1688. Scott could never emotionally engage with the Covenanters but he did admire the romance of their despair. Jeanie Deans is a product of covenanting Scotland, as is Mr Bide-the-Bent in *The Bride of Lammermoor* and perhaps he redeemed himself in 'Wandering Willie's Tale' wherein all the great persecutors of the covenanters were gathered in hell with Sir Robert Redgauntlet, a scenario which would surely have satisfied the most devoted Covenanter – Middleton, Rothes, Lauderdale, Dalyell, Earlshall, Bloody Advocate Mackenzie and Claverhouse, 'as beautiful as when he lived, with his long, dark, curled locks streaming down over his buff coat, and his left hand always on his right spule-blade, to hide the wound that the silver bullet had made'.[30]

In James Hogg's *Brownie of Bodsbeck* (1818), brownies and demons turn out to be persecuted Covenanters sheltering from their tormentors in a cave. Hogg actually had little sympathy personally for the Covenanters whom he thought deluded (a view devastatingly explored in his *Confessions of a Justified Sinner* (1824) but he comes down in their favour at the end of the story. 'Deil care what side they were on' he cries to his

[28] Johnson, *Sir Walter Scott*; David Brown, *Sir Walter Scott and the Historical Imagination* (London, 1979); James Anderson, *Sir Walter Scott and History* (Edinburgh, 1981).

[29] George Gilfillan, *The Martyrs, Heroes and Bards of the Scottish Covenant* (London, 1853), 198.

[30] Walter Scott, *Redgauntlet*, The Melrose Edition, 99–100.

daughter who had aided the persecuted, 'ye hae taen the side o' human nature; the suffering and the humble side, on the side o' feeling my woman'.[31] Hogg's countryside around Ettrick and Yarrow was full of tales of the martyrs, but his folksy approach was, generally speaking, less well regarded than that of Scott. The Shepherd's critics accused him of mounting an attack on the aristocracy through his portrayal of Claverhouse. The empathy for his subjects which Hogg achieved, while finding himself not totally sympathetic towards them, was probably what Scott thought he was achieving in *Old Mortality*, but his instincts and prejudices let him down.

John Galt was moved to write *Ringan Gilhaize* (1823) because he thought that Scott had treated the defenders of the presbyterian church with too much levity, possibly even, ridicule. His own ancestors had been persecuted for their support of the covenant, one suffering banishment to Carolina. The story is told by Ringan, a Covenanter who recounts the adventures of his grandfather during the Reformation. One of McCrie's criticisms of Scott was that he had not spent enough space discussing how the Covenanters acquired their attitudes and prejudices.[32] Galt rather compensated on this count, though the novel was not regarded as a success (much to the mystification of its author) until comparatively recently. At the end of the story Ringan fatally shoots Claverhouse at Killiecrankie; the novel's concluding words are:

> Thus was an avenging vow fulfilled and thus was my native
> land delivered from bondage. For a time yet there may be
> rumours and bloodshed but they will prove as the wreck which
> the waves roll to the shore after a tempest. The fortunes of the
> papistical Stuarts are foundered forever. Never again in this
> land shall any king, of his own caprice and prerogative, dare to
> violate the conscience of the people.

In a postscript he added the memorable observation that,

> The English are a justice-loving people according to charter
> and statute; the Scotch are a wrong-resenting race according to
> right and feeling; and the character of liberty among them takes
> its aspect from that peculiarity.

---

[31] James Hogg, *The Brownie of Bodsbeck*, ed. Douglas Mack (Edinburgh and London, 1976), 3, 163.

[32] McCrie, *Vindication*, 26.

He proceeded to make his point by quoting *in extenso* the Declaration of Arbroath (1320), a momentous document that was central to the Whig tradition since it promoted the idea that a king was answerable to his subjects and so could be deposed; it advocated an elective kingship, and swore its signatories to fight to the death for freedom, which no honest person would ever lose save with life itself.[33]

A fair amount of published commentary was forthcoming in 1838 and 1843, the anniversaries respectively of the National Covenant and the Solemn League, the latter date, happily enough, proving to be the year of the Disruption, and one did not have to be a religious enthusiast to see parallels between the plight of the Free Church and of the 'Suffering Bleeding Remnant'. Lest any doubted, James Aikman's hugely influential *Annals of the Persecution in Scotland* had handily appeared in 1842: 'there is no testimony stronger than that of the Church in Scotland, whether we consider the fiery trials she has gone through, or the noble records her martyrs have left to the truth and faithfulness of God'.[34] If the Disruption can be interpreted as a nationalist gesture, it is also, of course, part of a long-standing tradition that can be traced to the very nub of the covenant – the relationship between church and state.

Robert Simpson's *The Banner of the Covenant* lamented the scarcity of historical materials: 'Tradition has in many cases supplied the deficiencies of history.' He was concerned to emphasise the atrocities perpetrated during the 'good-ill-time of persecution': 'the loss of property, of liberty and of life was the fate of thousands and thousands of virtuous and patriotic persons' who suffered imprisonment, transportation, billetting, unemployment and enforced vagrancy, but who nonetheless triumphed.

All the prisons they could fill with us, and all the ships they could freight with us, and all the gibbets they could hang us on, could never either exhaust or lessen our number; but the more we were afflicted the more we grew, and the design to destroy us, through the mercy of our God, proved always ruinous to the destroyers; and this must be acknowledged to

[33] John Galt, *Ringan Gilhaize: or The Covenanters*, 2 vols *The Works of John Galt*, ed. D. S. Meldrum and William Roughead (Edinburgh, 1936), ii, 322–3, 326–34. Edward J. Cowan, 'Identity, Freedom and the Declaration of Arbroath', in Dauvit Broun, R. J. Finlay and Michael Lynch (eds), *Image and Identity. The Making and Re-making of Scotland Through the Ages* (Edinburgh, 1998), 38–68.

[34] James Aikman, *Annals of the Persecution in Scotland, from the Restoration to the Revolution* (Edinburgh, 1842), ix.

the praise of God's clemency, and the condemnation of man's cruelty, that when they tried all ways possible to destroy us, and root us out from the earth – after they had hanged, shot, tortured, and banished for slaves all they could catch of us – they were further from their purpose than when they began.[35]

Thus grew the legend. When Simpson returned to the Killing Times in 1861, he chose to concentrate on the area between Muirkirk and Sanquhar, of which latter he was parish minister. He contended that the moors and hills separating Nithsdale and Clydesdale supported only two shepherds' cottages where once there had been twenty dwellings. His facts were shaky but he was attempting to suggest that the persecutions were responsible for the Lowland Clearances.[36] The hagiography continued. Another very influential work, which is still in print, was Alexander Smellie's *Men of the Covenant* (1901).

Volumes of verse, some execrable some elevating, usually combining moors and martyrdom, tumbled from the press, as did dozens of versions of the Persecution Story edited for children. John MacFarlane, editor of *The Harp of the Scottish Covenant* thanked Rob Wanlock of Montreal and the Rev. Duncan Crerar of New York for their help. The anthology included James Graham's much favoured 'The Sabbath', 'in solitudes like these/Thy persecuted children, Scotia, foiled/ A tyrant's and a bigot's laws'. In the same collection James Hislop's 'The Cameronian Dream' might be described as a blend of sacrifice and scenery, somewhere between William Blake and Rupert Brooke.[37] On the frontier of Upper Canada Alexander McLachlan, originally from Johnstone, Renfrewshire, celebrated the covenants. A Chartist, he regarded William Wallace and the Covenanters as part of his ideological heritage. In his poetic reveries he recalled Bothwell, 'where the Covenanting ranks/Were worsted sair', and celebrated the 'puir hunted Hillfolk wha fought not in vain'.[38]

A constant source of inspiration until the end of his short life was the legacy of Robert Louis Stevenson's covenanting ancestors. His first publication was on the Pentland Rising (1666). His last story, *Heathercat*, was set during the Killing Times. For his friend S. R. Crockett, the

---

[35] Robert Simpson, *The Banner of the Covenant* (Edinburgh, 1847), 13–19, 25.

[36] Robert Simpson, *Martyrland or The Perils of Persecution* (Glasgow, 1861), xx.

[37] *The Harp of the Scottish Covenant: Poems, Songs, and Ballads Relating to the Covenanting Struggle* (Paisley, 1895), vii, 18–19, 21–24.

[38] *The Poetical Works of Alexander McLachlan* (Toronto, 1900), 100, 115.

prolific novelist who produced many tales set in covenanting times, he wrote the beautiful lines:

Blows the wind today, and the sun and the rain are flying,
Blows the wind on the moors today and now,
Where about the graves of the martyrs the whaups are crying,
My heart remembers how.[39]

Lewis Grassic Gibbon, arguably Scotland's greatest twentieth-century novelist, was working on a novel of the Covenanters when he died.[40] That their literary potential has continued to fascinate is indicated by James Robertson's accomplished novel *The Fanatic* (London, 2000).

For over a hundred years historians have tended to shy away from the later Covenanters, leaving them almost exclusively to pious populists. J. K Hewison's study, that of yet another divine following a well-tramped path, was somewhat credulous and uncritical but still useful. Although the twentieth century spawned many biographies of the major participants in the movement which received obligatory, if cursory, treatment in standard histories, and although the first phase of the covenanting saga has received expert coverage, a satisfactory study of the later Covenanters is still lacking. A soulmate of Napier's, though shunning his extravagant rhetoric, Gordon Donaldson in 1965 was still debating with Robert Wodrow. Ian Cowan's book, of which much might have been expected, proved curiously detached and subdued.[41] Sadly, professional historians have completely failed to meet the challenge posed by the legend of the 'Suffering Bleeding Remnant'.

In 1853 the indefatigable George Gilfillan attempted to sum up the significance of the covenanters. Their legacy, in his view, included 'the folly of persecution for conscience' sake' and 'the influence of adversity

---

[39] *Robert Louis Stevenson: Collected Poems* ed. Janet Adam Smith, 2nd edn (London, 1971), 283–4. See Islay Murray Donaldson, *The Life and Work of Samuel Rutherford Crockett* (Aberdeen, 1989) and Edward J. Cowan, 'Intent upon my own race and place I wrote'; 'Robert Louis Stevenson and Scottish History', in Edward J. Cowan and Douglas Gifford (eds), *The Polar Twins* (Edinburgh, 1999), 187–214.

[40] Ian S. Munro, *Leslie Mitchell: Lewis Grassic Gibbon* (Edinburgh, 1966), 185. I owe this point to Hanne Tange.

[41] James King Hewison, *The Covenanters: A History of the Church in Scotland From the Reformation to the Revolution*, 2 vols (Glasgow, 1908; rev. edn. 1913); Gordon Donaldson, *Scotland: James V to James VII* (Edinburgh, 1965), Ian B. Cowan, *The Scottish Covenanters 1660–1688* (London, 1977).

and persecution in developing character'. Gilfillan, like most who wrote on the subject, was in no doubt about the covenanting achievement. First, they resisted tyranny, absolutism and popery, and in so doing anticipated the Glorious Revolution of 1688–9. Second, the covenanters were at the heart of an international resistance spreading from the Netherlands and Germany to North America. Third their histories provided the first real martyrology for the Scottish presbyterian church; if the Established church wished to plunder the Killing Times for inspiration, that was fine too.[42]

There is much more to be made of this topic, not least on the impact of the covenant in Ireland, the United States and elsewhere, including Scotland itself, where, arguably, the covenant continues, in some quarters, to stoke the fires of sectarianism. A beginning should involve the attempt to achieve something of a balance, to look at both sides of the picture, to place covenanting activities in some kind of context without special pleading and without slighting the equally intriguing histories and struggles of Catholics and episcopalians. The covenant was, in certain respects, a perversion. Things went desperately wrong. Fanatics and the righteous are never attractive but these people were not assassinated in the dark or a ditch; they faced the guns as they met their maker. They followed political principles which are still not absent in Scottish political debate. They ought to be considered ideal candidates for the type of historical enquiry which has not so far materialised. They represent the classic dichotomy between folk tradition and elite culture, and thus the eternal conundrum of History.

[42] Gilfillan, *Martyrs, Heroes and Bards*, 217–51.

CHAPTER 7

'What's in a Name?': Pedigree and Propaganda in Seventeenth-Century Scotland

David Allan

F amily history remains fantastically popular. A headcount would surely confirm that there are today more genealogists than academic scholars afoot in Scotland's repositories and research libraries; and an impressive proportion of the works optimistically classified as 'Scottish history' by the bookshops turns out to be attempts to entice the budding family historian.[1] This should not be entirely surprising, given the commercial capital now invested in Scottish kinship, fictitious and real: both tartan textile manufacturers and heritage tourism, to name just two profitable industries, derive obvious advantages from peddling the notion of meaningful blood ties between the now-scattered members of ancient Scottish dynasties. But if such activities have formed an important part of the relentless romanticisation of the Scottish past, usually attributed by cynical cultural historians to the effects of nineteenth-century Balmorality and the novels of Sir Walter Scott, then it is crucial to note that the desire to trumpet one's breeding was neither a unique product of that age nor at any time a peculiarly Scottish affectation.[2]

---

[1] Useful guides of this kind include David Moody, *Scottish Family History* (London, 1988); Joan P. S. Ferguson, *Scottish Family Histories Held in Scottish Libraries* (Edinburgh, 1986); and Margaret Stuart, *Scottish Family History: A Guide to Works of Reference on the History and Genealogy of Scottish Families* (Baltimore, MD, 1978).

[2] The theme of Scotland's reinvention as a tartan theme park, consistent with the expectations of Romanticism, has been widely discussed, but important treatments include Tom Nairn's discussion, epitomised by the observation, truer than it sounds, that 'we are still living in the Scotland of Sir Walter Scott', *The Break-Up of Britain: Crisis and Neo-Nationalism*, 2nd edn (London, 1981), 149. See also Murray Pittock, *The Invention of Scotland: The Stuart Myth and the Scottish Identity, 1638 to the Present* (London, 1991) for a more recent and influential view.

For all the monumental labours of Sir William Fraser in particular, with his definitive late Victorian works on several dozen aristocratic houses, recognisably similar activities were being undertaken a century before, by men like Andrew Gordon, David Symson and William Buchanan.[3] Even earlier, genealogical study had already produced several Scottish texts still deservedly familiar to students of political thought and literature, including David Hume of Godscroft's *History of the Houses of Douglas and Angus* and Sir Robert Gordon of Gordonstoun's *Genealogical History of the Earldom of Sutherland*, both of them dating from the 1620s.[4] This chapter will ask why it was that seventeenth-century Scots increasingly wrote such works.[5] We shall find that the craze for genealogy was in certain respects a response to pressures which were producing comparable reactions in other contemporary European societies. But this quite remarkable outpouring of antiquarian and scholarly endeavour also goes a long way towards explaining what the Scots were doing between the celebrated historical productions of the sixteenth-century Renaissance and the 'historical age' confidently detected by David Hume in the third quarter of the eighteenth.[6]

An important function of genealogy in all societies is neither profound nor especially obscure: the stressing of a latent unity between now-distinct individuals or families, the better to encourage a sense of mutual affinity and the recognition of common interest.[7] As Allan Macinnes has argued for the early modern Highlands, 'a pretentious veneration for genealogy' can provide a surprisingly effective bond, even 'offsetting the

---

[3] David Symson, *A Genealogical and Historical Account of the Illustrious Name of Stuart, etc.* (Edinburgh, 1712); C. A. Gordon, *Concise History of the Ancient and Illustrious House of Gordon* (Aberdeen, 1754); William Buchanan, *History of the Ancient Surname of Buchanan and of Ancient Scottish Surnames, More Particularly the Clans* (Glasgow, 1793). On Fraser, see Gordon Donaldson, *Sir William Fraser: The Man and his Work* (Edinburgh, 1986).

[4] There is even a recent modern edition of one of these works: David Hume, *The History of the House of Douglas* ed. D. Reid, 2 vols (Edinburgh, 1996), the original having first been published in 1643–4, about ten years after its author's death. Like Hume's, Gordon's was a posthumous publication: Sir Robert Gordon, *A Genealogical History of the Earldom of Sutherland* (Edinburgh, 1813).

[5] Although this phenomenon has not escaped the attention of other scholars, its explanation has, oddly, never been attempted. For example, William Ferguson has recently noted how Scottish dynasties in the 1680s 'sometimes went to extraordinary lengths to boast, and often to augment, their family trees': *The Identity of the Scottish Nation: An Historic Quest* (Edinburgh, 1998), 152.

[6] *Letters of David Hume*, ed. G. Birkbeck-Hill (Oxford, 1888), 155.

[7] For Scotland this view has been advanced in J. Triseliotis, 'Identity and Genealogy', *Scottish Genealogist*, XXXIV (1987), 272–6.

loss of unified clan leadership' in so large, complex and scattered a kinship grouping as Clan Donald.[8] Thus a natural desire to counteract the centrifugal effects of intermarriage and physical migration upon what it was advantageous to present as a cohesive kin identity almost certainly lay behind many seventeenth-century Scottish genealogies and family histories. In effect, their extraordinary inclusivity and comprehensiveness were a reflection of the wish to demonstrate the widest possible extension of familial association, mutual obligation and manifest nobility across time and space.

A Lowland genealogy which renders this expansiveness strikingly visible is Edinburgh University Library's manuscript copy of the 'Genealogy of Cunningham', attributed to William Colquhoun and dating from approximately 1602.[9] Purporting to be 'Ane genlligie of ye hounourabill name of coninghame frome thair first progenatoure Neill coninghame', the document sketches out an extensive kinship network centred upon Ayrshire but reaching out to the Lothians and Fife, a literal tree of common descent and intermarriage incorporating numerous lairds still prominent in the early seventeenth century – including Warristoun, Robartland, Glengarnock and Barns – as well as several important noble relations, through marriage, such as the Kennedy earls of Cassillis, and the Montgomeries, earls of Eglinton. The overriding message would presumably have been clear to contemporaries, and remains so to anyone who examines this beautifully-crafted manuscript today: the Cunninghams and their kin, wherever and whenever they were to be found, were a coherent unit, its members deriving unique strengths from, and owing unique mutual obligations because of, their possession of this revered name.

The Drummonds provide an even more dramatic instance of genealogy acting at its simplest, as a unifying force across a large and diverse kinship grouping, and it does this not least because several of its histories survive from the period. Clearly the most famous example is the work of the extended family's most celebrated individual, William Drummond of Hawthornden, a distant descendant of the Drummonds of Stobhall and, curiously, the former betrothed of the late daughter of Cunning-

---

[8] Allan Macinnes, *Clanship, Commerce and the House of Stewart, 1602–1788* (East Linton, 1996), 3.

[9] William Colquhoun, 'Genealogy of Cunningham' (Edinburgh: EUL, La. Charter 1430 (90 Box 2)). There is also a surviving seventeenth-century genealogy of the Cunninghams in Edinburgh: NLS, MS. 3033.

ham of Barns. It is well known how implausibly proud the poet was of his remote ancestral links, through Annabella Drummond's marriage to King Robert III in 1367, with the Scottish royal line – an inflated sense of dynastic propinquity which further encouraged Hawthornden in his support of Charles I. The extent of Drummond's obsession with pedigree is amply shown by his engagement in the dispute in 1632 over the earl of Menteith's claim to the Earldom of Strathearn, the incautious early acceptance of which by the king seemed to imply that Robert II should not have been succeeded by Robert III and the Stuart sons of Annabella Drummond but by the heirs of his other son, David, earl of Strathearn, ancestor of the modern earls of Menteith. Yet his manuscript history of the Drummond family, closely related to his inevitably Drummond-filled *History of Scotland*, was its principal expression.[10] This text is not alone, however, for other contemporary efforts at Drummond genealogy (including one by John Freebairn, minister of Maddertie) were collected and copied by the antiquary Robert Mylne and survive severally in Edinburgh in the National Library of Scotland.[11] A further Drummond genealogy also exists in the National Library, itself a part-copy of 'The genealogie of the most noble and ancient house of Drummond' by a kinsman of the poet, another William Drummond, 1st Viscount Strathallan, compiled in 1681.[12] With numerous distinguished stems – led by the earls (later dukes) of Perth and the lords Maddertie, and also including the Drummonds of Blairdrummond, Cargill, Carnock, Riccarton and Hawthornden – spread right across the kingdom from the Highland marches of Perthshire, through Fife and almost to the gates of Edinburgh itself, the Drummonds evidently saw genealogy as a constructive influence, one which vitally emphasised the antiquity, the royal connections, the high social status and the enduring political significance of their name.

A different example, that of the Gordon family, emphasises that throughout Scotland some of the furthest-flung and most complex kinship networks were contributing to this early seventeenth-century upsurge in family history writing, attempting to impose a powerful sense of retrospective order on a highly dispersed social reality. Again numerous contemporary manuscripts have come down to us, though,

[10] David Masson, *Drummond of Hawthornden* (London, 1873), esp. 176–7, 185–93, 216–23, 449.
[11] Edinburgh: NLS Adv. MS. 16.1.1, 34.6.9 and 73.1.17.
[12] Edinburgh: NLS Adv. MS. 34.3.14.

as with the Drummonds, these are perhaps secondary to a single famous text, Gordon of Gordonstoun's *Genealogical History*, composed during the 1620s and intellectually the most interesting family history written in seventeenth-century Scotland. Brutally frank, unashamedly *politique* and specifically designed by its author to act as a practical education in aristocratic politics for his inexperienced young nephew John, 13th earl, it sought to describe affairs as they were and as they needed to be conducted – and not, as conventional humanism pre-scribed, as one might ideally have wished them to be. In Gordon's words:

> It is aneugh in histories (as ane old writer sayeth), iff maters be rehearsed plainlie as they are done, and recorded without any lie, that there be nothing related without evident apparence of truth, or aganiest commoun sense and reasone.[13]

His troubling, sometimes amoral, vision of the place of the earls of Sutherland in Scottish history is indebted above all to the new editions of Tacitus that he had purchased and that were then exerting such a strong influence over European historians and political thinkers.[14] But however uncomfortable its emphasis on *actualité*, which ensured its withholding from public view until the nineteenth century, the text seems to have enjoyed something of a minor celebrity in private circulation within the family. Certainly the extant manuscripts after nearly four hundred years of continuous attrition, today numbering at least five if one includes copies of the loose Latin translation produced by Gordon's colleague Alexander Ross, suggest that very considerable importance was attached by the

---

[13] Gordon, *Genealogical History*, 13.

[14] On the Roman historian's re-emergence at the turn of the seventeenth century, see C. O. Brink, 'Justus Lipsius and the Text of Tacitus', *Journal of Roman Studies*, 41 (1951), 32–51; A. Momigliano, 'The First Political Commentary on Tacitus', *Journal of Roman Studies*, 37 (1947), 91–101; J. H. Whitfield 'Livy > Tacitus', in R. R. Bolgar (ed.), *Classical Influences on European Culture*, AD1500–1700 (Cambridge, 1976), 281–93; P. Burke, 'A Survey of the Popularity of Ancient Historians, 1450–1700', *History and Theory*, 2 (1966), 135–52, and his 'Tacitism', in T. A. Dorey (ed.), *Tacitus* (London, 1969), 149–71; and R. C. Schellhase, *Tacitus in Renaissance Political Thought* (Chicago, 1976). Precisely because of Tacitus' focus on the conduct of individual emperors, politicians and courtiers, his style and insights translated especially well into the genre of the genealogical history of aristocratic dynasties.

family to the physical survival and necessarily furtive study of this extraordinary genealogical work.[15]

Not surprisingly, however, other Gordon genealogies were produced in the seventeenth century, fully reflecting the diffuse nature of a family name whose bearers included not just the earls of Sutherland in the far north but the earls of Huntly in the north-east and several other extremely distinguished stems. The Huntlys, for example, were the subject of the cartographer Robert Gordon of Straloch's 'Origo et progressus familiae Gordoniorum de Huntley in Scotia', a copy of which is now in the National Library of Scotland.[16] An anonymous hand – possibly the Catholic priest David Burnet – was responsible for the slightly later 'The pourtrait of true loyalty exposed in the family of Gordon', from around 1691.[17] A manuscript now in Aberdeen University Library represents itself as a 'Genealogy of the House or Family of Gordon' from around 1644, and contains an extensive list of members of both the main and cadet lines of Huntly, including the Gordons of Lochinvar, Cluny, Essy and Buckie.[18] A 1594 genealogy of the Huntlys also survives in the National Library, an impressive collection of Scottish noble family trees ascribed to the great English genealogist and historian William Camden.[19] And, taking up and propagating an even older genealogical work, there is the 'De origine et incremento Gordiniae familiae' by the Piedmontese scholar resident at Kinloss Abbey, Joannes Ferrerius, written around 1545, which seems to have been widely copied during the early seventeenth century, with surviving versions being dated to 1613 and 1624.[20]

Similar patterns of both new genealogical studies and the enthusiastic multiplication of existing texts are found elsewhere in seventeenth-century Scotland, though nowhere more suggestively than in the case of the Campbells. Their example is crucial because, as the most extra-vagantly acquisitive and materially successful kinship grouping in the

---

[15] An original 1630 version of Gordon's work survives as Edinburgh: NLS, Adv. MS. 34.3.3. Two of Ross' translations (dated 1631) exist in Adv. MSS. 34.1.6 and 34.6.18, and two further texts of 'Southerlandie Comitum Annales' from Aberdeen: AUL MS. 2049 and Oxford: Bodleian Ms. Top.Sutherland.c.1. An original and two later copies of Gordon's text were also recorded at Dunrobin by Victorian visitors: see HMC, *Second Report* (London, 1874), 179.

[16] Edinburgh: NLS Adv. MS. 34.6.23.

[17] Edinburgh: NLS Adv. MS. 34.6.11.

[18] Aberdeen: AUL MS. 908.

[19] Edinburgh: NLS Adv. MS. 33.2.36.

[20] Edinburgh: NLS, Adv. MSS. 35.5.5A and 34.6.18.

kingdom during the early modern period, the Campbells' fondness for pedigree and lineage should emphatically dismiss any lingering thoughts that genealogy was simply an antiquarian indulgence, offering comfort and consolation to backward-looking, failing or fragmenting family networks. On the contrary, the rise of the Campbells as major land-owners, substantial political figures and peers of the realm in different parts of sixteenth- and seventeenth-century Scotland shows that gen-ealogy was a vital tool in the self-fashioning of an emergent modern elite, a potent propaganda weapon providing identity, unity and historical legitimation to the various strands of a powerful kinship network successfully 'on the make'.

One Clan Campbell genealogy from the later seventeenth century, for example, survives in the National Library of Scotland.[21] Reflecting the pivotal position of the principal Campbell dynasty in the west of Scotland on both sides of the Highland Line, there is also in the same collection a verse genealogy of Archibald, marquess of Argyll, dated 1690–1 but containing poetry attributed to the early 1640s, significantly composed in Gaelic.[22] Whether as earls (or in one case a marquis) of Argyll at Inveraray, as earls of Breadalbane in Glenorchy, as earls of Loudoun in Ayrshire, as lairds of Cawdor near Inverness or Craignish in Argyllshire, all Campbells were able to bask proudly in the glow of an ancient and heroic pedigree. Partly Gaelic in origin but increasingly anglicised, a changing character which reflected the conscious mutation of its leading members from west Highland chieftains to national leaders, their genealogy – however bogus in certain particulars, however implausible in its remoter reaches – lent them distinction and status during their relentless rise.

An inevitable consequence of this tendency to employ surveys of the past to reinforce kin identity and to enhance the family's social standing was that a conflation could occur between genealogy and national

---

[21] Edinburgh: NLS Adv. MS. 32.6.13.

[22] Edinburgh: NLS Adv. MS. 72.1.36. On the Campbell genealogies, see W. Gillies, 'The Invention of Tradition, Highland-Style', in A. A. Macdonald, M. Lynch and I. B. Cowan (eds), *The Renaissance in Scotland: Studies in Literature, Religion, History and Culture* (Leiden, 1994), 144–56, which discusses the Gaelic Adv. MS. 72.1.36, as well as the miscellaneous Adv. MS. 72.2.2., which includes another Campbell genealogy from the second half of the seventeenth century; W. D. H. Sellar, 'The Earliest Campbells – Norman, Briton or Gael', *Scottish Studies*, 17 (1979), 109–25; his 'Highland Family Origins – Pedigree Making and Pedigree Faking', in L. Maclean (ed.), *The Middle Ages in the Highlands* (Inverness, 1981), 103–16; and E. J. Cowan, 'Clanship, Kinship and the Campbell Acquisition of Islay', *Scottish Historical Review*, 58 (1979), 132–57.

history. This was certainly the case with pre-eminent regional families such as the Drummonds, whose contribution to Scotland's very survival during the later Middle Ages had been considerable: Hawthornden's *History of Scotland* is a text which positively invites us to read it in this way, and, according to Arthur Williamson, a preference for seeing Scotland's history as a succession of specifically dynastic achievements was a characteristic which increasingly set Jacobean Scots apart from their English counterparts, who frequently expressed the struggle for English liberty in terms of the institutional histories of law and parliament.[23] Hume of Godscroft's *History* is probably the best example of this distinctive Scottish approach; it is ostensibly a recapitulation of the deeds of individual Douglases but without any shadow of a doubt really a full-scale history of Scotland, with the patriotism and skill of the earls of Douglas and Angus, particularly in wars with England, inevitably to the fore throughout.[24] As George Crawfurd, an early eighteenth-century collector of Scottish genealogies, observed of this great work:

> Of this noble family there is a particular Historie wryte by a very learned [man?] who equalizes them to any of the ancient Roman familys and gives them the preference to all others in Europe those of crowned heads excepted.[25]

[23] Arthur Williamson, *Scottish National Consciousness in the Age of James VI: The Apocalypse, the Union and the Shaping of Scotland's Public Culture* (Edinburgh, 1979), esp. 7. See also Colin Kidd, *Subverting Scotland's Past: Scottish Whig Historians and the Creation of an Anglo-British Identity, 1689–c.1830* (Cambridge, 1993), 165.

[24] On the publication of this text, see G. P. Johnston, 'The First Edition of Hume of Godscroft's History', *Papers of the Edinburgh Bibliographical Society*, 4 (1899–1901), 149–71. There is evidence that the Douglases' genealogy, cast in effect as the nation's history, enjoyed some wider currency, for there survives in Aberdeen: AUL MS. 2092, fos. 55r–65r, which is an anonymous seventeenth-century commonplace book, what seems to be a transcript of the skeleton lineage around which Hume developed his narrative. Whether this was used by Hume or post-dates his work and derives from the published *History* is unclear.

[25] [George Crawfurd], 'The Accompt of the FFamily [sic] of Douglas for the Peerage of Scotland By G.C.', (Edinburgh: EUL MS. Dc.1.65): 1. Crawfurd's manuscript also incorporates 'The Genealogie of the Trustie Noble and Ancient Surname of Douglas', which traces the name back to the year 767 and emphasises its connections, through marriage, with such luminaries as the Duke of Lennox and the earls of Abercorn, Mar, Seaforth, Errol and Dunfermline, 2. The notion that the Douglases derived their special status in Scottish life in part from their great antiquity was an important feature of their genealogies, as repeated, for example, in William Dunlop's collection from the 1670s or 1680s, 'Genealogies of the Nobilitie of Scotland', now Edinburgh: EUL MS. Dc.1.64.

But even lesser lights, such as the Lyons, lords of Glamis, conceived of their own ancestors in the same grand style, one of their genealogies being compiled in 1627 and filled with numerous improbable allusions to national greatness – a leaden roll-call of royal kinsmen, eminent marriages, high-ranking offices of state and predictably selfless patriots.[26] Such emphatic visions of dynastic significance within the nation's collective history, founded on unimpeachable antiquity and the subsequent demonstration of what at times could appear to be genetically-programmed virtue, were the orthodox way in which genealogists presented their family's past to their Scottish noble patrons, and, through the circulation of manuscripts, possibly to an interested elite audience. Some of the reasons why else they may have done so, and the problem of why the assertion of identity and kinship suddenly seemed to take on greater importance around and after 1600, occupies the remainder of this chapter.

In further explaining the marked seventeenth-century expansion of Scottish family history writing it rapidly transpires that we are dealing with a topic on which, in keeping with recent historiographical fashions, there are a range of European, British and also internal Scottish factors on which we can plausibly draw. For the Scots were certainly not alone in turning to genealogy with a vengeance from the last years of the sixteenth century. Lawrence Stone, for example, describes English landed society in the time of Elizabeth as being swiftly overtaken by 'a fad, a craze, a quasi-intellectual hobby for the idle rich . . . the welding of a homogenous group of seemingly respectable lineage from a crazy patchwork of the most diverse, and sometimes dubious, origins'.[27] This enthusiasm had already reached such ludicrous heights by the arrival of James VI and I that, faced with the particularly fatuous but endlessly repeated claims of the 6th lord Lumley to possession of an

---

[26] [John Lyoune?], 'The Pedegrie of the house of Glammiss' (Glasgow: GUL MS. Gen. 240). This text is largely a verbatim copy of a 1627 genealogy extant at Glamis, attributed to John Lyoune, though the Glasgow version also has a unique continuation.

[27] Lawrence Stone, *The Crisis of the Aristocracy, 1558–1641* (Oxford, 1965), 23. Other works touching on the late Tudor and Stuart predilection for pedigree include his *An Open Elite? England, 1540–1880* (Oxford, 1984); F. Heal and C. Holmes, *The Gentry in England and Wales 1500–1700* (Basingstoke, 1994), esp. 20–2, 34–7; A. R. Wagner, *English Genealogy*, 2nd edn (Oxford, 1972), esp. 361–74; and M. Maclagan, 'Genealogy and Heraldry in the Sixteenth and Seventeenth Centuries', in Levi Fox (ed.), *English Historical Scholarship in the Sixteenth and Seventeenth Centuries* (London, 1956), 31–48.

ancient pedigree, the exasperated Scot is reported finally to have snapped: 'I did na ken Adam's name was Lumley'.[28]

Similar observations, however, could have been made in relation to bogus ancestor-worship in the Netherlands: the turn of the seventeenth century saw the gentry of the newly-liberated Dutch republic 'devoting a great deal of time to writing genealogies and listing pedigrees'.[29] France, too, experienced an explosion of this kind of scholarship, Jay Smith recently establishing that a scant two printed and two unpublished genealogical works emerging during the 1550s had been dwarfed by the decennial output of twenty-seven printed works and fourteen manuscripts in the 1630s.[30] Clearly in all of these environments the verification (or, as was so often the case, the creation) of an honourable and ancient descent was in general desirable, as in Scotland and England, because of the affirmation of status which kinship brought in a society where wealth and power rested on heredity, and thus ultimately because of the legitimacy and commensurate entitlements which it could help to confer. But these parallel developments also mean that any explanation of Scottish trends must at least to some extent take cognisance of the explanations advanced for the explosion of genealogical interests elsewhere in Britain and Europe.

One point on which many scholars of contemporary Europe are agreed is that this was an age during which traditional landed elites confronted an uncertain future – whether the full-blown 'General Crisis of the Seventeenth Century' or a rather less severe and more regionally-specific downturn in fortunes.[31] Above all there are some reasons to think that

---

28 Stone, *Crisis*, 24.

29 Sherrin Marshall, *The Dutch Gentry 1550–1650: Family, Faith and Fortune* (New York, 1987), 2.

30 Jay M. Smith, *The Culture of Merit: Nobility, Royal Service and the Making of Absolute Monarchy in France, 1600–1789* (Ann Arbor, MI, 1996), esp. 57–8. See also Orum Ranum, *Artisans of Glory: Writers and Historical Thought in Seventeenth-Century France* (Chapel Hill, NC, 1980), esp. 3–6 and, for the wider background, Davis Bitton, *The French Nobility in Crisis, 1560–1640* (Stanford, CA, 1969).

31 See, for example, on the European scene, H. R. Trevor-Roper, 'The General Crisis of the Seventeenth Century', in his *Religion, the Reformation and Social Change* (London, 1967), 46–89; T. K. Rabb, *The Struggle for Stability in Early Modern Europe* (New York, 1975); G. Parker and L. M. Smith (eds), *The General Crisis of the Seventeenth Century* (London, 1978); T. H. Aston, *Crisis in Europe, 1560–1660* (London, 1965); H. Kamen, *The Iron Century: Social Change in Europe, 1560–1660* (London, 1971); V. G. Kiernan, *State and Society in Seventeenth-Century Europe, 1550–1650* (London, 1980), and P. Zagorin,   /over

the western European aristocracy faced a demographic crisis during the seventeenth century, which had certain practical implications for genea-logical studies. For it meant, as Philip Hicks has recently argued, that 'family continuity could depend upon the preservation of family docu-ments pointing to a distant relative who could inherit the estate intact'.[32] This downturn in biological fortunes had its origins in the later sixteenth century and continued well into the eighteenth, but Stone's studies suggest that the proportion of English property-owners dying without male sons effectively doubled during the phase of steepest increase – from just 20 per cent in the period before 1550 to 41 per cent across the decades 1650–99.[33] Although this simultaneous crisis in nuptiality, fertility and mortality peaked in the fifty years before 1700, acceleration into it was, intriguingly, at its most dramatic and disorienting in the early decades of the seventeenth century: for example, of the sixty-three noble families in England in December 1559, twenty-one had already failed in the male line by December 1641 and twenty-six by December 1659 – an alarming extinction rate, if one takes Stone's definitions at face value, of 40 per cent in a century.[34] Direct patrilineal transmission of titles and property might thus have come to seem increasingly unreliable as a mechanism for family survival. An authenticated genealogy, cataloguing other potential suc-cessors and indicating the precise nature of their respective claims, even if it comprised little more than crude lists of names or a basic family tree, was no harmless diversion, no mere amusing affectation. In vulnerable times, and particularly in a society such as Scotland's where elaborate entails were increasingly being employed to determine patterns of inheritance, it could amount to a fully comprehensive insurance policy against genetic or pathological misfortune.

Many Scottish works probably fall to some extent into this essentially

cont'd   Rebels and Rulers, 1500–1660, 2 vols (Cambridge, 1982). The British Isles have been the subject of attempts to assess their levels of participation in the Europe-wide crisis of the seventeenth century, as for example D. Roy, 'England turned Germany?: the Aftermath of the Civil War in its European Context', Transactions of the Royal Historical Society, 28 (1978), 127–44, M. Lee, 'Scotland and the "General Crisis"', Scottish Historical Review, 63 (1984), 136–54, and A. Clarke, 'Ireland and the "General Crisis"', Past and Present, 48 (1970), 79–99.

[32] Philip Hicks, Neoclassical History and English Culture: From Clarendon to Hume (London, 1996), 50.

[33] Stone, Open Elite, 101–4 and Table 3.7. These data are broadly confirmed by the definitive demographic study of the elite, T. H. Hollingsworth, The Demography of the British Peerage, Supplement to Population Studies, xviii (1964).

[34] Stone, Crisis, 169.

functional category, even though, in the absence of an equivalent to Stone's English study, it is unclear how far Scotland's elite was a participant in, or merely a nervous observer of, this European demographic phenomenon. Either way, genealogy existed at one level merely as the meticulous recording of descendants and kinsmen to the nth degree, the better to ward off biological disaster and underpin a system of entailed inheritance. For example, the collections of Camden, aptly catalogued by the National Library of Scotland as 'Genealogical trees of the Scottish nobility', are little more than this, a straightforward list of ancestors designed to indicate succession and degrees of propinquity, albeit gorgeously illustrated with ornate heraldic devices.[35] Important parts of the surviving work of Sir James Balfour of Denmilne must have been capable of serving a similar function: they were family trees of the royal dynasties, nobility and landed gentry gathered together by a scholar (who, after all, became Lord Lyon King of Arms, and thus Scotland's leading heraldic authority), in effect preserving an accurate account of kinship and affinity among those possessing titles and heritable property in the kingdom.[36] Some beautiful sixteenth-century manuscript genealogies from Scotland, incorporating lavish heraldic illustrations of arms even for many of the less significant members of the propertied class, survive in the Bodleian Library, Oxford, suggesting that this desire to record descent and entitlement was already becoming endemic in landed society as early as the last days of James V.[37] It is

---

[35] Edinburgh: NLS Adv. MS. 33.2.36.

[36] Examples of Balfour's collections include 'Genealogical Trees of the Scottish Kings from 1061 to 1624' (Edinburgh: NLS Adv. MS. 15.2.13.); 'Genealogies of the Scottish Nobility' (Adv. MSS. 33.2.38–41.); and the copy of his 'Genealogies of Peers of Scotland, and Lists of Baronets and Landed Gentry' (in Adv. MS. 22.2.14.).

[37] The Bodleian's collections are particularly interesting for the relatively early evidence of Scottish noble genealogy which they contain. 'Coloured Sketches of the Arms of the Nobility and Gentry of Scotland' (Ms. Greaves. 52), for example, has been authoritatively dated to no later than the death of Mary of Guise (i.e. 1560) on the basis of internal evidence. Similarly 'An Account, in English, of the Nobility of Scotland, c.1577' (Ms. Dodsw. 20) seems to be a product of James VI's adolescence and 'Full-page Sketches of Arms of the Nobility of Scotland' (Ms. Wood. c. 9) can be provisionally dated to 1588 – the latter text being particularly intriguing because, as well as the usual suspects from the titled aristocracy, its unknown author has again troubled himself with the arms of numerous minor families such as Armstrong of that Ilk and Turnbull of that Ilk. The Bodleian also houses several Scottish genealogical manuscripts from the seventeenth century belonging to particular families, including 'Notes and Drafts by Johnston, mainly for a History of the Bruce Family' (Ms. Top. gen. c. 54), attributed to the Restoration antiquary Nathaniel Johnston.

unsurprising, therefore, that other lengthy but very basic genealogical compilations for Scotland's elite as a whole continued to appear well into the next century, having accelerated to new heights through the reign of James VI. 'Lord Ochiltree's collections' and William Dunlop's 'The genealogie of noble families of Scotland', for example, seem to have had the very simple purpose of setting out to preserve for all time – for use by the king, by the families themselves, by succeeding generations, and probably by the legal experts retained by all three – the precise relationship between individual family members.[38]

The painstaking care which this involved was amply justified, conclusive proof of pedigree providing vital legal evidence in some acrimonious inheritance disputes. The Gordons' repeated declarations about their status in right of the earldom of Sutherland, for example, need to be read in the light of the uncomfortable knowledge that they had secured that ancient title only through a marriage with a Sutherland heiress, herself empowered by the insanity of one brother and over the opposition of another, as recently as 1515: Gordon of Gordonstoun's work was therefore in part an attempt to legitimise a controversial act of dynastic acquisitiveness which had taken place barely out of living memory.[39] During the great eighteenth-century battles over title to the earldom, ironically provoked by the aggressive claims of Gordonstoun's own descendant and only finally resolved in 1771 with the vindication in the House of Lords of yet another countess of Sutherland in her own right, eager recourse was inevitably had to the genealogical materials stored up over the previous two centuries, which provided compelling evidence of earlier instances of descent in the female line.[40] Similarly the 'Genealogicall and Historicall Account of the Family of Craignish', written early in the eighteenth century, may be seen as reinforcing the tenure of the descendants of Campbell of Barrichbeyan whom the earls of Argyll had inserted in the early seventeenth century following the sad demise of the direct line of Craignish.[41]

---

[38] 'Lord Ochiltree's Collections' (Edinburgh: NLS Adv. MS. 34.3.18.); William Dunlop, 'The Genealogie of Noble Families of Scotland', vol. ii, 1693 (Adv. MS. 34.3.7.).

[39] Sir James Balfour Paul (ed.), *The Scots Peerage* (Edinburgh, 1911), VIII, 334–7, 359–60.

[40] Gordonstoun's descendant, another Sir Robert Gordon of Gordonstoun, even produced his own genealogical treatise to back his arguments, *In the Question Concerning the Peerage of Sutherland* (n.p., 1771).

[41] Alexander Campbell, 'Genealogicall and Historicall Account of the Family of Craignish', *Scottish History Society: Miscellany IV* (Edinburgh, 1926), 117–299. On the Barrichbeyan transfer, see Macinnes, *Clanship*, 12.

A second and similarly problematical pattern which emerged across much of western Europe during the later sixteenth century, and from which it is unlikely that the Scottish elite were wholly exempt, was the economic stress to which the landed classes were subjected. This, as described by many historians, took on the usual grim proportions: poor harvests, rising prices (particularly of foodstuffs), mounting expenditures through a growing emphasis on conspicuous consumption, high interest rates and greater technical legal exposure to creditors, fixed incomes limited by traditional long-term tenancies, and ever-increasing tax demands from the burgeoning modern state.[42] The effect on individual elite families in western Europe was to bring about critical levels of indebtedness for many, anxiety for almost all and outright bankruptcy for some. In ways which are perfectly understandable, material pressures of this kind could lead directly to the extravagant assertion of pedigree. For families in decline, genealogy, particularly where demonstrably accurate, offered a modicum of consolation, an honourable figleaf in times of advancing financial nakedness; for those on the make (because every impecunious seller of an estate required a cash-rich purchaser), genealogy, especially at its most creative, could conversely provide a quick route to assimilation and acceptance within a pedigree-obsessed elite.

In France, for example, the crude economic pressure provided by rising royal taxation, further encouraged by the Bourbon monarchy's own periodic *recherches* into the credentials of those claiming exemption, stimulated an increasing and perfectly understandable concern among the *noblesse* for the accurate recording of their family genealogies.[43] Fiscal privileges, together with the associated exclusive rights of political participation, seem similarly to have borne heavily upon the thinking of gentlemen-genealogists in the Netherlands as they set about establishing definitive 'proof of nobility'.[44] In Scotland debt has had a greater profile in recent studies of the elite economy. Keith Brown has shown how once great aristocrats like the earls of Atholl, Crawford and Caithness were bankrupted in the early seventeenth century, along with such recent peerage creations as the earls of Lothian and Tullibardine.[45] Partly as a consequence, 'a good deal of land was changing hands in the early seventeenth century', both within the nobility and through the

[42] Stone, *Crisis*, 183–9.
[43] Smith, *Culture*, esp. 60–1.
[44] Marshall, *Dutch Gentry*, 3.
[45] K. M. Brown, 'Noble Indebtedness in Scotland between the Reformation and the Revolution', *Historical Research*, LXII (1989), 260–75.

encroachments, especially around Edinburgh, of socially-ambitious urban and mercantile purchasers.[46] Whether new money or old, and whether rising or declining, members of the Jacobean landed elite, nobles and gentlemen alike, might well have responded to such instability with an enhanced focus on pedigree.

A third phenomenon for which there exists copious evidence elsewhere in the British Isles and Europe is the partial convergence of national elites towards certain cultural norms – not least as military and royal service, increasingly open to merit as well as birth, gradually ceased to be the exclusive, defining characteristics of the aristocratic elite. Broadly this process saw the successful bedding-in of the Renaissance which had spread contagiously across northern Europe during the sixteenth century: taste, breeding, manners, conduct and such tangible affectations as art and heraldry became the new distinguishing features of nobility. Historical scholarship itself received a powerful impetus from this process, a competent knowledge and understanding of the past rapidly becoming a necessary educational and recreational attainment for the respectable member of the elite. As noble literacy expanded in Scotland, the price of both paper and print decreased, and a corresponding curiosity about the past also quickened, history as a literary genre reached new heights of popularity.[47] An edifying, didactic discipline – 'it makes men ripe and aged in knowledge, though they be children in years', promised Gordon of Gordonstoun's associate Alexander Ross – history appeared uniquely equipped to furnish its devotees with a vital mixture of practical knowledge and moral instruction.[48]

To a European elite which enthusiastically embraced this persuasive cultural vision, it was also natural that the study of their own family's origins in particular should gain an enhanced status: therein, wrote Drummond of Hawthornden, 'consisteth a part of the knowledge of a mans [sic] own self'.[49] Indeed no forms of history seemed more relevant and more instructive to an aristocratic or gentlemanly audience – and certainly no exploits more worthy of permanent preservation and

---

[46] Ibid., 269. K. M. Brown, 'Aristocratic Finances and the Origins of the Scottish Revolution', *English Historical Review*, CIV (1989), 46–87.

[47] See, on the growing role of history in Scottish public life, Williamson, *Scottish National Consciousness*; Kidd, *Subverting Scotland's Past*; David Allan, *Virtue Learning and the Scottish Enlightenment: Ideas of Scholarship in Early Modern History* (Edinburgh, 1993).

[48] Alexander Ross, *The History of the World – The Second Part in Six Books* (London, 1652), a1r.

[49] William Drummond, *History of Scotland* (London, 1655), 245.

celebration – than those of their own forbears. Such texts seemed, as yet another Gordon family historian would later aver, 'in some Measure . . . [to] contribute to raise in them a generous Emulation of their illustrious Ancestors'.[50] In Scotland they also provided an alternative focus of attention in a family's insistent claims to authority and respect, increasingly supplanting violence and the feud as means to these most desirable of ends.[51] To such motivation we may also partly ascribe some of the most important surviving examples of genealogical literature, important not least because they go beyond the mere compilation of lists, becoming substantial literary endeavours in their own right, by turns narrative and analytical: both Gordon of Gordonstoun's *Genealogical History* and Hume of Godscroft's *History* were extended treatises of this type, in which the dead family served as the principal subject both for emulation by the living generation of the line and, it was hoped, for reverential acknowledgement by others.

Turning to more specifically British and Scottish processes which might help to explain the upsurge in genealogical activity, the changing nature of the landed elite, who at this time formed its principal constituency, brooks inevitably large. This was, after all, a society whose upper echelons grappled with a palpable contradiction: a tenacious social theory of timeless order and finely-graded hierarchy was everywhere cut across by a social reality formed by rising and falling fortunes, unexpected creations and unavoidable extinctions, enforced sales and opportunistic purchases. Such fluctuations needed to be explained, or at least their more offensive deviations smoothed over, in such a way that they would appear consistent with the accepted governing principles of heredity and lineage. Given the shamelessness with which even copper-bottomed aristocrats embellished their own genealogies (was the earl of Argyll not a descendant of King Arthur himself?), it should be no surprise that brazen *arrivistes* and *nouveaux riches* proved adept at fabricating for themselves impressively antique credentials. This was fortunate, for the reigns of James VI and Charles I saw some significant changes in the ranks of the Scottish elite.[52] And genealogy was potentially one of the chief means by which such unwelcome turbulence could be moderated.

[50] William Gordon, *The History of the Ancient, Noble, and Ilustrious Family of Gordon*, 2 vols (Edinburgh, 1726–7), I, vi.
[51] K. M. Brown, *Bloodfeud in Scotland, 1573–1625: Violence, Justice and Politics in an Early Modern Society* (Edinburgh, 1986). See also his 'Aristocratic Finances', esp. 47.
[52] M. Meikle, ' "The Invisible Divide". The Greater Lairds and the Nobility of Jacobean Scotland', *Scottish Historical Review*, LXXI (1992), 70–87.

For example, between James' British accession in 1603 and the outbreak of the English Civil War in 1642 the Scottish peerage increased substantially in size, and its character was altered forever, by the induction of new families and the sudden promotion of others. James' creations often amounted to reward for services rendered by loyal officials and allies – sometimes the younger sons of existing peers – like his Chancellor, Alexander Seton, ennobled in 1605 as earl of Dunfermline, his Lord President, Thomas Hamilton, successively earl of Melrose (1619) and earl of Haddington (1627), and Thomas Erskine, one of his saviours in the Gowrie conspiracy, rewarded with the earldom of Kellie in 1619. Other earldoms lavished on his countrymen by James included Tullibardine, Kinghorn, and Lothian (all 1606), and Roxburgh (1616). Under Charles new titles continued to shower down: John Stewart became earl of Traquair in 1633, having only recently been elevated to a lordship; Sir William Alexander, Charles' Secretary of State, found himself an earl (Stirling) that same year, as did his friend and another experienced courtier, Sir Robert Ker (Ancram). By 1641, with a curious inverse logic which saw peerages also being used to mollify former adversaries, the covenanting commander Alexander Leslie was entering gratefully upon the freshly-minted earldom of Leven.

With these fortunate Stuart servants (or, in certain cases, enemies) intruding into the upper reaches of the titular elite, more established members inevitably sought to protect their own positions by trading up: lords Drummond and Home obtained earldoms in 1605 (Perth and Home respectively); the 2nd lord Buccleuch, inheritor of a title only created in 1606, had acquired an earldom by 1612; lord Mackenzie of Kintail became earl of Seaforth in 1623; lord Thirlestane received the earldom of Lauderdale the following year; lord Kinloss became earl of Elgin in 1633; two lords Ogilvie each secured earldoms (Findlater in 1638 and Airlie in 1639); George Gordon, previously mere 6th earl of Huntly, had obtained promotion to a marquisate in the 1590s, an entirely new distinction in Scotland, and so Archibald Campbell, 8th earl of Argyll and another of the king's briefly-reconciled opponents, was presumably delighted to do likewise in 1641. Overall – and very similar patterns are found in England, at least until the eclipse of Buckingham in 1629, and in the France of Louis XIII – the result of these changes in both the size and the composition of the peerage, added to the Europe-wide processes which we have already discussed, was considerable upheaval in the established systems of precedence, place, office, status, mutual respect and political influence by which individual members of the elite traditionally related to each other and, even more crucially, to the Crown.[53]

These changes may well have meant that, just as for the expanding gentry of later Elizabethan England, family history was of greater utility to the re-modelled nobility of early seventeenth-century Scotland. As Stone observes in linking intellectual fashion to unsettling social change south of the border:

> Genuine genealogy was cultivated by the older gentry to reassure themselves of their innate superiority over the upstarts; bogus genealogy was cultivated by the new gentry in an effort to clothe their social nakedness, and by the old gentry in the internal jockeying for position in the ancestral pecking order.[54]

Whilst the pictures this conjures up of competitive fabrication among the ermined classes are faintly pleasing, when translated to the paranoid world that was the Jacobean and Caroline court, when superimposed upon the fears and anxieties particularly of a Scottish elite which had grounds for suspicion that *real* influence and *real* prestige were beginning to slip away to London and the English elite, frantic activities in genealogical composition, whether practised by new or old members of the peerage, were in truth indicative of a pervasive lack of self-confidence.

It is difficult not to see the proliferation of assertive Drummond genealogies, for example, as the natural response of an august old family, at last raised to an earldom but acutely conscious of the fact that its long-overdue elevation had taken place in the company of an army of vulgar time-servers and pen-pushers. Similar mixed feelings, of dynastic relief mingled with simmering resentments, may explain the unsubtle triumphalism audible in the 'True Historie of Several Honourable Families of the Name of Scot', a metrical verse promoting a distinguished Border house belatedly elevated to the earldom of Buccleuch, written by Walter Scott of Satchells, who had himself been a companion of the fortunate 1st earl.[55] David Reid likewise suggests that Hume's *History* was published not least because, after the elevation of the Huntly Gordons and the Hamiltons to the marquisate, the reassertion of historic

[53] Smith, *Culture*, 93–124.
[54] Stone, *Crisis*, 23.
[55] Walter Scott, *A True Historie of Several Honourable Families of the Name of Scot*, 2 pts (Edinburgh, 1776).

Douglas precedence within the peerage (culminating in the 11th earl of
Angus himself finally becoming a marquis in 1633) had for several
decades past become a family obsession.[56] For all the brashness and
bombast which characterised confident-seeming texts like 'A breviat of
the genealogie of the honourable surname of the Lesleyes', the 'Genealogy of the Mackenzies' or the numerous copies of Maitland of Lethington's mid-sixteenth-century 'The historical genealogie of the . . . house
of Seton' which were now being made, the very same processes which
had seen men of these surnames catapulted spectacularly into the
earldoms of Leven, Seaforth and Dunfermline (indeed Maitland's
own descendants now exulted in the earldom of Lauderdale) had also
undermined the most precious quality of aristocracy – its seeming
stability, which brought with it effortless superiority, guaranteed precedence and entitlement – to which all continued to aspire.[57]

As if James' and Charles' gently inflating peerage were not enough to
worry traditionalists and *parvenus* alike, the Union of the Crowns was a
source of further uncertainty and foreboding among the Scottish elite. A
fortunate few were, of course, able to take up residence in London and
could believe themselves men of unrivalled influence and station. Some,
like Stirling and Ancram, even owed their peerages to professional success
at the Whitehall court. But for others there was a nagging fear of royal
anglicisation, one disturbing aspect of which was their own monarch's
sudden exposure to the mighty influence of the great English nobility.[58]
The English customs and practices adopted by the court are alleged to
have offended Scottish sensitivities.[59] In an intensely status-conscious
society, where ritual and formality were presumed to express fundamental
political and social values, an increasingly Baroque style of kingship

---

[56] Hume, *History*, x–xi.

[57] [Sir James Balfour?], 'A Breviat of the Genealogie of the Honourable Surname of
the Lesleyes . . . togither with some of ther Cadets': NLS Adv. MS. 17.2.4;
John Mackenzie of Applecross, 'Genealogy of the Mackenzies', NLS Adv. MS.
34.6.27; copies of the 1545 work of Sir Richard Maitland of Lethington, 'The
Historical Genealogie of the . . . House of Seton', Adv. MS. 34.7.4. and in
31.2.2 (i), 34.3.16. and 34.6.19.

[58] K. M. Brown, 'The Scottish Aristocracy, Anglicisation and the Court, 1603–38',
Historical Journal, 36 (1993), 543–76.

[59] See David Stevenson, 'The English Devil of Keeping State: Elite Manners and
the Downfall of Charles I in Scotland', in R. Mason and N. Macdougall (eds),
People and Power in Scotland (Edinburgh, 1992), 126–44. Many previously
influential Scots came to fear marginalisation and loss of power after James'
accession, as Jenny Wormald notes: 'James VI and I: Two Kings or One?',
History, 68 (1983), 187–209.

supposedly alienated many of the Stuart monarchy's traditional supporters in Scotland, convincing them – rightly or wrongly – that their own
interests had been relegated, their Scottish name and titles devalued.
Some embraced the exaggerated 'distancing' and formalism of the court,
in the process developing an even greater self-importance to which a
fashion for genealogy could obviously cater.[60] Others, less confident and
still hankering after recognition, found that they needed to engage in an
unseemly struggle for office and precedence with a much larger number of
usually condescending and often ferociously resourceful English rivals.

This too may explain certain features of the seventeenth-century
Scottish obsession with family history, and particularly – as with James
VI himself – with the coining of ever more incredible superlatives,
designed to impress a sceptical English audience.[61] If the Douglases, for
example, really did wish in the 1620s to be seen as superior in antiquity
to all other houses in Europe, then the flourishing of the claim that they
had originated as early as AD 767 may well have owed a lot to the desire
to better the pretensions of their English counterparts. Similarly the
Drummonds' claim to have originated in the embassy to Scotland of
Maurice, a Mongolian prince from Hungary, during the reign of
Malcolm Canmore, loudly trumpeted by their seventeenth-century
genealogies, can only have been calculated to impress an ever-wider
audience of potential allies and rivals on a widening British stage. The
travails of Sir Maurice Drummond, for example, gentleman-usher to
Queen Henrietta Maria and by 1637 embroiled in a bitter struggle for
precedence with James Hay, earl of Carlisle and viscount Doncaster,
were typical of the intensified difficulties which inspired such a determined attachment to ancient pedigree among the Scottish elite.[62] With

---

[60] Brown, 'Aristocratic Finances', 47–8.

[61] On James' multi-faceted public image, see Maurice Lee Jnr, *Great Britain's
Solomon: James VI and I in His Three Kingdoms* (Urbana, IL, 1990), esp. 153,
and David Allan, 'Prudence and Patronage: The Politics of Culture in
Seventeenth-Century Scotland', *History of European Ideas*, 18 (1994), esp. 472.

[62] Sir Maurice's problems elicited supportive correspondence from Drummond of
Hawthornden, later printed in William Drummond, *Works*, eds John Sage and
Thomas Ruddiman (Edinburgh, 1711), 145–6. On this controversy at court, see
Kevin Sharpe, 'The Image of Virtue: The Court and Household of Charles I,
1625–1642', in David Starkey (ed.), *The English Court: From the Wars of the
Roses to the Civil War* (London, 1987), 245; also, for background, Caroline M.
Hubbard, 'The Role of a Queen Consort: The Household and Court of
Henrietta Maria, 1625–1642', in R.G. Asch and A. M. Birke (eds), *Princes,
Patronage and the Nobility: The Court at the Beginning of the Modern Age, c.
1450–1650* (Oxford, 1991), 393–414.

an expanded Scottish peerage and sudden exposure to the competitive environment of the Stuart British court, unhistorical wishful-thinking of this sort was, perhaps, neither careless nor pointless. It represented the best efforts of Scotland's elite to secure their positions and perquisites in an increasingly turbulent and uncertain world.

It is plain, above all, that kinship and family name were critical social and political facts in seventeenth-century Scotland, a circumstance loaded with far-reaching cultural implications. Perhaps it was ever thus. But that family history and genealogy enjoyed a very substantial upsurge in popularity at that time owed something to rather more transient historical processes. Demographic pressures, social and economic change, and the assimilation of Renaissance values were producing the same response across western Europe: Scotland, conceivably for similar reasons, was no exception in its propitiousness for such studies. Less universal was the impact of an expanding and changing peerage, though this affected English contemporaries too. Most specifically of all, James VI's good fortune in 1603, a happy accident ironically brought about by his own luminous pedigree, had the unforeseen consequence of destabilising the status, and so threatening the precarious self-regard, of his countrymen. Despite such threats, indeed almost certainly because of them, Scotsmen clung to their family identities, their impressive lineages, their noble ancestries, with renewed tenacity. 'A rose by any other name would smell as sweet' an English dramatist had recently had his Italian protagonist suggest.[63] As one can readily appreciate today, when admiring the unstinting effort which must have gone into the 'Memoirs of the family of Rose of Kilravock', compiled by Hugh Rose in the later seventeenth century, such opinions would have cut little ice among the Scots.[64]

I would like to thank Keith Brown and Hamish Scott for advice on this essay, and audiences at the Scottish History seminar at the University of Edinburgh and at the Strathclyde-Glasgow seminar series out of which this volume emerged.

---

[63] *Romeo and Juliet*, II, ii, 43–4.
[64] Copy of Lachlan Shaw, late eighteenth-century abridgement and continuation of Hugh Rose, 'Memoirs of the Family of Rose of Kilravock' (Edinburgh: Adv. MS. 32.6.7).

CHAPTER 8

The Ideological Uses of the Picts, 1707–*c*.1990

Colin Kidd

'I t is nationalism which engenders nations, and not the other way round. Admittedly, nationalism uses the pre-existing, historically inherited proliferation of cultures or cultural wealth, though it uses them very selectively, and it most often transforms them radically. Dead languages can be revived, traditions invented, quite fictitious pristine purities restored.'[1] The late Ernest Gellner's pronouncement on the ficticity of national identities stands at the modernist extreme of an exciting and highly relevant debate about the provenance of nationalism. On the one hand, primordialists point to the historic continuity of ethnic and national groups from medieval, and, sometimes, ancient times:[2] on the other, modernists point to the ways in which during the nineteenth and twentieth centuries the subethnic and highly localist peasantries of eastern Europe and Caucasia were transformed into ethnic nations, not least through the offices of nationalist intellectuals who endowed them with invented national pasts and distinctive written languages.[3]

[1] E. Gellner, *Nations and Nationalism* (Oxford, 1983), 55–6.

[2] See e.g. A. D. Smith, *The Ethnic Origins of Nations* (Oxford, 1986); A. Hastings, *The Construction of Nationhood: Ethnicity, Religion and Nationalism* (Cambridge, 1997).

[3] C. Hann, 'Intellectuals, Ethnic Groups and Nations: Two Late Twentieth-Century Cases', in S. Periwal (ed.), *Notions of Nationalism* (Budapest, 1995); S. Astourian, 'In Search of their Forefathers: National Identity and the Historiography and Politics of Armenian and Azerbaijani Ethnogeneses', in D. V. Schwartz and R. Panossian (eds), *Nationalism and History: The Politics of Nation Building in Post-Soviet Armenia, Azerbaijan and Georgia* (Toronto, 1994); N. Ascherson, *Black Sea: The Birthplace of Civilisation and Barbarism* (London, 1995); F. Mount, 'How to Invent your own Nation', *Times Literary Supplement*, 17 November 1995, 34.

Despite their scepticism of primordialist claims, modernists recognise the need for compelling stories of ethnogenesis. In answer to the question 'Do nations have navels?', Gellner conceded that 'some nations possessed ancient navels', but argued that more 'have navels invented for them by their own nationalist propaganda, and some are altogether navel-less'.[4] By Gellner's lights, Scotland is an anatomical freak, a nation with two navels: one an authentic historic navel representative of a deep continuity from the Middle Ages of a lively Scottish national consciousness, the second involving modern retailoring of some scanty rags bequeathed from the ancient past. Traditionally, the Scots – a historic nation whose consciousness can be clearly documented from at least the turn of the fourteenth century – have traced their ethnogenesis back to the ancient west Highland settlement of Dalriada by Gaelic Scots from Ireland, and beyond.[5] However, the shadowy Picts of Scotland's distant past have offered an alternative navel – ancient, yet also largely fabricated – for disaffected intellectuals. From the early eighteenth century through to the late twentieth century a variety of groups in quest of aboriginal historical legitimation, not only Scottish nationalists, but also Jacobites, celtophobic champions of Lowland Scots, a noted Marxist-Diffusionist, and, most recently, Ulster loyalists, have appropriated and reshaped an elusive Pictish antiquity to serve contemporary ideological needs.

Before the eighteenth century the Picts held very little ideological significance. From the fourteenth century the established identity of the Scottish nation was based upon the history of the Dalriadic Scots from the supposed foundation of their monarchy in the west Highlands in 330 BC. This version of Scottish ethnogenesis was set out around 1370 in the chronicle of John of Fordun, given a humanist gloss by Hector Boece in his *Scotorum Historiae a prima gentis origine* (1527), and given a radical anti-monarchical spin by George Buchanan in his *De Iure Regni apud Scotos* (1579) and *Historia rerum Scoticarum* (1582).[6]

Within this scheme of Scottish history, the Picts were generally believed to have been extirpated during the reign of Kenneth MacAlpin. Without any continuing influence on medieval and early modern Scotland, the Picts, their manners and their institutions, were an irrelevance.

[4] E. Gellner, *Nationalism* (London, 1997), ch. 15, 'Do Nations have Navels?', 96.
[5] C. Kidd, *Subverting Scotland's Past* (Cambridge, 1993), ch. 2; W. Ferguson, *The Identity of the Scottish Nation: An Historic Quest* (Edinburgh, 1998), ch. 3.
[6] R. A. Mason, 'Scotching the Brut: Politics, History and National Myth in Sixteenth-century Britain', in Mason (ed.), *Scotland and England 1286–1815* (Edinburgh, 1987); Ferguson, *Identity of the Scottish Nation*, chs 4, 5.

In antiquarian circles, however, there was a growing interest in the Picts from the late seventeenth century. Sir Robert Sibbald (1641–1722), for example, discussed the Picts in works such as his *History, Ancient and Modern, of the Sheriffdoms of Fife and Kinross* (1710), while in 1706 there appeared a *History of the Picts* which has been attributed to Henry Maule of Melgum.[7]

The Picts first achieve ideological salience in the work of an emigré Jacobite priest, Father Thomas Innes (1662–1744), whose *Critical Essay on the Ancient Inhabitants of the Northern Parts of Britain, or Scotland* (1729) shattered the prevailing paradigm of Scottish ethnogenesis. By comparing regnal lists and detecting scribal errors in the transcription of Gaelic royal names by Latinate Lowland monks, Innes, influenced by the new diplomatic scholarship pioneered by Jean Mabillon and the Maurist Benedictines, was able to show that the eleventh- and twelfth-century chronicles of Veremundus and the Highlanders John Campbell and Cornelius Hybernicus, upon which Boece had relied, were forgeries from no earlier than the fifteenth century. Thus Innes showed that the king-lists before the era of Fergus MacErch right back to the founding monarch Fergus MacFerquhard were unreliable. Innes also explained the ideological impetus behind these hoaxes, namely to provide precedents for the violent removal of James III in 1488, and the patriotic legend of Scottish origins that, emerging during the War of Independence, had been consolidated in Fordun's late fourteenth-century chronicle. As a result, the historical evidence for the Whig interpretation of Scotland's ancient constitution lay in tatters. However, Innes' scrupulous scholarship was vitiated by his committed Jacobitism, and he took the opportunity to replace the discredited Whig history of the Dalriadic Scottish monarchy with a royalist account of the ancient Picts. Not only was this Pictish history founded upon a shaky king-list which contained a mixture of bogus and *bona fide* materials, but it extended even further back into the mists of antiquity – to a legendary King Cruithne – than the origin myth Innes had just exploded. On this basis, the otherwise sceptical Innes proclaimed Scotland the oldest monarchy in Europe. The hereditary Pictish kingdom had been united to the kingdom of the Scots by Kenneth MacAlpin on the un-whiggish basis of

---

[7] Robert Sibbald, *The History of the Sheriffdoms of Fife and Kinross* (Edinburgh, 1710), 4–18, in Sibbald, *A Collection of Several Treatises in Folio* (Edinburgh, 1739); [Henry Maule], *History of the Picts* (Edinburgh, 1706). For the place of the Picts in early modern Scottish historiography, see W. Ferguson, 'George Buchanan and the Picts', *Scottish Tradition* (1990–1), 18–32 and *Identity of the Scottish Nation*.

blood and conquest. MacAlpin traced his descent in both the Pictish and the Scottish royal lines, and had conquered – without extirpating – the Pictish kingdom. Innes even aired the notion that the Stewarts themselves were of Galloway Pictish stock.[8]

Innes' Pictish fantasy failed to take hold as the dominant Jacobite treatment of the Scottish past. Just as Scottish Whiggism was indebted to the myth of the elective Scottish monarchy, so the existing royalist-Jacobite interpretation of the Scottish past, formulated by Sir George Mackenzie of Rosehaugh in the 1680s, drew upon an anti-Buchananite reading of the same disputed events of Fergus MacFerquhard's inauguration in 330 BC and the operation of the royal succession thereafter within the kingdom of Dalriada.[9] Innes had pulled the rug out from beneath *both* Whig and Jacobite propagandists. Some Jacobite historians, including the episcopalian champion Walter Goodall (d. 1766), attempted to undo Innes' deconstructive scholarship. Goodall turned to geography – in particular to the exegesis of geographical expressions used by classical commentators and poets, most notably Claudian (c.370–410) – to retrieve the claim that in ancient times there had been a Scottish monarchy in the territory of Scotland. Claudian's *Panegyric on the Fourth Consulship of the Emperor Honorius* seemed to indicate that the Scoti had been located across the sea in an ice-bound Ierne.[10] The Ierne of the ancients, according to Goodall and to the Whiggish school of historical geography represented by Alexander Taitt, both of whom wished to conserve the old legend of Scottish origins, was not Ireland, but Strathearn, or more generally, Scotland north of the Forth and Clyde. Against the scepticism of Innes, Goodall and Taitt held that the Scots had been in Scotland during the disputed centuries prior to the accession of Fergus MacErch.[11] Thus, although Innes had succeeded in undermining the powerful myth of Scottish origins which had formed the basis of the nation's identity between the fourteenth and the eighteenth centuries, he had not managed to establish a new Pictish identity. The Picts remained peripheral within

[8]   Thomas Innes, *A Critical Essay on the Ancient Inhabitants of the Northern Parts of Britain, or Scotland* (1729: Edinburgh, 1879), esp. 72, 80, 94–5, 104, 163–7, 407.

[9]   George Mackenzie, *A Defence of the Antiquity of the Royal Line of Scotland*, in *Works*, ii, 370–8; Mackenzie, *The Antiquity of the Royal Line of Scotland, further Cleared and Defended*, in *Works*, ii, 404–10.

[10] W. Barr (ed.), *Claudian's Panegyric on the Fourth Consulate of Honorius* (Liverpool, 1981), 30–3.

[11] Walter Goodall, *An Introduction to the History and Antiquities of Scotland* (trans. from the Latin of 1739: Edinburgh, 1773), 2–16, Alexander Taitt, *The Roman Account of Britain and Ireland in Answer to Father Innes* (Edinburgh, 1741).

the nation's historic consciousness, though, as we shall see, still ripe for ideological appropriation.

From the late seventeenth century there had been some antiquarian speculation that the Picts had been a people of Germanic or Gothic extraction.[12] In the course of the eighteenth century some champions of Lowland Scots used this misidentification to argue for the common ethnic roots of the English and Scottish peoples, which provided, by extension, an additional justification for the Union of 1707. The antiquary and politician Sir John Clerk of Penicuik (1676–1755) had been active both in negotiations and as a pamphleteer on the incorporating unionist side during the reign of Queen Anne. Subsequently, he wrote a Latin manuscript treatise, 'Historia de imperio Britannico', which recounted – in unionist terms, of course – the story of Britain from ancient times through to the Union of 1707. During the disturbance of 1745 Clerk took the precaution of hiding this Whiggish work down a coalmine on his estate.[13] A few years before the Jacobite rebellion Clerk also wrote a less well-known paper for the Philosophical Society of Edinburgh entitled 'An Enquiry into the Ancient Languages of Great Britain'. Clerk advanced the bizarre philological claim that Scots had not been imported by the Saxons, but was indigenous. Neither the 'imaginary extension' of the kingdom of Northumbria, nor the marriage of the Saxon princess Margaret to Malcolm Canmore, nor the 'inroads' of Edward I 'had any manner of concern in the introduction of the Scotch Saxon language. We must carry it much higher, or contradict all that antiquity can produce for its origin.' The language spoken by more than three-quarters of the inhabitants of eighteenth-century Britain, the people of England and the Scottish Lowlands, was in essentials the same spoken by their ancient British ancestors at the coming of Julius Caesar. Even in ancient times, according to Clerk, the Celtic languages had been confined to the Scottish Highlands, Ireland, Wales and Cornwall. Clerk's argument cleverly promoted a shared British identity without sacrificing pride in the Scottish past. Not only was Scots an ancient

---

[12] See e.g. James Wallace, *An Account of the Islands of Orkney* (London, 1700), 105–7; Christopher Irvin, *Historiae Scoticae Nomenclatura Latino-Vernacula* (Edinburgh, 1682), 186; *Britannia* (1695 edn), 1081.

[13] I. G. Brown, 'Sir John Clerk of Penicuik (1676–1755): Aspects of a Virtuoso Life' (Cambridge University Ph.D., 1980); D. Duncan, 'Introduction', Sir John Clerk of Penicuik, *History of the Union of Scotland and England*, ed. and trans. D. Duncan, Scottish History Society (Edinburgh, 1993).

native of Scotland, but Clerk claimed that it remained purer and less corrupt than English.[14]

Clerk's position was shared by other scholars in this field. The Reverend Lachlan Shaw in his *History of the Province of Moray* (1775) argued that the Picts had come originally from Scandinavia, and that the Pictish tongue, like English, Saxon and Danish, was one of 'the various dialects of the Gothic and Teutonic languages'. Even in north-east Scotland to this day, Shaw claimed, 'the illiterate peasants use the broad Scottish or Buchan dialect, which is manifestly the Pictish'. Indeed, the ancestors of Clan Chattan, a confederal grouping which included the Macphersons, were, Shaw believed, the ancient north German tribe of Catti mentioned by Tacitus in the *Germania*.[15] Curiously, the primary begetter of the Ossianic cult, James Macpherson (1736–96), also considered the historic ethnic origins of his clan to be Germanic.[16] Macpherson's obituary in the *Scots Magazine* is evidence for the wide currency of this view: 'This gentleman was descended from one of the most ancient families in the north of Scotland, being cousin-german to the Chief of the clan of the Macphersons, who deduce their origin from the ancient Catti of Germany.'[17]

In the late eighteenth century these idle antiquarian speculations were to fuel the racialist Lowland-focused Scoto-Britishness of John Pinkerton (1758–1826). Although in some respects conventionally patriotic, not least through antiquarian labours into Scottish literature and artefacts, Pinkerton championed only – what he believed to be – the dominant non-Celtic aspects of the Scottish past. Curiously, it was Pinkerton's interest in middle Scots literature which first drew him to the Picts. A convinced opponent of the cult of Ossian and its underlying historicity, Pinkerton was keen to nail the offensive assumption that Scotland's ancient high literature was Gaelic, as displayed in fragments of an epic dating from the third century AD. Moreover, aware of the prejudices that Scots was a mere 'dialect of the English' and that the achievement of the Makars had been built upon imitation of Chaucer, Pinkerton endowed Scots literature with an ancient Pictish pedigree in his 'Essay on the origin of Scotish poetry', appended to his edition of *Ancient Scotish Poems* (1786). Scots and

---

[14] John Clerk, 'An Enquiry into the Ancient Languages of Great Britain; Being the Copy of a Paper Intended for the Philosophical Society at Edinburgh, 1742', in John Nichols (ed.), *Bibliotheca Topographica Britannica*, 8 vols (London, 1780–90), iii, 362–84.

[15] Lachlan Shaw, *The History of the Province of Moray* (Edinburgh, 1775), 50, 167.

[16] C. Kidd, 'Macpherson, Burns and the Politics of Sentiment', *Scotlands*, 4 (1997), 29; C. Kidd, *British Identities before Nationalism* (Cambridge, 1999), 201–2.

[17] *Scots Magazine*, 58 (April 1796), 221.

English, maintained Pinkerton, were both of ancient Scandinavian provenance, the former through the Picts from whom 'the whole inhabitants
of the low and rich countries of Scotland are descended': 'the Picts coming
from the north of Scandinavia, and the Saxons from the south, the
languages were as nearly allied as Scottish and English.' However, as
the Picts had migrated to Britain, Pinkerton argued, four or five centuries
before the Saxons, the Scots-Pictish tongue, though a 'sister language' of
the Saxon-English, was purer and less corrupt, because it was 'an elder
daughter of the Gothic and more like the mother'.[18]

Pinkerton went on to establish the place of the Picts within a wider
European context. In his *Dissertation on the Origin and Progress of the
Scythians or Goths* (1787) he related the history of Europe largely in
terms of the westward expansion from Asia of a superior race of Gothic
Scythians who encountered in Europe the savage Celts. 'As the history
of North America is the history, not of the natives, but of the English
there,' wrote Pinkerton, 'so the history of Europe is that of the Goths in
Europe.' The Picts of ancient Caledonia, or the Piks, as Pinkerton came
to refer to them, were, of course, Gothic Scythians, traced from the
Peukini of the Danubian region. Their Lowland descendants were tall,
fair and industrious, in sharp contrast to the small, dark lazy Celts of the
Highlands. Yet, the union of Scot and Pik, through what Pinkerton
ascribed to the conquest by the Piks under Kenneth MacAlpin of the
Dalriadic Scots, had been followed by the gradual loss of the Pictish
name, until in the eleventh century Scotia, the former name of Ireland,
had been applied to Scotland, a 'confusion' arising from 'the vanity and
affectation of the Irish clergy who were established in Scotland, and
were the sole instructors of the people'. 'Had the old name of the
country, Pikland, been retained,' lamented Pinkerton in his *Enquiry into
the History of Scotland* (1789), 'the fables of the Highland bards would
never have been infectious.' As it was 'a line of dunces' controlled and
distorted the nation's historical memory. Moreover, this new Scottish
identity – 'a Celtic edifice of falsehood and nonsense' – was consolidated
during the propaganda debates of the War of Independence: 'After 1301
no nominal Scottishman would have sought to honour the Piks, though
his real ancestors, at the expense of the Scots, his name-fathers.'
However, Pinkerton, conscious that 'two words, Scots and Scotland

---

[18] John Pinkerton, 'An Essay on the Origin of Scottish Poetry', in Pinkerton (ed.),
Ancient Scotish Poems, 2 vols (London, 1786), i, lii–liii; P. O'Flaherty, 'John
Pinkerton (1758–1826): Champion of the Makars', *Studies in Scottish Literature*,
xiii (1978), 159–95; Ferguson, *Identity of the Scottish Nation*, ch. 12.

have hitherto totally ruined our history', aimed to restore to Scotland her lost – and considerably more eminent – Pictish identity.[19]

Pinkerton's outrageous and polemical scholarship led to a minor flurry of interest in the Picts. In 1818 the thoughts of some earlier authorities on the Picts were reissued in a single volume as *Miscellanea Pictica*.[20] Sir Walter Scott, who devoted a substantial article in the *Quarterly Review* to the Pictish debate, was a convinced opponent of Pinkerton.[21] However, in Scott's novel *The Antiquary* the eponymous hero, the Whiggish Jonathan Oldbuck of Monkbarns, is a Pinkertonian, while Oldbuck's antiquarian sparring partner, the Tory Sir Arthur Wardour, is an upholder of the Chalmers–Ritson thesis. Oldbuck and Wardour disagree strongly not only over whether the Picts were Gothic or Celtic, but over the vexed issue of what to call them. Wardour refers straightforwardly to the Picts, but Oldbuck presents a parody of Pinkertonian nomenclature insisting that the Picts be known either as the Piks, Pikar, Pihar, Piochtar, Pioghter, or Peughtar.[22] Although Pinkerton had some powerful detractors, including George Chalmers, author of the monumental *Caledonia* (1807–24) and the Northumbrian Joseph Ritson, who contested his claim that the Picts were of Gothic rather than Celtic descent,[23] there were several influential defenders of Pinkerton's thesis, though not of his virulent anti-Celtic racism. The most prominent Pinkertonians, unsurprisingly, were to be found among the champions of the Scots language, figures such as John Jamieson (1759–1838), renowned as the compiler of *An Etymological Dictionary of the Scottish Language* (1808) and James Sibbald (1745–1803), who authored a *Chronicle of Scottish Poetry* (1802).[24] As Pinkerton

[19] John Pinkerton, *Modern Geography*, 2 vols (London, 1802), i, 146; Pinkerton, *An Enquiry into the History of Scotland* 2 vols (1789: Edinburgh, 1814), i, 232, 234, 238, 251, 254, 339; ii, 35.

[20] *Miscellanea Pictica* (Edinburgh, 1818) included Maule's *History of the Picts* and Sibbald's discussion of the Picts extracted from his *History of Fife and Kinross*.

[21] Walter Scott, 'Ancient History of Scotland', *Miscellaneous Prose Works*, 28 vols (Edinburgh, 1834–6), xx, 319–67.

[22] Scott, *The Antiquary* (1816), ch. 6.

[23] George Chalmers, *Caledonia* (1807–24); Joseph Ritson, *Annals of the Caledonians, Picts and Scots*, 2 vols (Edinburgh, 1828); B. H. Bronson, *Joseph Ritson, Scholar-at-Arms* (Berkeley, CA, 1938), i, 200–14.

[24] John Jamieson, 'A Dissertation on the Origin of the Scottish Language', in Jamieson, *An Etymological Dictionary of the Scottish Language*, 2 vols (Edinburgh, 1808); Alexander Murray, 'Observations on the History and Language of the Pehts', *Archaeologia Scotica: or Transactions of the Society of Antiquaries of Scotland*, ii (Edinburgh, 1822), James Sibbald, 'Observations on the Origins of the Terms Picti, Caledonii and Scotti', in Sibbald, *Chronicle of Scottish Poetry*, 4 vols (Edinburgh, 1802).

had hoped, a Pictish descent conferred an ancient legitimacy on the Scots tongue, which was much valued by those involved in its preservation.

The line taken by Pinkerton was widely influential within the higher ranks of British physical anthropology, surfacing in the work of James Cowles Prichard and T. H. Huxley.[25] Pinkertonian ideas also helped to shape the anti-Celtic Teutonic racialism of nineteenth-century Lowland Scotland. As late as the 1870s the nationalist historian William Burns complained in his *History of the War of Independence* about 'one class of antiquarian writers whose mission seems to be, to set up the Pictish people of olden time as against the Scots'. In the eyes of Burns, these 'Pictish advocates' who saw the Scots as a 'contemptible race', together with Saxonist racialists, undermined the very idea of Scottish nation-hood.[26]

In the course of the nineteenth century the matter of the Picts became confined more narrowly to internal debates within historical and anthropological circles, not least those surrounding the work of W. F. Skene.[27] However, John Buchan's gruesome tale 'No Man's Land' (1899: published in collection of 1902), which related the experiences of a philologist who encounters the lost race of Picts, pointed to the mythic potential of the Picts for Scottish writers.[28] Indeed, the Picts became something of an obsession for writers during the literary renaissance of the 1920s and 1930s. Not only did this ancient people become prized totems of an emergent nationalist intelligentsia, but they were also endowed with a Marxist significance.

The importance of the Picts is captured in the title of the short-lived nationalist literary periodical the *Pictish Review* (1927–8). Its editor was the proponent of a Roman Catholic and Gaelic Scottishness Ruaraidh Erskine of Mar, while Christopher Grieve (Hugh MacDiarmid) also featured prominently. Erskine of Mar's first editorial declared the unashamedly – but obscure – Pictish outlook of the journal:

[25] James Cowles Prichard, *Researches into the Physical History of Man* (1813: reprint, with introduction by G. W. Stocking, Chicago and London, 1973), 506–7; 'Professor Huxley on Political Ethnology', *Anthropological Review*, viii (1870), 199.

[26] William Burns, *The Scottish War of Independence*, 2 vols (Glasgow, 1874), i, 9–10.

[27] J. Anderson, 'William Forbes Skene: *Celtic Scotland* versus *Caledonia*', *Scottish Historical Review*, 46 (1967), 140–50; R. M. Dorson, *The British Folklorists* (London, 1968), 408; Ferguson, *Identity of the Scottish Nation*, ch. 13.

[28] John Buchan, 'No-Man's-Land', in Buchan, *Supernatural Tales* (Edinburgh, 1997).

As its name implies, the *Pictish Review* has been set on foot in order to present a Pictish view of things in general; to re-elucidate the values implicit, and explicit, in Pictish history and civilization; and further, to impart a turn to current affairs, and the interpretation of them, which shall be conformable to the genius and inherited tendencies of the Pictish nation. In fine, we propose to restore the name of Pict to the politico-cultural map of Scotland, from which it has been banished, for no good reason apparent to us.[29]

However, despite its name and this proposal to recover a lost Pictish-ness, the *Pictish Review* was decidedly not an antiquarian enterprise, as Grieve made clear in the first issue:

The Scottish spirit has been largely dissipated in mere antiquarianism. The kilt has become of more importance than the Gaelic language and culture. At the opposite pole of our national tradition Scots Vernacular revivalists are more concerned with making lists of words than with utilising them in the creation of literature, and most of their conceptions of Scots matters spring from the decadent post-Burns period, and takes no account of the golden age of Dunbar and the Auld Makars.[30]

The *Pictish Review* would encourage a rejection of decadence, of the kitsch Scottishness represented by the Burns cult which Grieve so despised, and in some measure of the bogus Highlandism of tartanry and sentimental Jacobitism.[31] Thus although Erskine of Mar was a Gaelic enthusiast whose values were reflected in the pages of the *Review*, the identification of the journal with the Picts acted to distance it from the worst excesses of kitsch Gaelicism. The Picts represented an alternative to the fetishising of the familiar in Scottish history: Mariolatry, Jacobit-ism, and the cult of the Bard. Instead the Picts stood for authenticity in the Scottish past, for historic values untainted by the sentimental modern co-option of historical colour. Moreover, the Picts were also

[29] *Pictish Review*, no. 1 (Nov. 1927), 1.
[30] C. M. Grieve, 'Towards a "Scottish Idea"', *Pictish Review*, no. 1 (Nov. 1927), 1–2.
[31] A. Bold, *MacDiarmid: Christopher Murray Grieve, A Critical Biography* (1988: London, 1990), 221–2, 264–5; R. Watson, *MacDiarmid* (Milton Keynes, 1985), 13–14.

capable of inspiring the reintegration of Scotland, a Celtic people who transcended the Highland–Lowland, Gaelic–Teutonic split. Pagan Pictishness also suggested an alternative to the sterile presbyterianism against which Scotland's emergent secular intelligentsia railed, and which, of course, held very little appeal for Erskine of Mar, who wished to restore an organic pre-Reformation Scottishness.[32]

Such themes recur in the work of Neil Gunn (1891–1973), whose novels are characterised by a passionate concern with rootedness, ancestry and the disintegration of historic communities. Gunn was openly nationalist. He joined the National Party of Scotland (NPS) in 1929, and would serve on its Council and that of the successor Scottish National Party (SNP) created by the fusion of the NPS and the Scottish Party in 1934. Gunn was also an opponent of Calvinist repression, against which pagan antiquity offered an alternative belief system. Moreover, while a champion of Gaeldom and of the long-suffering peoples of northern Scotland, he was reluctant to insert a divisive wedge between Highlands and Lowlands.[33]

Born and brought up in the fishing village of Dunbeath in Caithness, Gunn was deeply influenced by his locality and its history. Among his novels *Butcher's Broom* (1934) deals with the Highland Clearances, and *The Silver Darlings* (1941) with those cleared to the coastal communities whose precarious livelihoods depend upon fishing for herring, the silver darlings of the title. However, Gunn was also fascinated by the remote past, and he acknowledged a Pictish ancestry and identity, partly in sport, partly as an act of local piety.[34] The shadowy Picts and their struggles formed the subject of his novel *Sun Circle* (1933).

Compressing the threatening arrivals in the far north-east of both Christianity and the Vikings into the same vague distant epoch, *Sun Circle* depicts a Pictish world in crisis. The Picts live in separated tribal communities, the Ravens on the coast, inland the aboriginal and

---

[32] Erskine of Mar, 'Culture and Presbyterianism', *Pictish Review*, no. 4 (Feb. 1928), 45; R. Finlay, *Independent and Free: Scottish Politics and the Origins of the Scottish National Party 1918–1945* (Edinburgh, 1994), 31–3.

[33] F. R. Hart and J. B. Pick, *Neil M. Gunn: A Highland Life* (1981: Edinburgh, 1985), 109–15. For evidence of Gunn's active involvement in nationalist politics, see Finlay, *Independent and Free*, 115–17, 178–80.

[34] Hart and Pick, *Gunn*, 14. Distant antiquity – and its mystical continuities with the present – was a preoccupation of Gunn's. In his novels the presence near modern Highland communities of standing stones and chambered cairns symbolised these deep connections. An excellent example is *The Silver Bough* (1948: Glasgow, 1985).

dwarfish Finlags, to the south the hostile Logenmen, who see in seaborne Viking marauding a chance to launch their own raids upon the Ravens' cattle. The Ravens have become nominal Christians, the local priest Molrua exerting authority through Silis, the fanatical wife of the local chief – and hen-pecked pagan – Drust. Under the Christian surface of Raven society, the old ways of Druidism persist, and under threat of Viking invasion, the men of the tribe repair to the pagan grove and the rites of the Druid Master. The novel is seen largely through the eyes of the Master's perceptive young disciple, Aniel (a scarcely disguised Neil Gunn), who finds himself disaffected from the harsh sacrificial demands of the dark gods, enjoys what seems an inordinate number of vivid – but wholesome – Lawrentian orgasms with the Pictish heroine Breeta (who narrowly escapes sacrifice herself), and witnesses the passing of the old society, its leaders massacred by the Vikings.[35]

Although Gunn is critical of the intolerant Druid Gilbrude, in general, the old pagan rites are used as a foil for an intrusive Christian doctrine less integral to the ways of the community. Among the Pictish folk, who did not have to endure the oppressions of Calvinist Scotland, sexuality had been natural and guiltfree. The moral values of the pagan Picts, moreover, were instinctive. The Picts took 'no heed of the morrow' in their giving, with no regard to a future reward in heaven:

> [A]nyone being rewarded by man or god for giving to the poor
> would grow hot with shame. A young hunter comes with a
> piece of flesh to an old woman . . . By giving to the old woman
> you have defeated the malignant, and smile in your strength,
> and your heart grows warm and your youth invincible . . .
> What sort of people, then, did Christ live amongst that he had
> to tell them to give to the poor . . .?[36]

Above all, paganism was in the blood, an autochthonous religion which answered the needs of the people. The Christian God was 'a white pale god, pleasant in the sun', but without power in times of turmoil and crisis:

> A puny crying god, who was himself sacrificed. No power in
> him, no fierceness; no storm set in black brows, no wind-
> thrashing vengeance, no terror; no sacrifices to be made to him,

---

[35] Neil Gunn, *Sun Circle* (1933: Edinburgh, 1996).
[36] Ibid., 85.

no appeasement, no dark drink. What did he know of the flesh and the vitals? And what of the cravings in the loins and in the womb of the earth?

The pagan religion of the Picts, on the other hand, 'went deeper . . . It ran with their blood as it had run with the blood of their ancestors.'[37]

There is also an implied contrast between the Picts and the conquering imperialists of modern Britain. Gunn perceived in this 'dark intricate people', with their love of music and fun, a stoic resignation. The ambitions of this 'affectionate people, desiring peace rather than strife' were confined to 'a profound persistence rather than a conquering or leading'.[38]

Gunn's nationalist concerns with the loss of organic community find a distorted echo in the Marxist-Diffusionism of James Leslie Mitchell (1901–35), better known by his occasional pen-name, Lewis Grassic Gibbon. Mitchell was no nationalist, though an elegiac lament for the passing of an older Scotland can be detected in *Sunset Song* and the successor novels of *A Scots Quair*. Other loyalties overrode his patriotism. Throughout his oeuvre, in his Scottish novels, his overseas tales, his science fiction and in his ethnographic writings, Mitchell showed himself a loyal Diffusionist.[39] In particular, he was a disciple of the chief prophets of Diffusionism, Grafton Elliot Smith (1871–1937), an Australian-born anthropologist, who served as Professor of Anatomy at Manchester, and later at University College, London, and W. J. Perry (1887–1950), reader in cultural anthropology at UCL.[40] Basically, Diffusionists believed that all civilisation originated on the rich fertile banks of the upper Nile where primitive nomads first adopted a settled way of life, which gradually spread into other regions. Settlement,

---

[37] Ibid., 191.

[38] Ibid., 267.

[39] D. F. Young, *Beyond the Sunset: A Study of James Leslie Mitchell (Lewis Grassic Gibbon)* (Aberdeen, 1973), 2–3, 7–30; K. Dixon, 'Letting the side down: some remarks on James Leslie Mitchell's vision of history', *Etudes écossaises*, I (Grenoble, 1992); D. Gifford, *Neil M. Gunn and Lewis Grassic Gibbon* (Edinburgh, 1983).

[40] G. Stocking, *After Tylor: British Social Anthropology, 1888–1951* (London, 1996), 208–20; H. Kuklick, *The Savage Within: The Social History of British Anthropology, 1885–1945* (Cambridge, 1991), 55. For Mitchell's view of Elliot Smith, see his typescript 'Grafton Elliot Smith: A Student of Mankind', published in Young, *Beyond the Sunset*, Appendix I, 141–5. Young also notes, 7, that Elliot Smith wrote a 'flattering' introduction to Mitchell's anthropological work *The Conquest of the Maya* (1934).

however, also brought – in time – property, states for the defence of property, and thought control in the form of religion. Writing in the 1930s, Mitchell had fixed opinions about where civilisation had led humankind, to the Great War, to the Depression and to the drabness – for the majority – of urban life. To Mitchell Marxism and Diffusionism offered complementary analyses of the ills of modern society, which he dramatised in various different genres, including the science-fiction tale *Three Go Back* (1932), in which the three surviving passengers – a lady novelist whose lover had been killed in the Great War, an arms manufacturer and the leader of the League of Militant Pacifists – of an airship downed over the Atlantic in a seismic timewarp find themselves twenty-five thousand years back into the past on the unstable continent of Atlantis. There they encounter a race of Cro-Magnards – peaceful, egalitarian, stateless, religionless, guiltless and freeloving (by way of consensual seasonal mating exchanges). Identified as the first future Europeans, these Cro-Magnards – significantly – speak a non-Indo-European tongue, a form of proto-Basque. (In 1892 the eminent Celticist Sir John Rhys had proposed the influential thesis that Pictish – like Basque – had been a non-Indo-European language.) Though struggling against the elements, ferocious sabre-toothed tigers and savage Neanderthals, the Cro-Magnards of Atlantis are a happy un-corrupted people free from the taint of agrarian-religious civilisation which will arise along the Nile around 4000 BC.[41]

Marxist-Diffusionism also surfaced in *A Scots Quair* and helped to shape Mitchell's distinctive interpretation of Scottish history, found in an essay entitled 'The Antique Scene', which Mitchell contributed to a volume co-authored with Hugh MacDiarmid. Scotland's first inhabitants during the Golden Age of nomadic peoples which preceded the spread of the Archaic Civilisation from Egypt were hunters of pre-dominantly Maglemosian stock – 'dark and sinewy and agile' – who had the good fortune to be 'cultureless', lacking both religion and social organisation. Eventually newcomers brought the Archaic Civilisation to Scotland, establishing agriculture and the religion of stone circles. However, this early stage of civilisation was 'singularly peaceful and

---

[41] James Leslie Mitchell, *Three Go Back* (1932: London, 1986), for Diffusionist analyses see esp. 90–1, 119, 124–5, 136–7, 142, 156, 171, 174–7, 202. A more recent edition of *Three Go Back* was published in Edinburgh in 1995. Mitchell also provided a futuristic complement to the Diffusionist arguments presented here in his novel *Gay Hunter* (1934: Edinburgh, 1989), see esp. 80, 91, 104, 106–7, 115, 143. For the emergence of the non-Indo-European hypothesis, see K. Forsyth, *Language in Pictland* (Utrecht, 1997), 8.

undisturbed', a tranquillity shattered with the advent of bronzework, the ability to wage 'organized warfare', and its savage practitioner, the ferocious Kelt. In Scotland a 'conquering military caste' of Kelts imposed themselves as overlords upon a population of peaceful Maglemosian-Mediterranean Picts, but contributed nothing of value to a culture 'miscalled Keltic'. The vast majority of the Scottish population remained Pictish – though from the ninth century were no longer known as such, an amalgam of the land's peaceful pre-Keltic inhabitants, while Scotland was ruled by a 'thin strand' of alien Normanised Keltic gentry, 'one of the great curses of the Scottish scene, quick, avaricious, unintelligent, quarrelsome, cultureless and uncivilizable'.[42]

In *Sunset Song* Mitchell celebrates the values of this ancient Pictish stock – the only hope for the regeneration of Scotland – even as the Old Peasant Scotland disappears in the face of relentless commercialisation, a process hastened by the Great War, which effects the mobilisation, and then the slaughter, of the flower of rural manhood. In the rural community which he describes, Mitchell contrasts the remnants of the Elder People of Pictish stock, with their deep attachment to the land and to farming as a way of life, with the allegiance of incoming carpetbaggers to the cash nexus. Continuity is symbolised by the circle of stones at Blawearie to which Chris Guthrie repairs to meditate and within which her new husband, the radical Reverend Colquohoun, dedicates a memorial to the four young men of Kinraddie – 'the Last of the Peasants, the last of the Old Scots folk' – who died in the Great War: 'It was the old Scotland that perished then, and we may believe that never again will the old speech and the old songs, the old curses and the old benedictions, rise but with alien efforts to our lips.' Scotland's best hope for organic renewal is to tap the roots of her original Pictish stock, but, deeply pessimistic, Mitchell retreats into elegy and, eventually, despair, in the face of an all-encroaching so-called civilisation.[43]

Another aspect of these interwar anxieties about Scottish identity was the fear that Scotland's traditional presbyterian ethos was threatened by the values associated with an immigrant Irish Catholic population. During this period anti-Catholic political movements emerged in the cities, most notably John Cormack's Protestant Action in Edinburgh.

---

[42] Lewis Grassic Gibbon, 'The Antique Scene', reprinted in Gibbon, *The Speak of the Mearns* (Edinburgh, 1994), esp. 92–5.

[43] Lewis Grassic Gibbon, *A Scots Quair* (1932–4: Harmondsworth, 1986), *Sunset Song*, 193; Young, *Beyond the Sunset*, 14, 91–103; Gifford, *Gunn and Grassic Gibbon*, 79–81, 87.

Hibernophobic prejudice was not confined to the Protestant working class, but was shared by the more respectable members of the Scottish establishment. Andrew Dewar Gibb (1888–1974), the Regius Professor of Private Law at Glasgow University between 1934 and 1958 and founder of the Scottish Party, articulated a nationalism of the right which included denigration of what he perceived as the alien and deleterious Irish Catholic presence in Scottish society. Even ministers of the kirk inveighed against the Irish menace, and a virulently nativist report was presented to the General Assembly in 1923.[44] It may be no more than a coincidence that Francis Diack, one of the leading Pictish scholars of this era, should underplay the arrival of the Dalriadic Scots from Ireland in the making of Scottish culture. Building on the arguments of Skene, Diack argued, that the language of the Picts was Old Gaelic. From his investigations of toponyms and Pictish inscriptions, Diack showed that, far from being an Irish importation, Gaelic was the indigenous language of the 'native Cruthni', or Picts. One would hestitate to ascribe broader ideological motives to Diack's highly technical scholarship were it not for the insistence upon a 'non-Dalriadic', and hence 'non-Irish', provenance for Scotland's Celtic culture:

> If the foregoing analysis is correct, there is not the least trace of anything that can be called un-Goidelic in the history of the sources from which it is derived. There is plenty, it is true, that is un-Irish, but that is merely an awkward fact for the theory that explains Scottish Goidelic, language and place-names, as an importation from Ireland within historical times.[45]

Since the 1920s and 1930s the Picts have not featured prominently in the Scottish political firmament, though Neal Ascherson has reported on the

[44] Finlay, *Independent and Free*, 94; Finlay, 'Nationalism, Race, Religion and the Irish Question in Inter-War Scotland', *Innes Review*, xlii (1991), 46–67; S. J. Brown, '"Outside the Covenant": The Scottish Presbyterian Churches and Irish immigration 1922–38', *Innes Review*, xlii (1991), 19–45; T. Gallagher, *Glasgow, the Uneasy Peace: Religious Tension in Modern Scotland* (Manchester, 1987); I. Maver, 'The Catholic Community', in T. Devine and R. Finlay (eds.), *Scotland in the Twentieth Century* (Edinburgh, 1996), esp. 276–9.
[45] F. C. Diack, 'Place-names of Pictland', *Revue celtique*, xxxviii (1920–1), 109–32, and xxxix (1922), 125–74, quotation at 173; Diack, 'A Pre-Dalriadic Inscription of Argyll: The Gigha Stone', *Scottish Gaelic Studies*, I (1926), 3–16; W. M. Alexander, 'Obituary of Francis C. Diack', *Scottish Gaelic Studies*, V (1938–42), 183–4; Ferguson, *Identity of the Scottish Nation*, 296.

activities of a Pictish fringe-grouping, a certain Robbie the Pict has figured in various nationalist protests and the profile of Scotland's Pictish heritage has been raised by such bodies as the Groam House Museum in Rosemarkie and the New Age-inspired Pictish Arts Society.[46] Although some modern Scots still seek in the Pictish past something of a pointed alternative to Highlandism, contemporary dreams of the Picts tend to have cultural or anthropological rather than overt political significance.[47] Nevertheless, across the North Channel among the Scots-British of Northern Ireland the Picts have proved useful to a new and formidable breed of propagandist among the ranks of the Ulster Defence Association (UDA).

In the late 1970s a group of loyalists tried to break free from the sterile negativity of the unyielding Unionism which had succeeded the liberal experiments of Terence O'Neill and Brian Faulkner. Ironically, one of the leaders of this new-style loyalist thinking was Glen Barr, the organiser of the successful Ulster Workers' strike of 1974, which had brought down the powersharing Sunningdale administration.[48] In 1978 the New Ulster Political Research Group (NUPRG), which included Barr and Harry Chicken, the most innovative thinker among the loyalists, published *Beyond the Religious Divide* (1978), a document which advocated negotiated independence for Ulster as a sovereign state within the European Community. The NUPRG envisaged Ulster nationhood in civic rather than ethnic terms, as a means of bridging the sectarian divide and liberating Ulster politics from the divisive irredentism and colonialism of external nationalist allegiances. Free from British and Irish entanglements, the new Ulster would have a liberal constitution and a Bill of Rights.[49] Barr, in particular, spoke of awakening both sections of the community in Ulster to a shared interest and identity: 'The only common denominator that the Ulster people have, whether they be Catholic or Protestant, is that they are Ulstermen. And that is the basis from which we should build the new life for the Ulster people, a new identity for them.'[50]

[46] N. Ascherson, 'Picts', in Ascherson, *Games with Shadows* (London, 1988), 279–82; Forsyth, *Language in Pictland*, 5.

[47] A. Jackson, *The Symbol Stones of Scotland* (Stromness, 1984); Jackson, *The Pictish Trail* (Kirkwall, 1989).

[48] S. Bruce, *The Edge of The Union: The Ulster Loyalist Political Vision* (Oxford, 1994), ch. 1.

[49] S. Bruce, *The Red Hand: Protestant Paramilitaries in Northern Ireland* (Oxford, 1992), 231–2; Bruce, *Edge of the Union*, 101–3.

[50] Quoted in Bruce, *Edge of the Union*, 102.

There was a historical dimension to this quest for an Ulster identity. The Pictish fantasies of Ulster loyalists were nourished by the antiquarian investigations of an influential amateur historian, Ian Adamson, by profession a hospital doctor and in politics an Ulster Unionist, under whose colours he was elected to the Northern Ireland Assembly in 1998 as a representative for Belfast East, having previously been Lord Mayor of Belfast. In his books *Cruthin: The Ancient Kindred* (Belfast, 1974; whose second edition has a preface by Glen Barr) and *The Identity of Ulster: The Land, the Language and the People* (Belfast, 1982) Adamson set out the argument that Ulster had historically been a distinct society. Indeed, in direct challenge to the claims of the history and mythology of Irish nationalism, Adamson contended that Ireland had first been settled by the Cruthin, a branch of the Scottish Picts, and then by the ancient British Fir-Bolg, long before the arrival of the Gaels. Although these latecomers had eventually established a Gaelic supremacy throughout most of Ireland, their sway had not reached into the north-east corner of the island where an Ulster confederacy composed of the Cruthin and the Fir-Bolg tribes of Dalriata and Ulaid maintained their ancient non-Gaelic Irish way of life. Moreover, Cu Chulainn, the hero of the *Táin Bó Cuailnge* (The Cattle Raid of Cooley), whose death had been used by Padraic Pearse as the defining ancient exemplar of nationalist blood sacrifice, was identified by Adamson as a hero not of the Gaels, but of the Ulster Cruthin at war with the raiders of Connacht. In time, according to Adamson, the Cruthin were gradually pushed further back to Antrim and Down, and began to emigrate in numbers to Lowland Scotland, especially after the watershed defeat at Moira in AD 637. Nevertheless, although driven out of Gaelic Ireland, the Lowland Scottish descendants of the Pictish Cruthin would return to the homeland in the seventeenth century.[51]

Adamson's work had a resonance in Ulster Protestant culture well beyond antiquarian and historical circles. In 1986 – in the aftermath of the Anglo-Irish agreement – the junior branch of the Ulster Unionist Party produced a pamphlet which rehearsed the Adamson line on Cu Chulainn and the ancient Ulster past.[52] Cu Chulainn even became the

[51] A. Buckley, "'We're trying to find our identity": Uses of History among Ulster Protestants', in E. Tonkin, M. McDonald and M. Chapman (eds), *History and Ethnicity* (London, 1989); H. J. Morgan, 'Deceptions of demons', *Fortnight*, no. 320 (Sept. 1993), 34–6.

[52] A. Buckley, 'Uses of History among Ulster Protestants', in G. Dawe and J. Foster (eds), *The Poet's Place: Ulster literature and Society. Essays in Honour of John Hewitt, 1907–87* (Belfast, 1991), 269.

unlikely subject of a Protestant mural.[53] The appeal of the Cruthin is not difficult to appreciate. Their story legitimised the Protestant presence in Northern Ireland. According to this myth of Ulster Protestant ethnogenesis, the modern descendants of the Cruthin were not colonial oppressors, but natives of Ulster, whose presence in Ireland pre-dated that of the Gaels. Moreover, if Ulster had historically been the distinctive non-Gaelic seat of the Pictish Cruthin and British Fir-Bolg, then partition became less of an affront to the logic of Irish nationalist unity. Indeed, the Adamson thesis directly subverted the notion advanced by nationalists that ancient Irish culture was homogeneously Gaelic. Not only did the Cruthin provide the basis for a non-religious form of identity, but their P-Celtic links (possibly as a Celticised people of pre-Indo-European origin) suggested a way forward for Ulster Protestants – traditionally hostile to Eire and all things Gaelic – which was anti-nationalist without being anti-Celtic. Moreover, the ambivalent associations of the Cruthin, linked historically both to Ireland and to mainland Britain, reflected something of modern Ulster Protestantism's overlapping identities, rooted in an Ireland whose nationalism it despised while proclaiming a version of Britishness which mainland Britons had long abandoned. Indeed, Michael Hall, one of Adamson's loudest supporters, has pointed out the cross-community significance of the Cruthin thesis (which was acknowledged in spite of its Unionist provenance by the late Roman Catholic primate Cardinal Tomás Ó Fiaich, himself a noted antiquary): 'Republicans could strengthen their case by convincing the Protestant community of their obvious Irishness, while Loyalists could help convince their Catholic fellow-countrymen that they too have ancient links with mainland Britain.'[54]

The myth of the Cruthin may also have received some reinforcement from a related set of ideas which were also circulating on the margins of Ulster Protestant society. British Israelism was espoused by the late Reverend Robert Bradford, a Vanguard Assemblyman and Official Ulster Unionist MP, and it also flourished in the Covenant Peoples' Fellowship and the Pentecostalist Churches of God. Moreover, during the 1960s there existed a paramilitary group called Tara, which maintained British Israelite ideas. The British Israelites also challenged the rhetoric of Irish nationalism by claiming to be the true ancient pre-Gaelic inhabitants of Ireland. The British of the mainland, America and

---

[53] Morgan, 'Deceptions of Demons', 35.
[54] M. Hall, *The Cruthin Controversy* (Newtonabbey, 1998), 22–4. I should like to thank Colin Armstrong for a gift of this pamphlet.

the white Commonwealth, they claim, are the pure descendants of the northern kingdom of Israel who spread into northern Europe after the death of Solomon, reassembling in the British Isles, the lands promised to Abraham and Jacob. The rest of the Jews, apart from the line of Benjamin of which Jesus came, were corrupted by intermarriage. During the Babylonian exile the prophet Jeremiah and the daughters of Zedekiah, last of the pre-Exilic kings of Judah, brought the Ark of the Covenant to Antrim, and thence to Tara in County Meath, the scene of Irish royal coronations, along with the Stone of Destiny. Ancient Ireland was inhabited by these Israelites who were driven out to Scotland by the invading Gaels, a half-Canaanite, half-Israelite people, and the British Israelites took with them the Stone of Destiny, upon which sat Queen Elizabeth II who traces her descent through the Israelite kings of Scotland and Ireland to the biblical King David.[55]

However, it was the UDA who did most to adopt Adamson's ideas about the Cruithin. As Steve Bruce, the leading sociologist of the loyalist phenomenon, records, articles on the Cruithin became a prominent feature of the magazine *Ulster*, while visitors to headquarters received from Andy Tyrie, the head of the UDA, complimentary copies of Adamson's books. The Red Branch Knights – the companions of Cu Chulainn – became a UDA *nom de guerre*. Nevertheless, despite official endorsement by the UDA, its rank and file preferred 'outward bound and arms training' to the night schools laid on in Cruthinic history.[56]

The problem was not simply that the Cruithin were too remote for a province living symbolically in the late seventeenth century, nor that Adamson's antiquarian writings were too arid and technical for the Protestant working class. There was also a problem with the very matter of Ulster deployed to bridge the sectarian divide. Bruce believes that the ancient Celtic associations of the Cruithin rendered them virtually indistinguishable in Ulster Protestant eyes from the detested Gaels. An unnamed senior Ulster Volunteer Force (UVF) source told Bruce that he 'might have gone for an independence line if Adamson hadn't tried to dress it up with all the Cruithin stuff. A load of Celtic mythology was not going to help anyone here and now.'[57]

---

[55] Buckley, 'Uses of History among Ulster Protestants', in Dawe and Foster (eds), *The Poet's Place*, 267–8. For modern myths and exaggeration surrounding British Israelite excavations at the mounds of Tara, see H. Butler, 'The British Israelites at Tara', in Butler, *The Sub-Prefect Should Have Held his Tongue and Other Essays*, ed. R. F. Foster (Harmondsworth, 1990), 68–70.

[56] Bruce, *Red Hand*, 235.

[57] Ibid.

The UVF drew on a rather different interpretation of Ulster history from that espoused by the UDA. UVF propagandists focused on the early decades of the twentieth century, especially Carson's resistance to Home Rule and the fervent participation of loyal Ulstermen in the First World War.[58] In the turmoil of Northern Ireland, as in Scotland between the eighteenth and twentieth centuries, the Picts were available to offer an alternative counter-identity to mainstream values, but remained too peripheral to sustain a credible, enduring identity.

Yet, in spite of these failures, the assumption clearly persisted that the Picts were the autochthonous people of northern Britain and that, as a consequence, any claim to aboriginal authority must confront an ancient Pictish presence. The argument that each generation re-created the Pictish past to meet its own ideological needs tells only half of a fascinating story; for there are consistent threads which join the various episodes we have studied. In each case the Picts – representing a suppressed aboriginal truth – were deployed to unmask a form of false consciousness about national origins. More-over, in almost every case the ideological error to be exposed was a myth of Gaelic origins. For Lowland Scotland and its Ulster colony an elusive Pictishness provided an alternative 'navel' of nationhood – at best Gothic, at worst P-Celtic or pre-Indo-European – to Q-Celtic Irish Gaelicism. In their different ways the Jacobite Innes and the Teutonist Pinkerton were convinced opponents of the ways in which Irish antiquaries – and their Scottish dupes – claimed Scotland's ancient past as an offshoot of their own.[59] Even during the Celticist literary Renaissance of the 1920s and 1930s there was some unease about the debasement of Gaeldom in a kitsch tartanry. Just as MacDiarmid, a nationalist critic of bogus Scottishness, turned to Dunbar to liberate literary Scots from a bourgeois Burns cult,[60] so he and others saw in the Picts an authentic Celtic past untainted by commodification. Moreover, for a generation in search of organic wholeness the Celtic Picts, unlike the Gaelic Scots, were not associated with the running sore of Scotland's Highland–Lowland division.[61] Though every age has had a different story to relate about

---

[58] Ibid., 234.
[59] Innes, *Critical Essay*, esp. bk II; Pinkerton, *Enquiry*, ii, 243.
[60] Bold, *MacDiarmid*, 204.
[61] R. Watson, 'Visions of Alba: The Constructions of Celtic Roots in Modern Scottish Literature', *Etudes écossaises* I, 256.

this obscure ancient people, the Picts have enjoyed an uncelebrated salience within various debates about the origins and nature of the relationships between the various communities and ethnic stocks within 'these islands'.

I should like to thank Katherine Forsyth, Steve Driscoll, Colin Armstrong, Dauvit Broun, Hanna Tange, Ian McBride and Ewen Cameron for various references and suggestions.

CHAPTER 9

The Jacobite Cult

Murray G. H. Pittock

The 'Tartan Curtain', 'Balmoralisation', 'Scotch Myths' and so on are all terms which have been used to emphasise the scope and profundity ofthe influence of the tartan cult after 1800, or more precisely 1822, the occasion of George IV's visit to Scotland.[1] They are also words which have been used as a currency of scorn, indicative of the perceived factitiousness of the process they are describing. It is said that presenting Scotland as essentially 'Highland' is a nineteenth-century fabrication; that such fabrication trivialised Scottish history, and, by trivialising it, marginalised it. To reclaim the underlying historicity of Scotland, it is thus necessary to exorcize the influence of the villains who invented this particular system of cultural representation, shortbread-tin Scotland. The usual suspects are Stewart of Garth, the Sobieski Stuarts and, of course, Sir Walter Scott.[2]

This tartan cult stressed particular aspects of Scottish experience: royalism, Highland dress, militarism, hardihood, physical strength and virility. It had little to say of the covenants, mercantilism, industrialisation, the ideas of the Scottish Enlightenment or the culture of urban Scotland. Politically, it was closely linked to the Jacobite century (1688–1788), and sought (particularly in the version essayed by Sir Walter Scott) to finally rehabilitate the losing side, on condition that its apparatus of representation would in future always be displayed severed

---

[1] 'Balmoralised' is itself almost a century old at least; for a discussion of these ideas, see Murray G. H. Pittock, *Poetry and Jacobite Politics in Eighteenth-Century Britain and Ireland* (Cambridge, 1994), ch. 7 and *The Myth of the Jacobite Clans* (1995: Edinburgh, 1999), ch. 4.

[2] Cf. John Prebble, *The King's Jaunt* (London, 1988) and T. M. Devine, *The Scottish Nation, 1700–2000* (London, 1999).

from any political content. Scottish (misplaced) loyalty to the Stuarts would be the symbolic avatar of their (appropriate) loyalty to the Georges; the Wrong but Wromantic exploits of the Jacobites would become the right-thinking heroics of Scottish troops in the Napoleonic Wars. Instead of being ashamed of the Jacobite century, it could be acknowledged in terms of a continuing tradition of loyalty and valour, now happily transferred to a better cause. It is this historical turn to which Scott returned again and again in his fiction: in *The Antiquary*, for example, the Catholic earl of Glencairn comes out of his reclusive broodings on the past to lead the militia against the French.[3]

Given that this was his aim, Sir Walter chose an apposite moment. Scottish troops had won themselves considerable popularity in the Napoleonic Wars; the last arrest for Jacobitism, in 1817, had finally set the seal on the fate of a movement which still gave a slight, if unrealistic *frisson* of fear to the sensibilities of the British Establishment;[4] and George IV, an unpopular king lacking image and authority, was the ideal receptacle for a rebranded version of Jacobite heritage. Flattered by the overriding metaphor of loyalty, enthralled by the fancy dress and the notion of himself as a chief of chiefs, each of whose clansman was a perfervid royalist, George was very likely to prefer his Scottish image to Gilray's picture of him picking his teeth among empty bottles while his turds swill around in a chamber pot. The Edinburgh visit, by contrast, was an enticing illusion, which flattered king and subject alike, though some did protest at Scotland's being turned into 'a nation of Highlanders'.[5] Others in England realised that the process reflected on the king's gullibility: in one cartoon called *The First Laird in Aw Scotia*, published in London, George appears together with his Svengali, Sir Walter, in full Highland garb, while the inhabitants of Edinburgh, dressed in the ordinary British fashions of the day, look on in amusement.[6]

So much is accepted, and much of what is written in this chapter concerning the 1822 visit owes a debt both to the ideas of John Prebble and Caroline McCracken-Flesher in this regard. But one thing which it is important to realise is that Scott's portrayal, while heightened and

---

[3] Cf. Murray G. H. Pittock, *The Invention of Scotland* (London and New York, 1991).

[4] Count Roehenstart, illegitimate son of Charlotte, Countess of Albany (the daughter of Charles Edward Stuart), was arrested in 1817.

[5] James Stuart of Dunearn, cited in Prebble, *The King's Jaunt*, 269.

[6] A copy of this print is kept in the Blaikie collection, Scottish National Portrait Gallery.

exaggerated, was not principally a fictive one. Few commentators have done Scott the justice of realising that he could not 'invent' a national myth single-handedly: rather he was re-animating a corpus of existing ideas and images. That this was so is of considerable importance. Because the 'Scottland' created by Scott has been held to be ersatz and false, relatively little attention has been given to the history, use and cultural context of its symbols. This chapter will make an attempt to redress this, not by attempting a full-scale discussion of the whole tartan cult, which requires greater scope, but by looking at it from the perspective of one of its most important areas: that of the representation of Jacobitism.

The Jacobites were not the first to use tartan as a symbolic representation of Scottishness in general. *Pace* those Scottish critics who have too readily followed Hobsbawm and Ranger in detecting in Scott the genesis of an 'invented tradition', tartan had been used as a visible symbol of old and traditional Scotland since the sixteenth-century ceremonies for Anne of Denmark's marriage to James VI, and Michael Lynch has detected it too at the court of James, Duke of Albany at Holyrood during the Exclusion Crisis.[7] In the Jacobite century which followed, tartan was the badge of authentic patriotism for Jacobite conspirators and ideologues and the outward sign of affection for traditional hierarchies and institutions: much as Scott used it, in fact. Bespoke tartan was provided for Sir John Hynde Cotton in Edinburgh in 1744; tartan portraits were used in English elections into the 1750s, and tartan as the Scottish patriot badge was used domestically in Jacobite celebrations such as Lady Bruce's dinner to celebrate Charles Edward's birthday in December 1746.[8] It was in this spirit too that the armies of 1715 and 1745, both around 50 per cent non-Highland in origin, were uniformed. Lowland units carried the targe, Lord Lewis Gordon accepted Highland clothes in lieu of money from Aberdeen, while even the Manchester Regiment wore tartan, as did at least some of the *French* officers in the army.[9] As the Atholl Whig Commissary Bisset remarked, 'lowlanders . . . are putting themselves in highland dress like the others'.[10] In such circumstances, it is unsurprising that there was (and remains) confusion as to whether Charles' was a

---

[7] Michael Lynch, *Scotland: A New History* (London, 1991), 299 and in conversation.

[8] Cf. F. Peter Lole, *A Digest of the Jacobite Clubs*, Royal Stuart Society Paper LV (London: Royal Stuart Society, 1999), 29, 45.

[9] Sir Bruce Seton, Bart, 'Dress of the Jacobite Army', *Scottish Historical Review*, 25 (1928), 270–81, still provides the best discussion of this. Cf. Pittock, *Myth of the Jacobite Clans*, ch. 2.

[10] Seton, 'Dress of the Jacobite Army', 273, 274, 277, 278, 279.

'Highland army': it was of course not so, but tartan was its national badge. In the controversy over the militia issue fifteen years later, some Lowland Scots may have taken advantage of (and indeed helped to generate) this confusion by pleading Lowland non-involvement in the rising in order to ingratiate themselves with the authorities.[11] Tartan was, however, clearly seen as an important part of national iconography in the death (or martyrdom, as it was regarded) of Lowland members of the Jacobite leadership. An account of the execution of Lord Balmerino in 1746 puts it thus: 'brave Balmerrony . . . in the midst of all his foes/ Claps Tartan on his eyes . . . A Scots Man I livd . . . A Scots Man now I die . . . May all the Scots my footsteps trace'. Tartan was the patriot identifier of Jacobite celebration and martyrdom alike.[12]

Tartan, then, was one of the elements of eighteenth-century patriot ideology restored to prominence by Scott. Another was the idea of Scotland's history as a struggle for liberty, usually expressed through a stress on the warlike and valorous qualities of true Scots, those who upheld the freedom of Scotland through 'countless warlike ages', as Burns put it. Such a language of brave struggle is a leitmotiv of patriot rhetoric in the eighteenth century, whether in the citation of the Declaration of Arbroath, as in James Anderson's *Scotland Independent* (1705), with its famous passage of commitment to defend Scotland 'as long as there shall but one hundred of us remain alive' or in the imagery used by anti-Unionists and Jacobites.[13] 'Are none of the descendants here of those worthy patriots who defended the liberty of their country against all invaders?' asked the Duke of Hamilton in November 1706, in 'consideration of the first article' of Union. Sixteen days later, those who conspired to burn the Articles at Dumfries wrote from their more humble social rank in the same terms: praising 'the sovereignty of this our native ancient nation . . . purchased and maintained by our ances-tors with their blood.'[14] The rhetoric of Jacobitism was similar. James

---

[11] Cf. Pittock, *Myth of the Jacobite Clans,* 32. Alexander 'Jupiter' Carlyle, for example, publicly claimed that the Jacobite army was 'from the most remote parts of the kingdom', while admitting in his memoirs the strength of Jacobite feeling in Haddingtonshire.

[12] 'A Song to the Tune of the Bonny Broom', Aberdeen University Library MS. 2222; printed as part of Murray Pittock, 'New Jacobite Songs of the Forty-five', *Studies on Voltaire and the Eighteenth Century,* 267 (1989), 1–75.

[13] Gordon Donaldson, *Scottish Historical Documents* (Edinburgh and London, 1974), 57.

[14] Daniel Szechi (ed.) with an introduction by Paul Scott, *'Scotland's Ruine': Lockhart of Carnwath's Memoirs of the Union* (Aberdeen, 1995), 160, 177–9.

Philp's epic on Viscount Dundee, *The Grameid*, emphasised 'glorious deeds and uncontaminated fidelity';[15] James VIII himself drew attention to 'a Nation always famous for valour', while the earl of Mar called for a breaking of 'the unhappy union' by 'force of arms', and thus restoring the 'free and independent' condition of an ancient and valorous Scotland.[16] Even Lord Lovat from the scaffold, speaking Horace's words, called to mind the Scoto-Roman ethos which underlay much of this discourse of liberty, with its emphasis on purity, simplicity and unity of purpose. '*Dulce et decorum est pro patria mori*' : in these words Lovat made his final statement as a Scottish nationalist and a Jacobite, calling to mind the bravery and simplicity of a noble and once uncorrupted nation. It was this discourse (against which its proponents set the 'bought and sold for English gold' motif of metropolitan corruption and loss of integrity which was itself a great Latin topos, the decline of Rome lamented by Juvenal) which Burns recalled in French revolutionary dress in 'Scots Wha Hae'.[17]

Apart from such bold attempts to revivify it with Jacobin modifications, this discourse foundered in the years after Culloden. It was Scott once again who bore significant responsibility for renewing its attractions. In his famous letter of 22 July 1822 to Macleod of Macleod, Scott wrote 'the King is coming after all. Arms and men [not learning, technological advance or industry, note] are the best thing we have to show him . . . Pray come and do not forget to bring the Bodyguard for the Credit of Old Scotland'.[18] Rehabilitation of this warlike image of traditional nationality was on the agenda: Alasdair Ranaldson's list of appropriate garb included 'Gun (or Fusee) . . . Broad Sword and Shoulder Belt . . . Target and Slinging Belt . . . A Brace of Highland Pistols . . . A "Chore Dubh" or Hose Knife called the "Skian" . . . A Powder Horn', in other words the full complement of a Jacobite officer's military accoutrements. The Royal Company of Archers appeared in a newly-authorised fancy military dress, and undertook their traditional role of being the king's bodyguard, while George was linked with Robert

---

[15] Discussed in Pittock, *Poetry and Jacobite Politics*, 41

[16] Colonel James Allardyce (ed.), *Historical Papers Relating to the Jacobite Period 1699–1750*, 2 vols (Aberdeen: New Spalding Club, 1895), I, 177, 188–9; Rev. W. H. Langhorne, *Reminiscences* (Edinburgh: David Douglas, 1893), 9; Pittock, *Myth of the Jacobite Clans*, 92, 96.

[17] James Boswell, *The Life of Samuel Johnson*, 2 vols (1906: Dent, 1946), I 105.

[18] Prebble, *The King's Jaunt*, 104, 105; cited in greater detail in Caroline McCracken-Flesher's discussion of 'George IV in Scottish Circulation, 1822' in her forthcoming book on Scott.

the Bruce.[19] Jacobite songs and Jacobite rhetoric lived again in the dress of the Union, whether in the air of 'When the king comes o'er the Water' or in the sets composed by Scott ('Carle, now the King's come') and others:[20]

> Hark, the pibroch's martial strain,
> Ca's the clans to Lothian's plain:
> Scotland's got her King again,
> Welcome Royal Geordie !
> 'George the Fourth's Welcome'[21]

'We are now all Jacobites, thorough-bred Jacobites, in acknowledging George IV,' stated the *Edinburgh Observer*, with breathtaking hypocrisy and candour. Scott designed the representation of Scotland as valorous and loyal,[22] its traditional patriotic discourses restored in a context which alienated them from their political meaning. As a result, they became means of emotive display, and in their turn expressed and confirmed the underlying message of the complex intellectual project popularised by Scott: that Scots were emotionally Celtic patriots, but intellectually Teuton Unionists. The discourses of that emotional patriotism were, by virtue of their use in military challenge to the Union in the preceding century, deeply involved with Jacobitism: hence the link of Scotland's traditional military valour to tartan, one endorsed by the British army, which had permitted tartan in its ranks during the thirty-five years when it had been effectively banned elsewhere.

Thus the renewal of Scotland's patriotic imagery by Scott and others was interwoven with a vision of the country which was to become closely bound up in at least one dimension with a Jacobite cult. It can be traced elsewhere: for example, the nineteenth-century enthusiasm for Bruce and Wallace as avatars of Union by virtue of their victories (which thus gained Scotland a negotiated Union, rather than forcing her into subjection) can be traced back to Scott and his Gothicist predecessors in the Scottish Enlightenment. But the manner in which the alluring images of Scotland = valour = a race of primitive heroes = Highlanders = Jacobites = Romance functioned in the nineteenth and early

[19] Prebble, *The King's Jaunt*, 92, 119, 248.
[20] Valentina Bold, '*The Royal Jubilee*: James Hogg and the House of Hanover', *Studies in Hogg and his World*, 5 (1994), 1–19.
[21] Ibid., 2 3.
[22] Prebble, *The King's Jaunt*, 123.

twentieth centuries draws us closely into the examination of what was an essentially Jacobitical cultus and is arguably the central matrix of a cultural experience derived from the efforts made to reintegrate anti-Union and pro-Stuart rhetoric and symbolism into a patriotic Scottish participation in the British polity and empire.

At the core of this lay a politics of location, which identified the central locus of Scottish patriot Jacobite valour as the Highlands. The location of Jacobitism as a discrete, remote 'Highland heritage' phenomenon was arguably underway as early as 1746, when brutal government action in the Gaidhealtachd was not matched in Angus, despite the presence there of public displays of Jacobite fervour (for example at Montrose on 10 June), and the continuing presence in the county of armed units, probably of the Forfarshire battalions.[23] Much of the Jacobite cult in the nineteenth century reinforced this intense sense of location, the confinement of patriot valour within narrow boundaries, boundaries often delimited by sublime landscape: the Soldier's Leap at Killiecrankie and the Queen's Views at the Tummel and throughout north and north-eastern Highland Scotland are both examples of this. In Scott's *Waverley* (1815), the more sublime the landscape, the higher the concentration of Jacobites in it: the decline of Jacobite fortunes is an actual as well as a metaphorical downhill journey. In Chapters 21 and 22, the two streams which mark the landscape in which Flora attempts to draw Waverley into her net of Jacobite sentiment famously symbolise the steady pacific virtues heralded by Britishness and the rough wild boisterousness of Scottish patriot Jacobitism uncontrolled by Saxon phlegm. Naturally, it is the Jacobite stream which occupies the higher and more sublime ground.

Similarly, although historical pageantry and the picturesque were key components of the early and mid-Victorian sense of history in general, it was in the Highlands that they reached their highest pitch, so that 'the Scottish Highlands, once the home and glory of the White Rose, became the most utterly Bal-moralized portion of the realm'.[24] On her first visit to Scotland in 1842, Queen Victoria asked for 'O wae's me for Prince Charlie' to be sung; subsequently she and Prince Albert symbolically adopted elements of a brave and hardy lifestyle in what she called her 'romantic little kingdom': stalking, eating bannocks and drying Prince Edward's socks over a peat fire. The Prince Consort was of course famously depicted standing over a burn spearing salmon with a leister,

---

[23] Pittock, *Myth of the Jacobite Clans,* 67–8.
[24] *The Royalist,* XII: i (1903), 3.

in deference perhaps to the same traditionalist fishing method adopted by Scott's most centrally nationalist Jacobite patriot, Redgauntlet. Both royals enjoyed the 'ancient way of hunting' on cleared land, re-enacting a legendary past in a country possessed of the distinctive but passive qualities of the picturesque. Victoria's patronage also 'effectively secured the development of the whole Highland Games industry after 1848'. At the same time, the queen and her husband seem to have enjoyed a frisson of antique violence: in 1842, they were met in Lochaber 'by 100 tenants in tartan, some armed with "Lochaber axes"; at Dunkeld, Highlanders "complete with claymores and battleaxes" were on show, "many . . . of gigantic stature"'. This combination of archaic weaponry and enormous, vigorous warriors were frequently reinforced in less impressive 'controlled environments for the pleasure of the onlooker'.[25] Thus 'Despite the fact that real Scots were often undernourished' and undersized, images of strength and vitality, linked to food and outdoor exercise, portrayed them as a hardy and huge race.[26] These images can be traced directly back to the government propaganda of 1745–6, with its envisioning of huge and virile barbarians ravishing a civilised English state. Transmuted through the work of Scott and his followers and allies, they became instead reassuring signs of the uncontaminated vigour at the heart of the global mission of the British race. The legacy of this kind of idealisation of a Jacobitical Scotland lives on today in 'the claymore-wielding Highlander of the "Crisp of the Clans" (Highlander Crisps), and the rippling muscles of his equally potent counterpart on Scott's Porage Oats'.[27] These images partake of the essential nature of kitsch, and its production of reified charisma: images of excitement and positive association reduced to the level of a commodity, the 'tartanry' despised by later generations of Scottish intellectuals. Scotland (and the Highlands as a synecdoche for Scotland) became a place of such charisma, one whose identity could be purchased, owned, collected and confined; an empty locale into which the

---

[25] Pittock, *Invention of Scotland*, 103; Delia Miller, *Queen Victoria's Life in the Scottish Highlands Depicted by her Watercolour Artists* (London, 1985), 8; John Glendening, *The High Road: Romantic Tourism, Scotland, and Literature 1720–1820* (Basingstoke, 1997), 231; Katherine Jean Haldane, 'Imagining Scotland: Tourist Images of Scotland 1770–1914', unpublished Ph.D. thesis, University of Virginia (1990), 9, 30, 31, 34, 273, 283, 334; Charles Kightly, *The Customs and Ceremonies of Britain* (London, 1986), 138.

[26] Murray G. H. Pittock, *Celtic Identity and the British Image* (Manchester, 2000), 39.

[27] Ibid.

desires of the incoming imagination could be poured. It was to these dimensions, the dimensions of heritage, that the language of Jacobite patriotism and valour and its tartan symbols were reduced.

But this is far from the whole story of the Jacobite cult in the nineteenth century. In the remainder of this chapter I am going to deal, not with the modification of Jacobite discourse in the interest of Scotland's integration into Britain, but rather with two different but closely related themes: the preservation by a colourful minority of a 'genuine' Jacobite language of adherence to the Stuarts and their Scottish tradition, and the more widespread phenomenon of the status of Jacobitism and its rhetoric as sources of nagging disquiet about the nature of Scottish identity itself.

In either case, the persistence of not only Jacobitical language but also Jacobitical interests is inexplicable unless we accept the continuing potency of the Jacobite discourse (hence Scott's need to expropriate it) in Scottish culture. The Sobieski Stuarts, Charles and John, claimed to be the legitimate heirs of the Stuart line in the early nineteenth century. Adopted by Lord Lovat, who in 1838 gave them 'an amazing Celtic Xanadu' on Eilean Aigas to live in, and by some of the more trustful members of the Highland societies, they remained a source of interest for over twenty years.[28] Symptomatic of the link between Jacobite rhetoric and the tartan as a patriot sign, much of their literary endeavours went into producing a standard work of reference on traditional clan tartans. Nor are or were they alone. Even in the 1980s and 1990s, Prince Michael has sought to gain status as the heir to Scotland's throne in a media climate apparently less unfriendly to his claims than to the legitimate allowances of the country's elected representatives. His book *The Forgotten Monarchy of Scotland* , argues that he is a direct descendant of Charles Edward Stuart by a late and private marriage to Marguerite, Comtesse de Massillan, and is full of much other choice information, including the news that the insurrection of 1820 was a Jacobite rising. *Forgotten Monarchy* made its way into the top ten best-selling titles in Scotland, indicative of the fact that, almost at the end of the second millennium, there remains an appetite for Jacobite discourse in almost any guise.[29]

[28] William Donaldson, *The Jacobite Song* (Aberdeen, 1988), 110, 113.
[29] HRH Prince Michael of Albany, *The Forgotten Monarchy of Scotland* (Shaftesbury, 1998). The Sobieski Stuarts and their interest in tartan are discussed on pp. 379–80. *Cf. George Skene, 'The Heirs of the Stuarts', Quarterly Review* (June 1847), 57–85.

Political neo-Jacobitism (Prince Michael is a nationalist of sorts and the Sobieski Stuarts wrote slightingly of the Union even at the Victorian noonday) was not confined however, to occasional colourful figures. In 1889, the major 'Exhibition of the Royal House of Stuart' made quite a stir in London, and ushered in an extraordinary period of neo-Jacobite activity: the Order of the White Rose (founded 1886), which bore considerable responsibility for the exhibition placed, despite the patron-age of Queen Victoria, the names of the post-1688 reigning monarchy in parentheses.[30]

The next year a journal, *The Royalist* (1890–1905), was launched, to serve the cause of 'Lawful Authority . . . the advancement of Legiti-mism as against Rebellion, Democracy, and Anarchy'.[31] It was linked to the Order of the White Rose, but its views were largely based on a Jacobite ethic, and did not, except in the outlook of a minority of activists, compass a restoration. That minority did, however, split off from the main body on 30 June 1891 to establish 'The Legitimist Jacobite League of Great Britain and Ireland', among whose aims was 'to support the claims of the elder and exiled branch of the Royal Family', and, rather late in the day, 'to gain the reversal of all attainders against the adherents of the Royal House of Stuart'.[32] Other journals, such as *The Jacobite* and *The Legitimist Ensign*, reflected these aims. Perhaps significantly, articles on Irish Jacobitism's nationalist tenden-cies appeared in the Jacobite press as the century drew to a close. Although there is no scope here to discuss the links between Jacobite rhetoric and Irish republicanism, they are demonstrable in figures as diverse as Roger Casement and Sean O'Casey. One example will suffice here. In 1896 *The Royalist* published an article, which discussed 'the King's son' and 'Kathleen-Ny-Houlihan' as part of a rhetoric of Irish national deliverance; at the same time, Maud Gonne was encouraging W. B. Yeats to form links with the neo-Jacobite mystic MacGregor Mathers (Count Glenstrae in the Jacobite peerage), who was supposed to be in command of 'shadowy Highlander organisations' which could be used in a pan-Celtic war effort.[33] Yeats was at this time responsible for the organisation of the Wolfe Tone centenary celebrations. In 1902 Yeats (with Lady Gregory) staged the passionately nationalist drama

---

[30] Ian Fletcher, *W. B. Yeats and his Contemporaries* (Brighton, 1987), 97.
[31] *The Royalist*, I:i, 2.
[32] 'Aims of the Legitimist Jacobite League of Great Britain and Ireland'.
[33] *The Royalist*, VII:3 (1896), 41–6 (43) ('Irish Jacobite Songs'); R. F. Foster, *W. B. Yeats: A Life* (Oxford, 1997), 157.

Cathleen Ni Houlihan, with Maud Gonne in the title role. Arthur Griffith, the founder of Sinn Fein, declared it more important than victory on the battlefield. Subsequently it became, for Yeats, the play which sent out 'certain men the English shot', the men of 1916. Gesture politics had their effect on the rehabilitation of Celtic heroism in Ireland.[34]

Whatever may have been the linkages of Jacobite rhetoric and Irish politics, in mainland Britain the supporters of the Legitimist League in particular undertook a programme of protest and political agitation:

> Its leading light, the Marquis de Ruvigny et Raineval (1869–
> 1922), whose *Jacobite Peerage* is still a standard work,
> engineered many demonstrations and protests by these more
> militant Jacobites. These even . . . found support in the House
> of Commons. When Gladstone's Bill to remove remaining
> disabilities from Roman Catholics was put forward in 1891, Sir
> John Pope-Hennessey wished to see the legislation extended to
> include the Royal Family . . . Questions were asked in the
> House of Commons; viciously anti-Jacobite letters appeared in
> the press, and MPs were quizzed by querulous constituents
> regarding secret Jacobite sympathies. Gilbert Baird Fraser [may
> have] stood for Parliament as a Jacobite in 1891; and on 2
> April that year, Herbert Vivian, one of the Legitimist leaders,
> issued an address to the electors of Bradford on the Jacobite
> issue. On 1 December, W. Clifford Mellor was adopted as the
> Jacobite candidate for North Huntingdonshire.[35]

Additional and sustained publicity was gained both through articles and press releases and via 'the war of the statues', an exercise in gesture politics whereby public monuments and particularly statues of the Stuarts and of Cromwell were praised or abused, decorated or removed, throughout the country. While neo-Jacobites 'demonstrated for the right to decorate Charles I's statue' and protested against the removal of James II and VII's statue from Whitehall, their opponents destroyed a statue of Charles II at Salisbury, and erected one to Cromwell at St

---

[34] Arthur Griffith, quoted in John Hutchinson, *The Dynamics of Cultural Nationalism* (London, 1987), 193; Yeats, 'Man and Echo', from *Last Poems*.

[35] Murray G. H. Pittock, *Spectrum of Decadence: The Literature of the 1890s* (London and New York, 1993), 98; Marquis de Ruvigny et Raineval (ed.), *Legitimist Kalendar 1895* (London, 1895), 59–60; Neo-Jacobite papers of Ian Fletcher, Reading University Library; cf. *The Royalist*, III:4.

Ives. From an Irish perspective, no less a figure than John Redmond, 'demanded the removal of Cromwell's statue "from the precincts of the House of Commons"'.[36] Numbers involved in these demonstrations could run into hundreds,[37] and notable persons involved in the neo-Jacobite movement included the earl of Ashburnham, the Hon. Stuart Erskine of Mar (later a prominent Scottish nationalist), Sebastian Evans, Ernest Dowson, Lionel Johnson, McGregor Mathers, Charles Augustus Howell and James McNeill Whistler. Henry Irving thought the general atmosphere sympathetic enough for it to be worth risking a revival of W. G. Wills's *King Charles the First* at the Lyceum, while the neo-Jacobites were notable enough to be regarded as worth satirising in *Punch* and the *Illustrated London News*. The novelist, barrister and parliamentary candidate Allen Upward (1863–1926) attacked the movement in two novellas, *High Treason* and *Mary the Third*, which take advantage of the fact that contemporary Stuarts were Bavarians by combining anti-Catholic and anti-German feeling. On Queen Victoria's death in 1901, the Princess of Bavaria was proclaimed as Mary IV and II, and posters were put up round London.[38]

There was a strong Scottish nationalist element among the Legitimist League, with associated groups such as the Flora MacDonald Club, Glasgow, the Royal Oak Club, Edinburgh, and the Mary Stuart Club of Lanark.[39] Among the leading Scottish neo-Jacobite figures were Stuart Erskine and the League's Scottish secretary Theodore Napier (1845–1928), who authored the League pamphlet on *The Royal House of Stuart: A Plea for its Restoration. An Appeal to Loyal Scotsmen* in 1898, in which he argued that Scotland is *'content to lick her chains'* and that 'no nation can ever be regarded as politically *free* that is prevented from making its own laws', as well as reciting the traditional Jacobite view that 'had the Revolution of 1688 never taken place, the present *Incorporating Union* . . . would never have occurred'.[40] In 1901 Napier began his own journal, *The Fiery Cross* (1901–12), to promote and publicise a political programme of determined nationalist activism which had already had some marked successes over the previous decade. Napier began the

---

[36] Pittock, *Spectrum of Decadence*, 99; *The Legitimist Ensign* 3 (1901), xii; *The Jacobite*, IV: 5 (1903), 33; IV: 7, 52; *The Legitimist Kalendar 1899*, 67; unsigned review of Allen Upward, *High Treason*, *The Jacobite* IV: 11, 12, 76.

[37] Foster, *W. B. Yeats*, 83.

[38] Ibid., 96–7, 101, 102.

[39] Lole, *A Digest of Jacobite Clubs*, 48, 53, 67.

[40] Theodore Napier, *The Royal House of Stuart*, Legitimist Jacobite League Publications no. 17 (Edinburgh and London, 1898), 17.

annual pilgrimage to Culloden on the anniversary of the battle; he criticised the Boer War, argued that Scotland's MPs failed to stand up for Scottish interests, and was the first to call for the establishment of a 'Scottish National Party'. On the inaugural Bannockburn Day demonstration of 1901, organised by the Scottish Patriotic Association (SPA), Napier 'denied his allegiance to Edward VII'.[41] Eleven hundred people subsequently signed a protest against Edward's title, and a vote was obtained in the Convention of Royal Burghs; but this was dwarfed by the claimed 104,000 who signed Napier's 1897 Diamond Jubilee petition to Queen Victoria against the use of 'England' to describe 'Great Britain'.[42] It is interesting to note that the symbolic interest in the correct regnal number manifested in the Edwardian petition surfaced again in the campaign against EIIR pillar-boxes in the early 1950s. Napier aimed for a 'Union of the Celtic Races', and for the repeal of the Union of England with both Scotland and Ireland.[43] His style of symbolic patriotism had considerable appeal in the early days of modern Scottish nationalism (as can be seen in the Stone of Destiny removal in 1950 and the campaigns against the queen's use of the title 'Elizabeth the Second'). Napier's allies called for Scots to recall 'the spirit that animated the brave hearts of 1745', and there were signs that this outlook was gaining in popularity. By 1912, the year in which Napier retired to Australia, there were 15,000 at the Bannockburn Rally.[44] His marriage of neo-Jacobitical rhetoric with modern methods of campaigning and agitation had its influence on the nationalists of the Scottish Renaissance and on the language, style and outlook of Wendy Wood's Patriots (that is, Scottish Nationalists), and, perhaps beyond them, the *Sìol Nan Gaidheal* of the early 1980s. Most immediately, it was taken up by his fellow neo-Jacobite Stuart Erskine, an Irish-style Gaelic revivalist and proprietor from 1904 to 1925 of the paper *Guth na Bliadhna*. In this fashion the ideas of the neo-Jacobite revival fed directly into the Celtic communism and Jacobite romanticism of the first generation of modern Scottish nationalists.

William Donaldson has argued that the continuing fascination with Jacobitism among Scottish authors and songwriters after 1746 was a way

[41] *The Fiery Cross*, 1:1 (1901), 2, 3, 5; 1:3 (1901), 4, 8; 6 (1902), 5; 11 (1903), 2; 12 (1903), 2; G. A. Cevasco (ed.), *The 1890s: An Encyclopedia of British Literature, Art and Culture* (New York, 1993), 417; Pittock: 'Theodore Napier'.
[42] *The Fiery Cross*, 17 (1905), 2; H. J. Hanham, *Scottish Nationalism* (London, 1969), 121.
[43] *The Fiery Cross*, 1:1.
[44] *Ibid.*, 3, 7; Hanham, *Scottish Nationalism*, 126, 133.

of expressing continued hostility to the Union. Whether or not this was the case, there is undeniably a powerful obsession with the Jacobite period and its issues in Scottish literature. This both pre- and post-dates Sir Walter Scott, and the core approach to the subject is in general more sympathetic than his: among his full-length novels only in *Redgauntlet* does Scott arguably treat the defeat of the Jacobite interest with ambivalence, let alone regret (*The Highland Widow* offers a parallel in his shorter fiction, with its postcolonial stress on a struggle for loyalty and identity between coloniser and colonised). Both significantly belong to the last ten years of Scott's life, when such reservations as he had about Scotland's place in the Union intensified.

While Burns came of Jacobite ancestry, and both wrote and adapted Jacobite themes in nostalgic and French Revolutionary modes, his writing cannot itself, for all its transmutations, be entirely divorced from the period when Jacobitism was still a political threat. Burns belongs more with Fergusson than with his successors, and friends in Fergusson's circle may have produced one of the earliest printed collections of Jacobite song, *The True loyalist*, which appeared in 1779. What is of greater interest is not the survival of Jacobite rhetoric and discourse so late, but its endurance and afterlife when the cause was, as Redgauntlet tells us, 'lost for ever'. As it was, it survived as an expression of self-doubt, a discourse and way of writing about Scotland which emphasised the country's divided identity, both Scottish and British, and the abandonment of the historic values of its past: indeed, this use of the Stuart dynasty can arguably be traced back as far as the writing of William Drummond in the early seventeenth century. Whether or not these assessments and their manner were accurate is perhaps less important than their central place in some of the imaginative constructions which themselves helped to keep the idea of 'Scotland' alive in the nineteenth and twentieth centuries.

James Hogg offered an oblique criticism of Scott's Panglossian tendencies by drawing attention both to Jacobite radicalism and the suffering of the Highlands in a manner which emphasised their continuing relevance for the plight of Scotland. His *Jacobite Relics of Scotland* (1819–21), collected at the behest of the Highland Society of London, caused offence by being insufficiently bowdlerised – by their authenticity and Scottishness in fact. Hogg also wrote a number of the songs himself: in one, 'Donald Macgillivray', which he slyly called 'a capital old song, and very popular', he introduces the Jacobite cause through the personae not of Highland chiefs, but of Lowland tradesmen. Donald is invited to 'come like a cobbler . . . come like a weaver', in a land whose 'makings were naething'. He will deliver Scotland from poverty, and the language in which this is promised is more redolent of the contemporary complaints of Lowland radicals than of the language of the Jacobite risings. The radicalised weavers of 1820 lurk only just behind Hogg's lines.[45]

Just as Hogg makes allusion to contemporary radicalism in 'Donald Macgillivray', so he opens up criticism of the Highland Clearances, not only in his poetry, but in the way in which he describes the aftermath of the 'Forty-Five' in *Three Perils of Woman*, which portrays a miserable land, a corrupt professional class and the death of one of the heroines and her child. Hogg asks 'Is there human sorrow on record like this that winded up the devastations of the Highlands?' The answer is again lurking in the background: yes. That the Clearances are the target is made all the more likely by the fact that Hogg's more explicit writing on them cites their effect on Jacobite clans and areas.[46]

Hogg also sets his most famous *Private Memoirs and Confessions of a Justified Sinner* (1824) at the time of the Union. The Wringhims are Whig presbyterians; the Colwans episcopalian royalists. Both have their vices: but it is Robert Wringhim's dogged antinomianism which destroys 'natural ties and relationships in order to fulfil a barren, self-destructive ideology'.[47] He loses his life and his soul, but not before he has destroyed the fabric of the life around him. These ideas, of a divided national self and the destructiveness of the impenetrable ideological self-congratulation of presbyterian Whiggery, were seminal in later Scottish fiction. In *The Master of Ballantrae* (1886), R. L. Stevenson portrays a Scotland divided by the Jacobite period, one side demonised by suffering, the other by complacency, while in *Kidnapped* and *Catriona* he presents a simpler picture of Jacobite honour and spontaneity against presbyterian caution, greed and hypocrisy. John Buchan's *Witch Wood* (1927), set in Montrose's Year of Victories, traces the division and destruction of an organic Scottish pre-Reformation identity by the bigotry-induced guilt of a society which massacres defenceless Irishwomen and pollutes charity and spontaneity with accusation and hypocrisy: like Hogg, Buchan probably intended contemporary reference to kirk of Scotland anti-Irishness in the 1920s.

[45] James Hogg, *The Jacobite Relics of Scotland*, 2 vols (Paisley, 1874), I, 100.

[46] James Hogg, *The Three Perils of Woman*, 3 vols (London, 1823), iii, 335, 339, 371.

[47] Murray G. H. Pittock, 'James Hogg and the Jacobite Cause', *Studies in Hogg and His World*, 2 (1991), 14–24 (17).

Likewise, J. M. Barrie's *Farewell, Miss Julie Logan* (1932) suggests that
fear of and desire for the lost organic identity of Stuart Scotland drive
the hero, a minister, insane. The link between Jacobitism and the
Clearances is made again in Neil Gunn's *Butcher's Broom* (1934). Even
in John Galt's *The Entail* (1829), the names Charles and George
respectively signify a carefree and a counting-house ethos. In Violet
Jacob's *Flemington* (1911), the difficulty of avoiding betrayal of one side
or the other in a divided Scotland is emphasised. On a slightly more
popular level, the 1850s Jacobite romances of James Grant live again in
twentieth-century novels and plays such as *The Romance of the White
Rose, The White Cockade, Chasing Charlie* and Malcolm Macinnes's
The 'Forty-Five (1923).

When in *The Albannach* (1932), Fionn MacColla wanted to stress the
need for a reawakened Scottish consciousness and the recovery of its
historic links with Ireland, it was again to the Jacobite period he turned.
The moment of truth comes when an Irish priest recites an *aisling* of
Aoghan Ó Rathaille's calling for the return to Ireland of the Stuart
prince, 'a man the most fine . . . of Scottish blood'. In *The Bull Calves*
(1947), Naomi Mitchison again tackles the question of divided identity
through an examination of the Jacobite period, while Compton Mackenzie in *Prince Charlie* (1932)[48] mused on the wonderful things that
might have happened if only Charles Edward had prevailed in 1745: 'the
long martyrdom of Ireland would have been averted. The decline of
Scotland into a provincial appendage would have been avoided.' From a
totally different part of the political spectrum a recent (1994) Scottish
socialist discussion paper set out to enquire 'Jacobite or Covenanter –
Which tradition?', terms which would alike have been meaningless to
their comrades south of the border, but which provide yet another
dimension of the use of Jacobite rhetoric and the Jacobite analysis in the
most unlikely places.

A similar deep and returning interest in the Jacobite period can be
found in poetry, particularly at the turn of the century, with works such
as A. C. MacDonell's *Lays of the Heather* (1896) and Douglas Ainslie's
Song of the Stewarts (1909). There is a long tradition of ersatz Jacobite
song, ranging from W. E. Aytoun's *Lays of the Scottish Cavaliers* to the
Corries' 'Roses of Prince Charlie', which gives a definitively modern
nationalist edge to its central symbol, the White Rose. This Jacobite
image was transformed once more into a national symbol in the early
mid-twentieth century: this was the course recommended by an early

---

[48] Compton Mackenzie, *Prince Charlie* (Edinburgh, 1932), 75, 155, 197.

article in *The Scots Independent*. Hugh MacDiarmid, always willing to see the Jacobites as avatars of 'the Gaelic Commonwealth Restored', helped to confirm the transformation of the White Rose into a national rather than a dynastic symbol, 'the little white rose of Scotland' in line with the nationalist claims of Scottish Jacobitism. In 1947, the nationalist Claim of Right to the United Nations specifically stressed the role of Jacobitism as one with 'appeal to Scottish patriotism', and the Jacobites as having a 'definite pledge to abrogate the Treaty of Union of 1707'.[49] Thus it came to be the case that both at the first sitting and at the official opening of the Scottish parliament, SNP members wore a white-rose buttonhole, a move which attracted interest among the most distinguished visitors that day.[50]

In broader terms, the struggle between Scottishness and Britishness that began in 1559–60 and ended in 1746 is at the heart of the 'universal landscape' of Edwin Muir's writing.[51] In 'Scotland 1941', the felling of 'the ancient oak of loyalty' (the oak is a Stuart badge) is a key to the collapse of Scotland, once again, into a country which has sold its organic soul ('We were a tribe, a family, a people') for 'pride of pelf'. The advantages in trade and commerce accruing from presbyterian acquiescence in the Treaty of Union and the Hanoverian succession have led to a Scotland of 'smoke and dearth and money everywhere "This towering pulpit of the Golden Calf".[52] This theme is part of Scottish literature's central critique of its own past. It surfaces again in Sydney Goodsir Smith's references to 'the Union's faithless peace' and its link to the 'cheated race' of the Stuarts, or in George Campbell Hay's call for national renewal in 'Feachd a' Phrionnsa' ('The Princes Army'). Muir's characterisation of the state of modern Scotland as 'Scotland's Winter' is perhaps also present in Iain Crichton Smith's image of 'dizzying snow' in his poem on Prince Charles, although Crichton Smith's outlook (seen also in 'John Knox' and 'Culloden and After') is not so decidedly one-sided as Muir's. Tom Scott's poem on 'Scotland 1967' describes the loss of a 'Stewart capital' in 'yon fell trap' set by England; elsewhere he follows Muir in seeing the Reformation 'as weed

[49] Cf. Hugh MacDiarmid, 'A Scots Communist looks at Bonny Prince Charlie', *Scots Independent* (August, 1945), 1; *Scots Independent* II: 8 (1928), 125–6; III: 2 (1929), 143; IV: 7 (1930), 85; October (1947), 1.

[50] Request to the author for a history of the white rose emblem from Holyrood Press Office, 2 July 1999.

[51] P. H. Butter, *Edwin Muir: Man and Poet* (Edinburgh and London, 1966), 6.

[52] Murray G. H. Pittock, ' "This is the Place": Edwin Muir and Scotland', *Scottish Literary Journal*, 14:1 (1987), 53–72 (66); Pittock, *The Invention of Scotland*, 140.

that chokes the grain'.[53] In this continuing framework of reference the twent-first century has tended to politicise what to earlier writers like Lady John Scott (1810–1900) was simply sentiment. In such a manner Jacobite discourse and the Jacobite critique revivify the patriot dimension on which once it drew, and which was sidelined in its restoration as a colourful variety of imperial localism in the early nineteenth century. In the last seventy-five years its rhetoric has become increasingly part of a culture of disquiet in Scotland; and in this process, the Jacobite cult remains both irritating kitsch and a language of identity, which in one sense or another it has been for 300 years. It still, however, both leads us back to the Scottish past and blocks us off from it: for the discourse of Scottish patriotism, the Scottish court and Scottish high culture is distorted for us by its adoption in the partisan struggles which brought the Scottish state to an end and helped to confirm the stable dominance of its British replacement.

[53] Sydney Goodsir Smith, *Collected Poems* (London, 1975), 47; Iain Crichton Smith, *The Exiles* (Manchester and Dublin, 1984), 26; George Campbell Hay and Tom Scott, quoted in Pittock, *The Invention of Scotland*, 145, 152; cf. also Christopher Whyte, 'Tom Scott: An Imagined World', in *Chapman*, 47–8 (1987), 7–13 (9).

CHAPTER 10

Queen Victoria and the Cult of Scottish Monarchy

Richard J. Finlay

H istorians of modern Britain have long recognised the cultural, social and political significance of the monarchy.[1] Indeed, as the institution was modernised and updated, it came to play an increasingly important symbolic role in defining Britain and its imperial identity in the Victorian era. As the apparent political power of Victoria diminished as Britain ambled on its way towards greater democracy, her symbolic power increased. The use of the monarchy as a symbol of British power and prestige is perhaps one of the most popular and enduring cultural icons of the Victorian era. Victoria, whether as the middle-class embodiment of the 'mother' of the nation or the altogether more resplendent Empress of India, was largely omnipresent in British society (apart for a prolonged period of mourning for the death of Albert in 1861). David Cannadine has noted how the institution of the monarchy was reinvented to accommodate the greater symbolic demands of Victorian Britain.[2] Yet, historians of Scotland have not focused on the effect of this most potent British cultural symbol, which, along with parliament and the military, combined to produce a 'holy trinity' of British institutions which could

---

[1] F. Hardie, *The Political Influence of the British Monarchy, 1868–1952* (London, 1970); J. L. Lant, *Insubstantial Pageant: Ceremony and Confusion at Queen Victoria's Court* (London, 1979); David Cannadine, 'The Context, Performance and Meaning of Ritual: The British Monarchy and the Invention of Tradition', in E. J. Hobsbawm and T. Ranger (eds), *The Invention of Tradition* (Cambridge, 1983); W. M. Kuhn, 'Ceremony and Politics: The British Monarchy 1871–1872', *Journal of British Studies*, April 1987; W. L. Arnstein, 'Queen Victoria Opens Parliament: The Disinvention of Tradition', *Historical Research*, 63 (1990).

[2] Cannadine, 'Context, Performance and Meaning of Ritual', in Hobsbawm and Ranger (eds), *Invention of Tradition*.

arguably match and balance the Scottish institutions of law, religion and education to produce a reasonably harmonious Scottish/British identity in Scotland.[3] While politics and the military are increasingly receiving historical attention, the monarchy has been strangely absent from Scottish historical enquiry in the British era. This is a situation which is all the more strange given the tendency to focus on Scottish notions of kingship and Jacobitism during the first half-century of the Union with England.[4] Indeed, more work has gone into charting the activities of the remnants of Stewart loyalism in Scotland in the nineteenth century than has been carried out on the activities of the British monarchy in Scotland.[5] After 1746 monarchy vanishes from the Scottish historical record with only minor appearances thereafter. Without the Stewarts, it would appear, monarchy has no place in Scottish history, other than to denounce the phoniness of 'Balmoralism'.[6]

There are good reasons for regarding this as an odd state of affairs. First, as many have noted, the nineteenth century witnessed the definition of Scottish national identity in which tartanomania and Highlandism predominated.[7] There were fewer better exponents of

[3] See Michael Fry, *Patronage and Principle: A Political History of Modern Scotland* (Aberdeen, 1987); Graeme Morton, *Unionist Nationalism: Governing Urban Scotland 1830–1860* (East Linton, 1999).

[4] M. G. H. Pittock, *The Myth of the Jacobite Clans* (Edinburgh, 1995); M. G. H. Pittock, *Jacobitism* (Basingstoke, 1998); B. P. Lenman, *The Jacobite Risings in Britain, 1689–1746* (London, 1980); B. Lenman, *The Jacobite Clans of the Great Glen 1650–1784* (London, 1984); D. Szechi, *The Jacobites, Britain and Europe 1688–1788* (Manchester, 1994); F. McLynn, *The Jacobites* (London, 1985); E. Cruikshanks and J. Black (eds), *The Jacobite Challenge* (Edinburgh, 1988).

[5] M. G. H. Pittock, *The Invention of Scotland: The Stuart Myth and the Scottish Identity, 1638 to the Present* (London, 1991), 120–33.

[6] For the historiographical longevity of Jacobitism as a Scottish phenomenon see footnotes 4 and 5 as well as R. Forbes, *The Lyon in Mourning* (Edinburgh, 1896); A. Cunninghame, *The Loyal clans* (Cambridge, 1932); G. P. Insh, *The Scottish Jacobite Movement* (London, 1952); Sir Charles Petrie, *The Jacobite Movement* (London, 1959). On the denounciation of 'Balmoralism' see George Scott-Moncrieff, 'Balmorality', in D. C. Thomson (ed.), *Scotland in Quest of its Youth* (Edinburgh, 1932); Oliver Brown, *Hitlerism in the Highlands* (Glasgow, 1944); Tom Nairn, *The Break-Up of Britain* (London, 1987 edn); Cairns Craig, *Out of History* (Edinburgh, 1989).

[7] P. Womack, *Improvement and Romance: Inventing the Myth of the Highlands* (Basingstoke, 1989); W. Donaldson, *The Jacobite Song: Political Myth and National Identity* (Aberdeen, 1988); J. Prebble, *The King's Jaunt: George IV in Scotland, 1822* (London, 1988); T. M. Devine, *Clanship to Crofters' War* (Manchester, 1994); Pittock, *The Invention of Scotland*.

this fashion than Albert and Victoria, who not only invented their own tartans, but were quite happy to wear the Stewart tartans without any sense of contradiction or even irony. Second, Victoria spent a great deal of time in Scotland and did more touring of the area than any major politician. The route from Stirling to the north-east is littered with monuments, statues and fountains opened by Victoria, whose regular appearance at numerous train stations on her way north ensured that a large number of her subjects were able to physically view their sovereign. The 1879 Mid-Lothian by-election is often heralded as a turning point in Scottish and British politics as the former prime minister and leader of the Liberal Party, William Gladstone, went out and spoke to the people at mass rallies. The public had to be courted and leaders had to be seen by the people. Yet Victoria had established this technique of mass meetings more than twenty years earlier. Third, the monarchy was a fundamental British institution; yet, in Scotland it was able to recast itself in native garb, using notions of the historical continuity of Scottish kingship to legitimise Victoria and Albert's special relationship with the Northern Kingdom.[8] The fact that the cult of Scottish monarchy in the Victorian era was an invented tradition does little to take away neither its success nor the public's willingness to accept it as truth. Furthermore, Scotland was not unique in this phenomenon. The Raj combined native and imported traditions to provide a veneer of authenticity and legitimacy to British rule with the monarchy as the focal point. The use of 'fake' historical traditions was one way of presenting British rule as a continuity of Indian history and not a break with the past.[9] While the use of invented tradition in India was more systematic, thorough and planned than was the case in Scotland, it can reasonably be argued that the lessons of the success of a tartan monarchy imprinted a future blueprint for the chameleon-like ability of the British sovereign to adapt to different localities, customs and cultures. From the great white mother of Africa to the Empress of India, the projection of royal authority in the heyday of Victorian imperialism clearly owed much to the Scottish experience. These are the issues that this chapter will explore to show how the British monarchy was legitimised as a major Scottish institution and an

[8] This point has been picked up more by 'British' historians than their Scottish counterparts. See K. Robbins, *Nineteenth Century Britain* (Oxford, 1988), 172–4 and B. Harrison, *The Transformation of British Politics 1860–1995* (Oxford, 1996), 90–1.

[9] Bernard S. Cohn, 'Representing Authority in Victorian India', in Hobsbawm and Ranger (eds), *Invention of Tradition*, 165–209.

important part of this phenomenon was the rethreading of links to the Scottish monarchy of the past.

The visit of George IV to Scotland in 1822 has been seen by many historians as the beginning of the rehabilitation of the monarchy in Scotland.[10] After all, it was the first visit to Scotland by a reigning British monarch for over a century and the event was stage-managed by Sir Walter Scott to cast the king in a peculiarly Scottish, and, in particular, Highland hew. The 'plaided panorama' as Scott's son-in-law, Lockhart, described it, was a highly theatrical reinvention of history.[11] The king was toasted as 'the chief of the chiefs' in recognition of the dubious claim that Scotland was a clan-based society. Even the Lowland elite, most of whom had little time for, nor understanding of, the Highlanders, other than to denounce them periodically for laziness, barbarity and being a general affront to civilisation, were ordered to don Highland costume.[12] Most of the tartans were invented and the whole process has been dismissed as a sham, especially as the visit coincided with a ferocious economic and cultural onslaught against the Gaels which would eventually lead to clearance, famine and emigration.[13] The event is also hailed as the start of the phenomenon of Highlandism or tartanism in which Scotland was cast in an essentially phoney Highland image. The shortbread tin image of Scotland was to endure right through the nineteenth and twentieth centuries and, certainly in the popular imagination, much of this has been bound up with the visit of George IV.

Yet, there are a number of problems with this thesis. Firstly, as Tom Devine has shown, Highlandism was growing from the late eighteenth century and the event was not as new as has been presented.[14] Indeed, tartan and the association of Scotland with Highland images seems to have been most pronounced in London and it could be argued that George's visit was essentially what a southern English aristocrat would expect to see in Scotland. Put crudely, Sir Walter was making sure that

---

[10] Bruce Lenman, *Integration, Enlightenment, Industrialization: Scotland 1746–1832* (London, 1981), 130–5; M. Lynch, *Scotland: A New History* (London, 1991), 355; M. G. H. Pittock, *The Invention of Scotland*, 88.

[11] The best account of this is Prebble, *The King's Jaunt*.

[12] See Rob Clyde, *From Rebel to Hero: The Image of the Highlander, 1745–1830* (East Linton, 1995), 1–49 for traditional views of the Highlanders.

[13] See T. M. Devine, *The Great Highland Famine: Hunger, Emigration and the Scottish Highlands in the Nineteenth Century* (Edinburgh, 1988), 1–33.

[14] T. M. Devine, *Clanship to Crofters' War: The Social transformation of the Scottish Highlands* (Manchester, 1994), 84–100.

his majesty was not disappointed and that Scotland lived up to his expectations. Second, it was a one-off visit of a fairly short duration and confined only to Edinburgh. No monarch would visit Scotland again for another twenty years, until Victoria arrived in 1842. Clearly, there is a danger of sketching in lines of continuity between the visit of George in 1822 to the explosion of Highlandism in the mid-Victorian period when no such continuity existed. Are we to assume that the visit of George IV had a delayed reaction which only came to fruition in the reign of Victoria?

While it may be said that the visit of George IV forged a link between the British monarchy and tartanry, it could be equally argued that it was a short-lived affair. Highlandism is largely absent from Scotland in the late 1820s and 1830s, which tends to suggest that the short visit of George IV and decades-long association of Victoria with Scotland were two unrelated and different phenomena. Furthermore, as a catalyst in the promotion of a Highland Scottish identity, longevity alone would suggest that Victoria was the more important. A third problem is that the visit of George IV was predominantly the fare of the Scottish aristocracy. As Catriona Macdonald points out in Chapter 11 of this book, the sorry affair of the king's treatment of Queen Caroline two years earlier had brought the monarchy into considerable disrepute. Furthermore, the key voices of censure were those of the church and the middle class, who would emerge in the Victorian period as the mouth-piece of Scotland and the queen's staunchest supporters. The period between George's visit in 1822 and Victoria's arrival in Scotland in 1842 was a time of heightened tensions between the middle class and the aristocracy. Disputes over patronage in the church, a bitterly fought campaign for the extension of the franchise to the middle class and the growing sense of frustration over the corn laws combined to sharpen anti-aristocratic sentiment in Scotland. The impact of the Irish and Highland potato famines in the second half of the 1840s was cited as evidence of the rapacious and self-centred nature of landlords. It was an episode in which, according to contemporary eyes, the Highland gentry emerged with little credit. The aristocratic Highlandism which accom-panied the visit of George IV to Edinburgh in 1822 seems badly out of kilter with the growing dominance of anti-aristocratic middle-class ideas and values in early Victorian Scotland. George and his cronies were associated with dandyism, something that could never be said about Victoria, the middle-class mother of the nation. Again what many have assumed is that the visit of George IV established the Scottish Highland identity in an undiluted and fixed form. A final difficulty of crediting

George's visit with the adoption of Highlandism is that in a society with a limited print media and poor internal communications, very few people actually witnessed George's tartan spectacular. Furthermore, it is worth noting that those who did were not overawed by what they saw and if anything, the whole episode was a source of ridicule and humour.[15] The coming of the railway age and the mass press coincided with the reign of Victoria and, as we shall see, both were necessary ingredients in the promotion of Highlandism and the popularity of Victoria. So also was her solemnity, which was an essential component for tartanry to be taken seriously.

The timing of the reinvention of Scottish monarchy coincided with the Victorian age of equipoise; a period of calm after the turbulence of the post-Napoleonic Wars era. Between 1815 and 1850, Scotland had witnessed a profound economic depression following the end of the Napoleonic wars, an insurrection in 1820, class conflict and industrial disputes throughout the twenties and thirties, a cholera epidemic in 1832, famine in the Highlands in 1846, the passing of the Reform Act in 1832, the growth of Chartism and bitter conflict in the church, which culminated in the Disruption of 1843 and its aftermath, all of which created a great sense of unease. For many contemporaries, it seemed as if Scotland was losing its distinctive national identity as the forces of modernisation ripped through the nation, in the words of Henry Cockburn, like an economic scythe.[16] Much of this national soul searching created the necessary environment ready for a royalist take-over. The belief that Scotland was disappearing created a fad for the collection of historical manuscripts and ballads before old Scotia was lost forever. Evidence of this sense of crisis in national identity seemed to be confirmed with the failure to complete the Scottish National Monument on Calton Hill, which was started in 1822, but had run into serious difficulties by 1828.[17] It was during this time when 'traditional' Scotland was disappearing that the novels of Sir Walter Scott and his rediscovery of the Scottish regalia in 1818 awoke a popular sense of history.[18] The conflict in the church sent many back to the past in pursuit

---

[15] See Prebble, *The King's Jaunt*, 269.

[16] Quoted in Paul Scott, 'The Last Purely Scotch Age', in D. Gifford (ed.), *The History of Scottish Literature, Volume 3: The Nineteenth Century* (Aberdeen, 1988), 17.

[17] Morton, *Unionist Nationalism*, 184–7.

[18] Carola Oman, *The Wizard of the North: The Life of Sir Walter Scott* (London, 1973); James Anderson, *Sir Walter Scott and History* (Edinburgh, 1981); C. Kidd, *Subverting Scotland's Past: Scottish Whig Historians and the Creation of an Anglo-British Identity, 1689–c.1830* (Cambridge, 1993), 247–68.

of a historical vindication for current objectives. The debate over the rights and wrongs of patronage was littered with historical examples.[19]

Even radicals were appropriating the figures of Bruce and Wallace in their quest for political reform.[20] The belief that there was a 'strange death of Scottish history' in the first half of the nineteenth century should only be applied to the writing of academic history.[21] In the popular imagination, it seemed to be everywhere. For many of today's cultural and literary critics, the creation of a 'sham' Scotland has been portrayed as a failure of historical nerve and a collapse into cultural degeneracy.[22]

While it is undoubtedly the case that the sentimentalisation of Scottish culture and history in the Victorian era created a tartan monster whose clutches have extended into the present, it should not blind the historian as to the reasons for its creation nor should value judgements as to what should or should not have happened interfere in the process of reconstructing the reasons why this phenomenon came to exist. Just as contemporary critics have deconstructed the tartan and kailyard myths for their own reasons, so too did the Victorians construct them. As a precondition for the reinvention of the monarchy in Scotland, the upsurge of a popular romantic interest in Scottish history was important for two reasons. First, it created the necessary fertile imagination that would be receptive to re-establishing imagined lines of continuity with the Scottish past, which was an essential prerequiste to the tartanisation of the monarchy. Second, the monarchy offered the possibility of a reconnection with the past that did not necessarily lead to conflict in the way that radical and conservative and free and established church readings of the past did. Just as Victoria was important in uniting the nation in the present, she could also unite the nation in the past through the veneration of the institution of monarchy. The product was a rather uncritical and sentimentalised version of the Scottish past, but that said, it was one that suited Victorian sensibilities.

During the second half of the nineteenth century, Victoria's visits to

[19] R. J. Finlay, 'Keeping the Covenant: Scottish National Identity', in T. M. Devine and J. R. Young (eds), *Eighteenth-Century Scotland: New Perspectives* (East Linton, 1999), 127–30; S. J. Brown and M. Fry (eds), *Scotland in the Age of Disruption* (Edinburgh, 1995).

[20] T. C. Smout, *A Century of the Scottish People, 1830–1950* (London, 1987 edn), 237.

[21] See M. Ash, *The Strange Death of Scottish History* (Edinburgh, 1980).

[22] Most famously, Tom Nairn, *The Break-Up of Britain* (London, 1981 edn); Cairns Craig, *Out of History* (Edinburgh, 1996).

216 RICHARD J. FINLAY

Balmoral were more or less annual events and were accompanied by much pomp and ceremony. The family purchased the Balmoral estate in 1852 and immediately commissioned architects to design and rebuild the castle, which was completed in 1855. The expansion of the railway system meant that a direct route through Scotland enabled the royal family to make many stopping-off tours and visits and thus increase their exposure to the population.[23] In 1849 for example, Glasgow and Perth were visited, which aroused keen public interest and excitement. Such public spectacles invariably had a Highland flavour, which meant that royal visits, which not only increased in number in the second half of the nineteenth century, but also became opportunities to demonstrate a distinctive Scottish take on the monarchy. The monarch's presence in Scotland helped to revitalise and promote the role of the Order of the Thistle. It provided increased ceremonial roles for the army and the volunteers, as well as the justiciary and the county sheriffs. The royal palace at Holyrood in Edinburgh regained some of its former presence as a result of Victoria's visits. Many towns and cities became regularly acquainted with royal visits and the considerable tartanorama that accompanied them and developed into tourist attractions in their own right. Royal visits were reported and recounted by the press especially the local press, which was able to inject a lot of local interest. Stirling, for example, received royal visitors in 1842, 1869, 1875, 1879 and 1891. In 1887 the queen opened a fountain, which was a lasting memorial to her visit. The fact that numerous statues, fountains, buildings and other civic monuments have Victoria's dedication is an ample testament to her presence within Scottish society at this time. Added together, Victoria was to spend over eighty months in Scotland, compared to the paltry five weeks allocated to Ireland.

The press were especially gratified by her majesty's sensitivity to Scottish customs and Scottish ways. Local authorities went out of their way to impress and the Provost of Perth had to ask the Lord Lyon for instruction on Scottish royal protocol. The publication of *Leaves from the Journal of Our Life in the Highlands* in 1868 and a follow up *More Leaves from the Journal of a Life in the Highlands* in 1883 allowed the reading public a fascinating insight into Victoria's passion for Scotland. In them, she described an ideal Highlands, which, although far removed from reality, was nevertheless flattering to Scottish sensibilities. Her

---

[23] T. C. Smout, 'Tours in the Scottish Highlands from the Eighteenth to the Twentieth Centuries', *Northern Scotland*, 5 (1983); J. Simmons, *The Victorian Railway* (London, 1991).

character descriptions of the Highlanders show them to be imbued with the traditional Victorian values of hard work, religiosity, sobriety (apart from the odd dram) and respectability. The *Journals* are also lavish in their praise of Sir Walter Scott, which undoubtedly helped to keep that author's particular romantic notion of Scottish history alive in the public imagination. There was no doubt that Victoria liked Scotland and this certainly endeared her to the Scottish nation. As she told her children's governess, Lady Lyttleton, 'Scotch air, Scotch people, Scotch hills, Scotch rivers, Scotch woods are all preferable to those of any other nation in the world.'[24] At a time when there was a desire for a sanitised Scotland free from the evils of urbanisation and industrialisation, Victoria's description of the Highlands was an ideal tonic:

> The scenery is so beautiful! It is very different from England: all the houses built of stone; the people so different, – sandy hair, high cheek bones; children with long shaggy hair and bare legs and feet; little boys in kilts. Near Dunkeld, and also as you get more into the Highlands, there are prettier faces. Those jackets which the girls wear are so pretty; all the men and women, as well as the children look very healthy. [25]

Also, while politicians such as Duncan McLaren and organisations such as the National Association for the Vindication of Scottish Rights in the mid-1850s bemoaned the lack parliamentary time and attention Scotland received, monarchical presence helped compensate. Indeed, one of the key complaints of the national Association for Scottish Rights was the improper use of Scottish heraldic devices. Petitions to her majesty pointing out the correct use of such devices was part and parcel of a resurgence of Scottish identity in the mid-nineteenth century in which the reclamation of Scottish monarchy was an important element.[26] A distinctive Scottish royal presence helped make the Scots feel part of the British state and empire. For many Scots at the time it seemed at last as if the monarchy had come home. Jacobites and Jacobitism rarely make an appearance in the Scottish historical record at this time, apart from the occasional denounciation of their tyranny and threat to liberty. The

---

[24] Quoted in Michael J. Stead, *Queen Victoria's Scotland* (London, 1992), 9.

[25] *Leaves from the Journal of Our Life in the Highlands* (1868, various editions); *More Leaves from the Journal of a Life in the Highlands* (1883, various editions); hereafter *Journal* and date. *Journal*, 1 September 1842.

[26] See Morton, *Unionist Nationalism*, 133–55.

Catholic Stewarts had no place in the presbyterian vision of Scotland's past.[27] Serendipity also played its part in Victoria's reclamation of the Scottish throne. The Highland Clearances were past their worse after the late 1850s, leaving the way open for the depiction of an idealised Highland way of life without the awkward brutal facts of eviction getting in the way and the Highlanders had helpfully turned themselves into a bastion of god-fearing presbyterianism. The Highland/Lowland divide was conquered by the Victorian creation of a strong identification of Scottishness with Highlandism, and the important point here is that Victoria was a significant part of this process. The Highland identity of Scotland was aided by a royal seal of approval.

A key element in the reinvention of the Scottish monarchy was Victoria's ability to reattach herself to the threads of Scottish history to create the appearance of historical continuity. Visits to historical sights were of great importance in the royal schedule north of the border, and Victoria made great play of her legitimacy to claim this history as her own. The royal castles, Fingal's Cave, Glencoe, Melrose, Dryburgh, Kelso and Dunfermline Abbeys and other places were part of the royal tour. Previous Scottish monarchs were described as her predecessors and she made no effort to describe them as specific Scottish monarchs, it was simply assumed. Her description of Jedburgh in 1867 gives a good example of her ease with Scottish history:

> King Malcolm IV died there; William the Lion and Alexander
> II resided there; Alexander III married his second wife,
> Joletta, daughter of the Comte de Dreux, there, and Queen
> Mary was the last sovereign who came to administer severe
> justice.[28]

On her visit to Inverness in 1873 much was made of the occasion because it was a place 'where no sovereign had been since my poor ancestress Queen Mary'.[29] The restoration of the Tomb of James III in Cambuskenneth near Stirling bears the simple inscription 'by a descendent, Victoria'.

Victoria actively incorporated many of the Jacobite myths into her own sense of Scottish identity. In 1875 she commented that:

---

[27] See R. J. Finlay, 'Myths, Heroes and Anniversaries in Modern Scotland', *Scottish Affairs*, 18 (1997), 108–26.
[28] *Journal*, 23 August 1867.
[29] *Journal*, 16 September 1873.

It was, as General Ponsonby observed afterwards, a striking scene. 'There was Lochiel' as he said, 'whose great grand uncle had been the real moving cause of the uprising of 1745 – for without him Prince Charles would not have made the attempt – showing your Majesty (whose great-great-grandfather he had striven to dethrone) the scenes made historical by Prince Charlie's wanderings. It was a scene one could not look on unmoved'.

Yes; and *I* feel a sort of reverence in going over all these scenes in this most beautiful country which I am glad to call my own, where there was much devoted loyalty to the family of my ancestors – for Stewart blood is in my veins, and I am now their representative, and the people are as devoted to me as they were to that unhappy race.[30]

Victoria used her own sense of self and her position as monarch as a means to attempt historical reconciliation between the Hanoverians and the Jacobites, and in so doing helped to lay one historical division to rest. In 1873 at Glenfinnan, the staging post for the 45 rebellion, she stated 'And here was I, the descendent of the Stewarts and of the very king that Prince Charles sought to overthrow, sitting and walking about quite privately and peaceably.'[31] Yet, the Jacobites were now safe to sentimentalise and many of the supposed qualities of loyalism and valour which had characterised the cause could now be incorporated and used by the Victorian monarchy. Writing in 1869, she claimed that the Scots were 'a high-spirited, intelligent and determined people, whose loyalty to herself, is exceeded by *none* – if it is equalled by any of her subjects'.[32] The same technique of historical reconciliation was evident in her visit to Bannockburn. It was described as the place where her two ancestors met in battle. In the person of Victoria, Anglo-Scottish enmity could be laid to rest. The queen demonstrated an awareness of the fact that she was the historical outcome of the Union of the Crowns, and by paying due deference to the Scottish royal line, no matter how remote her direct ancestry, Victoria reactivated the idea of a living Scottish monarchy.

Victoria was adept as utilising Scottish history and giving a lead in the reinvention of new traditions, or perhaps to be more accurate in giving old ones a new twist. The association with militarism and monarchy was

[30] *Journal*, 12 September 1875.
[31] *Journal*, 15 September 1873.
[32] Quoted in Harrison, *Transformation of British Politics*, 90.

presented as an authentic Scottish tradition. Taking up the myths of the loyal clans and their dedication to the Stewart cause, it was possible to integrate a mythic sense of Scottish militarism with the Queen as a figurehead. In 1859, a visit to open the Loch Katrine water works was the occasion of the first presentation of the newly created rifle volunteers (part-time soldiers) in British history.[33] volunteerism and monarchical loyalism were two strains in Scottish military tradition which were brought together in Victoria's reign. The volunteers were held up as an example of the virtues of civic society in that the use of non-professional soldiers was an antidote to the practice of despotic regimes. Further- more, that the ranks of the volunteers were drawn from the middle class and had a say in the appointment of their officers and leaders was an important factor in fusing the military tradition with a quasi-democratic ethos. Volunteerism represented the qualities of liberal Scotland. Yet, the fusion of civic virtue with loyalty to the monarchy enabled that other mythic Scottish tradition, the unthinking loyalty of the Scottish soldier, to be given a more acceptable and modern twist. The military was no longer seen as the exclusive preserve of the aristocracy. In 1881 Queen Victoria took the salute from 40,000 volunteers at Holyrood palace, demonstrating how monarch and militarism had became intertwined in the public imagination.[34] The decoration of Scottish soldiers at Balmoral and the queen's personal interest in 'her' Highland regiments further cemented the bond. The promotion of militarism in Scotland should not been seen purely as the tentacles of Britishness extending its grip into Scottish identity, but rather as a means for the Scots to bring their own reinvented tradition of military prowess to bear in their own creation of a British identity. Militarism enabled the fusion of two distinctive tradi- tions: the old romantic conservative loyalty bound up with Jacobitism and the new liberal civic militarism associated with presbyterianism. English observers were shocked by the fact that Highland soldiers embarking at Southampton chose to spend their time in church and reading the Bible rather than in the pubs and brothels.[35] The role of the monarchy as a military figurehead was an essential component project- ing the idea of a continuous loyal military tradition.

Presbyterianism was another facet which could have threatened the creation of a sense of historical continuity, given the fact that in the past

---

[33] *Glasgow Herald* 18 October 1859.
[34] *The Scotsman*, 26 August 1881.
[35] J. M. MacKenzie, 'Empire and National Identities: The Case of Scotland', *Transactions of the Royal Historical Society*, sixth series, 8 (1998), 226.

religion had been one of the main issues of dispute between the Scots and the monarchy. A point made more salient by the fact that many popular religious tracts made copious references to the covenanting struggle against the 'tyrannical' Stewart monarchy. The fact that Victoria chose to worship in the presbyterian church in Scotland was an essential precondition for popular support and demonstrated a clear break in monarchical tradition. Although Scotland was split by the Disruption of 1843, her support for the Established church, rather than the Free church was seen as natural, even neutral, given that the Free church also accepted the 'establishment' principle for most of the nineteenth century. Indeed, it was claimed in Free church circles that Victoria's endorsement of the Established church was a vital factor in shoring up its support. Victoria endeared herself to presbyterians by jumping to their defence against English encroachments, a factor which occasionally brought both sides of the Disruption together for a brief moment. Attempts to promote episcopalianism in Scotland and English ecclesiastical arrogance were firmly put down:

> When the Archbishop [of Canterbury] himself came to
> Scotland, and permits the Bishops to speak of '*the* Church' –
> implying as they do, that the *Scotch* establishment is *no*
> Church, and her Sacraments not to be considered as such,
> which they openly do – the case becomes *very grave*. Now the
> Queen takes a solemn engagement on her accession, to maintain
> the Established Church of Scotland and she will maintain it.
> But quite apart from this, the Queen considers this movement
> as most mischievous. The Queen will not stand the attempts
> made to destroy the simple and truly Protestant faith of the
> Church of Scotland.[36]

The *Journals* describe the presbyterian faith in approving terms and the queen attended Scottish baptisms and funerals. Accounts of the various sermons rendered in Craigie Kirk were likewise reported, with Dr Norman MacLeod and Dr Edward Caird coming in for especially high praise, often it must be said to the chagrin of English visitors. Both Gladstone and Disraeli had difficulty with Victoria's acceptance of the 'primitive' Scottish religion. Her espousal of presbyterianism won approval from the leader of the volunteerist United Presbyterian church,

[36] Queen Victoria, *Letters 1862–1878*, 3 vols, ed. A. C. Benson and Viscount Esher (London, 1907), i, 381.

John Cairns. Speaking on the occasion of her Jubilee in 1887, he tellingly contrasted Victoria with previous Scottish monarchs:

> Although we deny to a great and noble Queen like this any headship of any kind in the church of Christ, as our fathers denied it to the Stuarts. I as a Scotchman and a presbyterian am thankful not only for her recognition of men like Norman Macleod and Principal Tulloch, but for her goodness to men like Thomas Guthrie and George Middleton [both eminent Free Churchers] in their dying hours. In these things we see something deeper than womanly sympathy or native tolerance, even the Christianity which recognises everywhere the same divine image, and which, when it is set upon so lofty a throne, blesses both the country and the world.[37]

Similarly, Victoria urged the Home Secretary not to interfere with the Scottish education system on the grounds that 'there was enough trouble with one kingdom [Ireland] without experimenting with the most loyal and most intelligent other kingdom'.[38]

The projection of family life at Balmoral also helped to reinforce particular notions of Scotland that chimed in with the Victorian age of equipoise. The *Highland Journals* painted an image of the monarchy in Scotland which was less stuffy and formal than the royal court in London. Victoria was shown to visit locals and participate in the activities of ordinary people. There was deference and respect, which was homely and not overbearing. Visits to family cottages and a word with the locals was an effective way of breaking down class barriers. The fact that the royal family was instructed to shake hands with the servants at Balmoral was reported with approval in the Scottish press where notions of the meritocratic society had a firm grip.

The idea of a more democratic royalty in Scotland was given a further impetus by the figure of John Brown. Born into a humble background, Brown displayed those talents which were admired by meritocratic Scotland. He was a true lad o pairts.

> He has since, most deservedly, been promoted to an upper servant, and my permanent personal attendant. He has all the

---

[37] Alexander R. MacEwen, *The Life and Letters of John Cairns* (London, 1898), 774.

[38] Quoted in Harrison, *Transformation of British Politics*, 91.

independence and elevated feelings peculiar to the Highland race, and is singularly straightforward, simple-minded, kind-hearted and disinterested; always ready to oblige; and of a discretion rarely to be met with. He is now in his fortieth year. His father was a small farmer, who lived at the Bush on the opposite side of Balmoral. He is the second of nine brothers – three of whom have died – two are in Australia and New Zealand, two are living in the neighbourhood of Balmoral; and the youngest, Archie (Archibald), is valet to our own Leopold, and is an excellent trustworthy young man.[39]

The apparent contrast between the much freer and less formal way of life in Scotland and the English royal palaces helped to highlight an important difference in the nature of the monarchy in Scotland, which seemed to reflect the perception of a more democratic and egalitarian nation.

In many ways, the key to Victoria's popularity was her ability to absorb a wide range of identities and traditions which were then reflected back to her audience. She could be seen in a variety of different lights, all of which had their enthusiastic supporters. Although Queen of Britain and Empress of India, she was able in Scotland to project a distinctive Scottish identity. For conservative, aristocratic and traditional Scotland, the queen was a landholder and the pinnacle of hereditary aristocracy with all the grandeur, splendour, sports and pastimes that came with this. She was an upholder of the Established church and a friend to the Scottish nobility who livened up their social calendar. The queen was an ardent supporter of Scotland's military and imperial tradition, which was a vital source of aristocratic employment. But there was also another Victoria. She was a mother and woman who espoused good family values, as well as a preacher of morality, thrift, sobriety and hard work. Plainly dressed, sober and austere, the queen was able to project the monarchy in a fine middle-class image, which was even able to incorporate 'democratic' elements. Testament to Victoria's popularity is to be found in the widespread mourning of her death and the rancour created by her heir, Albert. Almost at a stroke, the 'playboy' prince was able to undo his mother's assiduous cultivation of the cult of Scottish monarchy by his crass insensitivity to Scottish history and tradition. By taking the title Edward VII, the new monarch was seen to demonstrate contempt for Scottish history, given that there had been no

[39] *Journal*, undated entry 16 September 1849.

Scottish monarch called Edward. The church and local authorities refused to recognise the numeral and public inscriptions simply used the title 'King Edward' with no number attached.[40] All of which demonstrated the remarkable impact Victoria had in giving the British monarchy a Scottish dimension.

[40] Finlay, 'Myths, Heroes, Anniversaries', 126.

'Their Laurels Wither'd, and their Name Forgot': Women and the Scottish Radical Tradition

Catriona M. M. Macdonald

> The gregariousness of the Scotch, – 'Highlanders! shoulder to shoulder', – the abstract coherency of the people as a nation, – their peculiar pride in the history of their country, – their strong exhilarating associations with battlefields on which the conflict terminated more than six hundred years ago, – their enthusiastic regard for the memory of heroes many centuries departed, who fought and bled in the national behalf, – are all well-known manifestations of a prominent national trait.
>
> Hugh Miller, *First Impressions of England and its People* (Edinburgh, 1870)

Since 1707, in the absence of independent statehood, the 'abstract coherency' of the Scottish people as a 'nation' has frequently been predicated on stylised readings of Scotland's past and complementary inferences regarding native sensibilities. As has been highlighted elsewhere, 'the historic sense' is often more vivid 'in the dispossessed than in those who are themselves the visible guardians of tradition'.[1] And indeed, in a very real sense, 'Scotland' has survived the Union and the subsequent emigrant diaspora as a set of shared values evoked by its history and personified in its heroes.[2]

Significantly, this association of principle and precedent has encour-

---

[1] The quotation in the title of this chapter is taken from Lady Anne Hamilton, *The Epics of the Ton: Or, the Glories of the Great World: A Poem in Two Books, with Notes and Illustrations* (London, 1807), line 13. M. A. Hamilton, *J. Ramsay MacDonald* (London, 1929), 131.

[2] See M. Ash, 'William Wallace and Robert the Bruce: The Life and Death of a National Myth', in R. Samuel and P. Thompson (eds), *The Myths We Live By* (London, 1990), 86.

aged the conflation of the discourses of radicalism and patriotism at various stages in Scotland's political evolution. Most particularly, the historicism of the Scottish Labour movement perpetuated this vision in the twentieth century. In 1924 James Maxton considered that Scotland was 'a nation which, above all, has the democratic spirit', and in her biography of Ramsay MacDonald, Margaret Agnes Hamilton considered that to the Scot, 'a sense of the dignity and equality of man is native'.[3] In arriving at such and similar conclusions, the influence of history was profound. William Haddow recounted that

> From the days of Wallace there has always been a
> Revolutionary Movement in Scotland, fighting at one time for
> religious *Liberty*, at another for political *Equality*, and for the
> past thirty years or so, for economic and industrial *Freedom*.[4]

In much the same way, in 1947, William Marwick chronicled a 'rebel tradition' in Scottish politics:

> Perhaps particularly associated with the South-West, this can be
> traced back to the Lollards of Kyle, with their analogies to the
> 'Communism' of the Reformation period. The Reformers and
> Covenanters were appealed to by protagonists of social and
> political change as their spiritual forebears. With this is curiously
> blended a Jacobite strain, which . . . may represent nostalgia for
> a pre-industrial society as well as fellow-feeling with a defeated
> cause; monarchism in Scotland also sometimes had a democratic
> flavour. Thomas Muir and the 'Political Martyrs' of French
> Revolutionary days illustrate the first modern phase. Working-
> class support is more clearly evident in the post-war agitation of
> which the abortive 'Radical Rising' . . . is the most dramatic
> instance. Regular working-class organisation operates in the
> political field in the struggle for the Reform Bill, and, in
> disillusionment with its results, in the rise of Chartism.[5]

---

[3] J. Maxton, *James Maxton and Scotland* (Glasgow, 1924), 2; Hamilton, *J. Ramsay MacDonald*, 142.

[4] W. Haddow, *Socialism in Scotland: Its Rise and Progress* (Glasgow, n.d.), 9. See also W. Stewart, *J. Keir Hardie: A Biography* (London, 1921), xix.

[5] W. H. Marwick, *Labour in Scotland: A Short History of the Scottish Working Class Movement* (Glasgow, 1947), 6. In contrast, Tom Johnston resolutely opposed attributing democratic motives to the covenanters; see *The History of the Working Classes in Scotland* (Glasgow, 1922), 86–90.

After 1707 reform movements in Scotland relied to a significant extent on the conflation of radical and patriotic discourses to ground their claims for representation and social justice.[6] At each stage of development, action was legitimated in the name of previous 'martyrs' and in the principles which they were judged to hold, and, incrementally, new heroes were created and associated with the longer fight for Scottish liberty. Thus we have David Lowe in 1919: 'The Scottish Labour movement was not founded on materialism. The instinct for freedom and justice which animated the Covenanters and the Chartists also inspired the Nineteenth Century pioneers.'[7]

While such historicism succeeded in locating successive radical movements in an emotive shared past, it also simultaneously replicated the bias of contemporary sexual conventions and the prevalent gendered perspectives of existing histories. Necessarily restricted by the parameters of historical knowledge, protogonists had little alternative. While, in the nineteenth century, popular notions of the exploits of the men of the National Covenant emphasised their valour, courage and commitment to principle, similar activities attributed to 'indignant' female covenanters, were said to have often 'carried them somewhat beyond the bounds of moderation', and of those whose names survived in the historical record, the majority appeared as the wives, sisters and mothers of their more famous menfolk.[8] Given the high profile of covenanting rhetoric in the reform movement after 1832, such limited readings of women's role are significant. More generally, as a consequence of radicalism's historicism, sites of female activity were disempowered and the feminine was frequently excluded from definitions of responsible citizenship. The near absence of women in the lineage of the Scottish radical tradition is thus as much the consequence of the movement's use of history as it is representative of the failure of a limited historiography.

Isolating male bias in the historian while underestimating that which

[6] Controversially, more recently P. B. Ellis and S. Mac A'Ghobainn have noted that 'The Scottish Radical tradition has always gone hand in hand with Scottish nationalism': *The Scottish Insurrection of 1820* (London, 1976), 296.

[7] D. Lowe, *Souvenirs of Scottish Labour* (Glasgow, 1919), 125. Indeed, in more recent years, such a perspective has found a ready echo in the historiography of the Independent Labour Party. As Knox explains: 'They were the twentieth century's embodiment of the spirit of the Covenanters, and often referred to themselves as such': 'The Red Clydesiders and the Scottish Political Tradition', in T. Brotherstone (ed.), *Covenant, Charter and Party* (Aberdeen, 1989), 95.

[8] Rev. J. Anderson, *The Ladies of the Covenant: Memoirs of Distinguished Scottish Female Characters, Embracing the Period of the Covenant and the Persecution* (New York, 1880), 15. See also Anderson's *Ladies of the Reformation: Memoirs of Distinguished Female Characters, Vol. i* (Glasgow, 1854).

appears in the rhetoric and historical sense of past protagonists has tended to misdirect recent efforts to write women into Scotland's political past and has encouraged a women's history which is frequently 'compensatory' in nature.[9] (Rather, men have not been alone in undervaluing the role of women in Scotland's past.)[10] In the context of the radical movement, the 'corrective' is more usefully sought in explaining the gendered roots of its historical sense than in a relentless search for 'exceptional women', or in amalgamating women's movements into the ancestral lineage of the radical tradition by focusing on a limited elite who were members of *both* suffrage and labour movements. This is a strategy which threatens merely to perpetuate the replication of radical myth-history in current historiography. Instead, in seeking an explanation as to why Scottish radicalism identified women as *different*, we get closer to understanding the evolving popular epistemology which dictated the parameters of the radical tradition itself. As Linda Kerber has noted, 'political systems and systems of gender relations are reciprocal social constructions'.[11]

The conflation of radicalism and patriotism clearly has a significant gender dimension which demands analysis as a contribution to understanding the manner in which ' "Scottishness" and national identity are linked to a discourse of sexuality'.[12] It is not enough to account for 'the lack of prominence given to Scottish women' in cultural nuances which have 'denigrated Scottishness', and a society which, being 'essentially repressive and lacking in confidence', has 'repressed' and 'ignored' the achievements of its 'weaker sections'.[13] Rather, conventional sites of Scottish empowerment have frequently necessitated the disempowerment of alternative voices, among them, those of Scottish women. What follows will attempt to explain the manner in which this paradox has been played out within the Scottish radical tradition by pointing to important and interrelated determinants of radicalism's gendered vision and our understanding of it: namely, the legacy of the Union settlement;

[9] See J. Hendry, 'Snug in the Asylum of Taciturnity: Women's History in Scotland', in C. Whatley and I. Donnachie (eds), *The Manufacture of Scottish History* (Edinburgh, 1992), 125–42; E. King, *The Hidden History of Glasgow's Women: The The New Factor* (Edinburgh, 1993), 11.

[10] See E. G. Murray, *Scottish Women in Bygone Days* (London, 1930); *A Gallery of Scottish Women* (London, 1935), 9–10.

[11] L. K. Kerber, 'Separate Spheres, Female Worlds, Woman's Place: The Rhetoric of Women's History', *Journal of American History*, 17 (1988), 39.

[12] A. Howson, 'No Gods and Precious Few Women: Gender and Cultural Identity in Scotland', *Scottish Affairs*, 5 (1993), 48.

[13] M. Bain, 'Scottish Women in Politics', *Chapman*, 28 (1980), 4.

the pervasive influence of Enlightenment doctrines of political economy; the periodisation of current historiography; the ascendancy of constitutionalism in radical rhetoric after 1820 and the self-styling of the Labour Party as the 'closure' of the radical meta-narrative.

focus lies with male contrib. to Enlightenment

THE NEGLECTED CENTURY

Amanda Vickery has recently identified the eighteenth century as a neglected period in the history of British women, while highlighting how, sitting as it does 'smack in the middle of the conventional "big picture" ', it promises much to those who research these years.[14] Moreover, as the originary period during which many assumptions regarding womanhood, manners, sexuality and Scotland's place in a 'greater' Britain were codified, it is critical in any understanding of the conventions which determined the marginalisation of women in Scotland's radical tradition. In this regard, the twin legacies of the Union and the Enlightenment are critical to our understanding.

what about the female entry into polite society?

Whether through a process of elimination as much as by intent, the Union of 1707 facilitated the association of patriotism and radicalism by determining the 'spaces' within which Scottish identity might be articulated, while denying it others more appropriate to an as yet partial British or Anglo-British identity. Scottishness in this new 'Britain' was welcomed only in so far as it reinforced principles and practices commonly associated with 'the rights of Englishmen' which held 'universal appeal'.[15] Nevertheless, it was possible for Scottish identity to act as the vehicle for liberalising tendencies in the British state: a claim for Scottish 'rights' would, by necessity, either require the reformation of the constitutional settlement or demand its more efficient operation in order to uphold the much-vaunted values of constitutional liberty. Either way, after 1746 there was less likelihood that such demands would run the risk of reinvigorating the dynastic claims of the Stewarts, and a greater probability that they would echo the democratic ideals of the American colonies.

The indeterminate nature of, and ambiguities inherent in, the traditions

---

[14] A. Vickery, 'The Neglected Century: Writing the History of Eighteenth-Century Women', *Gender and History*, 3 (1991), 211.

[15] See C. Kidd, 'North Britishness and the Nature of "Patriotism" in Eighteenth-Century Scotland', in E. A. Cameron and F. Watson (eds), *Proceedings of ASHS Annual Conference* (n.p., 1994), 57. See also R. J. Finlay, 'Keeping the Covenant: Scottish National Identity', in T. M. Devine and J. R. Young (eds), *Eighteenth-Century Scotland: New Perspectives* (East Linton, 1999), 122–33.

of English constitutionalism, interacting with a Scottish notion of popular sovereignty which had never acquired parliamentary form, made this more likely and allowed Scots to rework the 'traditional rhetoric of Scottish liberty' in constitutional guise.[16] Indeed, by 1819 a Whiggish reformer from Renfrewshire could – with little apparent fear of self-contradiction – celebrate his descent from Robert Bruce and his territorial debts to William Wallace, while at the same time offering to uphold the constitution 'by sacrificing myself, either for the royal or popular rights, when they are in danger of mob, or suffering from tyranny'.[17]

Despite the fact that successive Whig histories of Scotland's pre-Union past described a barbaric society and a culture of limited consequence,[18] the absence of 'an official cult of the hero' in Britain in the latter half of the eighteenth century – despite the desire of many British men and women to '[see] their politics in terms of personalities' – invested greater capital in the more palatable heroes of Scotland's past.[19] As successive British governments avoided 'evolving and propagandizing a secular all-inclusive nationalism', in fear of the popular participation it would doubtless necessitate, radicalism effectively appropriated such figures as Wallace, Bruce and Knox as their own, just as the secession churches stood as the guardians of the settlement of 1690 and the principles of the Covenanters.[20] There was thus, from the beginning, the potential for a reciprocal relationship between the rhetoric of Scottish rights and personal liberties. The Union settlement and its operation did not guarantee its evolution, but allowed it space to evolve.

With the geographic parameters of the nation redrawn, it fell largely to the philosophers and social scientists of the Scottish Enlightenment to sketch its historical evolution and its moral limits, and to prominent Scottish Whig politicians to realise the principles of political economy on the material plane of interest and party.[21] The association of the 'conjectural history' of the Enlightenment and what Henry Cockburn chose to term the 'philosophic Whiggism' of the politicians of the *Edinburgh*

---

[16] Ibid., p. 61. See also G. Morton, *Unionist Nationalism: Governing Urban Scotland, 1830–1860* (East Linton, 1999).

[17] *A Letter Addressed to the Honest Reformers of Scotland* (Glasgow, 1819), 21.

[18] See C. Kidd, *Subverting Scotland's Past: Scottish Whig Historians and the Creation of an Anglo-British iIdentity 1689–c.1830* (Cambridge, 1993).

[19] L. Colley, 'Whose Nation?: Class and National Consciousness in Britain 1750–1830', *Past and Present*, 113 (1986), 105.

[20] Ibid., 107, 108; Finlay, 'Keeping the Covenant', 123.

[21] See B. Fontana, *Rethinking the Politics of Commercial Society: The Edinburgh Review, 1802–1832* (Cambridge, 1985).

Review, the sculptors of the 1832 Reform Act, had a profound influence on the definition of the Scottish 'body politic' and the political traditions with which later reformers were forced to engage.[22] Premised as both were on a stadial vision of human development and the coincidence and interrelated nature of economic prosperity and civilised manners, the role of government was appreciated as the guardianship of economic progress – an eventuality which would be most efficiently realised if it truly reflected the distribution of power in society.[23] As Biancamaria Fontana has acutely observed, in and of itself political economy 'had no precise prescriptive content', but in encouraging appeals to presumed historical precedent, and offering a 'scientific' rhetoric of rational citizenship, it did much to determine the means and the language through which new interests asserted their rights to representation.[24] Indeed, as early as the 1790s, it has been suggested, 'rationalist argumentation was in the ascendant within popular radicalism' in Britain.[25] Yet, while the historicism and rationalism encouraged by 'enlightened' Whigs were potentially inclusive, they denied equal political rights for women and other social groups.

As Jane Rendall has made clear, the association of commerce with the accomplishments and manners of a civilised society cast woman in a different role to political power than her menfolk.[26] As the qualities of men and women in such a society were judged to be 'complementary', female 'difference' was simultaneously celebrated and circumscribed, and accorded secondary status in the operation of government while at the same time being eulogised as the source of moral virtue and domestic stability.[27] We can clearly see the influence of such a perspective in the following from Francis Jeffrey, which appeared in the *Edinburgh Review* two years before the first reform Act, 'Perhaps', he wrote:

> [Women] are . . . incapable of long moral or political
> investigations, where many complex and indeterminate elements

[22] Ibid., 6.

[23] Ibid., 7–8; J. Rendall, ' "The grand causes which combine to carry mankind forward": Wollstonecraft, History and Revolution', *Women's Writing*, 4 (1997), 157.

[24] Ibid., 180.

[25] J. A. Epstein, 'The Constitutional Idiom: Radical Reasoning, Rhetoric and Action in Early Nineteenth-Century England', *Journal of Social History*, 23 (1989), 565.

[26] See J. Rendall, 'Clio, Mars and Minerva: The Scottish Enlightenment and the Writing of Women's History', in Devine and Young (eds), *Eighteenth Century Scotland*, 134–51.

[27] Ibid., 137; See also J. Dwyer, *Virtuous Discourse: Sensibility and Community in Late Eighteenth-Century Scotland* (Edinburgh, 1987).

are to be taken into account, and a variety of opposite
probabilities to be weighed before coming to a conclusion.
They are generally too impatient to get at the ultimate results,
to go well through such discussions; and either stop short at
some imperfect view of the truth, or turn aside to repose in the
shade of some plausible error . . . Their proper and natural
business is the practical regulation of private life, in all its
bearings, affections, and concerns.[28]

Reinforced by the prevalent concerns and values of the Moderate clergy
and practical moralists of the late eighteenth century which were later
taken up in modified form by Scottish evangelicals, and buoyed by a
crystallising 'cult of womanhood', Jeffrey's sentiments highlight the
gendered legacy of the Scottish Enlightenment as it was played out on
the political stage of the early nineteenth century.

While Henry Meikle would claim in 1912 that the Enlightenment
'prepared the ground' for the seeds sown by the revolutionary movements
of the eighteenth century, it is clear that the same philosophical influences
made Scotland resistant to the most radical visions of continental and
colonial revolutionaries and had profound implications for Scottish
women. Painite claims to natural rights which, if interpreted in their
most inclusive sense, could have encompassed sexual equality in the realm
of politics, were rejected by many moderate reformers as they seemed to
imply the reinstatement of primitive equality and 'an economic programme which threatened the progress of . . . commerce, and its accompanying polished manners'.[30] Instead, many reformers grounded their
claims for representation in utilitarianism, political economy and historical precedent.[31] While at the level of popular politics, as Epstein has made
clear, such 'distinctions between . . . arguments based upon historical
precedent and those based on natural rights were rarely drawn very
sharply', the defensive rhetoric of constitutionalism and a commitment to

---

[28] F. Jeffrey, 'Felicia Hemans (circa 1830)', in *Essays from the Edinburgh Review*
(London, 1908), 131.

[29] See C. G. Brown, *Religion and Society in Scotland since 1707* (Edinburgh, 1997),
198; C. Hall, *White, Male and Middle-Class: Explorations in Feminism and
History* (Cambridge, 1992); M. LeGates, 'The Cult of Womanhood in
Eighteenth-Century Thought', *Eighteenth-Century Studies*, 10 (1976), 21–89.

[30] G. Claeys, 'The French Revolution and British Political Thought', *History of
Political Thought*, 11 (1990), p. 61. See also A. Clark, *The Struggle for the Breeches:
Gender and the Making of the British Working Class* (London, 1995), 141.

[31] Ibid., 80. See also Fontana, *Rethinking the Politics of Commercial Society*, 13.

commercial progress often set and 'sexed' the limits of the radical programme.[32] The Enlightenment legacy, conditioned by a constitutional inheritance which was favourably contrasted with the extremes of re-volutionary Jacobin France, in this way allowed for little more than a subordinate and supportive role for women in the reform movement.[33]

In light of such gender disparities, the conventional identification of 1789 (or 1792) as the birth of modern Scottish radicalism clearly stands in need of revision.[34] By positing a periodisation which overwhelmingly rests on a definition of politics which replicates the bias of the times, women's wider public and political role has been undervalued. That it is 'difficult to find any evidence of political activity or organisation among women . . . in respect of the movement known as the Friends of the People' is undeni-able.[35] Yet, by expanding our definition of what constituted politics in the eighteenth century, and by questioning contemporary Whig assumptions regarding the female role, we locate sites of female empowerment which challenge us to deconstruct the periodisation of radicalism's historical sense. For example, women's prominent role in the anti-patronage riots of the eighteenth century, which drew heavily on the rhetoric of the democratic basis of presbyterian church government, suggests an alter-native periodisation of protest to that advocated by the reform movement itself, and indeed by historical commentators.[36]

[32] Epstein, 'The Constitutional Idiom', 556, 565.

[33] See J. Epstein, 'Understanding the Cap of Liberty: Symbolic Practice and Social Conflict in Early Nineteenth-century England', *Past and Present*, 122 (1989), 75–118; Colley, *Britons*, 265.

[34] Examples of this perspective include: H. W. Meikle, *Scotland and the French Revolution* (Glasgow, 1912), 40; I. G. C. Hutchison, 'Glasgow Working-Class Politics', in R. A. Cage (ed.), *The Working Class in Glasgow, 1750–1914* (London, 1987), 98; E. W. McFarland, 'Scottish Radicalism in the Later Eighteenth Century: "The social thistle and shamrock" ', in Devine and Young (eds), *Eighteenth-Century Scotland*, 279.

[35] King, *Hidden History*, 63. Similarly, regarding Britain as a whole, M. I. Thomis and J. Grimmett have commented that 'with women's involvement, the pre-1816 years had produced little popular participation in political causes', *Women in Protest, 1800–1850* (London, 1982), 89.

[36] See K. Logue, *Popular Disturbances in Scotland, 1780–1815* (Edinburgh, 1979), 199; R. A. Houston, 'Women in the Economy and Society of Scotland, 1500–1800', in R. A. Houston and I. D. Whyte (eds), *Scottish Society, 1500–1800* (Cambridge, 1989), 137. In a similar sense, in the context of workplace relations, P. Sharpe has suggested that the 'boundaries of "early modern" and "modern", "pre-industrial" and "industrial" historical approaches unduly restrict our appreciation of women's work', *Adapting to Capitalism: Working Women in the English Economy, 1700–1850* (Basingstoke, 1996), 151.

The narrow historicist vision of the radical tradition refracted rather than replicated Scotland's past through the filter of changing contemporary influences and imperatives. In this regard, the constitutional and ideological experiences of the 'neglected century' determined a reading of the past of both Scotland and the radical movement in general, in which women were marginalised, at the same time as the reform movement itself was empowered with a rhetoric and philosophy with which to meet the commercial and political claims of the Establishment.

1820

As with the 1790s, in like manner, the year 1820 has occupied an important position in the periodisation of radical historicism and contemporary historiography. While J. O'Connor Kessack in 1907 lauded the accomplishments of the 'brave Radical working-men' of the 'war' of 1820, subsequent historians have reflected at length on the significance of the days in April when a provisional government for Scotland was announced by radicals on the streets of Glasgow.[37] In general, most would agree that during the spring and summer of 1820 the radical republicanism of a minority threatened the peace of the west of Scotland and, in defeat, subsequently confirmed the majority in their constitutional search for reform. Yet was this a significant turning point for Scottish women?

In 1820, a 'British Subject' composed an open letter to the Duke of Hamilton, warning him of 'the spirit of Radicalism' in the west of Scotland, and cautioned: 'Men, *and very many women*, old and young, are infected with this deadly mania.'[38] Despite such evidence, women's role in the activities of 1820 has seldom solicited much interest, although Elspeth King has noted that as a 'side effect', the failure of the 1820 rising 'wiped out the direct participation of women in political meetings, and indeed the very memory of that participation'.[39] Yet the legacy of 1820 for Scottish women was rather more complex and, until more far-

---

[37] J. O'Connor Kessack, *The Early Struggle for Political Freedom in Scotland* (Glasgow, 1909), 16. See Ellis and MacA'Ghobainn, *The Scottish Insurrection*; T. Clarke and T. Dickson, 'Class and Class Consciousness in Early Industrial Capitalism: Paisley 1770–1850', in T. Dickson (ed.), *Capital and Class in Scotland* (Edinburgh, 1982), 8–60; W. H. Fraser, *Conflict and Class: Scottish Workers, 1700–1838* (Edinburgh, 1988); Hutchison, 'Glasgow Working-Class Politics', 102–3.

[38] *A Letter to his Grace the Duke of Hamilton and Brandon . . . detailing the Events of the Late Rebellion in the West of Scotland* (Glasgow, 1820), 39. (My italics.)

[39] King, *Hidden History*, 65.

reaching research is completed on the early months of the year, is more usefully revealed in the six months between June and December – a period dominated by the 'Queen Caroline affair'.

Until now, little has been said of this phenomenon in Scotland. Indeed, in 1988 Hamish Fraser pointed to 'the irrelevancy of the Queen Caroline affair', which, he concluded, 'blackened the character of the Monarch without undermining the institution of monarchy'.[40] Yet, in recent years, the Queen Caroline affair has been considered by Anna Clark as significant in the history of British radicalism, partly because 'it established a place in politics for women's issues as well as for women activists'.[41] While Clark implies this analysis of 1820 holds good for Britain as a whole, what follows will attempt to assess the extent to which Scotland truly 'fits' *this* picture, or that implicit in the radical tradition itself.

While already 'married' to Maria Fitzherbert, George, Prince of Wales, married Caroline of Brunswick in 1795. According to Craig Calhoun, Caroline 'was no prize. The fastidious prince was saddled with a wife who did not bathe or change her linen very often, who lacked every vestige of the sophistication he cultivated.'[42] Nevertheless, one year later, a daughter was born to the royal couple – Princess Charlotte. With an heir presumptive secured, George and Caroline parted company, and in 1813, following two investigations into her love life, sponsored by her husband, Caroline abandoned Britain for a life in exile on the continent. This was the unlikely heroine of the reformers of 1820.

Sympathies aroused by Caroline's plight were evident before her removal to Italy, largely as a consequence of her close relationship with George III (a popular monarch, whose morality and family values were in sharp contrast to those of his eldest son), her ill-usage by her husband, and what was seen as her forced separation from her daughter.[43] Also, in the intervening years before her return to England, several events took place which would make Caroline an ideal *cause célèbre* in the aftermath of the Peterloo atrocity. In 1817 Princess Charlotte died in childbirth and became perhaps the first in a long line of royal female idols; the Prince of Wales was becoming known for his love of excess at a time when the country was suffering its worst recession in years; and in

---

[40] Fraser, *Conflict and Class*, 113. In such a conclusion, Fraser is joined by E. P. Thompson, who referred to the 'humbug of the Queen's cause', *The Making of the English Working Class* (London, 1980), 778.

[41] Clark, *Struggle for the Breeches*, 164.

[42] C. Calhoun, *The Question of Class Struggle: Social Foundations of Popular Radicalism during the Industrial Revolution* (Oxford, 1982), 105.

[43] M. Morris, *The British Monarchy and the French Revolution* (London, 1998).

March 1820 a Tory administration was returned to office as the prince prepared himself at last to occupy the throne vacated by his late father.[44] Despite the warnings of her counsel, and under the unlikely influence of Alderman Wood, the London radical, in June 1820 Caroline returned to England. Within weeks, having already dropped Caroline's name from the Anglican liturgy, the king's ministers prepared a Bill of Pains and Penalties against her, accusing her of adultery.

Protests in support of the queen's cause encompassed a significant proportion of the population and seemed to unify the country in a shared commitment to a legitimate British monarch and a revitalised constitution. Yet nationhood and history framed contrasting responses north and south of the border. Three principal features highlight such difference and illustrate the manner in which the complexity of the legacy of 1820 has been underestimated: of importance are the size, geographic distribution and class composition of support for the queen in contrast to the events of April; the high profile of Scots in the queen's defence and the use of Scottish history in her mobilisation of support in the north, and the role of religion and the law in shaping a unique Scottish response.

On the return of the queen to England, Henry Brougham recorded: 'It is impossible to describe the universal, and strong, even violent, feelings of the people, not only in London but all over the country, upon the subject of the Queen.'[45] And on 25 November, *The Scotsman* recorded that: 'Never since the foundation of the English monarchy did so great a proportion of the people interest themselves in a public question.'[46] In Scotland, the extent of the protests in favour of Caroline far exceeded those of the radical war, when measured both in terms of the numbers involved and their geographic distribution. True, petitions in favour of Caroline were slower to emerge in Scotland, possibly as a consequence of a cautious populace who, in the summer of 1820, were witness to the trials and executions of the protesters of April, but when they did emerge they replicated the enthusiasm of the English response. Petitions were presented to the queen from areas as far apart as Montrose and Stranraer, Aberdeen and Wigtown, as well as the more predictable areas of reforming interest: Edinburgh,

[44] See Colley, *Britons*, 279–80; F. Fraser, *The Unruly Queen* (London, 1996); T. Holme, *Caroline: A Biography of Caroline of Brunswick* (London, 1979); E. Parry, *Queen Caroline* (London, 1930); J. Richardson, *The Disastrous Marriage: A Study of George IV and Caroline of Brunswick* (London, 1960); E. A. Smith, *A Queen on Trial: The Affair of Queen Caroline* (Dover, 1993).

[45] H. Brougham, *The Life and Times of Henry Lord Brougham* (Edinburgh, 1871), 366.

[46] *The Scotsman*, 25 November 1820.

Glasgow, Perth and Paisley.[47] Moreover, areas involved in the illumina-
tions, festivities and rioting following the Lords' rejection of the Bill of
Pains and Penalties in November mirrored this geographic breadth of rural
and urban areas. Indeed, over ninety separate reports of such activities
have been identified from a range of contemporary newspapers.[48] Support
also crossed class divides. Lady Charlotte Lindsay, who gave evidence at
the queen's 'trial' wrote in July 1820: 'Not only the common people, but the
middle ranks, and also many of the upper class. . . are all warmly interested
for the Queen.'[49] In contrast to the regional specificity of the events
surrounding Peterloo and the radical 'war' of April 1820, the Caroline affair
was truly national in scope and, as it involved the queen consort of the head
of state, had the potential to involve all. The possibilities for the conflation
of patriotism and reform were thus greatly enhanced.

In the Scottish context, the personalities and imagery associated with
the affair made such possibilities more likely. Caroline's Attorney General
in the Lords was Henry Brougham, co-founder of the *Edinburgh Review*
and well-known Whig reformer.[50] While debate surrounds the role of self-
interest in his motivation, it is undeniable that his oratory and position in
party politics facilitated the close association of the queen's cause with that
of reform. Additionally, Flora Fraser has attributed the truly national
scope of support for Caroline to his skilful propaganda.[51] Lady Anne
Hamilton, sister of the reforming Lanarkshire MP, Lord Archibald
Hamilton, and Caroline's loyal lady of the bedchamber, also occupied
an important place in the dramatic line-up.[52] Appearing in a 'Scotch

---

[47] See *Glasgow Herald*, 18 September, 25 September, 16 October, 27 October, 3
November, 15 December, 22 December 1820; *Glasgow Courier*, 14 September
1820; *The Scotsman*, 7 October, 28 October 1820.

[48] Ninety-four separate incidents have been identified in the following from 1820:
Caledonian Mercury, *Edinburgh Weekly Journal*, *Glasgow Courier*, *Glasgow
Herald*, *The Scotsman*.

[49] Lady C. Lindsay to Miss Berry, 11 July 1820, in Lady T. Lewis (ed.), *Extracts of
the Journals and Correspondence of Miss Berry, Vol. iii* (London, 1865), 246. Such
sentiments were echoed by Edward Ellice, who commented that in England, 'The
middling classes, the shopkeeper and their families, are as much devoted to her
cause as the rabble': E. Ellice, to Earl of Durham, 14 September 1820, in A.
Aspinall (ed.), *Lord Henry Brougham and the Whig Party* (Manchester, 1927), 279.

[50] See Aspinall, *Lord Henry Brougham*: C. W. New, *The Life of Henry Brougham
to 1830* (Oxford, 1961).

[51] Fraser, *The Unruly Queen*, 408.

[52] Lady Anne Hamilton (1766–1846) was the eldest daughter of the 9th duke of
Hamilton and had been lady-in-waiting to Queen Caroline during her years in
exile on the continent. The author of *The Epics of the Ton*, the   /over

bonnet' in the caricatures which sensationalised the affair, Lady Anne
Hamilton was, perhaps, more influential as one of the many co-writers
who assisted in the composition of the queen's responses to the many
petitions which she received.[53] Added to these principal protagonists,
Lord Archibald Hamilton himself was prominent in calling for the
queen's name to be reinstated in the liturgy, and the support of Joseph
Hume, the radical Aberdeen Burghs MP, was significant in the early days
of the affair, as was the contribution of Lord Erskine, whose speech to the
Lords during the third reading of the Bill of Pains and Penalties was
perhaps his last notable contribution to a major political issue.[54]

Yet, in an age when political personalities could attract limited public
recognition, press reports, published petitions and the royal responses
were the major vehicles framing Scotland's response to the queen's
cause. Across all media, the queen's cause was made to resonate with a
radical interpretation of the nation's past and a complementary understanding of national sentiment and sensibility.

On 7 October, *The Scotsman* compared Caroline's case with that of
Wallace:

> When EDWARD the First got Possession of Scotland by force
> and fraud, his title was acknowledged by the nobles – the
> persons of *rank* and *respectability*. It was the *lower orders* who
> did not despair of their country, but proved every danger
> under the patriot WALLACE in fighting for independence.[55]

The deliberate association of the claims of patriotism and reform are
clear in this extract and is replicated when we look at many petitions.

When Major Cartwright, among other local worthies, presented the
Paisley petition of support to Queen Caroline, it was delivered in

cont'd   authorship of *The Secret History of the Court of England from the
Accession of George III to the Death of George IV* has also been attributed to
her. Throughout Caroline's ordeal she remained a loyal companion. See Lady
Charlotte Bury, *The Diary of a Lady in Waiting* (London, 1908), 310, 384.

[53] For an analysis of the artistic ornamentation of the affair, see T. W. Laqueur,
'The Queen Caroline Affair: politics as art in the reign of George IV', *Journal
of Modern History* 54 (1982), 417–66.

[54] See R. K. Huch and R. Ziegler, *Joseph Hume: The People's MP* (Ephrata,
1985), 23; Parry, *Queen Caroline*, 310. The Scottish connection was further
evident in other former female associates of the queen, notably Lady Glenbervie
and Lady Charlotte Lindsay, the daughters of Lord North.

[55] *The Scotsman*, 7 October 1820.

a barouche drawn by six greys, followed by another barouche
and four: on the driving box of the first, a person bearing a
large white silk banner device, Caledonia seated by an urn; on
the pedestal of which was inscribed: 'Scotia, the land of
Wallace, Bruce and Knox!' and underneath, on a scroll, the
national motto – 'Nemo me impune lacessit'.[56]

Paisley, only months before the site of a radical rising, was now
instrumental in grounding claims for reform in assertions of patriotic
loyalty and the legacy of a historic continuum.

Lady Charlotte Lindsay regretted that the queen's responses to petitions
in the late summer of 1820 had the hallmarks of intentions to 'please all
palates', being 'seditious for the Radicals, pathetic for the sentimental and
canting for the Methodists', and suspected the influence of Wood and
Hamilton in their composition.[57] Indeed, she conjectured that Caroline
seldom saw her answers until they appeared in the newspapers.[58] Yet the
heavy reliance on historicism in framing her case in Scotland is notable.
Take this, her response to the petitioners of St Andrews:

The free voice and unbiased suffrages of the enlightened
natives of Caledonia, wherever they could be heard, have
always been on the side of what is just, equitable and humane;
and I never can forget that it was the country beyond the
Tweed which nurtured such glorious vindicators of the freedom
and independence of their country, as a Wallace and a Bruce;
which gave birth to a Knox, who rescued this country from the
tyranny of the Court of Rome, and spread the light of
Reformation amongst the people.[59]

This may usefully be compared with the more contemporary emphasis
of her response to Paisley:

When I know what correct moral feeling prevails amongst the
natives of Scotland in general, and what progress political
knowledge has made among the Inhabitants of Paisley in

[56] *Glasgow Herald*, 27 October 1820.
[57] Lady Charlotte Lindsay to Miss Berry, 13 August 1820, in Smith, *A Queen on Trial*, 64–5.
[58] See Lewis, *Extracts of the Journals and Correspondence of Miss Berry*, 251. See also Richardson, *The Disastrous Marriage*, 142.
[59] *Glasgow Courier*, 14 September 1820.

particular, I am less surprised that my afflictions should have so warmly interested their tender sympathies . . . I am but too well convinced that deep distress has prevailed, and does prevail among the industrious Population of Paisley, and in other parts of the United Kingdom . . . Violence there has been; but that has not originated with the People. It has been instigated by the Enemies of the People. Secret agents and insidious emissaries have been busy in creating disloyalty.[60]

Throughout, the conflation of patriotism and reform were to the fore in the rhetoric of attempts to legitimate the queen's cause in Scotland. This, to a certain extent, was merely a variant on strategies used across the British isles, except that by mobilising material manifestations of Scotland's former independence – the law and the church – rhetoric acquired substantive and tangible manifestation.

Later, in Caroline's response to St Andrews, it was asserted that: 'Had I been either the highest or the lowest of Scotland, its laws would have afforded me . . . that sacred shield which has been withdrawn in England.'[61] (Here, Caroline was referring to the practice in Scotland whereby a list of witnesses was presented to the defence counsel in both criminal and civil cases.) Similarly, the removal of the queen from the liturgy and ill-advised orders that similar restrictions be placed on public worship in Scotland drew passionate protests from the north. As Henry Cockburn recounted: 'the presbyterians, who own no earthly head, kicked. Our whole seceders, and a great many of the established clergy . . . disdained this mandate and prayed for her all the more fervently that her husband's ministry declared that she was wicked.'[62]

As yet another exercise in the recapitulation of the radical tradition of Scotland, the rhetoric of the Queen Caroline affair highlighted the significance of the melodrama of national pageantry in the framing of radical claims. In the process, the affair did little to empower Scottish women in the sense Clark has suggested. Rather, the retreat into constitutionalism, which the Caroline affair marked, merely reaffirmed the separateness of female politics and confirmed their need of male protection.

On the surface, it would appear that there is much to commend Clark's proposal that the affair 'brought not only women but women's

[60] Queen's Answer to the Address of the Loyal Inhabitants of Paisley: Presented to Her Majesty 18 October 1820 (Paisley, 24 October 1820).
[61] Glasgow Courier, 14 September 1820.
[62] H. Cockburn, Memorials of His Time (Edinburgh, 1909), 350–1.

concerns into the centre of the dialogue of radical rhetoric' and 'decisively transformed radical notions of manhood'.[63] *The Scotsman* first addressed the question of the queen in June 1820, when it noted:

> The question[s] connected with the status and treatment of her Majesty . . . are less political than moral, and they engage the feelings of all, because they relate still more readily to domestic than to public affairs. The politician may speculate, the lawyer argue or quibble, and the courtier intrigue; but the MAN must feel: and the first and uppermost emotion this occasion is that which arises in every manly breast, where insult is offered to helpless woman – unmixed indignation.[64]

In August *The Scotsman* further elaborated on the melodrama of the unfortunate queen:

> Expelled from the roof and society of her husband, in the first years of her married life, while confessedly an innocent woman, and forced to remain in that state of cruel separation, her Majesty, even if she shall have subsequently erred, is to be pitied as much as blamed.[65]

Two months later, it referred to the proceedings in the Lords as 'unfeeling and unmanly'.[66]

Clearly, as Clark suggests, gender roles had been politicised, but women were still to be the recipients of a chivalrous concern which rested on their domestic role as wife and mother. True, many petitions gathered in support of the queen came exclusively from women, including one from several thousand 'Ladies of Edinburgh'.[67] Women were also often involved in the celebrations in November, following the abandonment of the Bill: in Auchinleck sixty females joined in a procession and the destruction of effigies.[68] But this was not the whole story. In Dumfries the Female Benevolent Society, who refused to

---

[63] Clark, *Struggle for the Breeches*, 171, 164. See also Clark, 'Queen Caroline and the Sexual Politics of Popular Culture in London, 1820', *Representations* 31 (1990), 47–68.

[64] *The Scotsman*, 17 June 1820.

[65] *The Scotsman*, 26 August 1820.

[66] *The Scotsman*, 28 October 1820.

[67] *Glasgow Herald*, 29 September 1820.

[68] *Caledonian Mercury*, 23 November 1820.

illuminate in honour of 'a woman who is a disgrace to her sex', threatened to dismiss their charity school and stop giving money 'to assist poor families in distress' if the mob broke any of their windows.[69] And in Edinburgh in November, 'only males, above twenty one were allowed to sign' a petition calling on the king to dismiss his ministers in light of recent events.[70]

The politicisation of female spaces was – as Clark admits herself – somewhat short-lived. While rumours circulated of a visit to Scotland by the queen in the summer of 1821, public interest and indeed patience with Caroline had ran out long before.[71] Only in Edinburgh and Paisley were symbolic gestures in support of the queen registered during the Coronation celebrations in 1821, and, in Paisley, this amounted to little more than an effigy bearing the slogan 'Am I forgotten?'[72] Indeed, only five months after her acquittal, the urban mob of Edinburgh and Glasgow had celebrated the king's birthday with their usual combination of squibs, bonfires, drunkenness and pistol shots.[73]

On reflection, then, perhaps Hamish Fraser's dismissal of the Caroline affair as an irrelevance has some credibility. The Scottish populace seemed to confirm Adam Smith's observation that despite having been brought to the highest state of resentment against their monarch, the people 'easily relapse into their habitual state of deference to those to whom they have been accustomed to look up to as their natural superiors'.[74] However, as we have seen, a closer look at the affair in Scotland reveals a more complex reality than its duration and limited long-term impact on conventional monarchical loyalty would suggest. Most importantly, the Caroline affair endorsed constitutionalism as the focus of the reform movement and highlighted the wide basis of popular appeal which this strategy could exploit.

In its appeal to the precedents afforded in history, constitutionalism sat neatly with the reform movement's historicist rhetoric, but, in turn, it restricted the potential of the movement to re-create politics anew. The

---

[69] *Caledonian Mercury*, 25 November 1820.

[70] Cockburn, *Memorials*, 354. In a similar way, until the 1830s, women in the movement for the abolition of slavery were excluded from signing many petitions, along with paupers and children, presumably, writes Clare Midgeley, 'because of their dependent status': *Women against Slavery: The British Campaigns, 1780–1870* (London, 1992), 23.

[71] *Edinburgh Weekly Journal*, 8 August 1821. Also, Smith, *A Queen on Trial*, 188.

[72] *Edinburgh Weekly Journal*, 25 July 1821.

[73] *Edinburgh Weekly Journal*, 25 April 1821; *Glasgow Herald*, 27 April 1821.

[74] A. Smith, *The Theory of Moral Sentiments* (Edinburgh, 1822), 70–1.

resolutions which were passed at the Pantheon meeting in Edinburgh in December 1820 and by the crowds who attended a meeting at the John Street Church in Glasgow some days later both focused *not* on a new politicised womanhood but on traditional complaints against the king's ministers, who, in their recent conduct, had attacked 'the constitutional privileges and liberties of the people'.[75] The *Scotsman* commented:

> The spirit of the country is raised – and every man who sets any value on the Constitution acquired by the Revolution of 1688, or who feels any regard for his own and the welfare of his family, is now exerting himself to rescue his Sovereign from the Councils of men who have acted equally as traitors to him and the Constitution.[76]

As Epstein has made clear, while the repertoire and idiom of constitutionalism was effective in 'rallying the mass force of popular radicalism', women's rights were not well served by it.[77] By embedding radical demands in a tradition in which the links between 'civil and political liberty with the rights of property' were strong, women were almost automatically excluded from their remit.[78] As a result, the Caroline affair – far from politicising women and women's issues in Scotland – was, if you like, a missed opportunity. By allowing for an expression of radical principle which, paradoxically, could be interpreted as loyalism, the events of the winter of 1820 reaffirmed the efficacy and popularity of constitutionalism as both a strategy and rhetorical device in the arsenal of reform for all classes.

This would have important implications for the radical movement of the 1830s and beyond, as Chartism reinforced the association of citizenship, rationality and masculinity, and the 'profoundly contractual' nature of separate spheres resonated with the constitutional idiom and specified the domestic ideals which confined women to limited roles in the movement.[79] In the process, more progressive voices in

---

[75] *Glasgow Herald*, 22 December 1820.
[76] *The Scotsman*, 16 December 1820.
[77] Epstein, 'The Constitutional Idiom', 558, 565.
[78] Ibid., 565. See also Epstein, 'Understanding the Cap of Liberty', 103.
[79] Colley, *Britons*, 277; A. Clark, 'The Rhetoric of Chartist Domesticity: Gender, Language and Class in the 1830s and 1840s', *Journal of British Studies* 31 (1992), 62–8. It should be noted, however, that there were at least twenty female Chartist associations in Scotland: see A. Wilson, *The Chartist Movement in Scotland* (New York, 1970); L. Wright, *Scottish Chartism* (Edinburgh, 1953), 43.

pursuit of female liberty in Scotland, such as that of Marion Reid, were marginalised.[80]

PRINCIPLE, PRECEDENT AND PERSONALITY

In 1838 representatives from the English reform societies were welcomed to Glasgow with a procession in which a party from Strathaven sported a banner said to have been carried by the covenanters at the battle of Drumclog.[81] Once more, the Scottish reform movement sought to associate itself with the nation's past at the same time as individual rights were asserted in the language of constitutional liberty.

The class composition of the reform movement changed dramatically after 1832, and – following 1867 – liberalism gradually abandoned its more radical tenets. But the emphasis on respectability and independence at the heart of the trade-union movement the warnings against revolution which the events on the continent in 1848 and 1870 seemed to offer, and the ascendancy of the British empire, which served to highlight the profitable utility of the constitutional status quo, guaranteed the perpetuation of constitutionalism and its attendant claims of historical precedent in the reform movement in all but its most 'extreme' guises.

In contrast to the English experience, the nature of poor law reform in Scotland in 1845 failed to stimulate the popular mobilisation of the female population, while, as in Britain as a whole, factory legislation and the activities of most trade unions continued to offer women a contradictory blend of chivalrous protection and economic exclusion.[82] Rather, overtly masculine discourses rooted in the rhetoric of the independent artisan reaffirmed the centrality of the family in the culture of the respectable working classes in Scotland as elsewhere.[83] At the same time, Owenite alternatives, promising the radical restructuring of gender

---

[80] Marion Reid, *A Plea for Woman* (Edinburgh, 1988). Born in Glasgow, the eldest daughter of a local merchant, Reid (née Kirkland) wrote *A Plea* in the 1840s. By 1852, it had run to five editions in the USA alone.

[81] Wright, *Scottish Chartism*, 34.

[82] See Clark, *Struggle for the Breeches*, 195, 267; E. Roberts, *Women's Work, 1840–1940* (Basingstoke, 1988), 56–7; M. Valverde, ' "Giving the Female a Domestic Turn": The Social, Legal and Moral Regulation of Women's Work in British Cotton Mills, 1820–1850', *Journal of Social History*, 21 (1987), 607–34.

[83] K. McClelland, 'Masculinity and the "Representative Artisan" in Britain, 1850–1880', in M. Roper and J. Tosh (eds), *Manful Assertions: Masculinities in Britain since 1800* (London, 1991), 74–91.

roles, were rejected in the 1880s, as 'the boundaries of the Socialist project narrowed' in pursuit of parliamentary representation and incremental social reform within the limits of the capitalist system.[84]

Clearly the inheritance of the Labour Party in Scotland was such as to discourage innovative responses to women's position in society, yet its historicist vision and constitutional rhetoric made such responses even less likely. Under Hardie and MacDonald, the Labour Party in Scotland proved unable to break the influence of history in the shaping of the radical agenda, indeed, it may be contested that they reinforced its hold. In the close association of Labour's leaders with the history of their native Scotland, and the identification of the Labour Party as the culmination of a history of protest and the expression of an innate sense of democracy, it may be suggested that a nineteenth-century vision of womanhood was – unwittingly or otherwise – carried into the twentieth century.

Labour's embeddedness in the history earlier outlined is easily shown. In 1906, while advocating the removal of 'the disabilities and restraints imposed upon woman', James Keir Hardie offered his own 'conjectural history' of women and revealed the legacy of his Enlightenment forebears:

> Amongst coloured peoples living in a state of nature and in a tribal environment which has evolved itself, and wherein custom is the only law, the woman . . . [is] her husband's drudge, and frequently a part of his wealth. In the military stage of social evolution, or the age of chivalry . . . woman is the weaker and more spiritualized sex, requiring to be protected by her lord . . . In modern life we get back to the savage stage. Woman of the working class is again the drudge who does the menial work.[85]

Yet, he added,

> I think it could be shown that the position of women, as of most other things, has always been better, more near equality with man in Celtic than non-Celtic races or tribes. Thus in Scotland a woman speaks of her husband as her 'man', whilst in Staffordshire he is always spoken of as 'the master'.[86]

[84] B. Taylor, *Eve and the New Jerusalem: Socialism and Feminism in the Nineteenth Century* (London, 1983), 285.
[85] J. Keir Hardie, *The Citizenship of Women* (London, 1906), 4.
[86] Ibid., 4.

Whether intentional or otherwise, Hardie's appeal to a 'scientific' understanding of women's role in society echoed the concerns of Scottish thinkers in the late eighteenth century, and – in relation to Scotland's exceptional status – replicated the insight of John Millar, Gilbert Stuart, Lord Kames and others who identified an uncommon quality in the manners of ancient Caledonia.[87] For MacDonald, such a scientific grounding to an otherwise sentimental appeal to national pride served a useful purpose by reinforcing claims to a lost golden age, while associating it still closer with the geographic roots of the contemporary Labour Party and its leadership.

Indeed, the Labour Party leadership was adept in the self-personi-fication of nationhood. Having recounted the words of Morton at the grave of John Knox, J. Ramsay MacDonald – significantly, a devotee of the writings of Hugh Miller – paid tribute to Keir Hardie at a memorial service in 1915:

> He [Hardie] associated himself with his Covenanting forefathers . . . when he read his Scottish history – that most splendid of all histories for the creation of moral muscle – when he read that history he felt his very blood tingle to his finger points. And when he united the religious heroism of his Covenanting forefathers with the magnificent lyrics of our Ayrshire poet – our Burns – and all the others that sung round about him . . . Hardie gathered them all up – his religion, his history, his lyricism – into his nature; he became the great seer that saw and saw deeply.[88]

Similarly, Mary Agnes Hamilton identified in Ramsay MacDonald and his writing, a 'romantic sense' belonging to many Scots:

> It is their secret. They pretend it is nationalism, but it is much deeper and wider than that. Their Socialism and their individualism spring from the same root: a sense of wonder, of the divinity even, attaching to personality . . . The Scot, wherever and in whatever station he is born, knows that Scotland belongs to him because he feels its history in his

---

[87] Rendall, 'Clio, Mars and Minerva', 141.

[88] R. Smillie et al., *Memoir of James Keir Hardie MP* (Glasgow, 1915), 22–3. See also Stewart, *J. Keir Hardie*, xvii, and C. Mackie, *Poem dedicated to the Memory of James Keir Hardie MP* (Kilmarnock, 1915), stanza 4.

veins. The people and the place belong together. No visible
landlordism can dissociate them. You feel this in Scott, you feel
it in Burns, you feel it in Carlyle, you feel it whenever a
Scotsman speaks from his heart, you feel it in MacDonald . . .
It is a reticent, a hidden feeling. That is partly why it
expresses itself more readily about the dead than about the
living, about the past than about the present.[89]

On occasion, even more rebellious proponents of socialism could also be
accorded their place in the radical lineage. The first stanza of Sidney
Goodsir Smith's 'The Ballant o John Maclean' is revealing in this respect:

> Muir and Wallace his prison mates,
>   Lenin and Connolly,
> None ither ever his maik,
>   But ithers there will be.[90]

Such accolades were exceptionally given to prominent women in the
movement. MacDonald's biographer offered the following observations
on Mary MacArthur:

Her father's people came from the Highlands; her mother's
from Aberdeen; the mingling of these potent strains will, to
those who know them, account for much . . . Countrywoman
of [Burns] she was, in the deepest fibre of her being, compact
of contradictions to those who do not know the Scot,
splendidly representative of national idiosyncrasy to those who
do . . . Through almost every Scot, in some form or other,
runs a vein of mysticism. It ran through her.[91]

Yet such historicism, aligned to a peculiar rootedness in place, did little
to empower 'exceptional' Scots, whose lives and beliefs could less easily
be subsumed in the drama of the nation's myth-history. For most
women, the historicism of the radical tradition was as exclusive in terms
of gender as it was inclusive in terms of nationhood.

[89] Hamilton, *J. Ramsay MacDonald*, 30–2. See also J. Ramsay MacDonald,
Wanderings and Excursions (London, 1934), p. 41, and *At Home and Abroad*
(London, 1936), 24–5.
[90] As quoted: *John Maclean and Scottish Independence* (John Maclean Society, n.d.), 3.
[91] M. A. Hamilton, *Mary MacArthur: A Biographical Sketch* (London, 1925), 3,
200, 204.

As the Labour Party styled itself at the end of the radical continuum, as its ultimate exemplar, its vision of womanhood is critical to understanding the gendered nature of the pervasive legacy of the radical tradition. Women clearly made significant inroads into the Labour movement through the Women's Labour Party (from 1888), the Scottish Co-operative Women's Guild (from 1892) and the Women's Labour League (from 1906), but the party's ambiguous position on issues such as the franchise and contraception reaffirm a limited vision of womanhood in the party at the opening of the twentieth century.

To a certain extent, the limits of Labour's vision of female potential were determined by its commitment to the parliamentary route to power in the union state and hence, in part, to constitutionalism. MacDonald was fervently attached to parliamentary methods, and despite the excited outpourings of the Clydeside MPs in the interwar years, most Scottish Labour MPs chose to work within the system – even if this meant delaying full universal suffrage, and compromising the movement's commitment to pacifism or devolved government for Scotland. The relatively limited support for truly socialist interpretations of social and political ills in Scotland, and the discouraging example of Maclean and later communist activists, seemed to indicate that there was little political capital to be made in appeals to a 'Scottish Workers' Republic' and little advantage to be gained in taking up unconstitutional methods.[92] Rather, Sir Patrick Dollan in 1943 would reflect that 'the principles of Constitutional Monarchy' inherent in Burns' 'songs of liberty', had 'since become so interwoven in our way of government that we think of the King and People as co-partners in the onward march for reform and progress'.[93] There seemed little necessity and great danger for Labour in the social engineering required to revolutionise the position of women.

From the same biographies that contextualise Labour's rise to power as the ultimate achievement of centuries of radical endeavour, descriptions of the wives and mothers of Labour leaders tell us much about the gendered ideals of the party and, by implication, offer these as a conclusive vision of 'radicalised' femininity.

Several unifying themes are apparent. Woman is foremost appreciated in her domestic environment. As MacDonald noted: 'she who seeks to mend the world is very often the woman who is most solicitous

---

[92] See J. Maclean, *In the Rapids of Revolution: Essays, Articles and Letters, 1902–1923* (London, 1978), 114, 218.

[93] P. Dollan, 'Introduction', in *Songs of Liberty by Robert Burns: A Selection by Sir Patrick Dollan* (London, 1943), vi.

in guarding her own hearth'.[94] We see this again in his biography of his wife Margaret, who is introduced initially through her home:

> I remember very vividly the reposeful dignity of her home, the calm detachment of the dining-room, the more lightsome and playful atmosphere of the morning room . . . The house abounded in charity. Pensioners blessed it; philanthropic institutions . . . were kept going by it. It was toned by . . . Puritan traditions of faith and service.[95]

In a very real sense Margaret *is* her domestic environment.

The ideal of woman as home-maker is seen again – in more prosaic terms – in William Gallacher's mother:

> She went out washing and had to slave for every penny she got . . . I used to feel it was a terrible thing that my mother should have to toil so endlessly. I made up my mind that as soon as I could work for her she would go out washing no more.[96]

In contrast to the working women of the Dundee mills, described by David Lowe as 'nearly all addicted to snuff and drink', most of the women who nurture Labour's leaders are temperance advocates, encourage their wards in the ways of self-improvement, and, except under exceptional conditions, very few continue in full-time work after marriage.[97] Instead, the ideal Labour wife is seen principally as a support to her husband. In 1878 Robert Smillie married Anne Hamilton. He recalled:

> Anne Hamilton has been an ideal wife to me, and without her my work as a miners' leader could never have been done. I always knew that, wherever my duties called me, however long they kept me away, the children and the home were cared for with uncomplaining devotion. Never an unnecessary hour did I spend outside the home circle, where peace and love have intensified with the passing years.[98]

[94] J. R. MacDonald, 'Introduction', in A. Popp, *The Autobiography of a Working Woman* (London, 1912), 9.
[95] J. R. MacDonald, *Margaret Ethel MacDonald* (London, 1912), 14.
[96] W. Gallacher, *Revolt on the Clyde: An Autobiography* (London, 1949), 1.
[97] Lowe, *Souvenirs of Scottish Labour*, 12.
[98] R. Smillie, *My Life for Labour* (London, 1924), 28.

Similar sentiments are evident in Hardie's early relationship with his wife, Lily, when she 'kept my home going, kept my children decently and respectably clothed'.[99] He told an ILP conference in Bradford in 1914:

> Comrades, you do well to honour her. Never, even in those days, did she offer one word of reproof. Many a bitter tear she shed, but one of the proud boasts of my life is to be able to say that if she has suffered much in health and in spirit, never has she reproached me for what I have done for the cause I love.[100]

There were, of course, exceptions to these general rules: not all labour leaders were 'lucky in love' – Harry McShane and John Maclean are cases in point – and female leaders of the movement are generally given credit for their labours in the public sphere.[101] But these biographies, and others, suggest that the personal experiences which framed Labour's ideas of womanhood outside the political sphere frequently confirmed conventional patriarchal convictions.

As Labour identified itself as the *end* of a radical continuum, these personal insights are important. They point to the perpetuation of restricted ideas of womanhood and a closure which was effected in the radical tradition at the beginning of this century with which future Labour women would have to deal. Alternative visions of radical woman were constricted. MacDonald's account of his wife is again instructive here:

> Her interest in women was not that of one who took sides in sex rivalry. Woman to her was something sacred, something different in essence from man. The woman was the mother, and, to her, motherhood contained everything that was holy . . . Her home was the source of her steadfastness and her energy . . . no woman's heart yearned more than hers for domestic quiet spent in the seclusion of home with personal friends and children around her . . . The home was her Paradise.[102]

[99] J. Keir Hardie, Speech to ILP conference, Bradford, 1914. As quoted in Stewart, *J. Keir Hardie*, 337.
[100] Ibid., 337.
[101] H. McShane and J. Smith, *No Mean Fighter* (London, 1978).
[102] MacDonald, *Margaret Ethel MacDonald*, 44, 233.

Even at its most inclusive, women's role in the Labour movement
opening decades of the twentieth century was quite literally tied
home, for example, in their association with the housing question d,
the First World War.[103] The reasons for this are complex, yet are p,
addressed in appreciating that, up to 1918, little in the radical tradi,,un
to which Labour appealed empowered women in any lasting sense.
Their spontaneous protests were identified as, at best, 'apolitical' and
what was offered in their stead denied the longevity of female radicalism
by denying it a history commensurate with that of their male colleagues.

CONCLUSION

While it may appear as something of a self-fulfilling prophecy informed
by the gift of hindsight, on balance it seems far from accidental or
coincidental that it was only with the reform of the Labour Party in the
late twentieth century, the realisation of a new vision of the union
relationship between Britain's component nations, and the constitutional reforms of the 1990s, that the position of women in radical
Scottish politics was transformed.

Until then, women were slow to emerge in leading roles in Scottish
parliamentary politics in the Labour interest: indeed, between 1918 and
1945, the Unionists put up more female parliamentary candidates than
the Labour Party.[104] And despite the high profile of women in the
Scottish National Party, their influence never proved sufficient to
dramatically recast the gendered nature of popular political conventions.[105] Indeed, between 1918 and 1992 – the last election before all-
female 'lists' were introduced by the Labour Party in some constitu-
encies – women had been returned in the Labour interest on only 31
occasions at general elections in Scotland, and only 77 female Labour
candidates had been offered for election.[106] While women maintained a
higher profile in local politics during this time, and exerted significant
influence in the Constitutional Convention in the 1980s and 1990s,

---

[103] See J. Smyth, 'Rents, Peace, Votes: Working-Class Women and Political
Activity in the First World War', in Breitenbach and Gordon (eds), *Out of
Bounds: Women in Scottish Society, 1800–1945* (Edinburgh, 1992), 174–96.

[104] C. Burness, 'The Long Slow March: Scottish Women MPs, 1918–45', in
Breitenbach and Gordon, *Out of Bounds,* 151–73.

[105] See C. Burness, 'Drunk Women Don't look at Thistles: Women and the SNP,
1934–94', in Cameron and Watson, *Proceedings,* 124–37.

[106] Ibid., 137 ('Table I).

following the Convention by issuing their own *Claim of Right* in 1991, the parliamentary record in the twentieth century clearly makes depressing reading.[107] Nevertheless, the entry of 47 women as members of the Scottish parliament in 1999 was heralded as the beginning of a new age for women in Scottish politics, particularly for those on the centre-left of the political spectrum who dominated the new cohort. But the need for positive discrimination at the party level to ensure a better gender balance in the new legislature only served to confirm the longevity of the traditions which had shaped radicalism in Scotland for many years.

The history of reform in Scotland and the experience of the 1990s seemed to indicate that in order for women to achieve greater political representation, the union, and the commitment of the left to it, had to be broken and remade; appeals to precedent had to be exchanged for promises of the future, and the constitutional legacy had to be reworked. In other words, a new radicalism was necessary to accommodate the female voice, and with it a new understanding of nationhood, history and political liberty. Ironically, in light of the pervasive influence of the past in the shaping of Scotland's radical tradition, Maxton's vision of a new Scottish parliament in 1924 may well offer the principal route to the empowerment of female radicalism: 'We will start with no traditions. We will start with ideals.'[108]

[107] A. Brown, 'Editorial: Women in Politics', *Scottish Affairs*, 5 (1993), 1–4; 'Women and Politics in Scotland', *Political Affairs*, 49 (1996), 27.
[108] Maxton, *James Maxton and Scotland*, 5.

CHAPTER 12

Tomorrow's Ancestors: Nationalism, Identity and History*

David McCrone

'The Scottish parliament, adjourned on 25 March 1707, is hereby reconvened.'

When Winnie Ewing, as mother of the house and temporary presiding officer, uttered these words on Wednesday, 13 May 1999 to open the Scottish parliament who could doubt the political potency of history: history regained? While one might take issue with the assumption that a devolved parliament is tantamount to the real thing – and no doubt Mrs Ewing was quite aware of that – this was the reclaiming of history. It was of course then reinforced by a number of MSPs prefacing their oath of allegiance by reference to an older claim of right to the sovereignty of the people rather than the crown, once more mobilising history in the interests of contemporary politics.

These are contentious issues, but central to the theme of this chapter: getting history right or wrong takes second place to the power, the charge, of history. Let us begin with the French historian Ernest Renan's phrase 'getting history wrong': Renan's famous essay 'What is a Nation?' places 'history' at the centre of the nationalist project, but it is a history which requires careful interpretation. 'Getting history wrong' is the precondition of nationalist history because it requires not only collective remembering but also collective forgetting. This 'forgetting,' said Renan, 'I would go so far to say historical error, is a crucial factor in the creation of a nation, which is why progress in historical

---

* A fuller account of the argument appears in McCrone, *Understanding Scotland: the sociology of a nation*, 2nd edn (London, 2001).

studies often constitutes a danger for [the principle of] nationality'.[1]

This makes it sound as though only nationalists are bad historians, but Renan was making a more general point. Renan was himself, as a French citizen, making a 'nationalist' claim, as he delivered his lecture at the Sorbonne in 1882, in the aftermath of the Franco-Prussian War after which Alsace and Lorraine were annexed by the Prussian state. Renan's remark that nationalism requires a 'daily plebiscite' was also made in the course of this lecture to counter the view that these territories were 'objectively' part of the Reich. Not so, said Renan, for governance requires the active and ongoing commitment of people – a 'daily plebiscite'. We will return to Renan's seminal essay later in this chapter, for he provided an analysis which was remarkably prescient and modern. 'To have common glories in the past, a common will in the present; to have accomplished great things together, to wish to do so again, that is the essential condition for being a nation.'

Let me take another example of the claim to history which might surprise us somewhat. In November 1993 the Secretary of State for Scotland, Ian Lang, wrote in *The Scotsman* newspaper that the historical event he would most like to have attended as a 'fly on the wall' was the battle of Bannockburn. He wrote: 'I would like to have been on the field of Bannockburn on 23–24 June 1314 to see the most decisive battle in Scottish history: the victory of Robert the Bruce's Scots over Edward II's English army'. What is going on here? Why should the leading Scottish politician of a party so thirled to defending the Union make such an ostensibly nationalist statement? The victory, wrote Lang, finally and firmly asserted Scottish nationhood. He concluded: ' From then on, as a nation, we have never looked back. So much so that it was our king James IV [sic] who succeeded to the throne of England in 1603: and it was his great grand-daughter – another Scot – who oversaw the Union of the nations of Scotland and England in 1707. That is the real legacy of Bannockburn, and it is one of which I am very proud. That is why I would like to have been there in 1314.'[2]

In many ways, the dissonance lies in our own judgement of these matters. These days we have grown used to a view that you cannot be a Unionist and a nationalist at the same time. The politics of our day have quite ruled out reconciling the two constitutional positions, reinforced by the fact that the Conservatives and the Scottish National Party are at opposite ends of the constitutional spectrum, and bitter political rivals.

---

[1] E. Renan, 'What is a Nation?', originally published in 1882, reprinted in H. K. Bhabha (ed), *Nation and Narration* (London, 1990), 11.
[2] *The Scotsman*, 27 November 1993.

And yet, as Graeme Morton's book of the same name spells out 'unionist nationalism' was at least the dominant political approach for much of the nineteenth century.[3] Ian Lang was simply restating its modern equivalent. Only because Scotland fought for and won its Independence in 1314 could it take its place ultimately as a sovereign and co-equal partner in the post-1707 British state. 'A Partnership for Good' was the title of the government's White Paper issued after its unexpected victory in 1992, and meant as a bulwark against the forces of Home Rule ranged against it. It did not last, and Lang and his fellow Conservative MPs were routed in 1997. 'No Lang noo' was the presumptuous but ultimately accurate slogan for his nationalist opponents in the debacle of that year.

That history should get caught up in the cut and thrust of modern politics surprises us little. And yet there is a deeper point than that. To paraphrase, it is not simply politicians never mind nationalists who get history wrong. 'History' is itself on the cusp of interpretation. It can lend itself to all sorts of uses and abuses. The 'facts are chiels that winna ding' school of history simply shakes its head and goes about its business, correcting the errors of a less well-informed public, but this is increasingly a forlorn task, and, above all, a rather thankless one in Scotland. History in Scotland is simply too central and too important an aspect of the politics of identity to be ignored in that way. For a start, there's simply too much of it about, and it is pretty thrawn. Willie McIlvanney touched on this in a newspaper article. Writing in The *Herald* on 17 March 1999, he commented:

> Not only was our history largely suppressed but those parts of it which were acknowledged were often taught in such a way that they seemed to appear suddenly out of nowhere. A sense of continuity was difficult to grasp. This was the pop-up picture school of history. Oh, look. There's Bonnie Prince Charlie. Where did he come from? And that's Mary Queen of Scots. Somebody cut her head off. Wasn't it the English?
>
> Moments of history isolated in this way from the qualifying details of context can be made to mean whatever we want them to mean. Our relationship to them tends to be impulsive and emotional rather than rational, since there is little for rationality to feed on. We see our past as a series of gestures rather than a sequence of actions. It's like looking in a massively cracked mirror. We identify our Scottishness in wilful fragments.

---

[3] G. Morton, *Unionist Nationalism: Governing Urban Scotland, 1830–1860* (East Linton, 1999).

We get a sense, then, of too much history rather than too little in Scotland, or, rather, the wrong sort. McIlvanney's explanation for this is that 'when a country loses the dynamic of its own history, the ability to develop on its own terms, its sense of its past can fragment and freeze into caricature. For a long time this was Scotland's fate.' The implication lies in that verb 'was', the past tense: history, however, stands every chance of being recharged as the present in contemporary Scotland.

Playing the game of history is a fairly common pursuit in Scotland. Visit any sizeable bookshop, and it will be by far the biggest section, somewhere between 'A hitchhiker's guide to but n' bens' and the 'Life and Times of the Midgie'. Much of this history gets written as a version of Scotland versus England, when even a cursory review of events and personages like Culloden, Glencoe, Mary Queen of Scots and so on indicates that life was much more complicated than that.

Nevertheless, historical events and processes can be threaded together in such a way as to present a continuous narrative. Pictish resistance to the Romans (and Saxons) reinforces the warlike reputation of the Scots, and allows film-makers to present the thirteenth-century Lowlander William Wallace as a third-century Pict. The Celts in general provide an important myth of origin, and an alternative set of values to southern Anglo-Saxons. The capture of St Andrew as Scotland's national saint owes more to the politics of ecclesiastical claims of the English diocese of York than to any actual connection of St Peter's brother, Andrew, with the northern kingdom. Claiming from the pope, Peter's successor, such high-level protection helped to see off the southern claim. It helped, too, that an apparition of St Andrew could be claimed by the Pictish king Hungus prior to his battle with the Anglian Athelstane in AD 345. Having recourse to the papacy in the fourteenth century by means of the self-styled Declaration of Arbroath helped to consolidate independence fought for at Bannockburn in 1314, even though the document only came to prominence at the end of the seventeenth century in a bid to stave off impending Union with England. Establishing legitimacy through history, this time as lineage, was the purpose of the deWit portraits of the early monarchs of Scotland in an attempt in the 1680s to shore up the regal claims of the late Stewart kings, Charles I and II.[4]

William Ferguson documents just how complex – and political – history

---

[4] S. Bruce and S. Yearley, 'The Social Construction of Tradition: The Restoration Portraits and the Kings of Scotland', in D. McCrone, D. Kendrick and P Straw (eds), *The Making of Scotland: Nation, Culture and Social Change* (Edinburgh, 1989).

can become. Explorations about founding peoples may seem arcane, but are central to debates about the national question.[5] In other words, what right does Scotland have to exist, and how can its existence be justified? Scotland's origin-myths have been a veritable battleground. Much rested on who the founding peoples were judged to be: the Scots or the Picts. John of Fordun in the fourteenth century tended to minimise the Pictish roots in favour of the 'Scots', that is, the Gaels from Ireland. The purport of his thesis was to counter English claims that thirteenth- and fourteenth-century Scots were Britons really, and hence descended from the same 'Trojan' roots as the English, so undermining Scotland's right to a political existence. Hector Boece, born in the second half of the fifteenth century, took the claim further forward by claiming that it was the 'Scots' who resisted the Romans, who conquered the Picts, and held out against the Norse and the English. He also subscribes to the 'forty kings' lineage of Scottish monarchs around whom much of the ideological battles over Scotland's origins were subsequently to rage. The Protestant reformer and historian George Buchanan in the sixteenth century was also a subscriber to the forty kings theory, and accepted that the 'Scots' had come from Ireland (not at all what our modern prejudices about staunch Calvinists would lead us to think).

Thomas Innes, Jacobite priest of the late seventeenth and eighteenth centuries, took the contrary view that the key founding peoples were the Picts, not the Scots (again, not what we would have predicted given Innes' religious politics). Innes helped to create what Ferguson calls Pictomania, which fed into the bizarre views of John Pinkerton a century later that not only were the Picts the true aboriginal peoples, but that they had Gothic (that is, Teutonic) roots – just like the English. James Macpherson of Ossian fame fell foul in the eighteenth century of massive anti-Scottish feeling in England, stoked by Pinkerton's celto-phobia, whose aim was to rubbish the origin-myths of the new junior partner in the British Union, the Scots. Ferguson makes the point that latter-day Unionists like Hugh Trevor-Roper were still employing celtophobic arguments to bolster their political beliefs.

We might be tempted to the view that all this is a travesty of proper history, and how on earth are we to judge claim and counter-claim. Ferguson argues that all post-Roman peoples had origin-myths in order to stake out their territorial claims as the empire collapsed. The medieval English appropriated the Brutus legend, of Trojan origin, from the

---

[5] W. Ferguson, *The Identity of the Scottish Nation: An Historic Quest* (Edinburgh, 1998).

Britons so that Edward I's claim to Scotland – heavily underwritten by Geoffrey of Monmouth's convenient interpretations – could be validated. It was no surprise then that the Scots mobilised the origin-legend of Gaidel Glas, who, depending on the version one reads, was either the husband or son of Scota, daughter of the Pharaoh of Egypt, and who came to Hibernia from Spain. The key point in all this is to emphasise that the Scots (and the Irish) were deemed to have quite different roots (Greek) from the English (Trojan).

Much of this strikes the modern reader as so much nonsense on stilts, but it has deadly serious import: whether or not Scotland had the ideological right to a distinct existence from England. After all, if the Scots were really the same people as their southern neighbours, then why should they have a separate state? Rubbishing the Ossianic myths also serves to validate political claims to the unity of these islands. The debate, of course, has moved on, but not perhaps as far we would like.

The *Braveheart* movie is a case in point. Critical and historical judgement about it is fairly negative. And yet, it has embedded itself in current political debates to a remarkable degree. The Scottish National Party takes by any account a civic rather than an ethnic view of nationalism, and yet it was happy to ride the wave of the Braveheart phenomenon, issuing leaflets outside cinemas with the message: 'Today it's not just bravehearts who choose independence – it's also wiseheads – and they use the ballot box.' On the other side were the words: 'You've seen the movie – now face reality.' To underline the message, Alex Salmond commented: 'The message is relevant today in that it is the Scots who are fighting for their independence the same way they are at the moment.'[6] In the slipstream of *Braveheart*, the SNP rose eight percentage points in the polls (the so-called 'Braveheart blip'), and membership applications rose to sixty per day. *Braveheart* might have been bad history, but it made good politics, at least for a time.

LIVING AND DEAD HISTORIES

All this might seem as so much froth to professional historians, but this would be to ignore or at least underplay the potency of history. Let us recall McIlvanney's comment about the impact of a country 'losing the dynamic of its own history' resulting in a fragmented and dislocated sense

[6] *Glasgow Herald*, 2 October 1995.

of the past. Recall too Marinell Ash's influential work in which she argued that Scottish history seemed to have 'died' at the point at which British history took over.[7] Her thesis that a concern, even an obsession, with the past was a compensation for the loss of a distinctive Scottish identity fitted into the view that Scotland was to all intents and purposes over:

> At the time that Scotland was ceasing to be distinctively and confidently herself was also the period when there grew an increasing emphasis on the emotional trappings of the past. This is the further paradox, and its symbols are bonnie Scotland of bens and glens, and misty shieling, the Jacobites, Mary Queen of Scots, tartan mania, and the raising of historical statuary.[8]

In Ash's argument we recognise the familiar view that history which is not allowed to flow along its 'proper' course takes on exotic and deformed shapes. There is perhaps something Whiggish about such a view, that history has a destiny with which one interferes with at one's peril.

Of course, all nations have 'histories' otherwise they would not exist as 'imagined communities'.[9] But history often does not have a future; it can be 'over'. In other words, we can find instances of 'dead' history which does not connect with present and future tenses, which is no longer deemed relevant. Similarly, history can be reconnected to the concerns of the present and future, and be made to 'live' again. This depends vitally on the use to which it can be put.

To exemplify this, let us examine the changing fortunes of Scottish and British 'history'. In the first case, it was deemed to have 'ended' in 1707, only to be reactivated in the second half of the twentieth century. In the case of Britain, the vitality of this 'forged' nation (as Colley describes it) seems to have ebbed away as a project for the future.[10] The two processes are clearly connected.

Scotland has no shortage of history; indeed, it can be argued that it has too much. By this we mean that for much of the past three hundred years Scotland was deemed to be 'over'. Its identity lay firmly in the past, obviously before the Treaty of Union of 1707, when it was an indepen-

---

[7] M. Ash, *The Strange Death of Scottish History* (Edinburgh, 1980).

[8] Ibid., 10.

[9] B. Anderson, *Imagined Communities: Reflections on the Origin and Spread of Nationalism* (London, 1996 edn).

[10] L. Colley, *Britons. Forging the Nation, 1707–1837* (Yale, 1992).

dent state. Thereafter, its elites came to believe that the future belonged to the political entity of 'Britain', whereas the past was Scottish.[11] This is best typified by the comment usually attributed to Walter Scott that the 'heart' was Scottish, but the 'head' British. In other words, while one could be culturally a Scot, politically progressive forces had to be British, for to be British was to be enlightened, rational and forward-looking. Construing identity as dual and complementary became the order of the day. As such, however, Scotland was 'over' by this time, and its history was deposited in the past. The future was British.

This line of historical thinking generated a powerful set of arguments, still extant today, that these constitutional processes led not only to a fragmented but a deformed history in Scotland. Terms like the 'Caledonian antisyzygy' are testament to an argument that the loss of a single historical dynamic generated a divided Scottish 'personality', the 'cringe', politics over culture, head over heart; Scotland, almost, as psychiatric condition.[12] All of this was mobilised in the past thirty years to explain the causes and consequences of the loss of Scottish statehood, and much of it was premised on a particular (one is tempted to say peculiar) view of the history of Scotland.

There was even a suspicion that Scotland was not really a nation anyway. Not only had its history come to an end, but it was lacking decent and distinctive cultural markers: language and religion being the obvious ones. Critics who would deny that Scotland was indeed a nation, and that nationalism in Scotland had any kind of future, fell back on instrumental and conjunctural explanations for the rise of nationalism (many preferred to call it 'regionalism') in the late twentieth century.

So far, so pretty depressing. Or is it? What this conventional critique lacks is any proper sense of perspective on two accounts: first, in the assumption that Scotland is in some fundamental way, unique or unusual; and second, that its own myth-history tells a simple and single story. Let us explore these in turn.

TRADITIONS AS INVENTIONS

The inventing of traditions, the title of a collection of essays edited by Hobsbawm and Ranger (1986), is nowadays treated with due suspicion,

[11] C. Kidd, *Subverting Scotland's Past: Scottish Whig Historians and the Creation of an Anglo-British Identity, 1689–c.1830* (Cambridge, 1993).
[12] T. Nairn, *The Break-Up of Britain* (London, 1977).

because we are better aware of the ways in which historical accounts are used as tools in the contemporary creation of political identities. We have grown used to the idea that history is not a product of the past, but a response to the requirements of the present. Indeed, we might say that all traditions are 'invented' in so far as they are constructed and mobilised for current political ends in some way or another. In this respect, there are no 'real' (as opposed to 'invented') traditions. The problem with this approach, however, is that it usually operates in a differential manner. The 'construction' of tradition is often a charge made against new or oppositional nationalisms rather than those of the 'centre', whose traditions are deemed matters of fact, because they are matters of power.

The conventional wisdom about inventing national traditions is that much of it occurred in Europe between the 1870s and the outbreak of the Great War in 1914. This, of course, was the period which saw the culmination of European national consciousness leading to its expression in 'world' warfare with its tragic consequences. In his useful review of 'mass-producing' traditions in this period, Eric Hobsbawm documents their role in state-building in the context of the extension of electoral democracy and the emergence of mass-politics. In d'Azeglio's famous phrase, 'We have made Italy; now we must make Italians'.[13] This was a particular problem for that state because the cultural raw material (language, symbolism and so on) was especially weak, and, we might argue with hindsight, never quite held together anyway, as the secessionary tendencies of the affluent north ('Padania') have made plain little over a century later.

The extension of the state into all corners of social life was typified by the simple postage stamp which became an implicit yet powerful icon of the nation, most obviously in the issue of historic stamps to celebrate jubilees and national occasions. In the case of the British state, it was not even thought necessary to put the name on the stamp, simply the head of the monarch, thereby reinforcing the sense of '*l'état, c'est moi*' quality of crown identity where people were defined as subjects rather than citizens. Postage stamps, along with coins and bank notes, as well as what Billig has called 'routine flags' served to deliver the 'banal' nationalism which the state required.[14] The supreme trick is to set up as the implicit national standard by a technique of non-naming.

---

[13] E. J. Hobsbawm, 'Mass-Producing Traditions: Europe 1870–1914', in E. J. Hobsbawm and T. Ranger (eds), *The Invention of Tradition* (Cambridge, 1986), 267.

[14] M. Billig, *Banal Nationalism* (London, 1995).

Thus, the British stamps do not mention the name of the state (being the first country to issue stamps is an obvious advantage); the English Football Association is 'the' FA, the English Rugby Football Union is simply RFU and so on. Other nationalisms were forced to be explicit about their naming by prefixing the national adjective ('Scottish', 'Irish', 'Welsh'), but the implicit standard was English which even denied its nationalism at all. (The parallels with implicit and explicit gendering are obvious.)

Where identities were or became problematic, these could not be taken for granted, as in the iconography of nationhood in Scotland, which has jealously guarded its bank notes and its national flag(s) from the taken-for-granted supremacy of the Anglo-British state, which has in any event allowed its state flag to become a symbol of English nationalism. In like vein, sporting occasions came to take on added political and cultural value from the late nineteenthth century as the nation was 'represented' in competition short of war. Thus the familiar social world, its dispositions, practices and routines, became habitualised and implicit, but carrying powerful messages about who 'we' are and where and who we had come from. Billig has captured this implicitness in his comment that 'the nation is flagged, but the flagging itself is forgotten as the nation is mindlessly remembered'.[15] The use of terms like 'we' and 'us' and 'around the country' acknowledge the sense of place. At the same time, the world is shrunk. The USA has its 'world series' in baseball (and Scotland its 'world pipe band championship'), so shrinking the world to the concerns of place and people.

MOBILISING HISTORY

The weight of research has been on the ways in which states mobilised national iconography in the nineteenth century with a view to strengthening political legitimacy at a time when extending the franchise was both necessary and risky for the status quo. Writers like Hobsbawm have no difficulty with such an interpretation, but tend to view similar uses by nationalists in the late twentieth century as inappropriate to the conditions of the times. Before we assess whether they are right or not, we ought to give some instances of the ways in which 'history' continues to be mobilised by nationalists today.

In their appeal to the voters of Quebec (slogan: *'Je me souviens'* – a

[15] Ibid., 143–4.

powerful form of Billig's banal nationalism which appears on all Quebec
car licence plates in the province) in the referendum in 1995 which it lost
narrowly, the Parti Québécois government mobilised the past as the ally
of the present as follows:

> The time has come to reap the fields of history. The time has
> come at last to harvest what has been sown for us by four
> hundred years of men and women and courage, rooted in the
> soil and now returned to it.
>   The time has come for us, tomorrow's ancestors, to make
> ready for our descendants harvests that are worthy of the
> labours of the past. May our toil be worthy of them, may they
> gather us together at last.[16]

The key descriptor in this passage is 'tomorrow's ancestors', which
encapsulates the seamless quality of the past, present and future, the
continuity and coherence of the people of Quebec moving, in Benedict
Anderson's phrase, 'up and down history'.[17] The images are those of
sowing and reaping in the 'fields of history', of 'harvests', of 'soil', of
'toil', of 'labours of the past' which cast a duty on the present incum-
bents and descendants of the early settlers four hundred years ago.
There can be little doubt what the present population was expected to
do, although insufficient of them did this duty to have Bill 1 pass.
    What we have here is an up-to-date example of what virtually all
states attempt, namely, the capturing of history in the national interest.
In Homi Bhabha's useful phrase, nations are like 'narratives' which tell
themselves and others stories about who they are and where they have
come from. History and the nation are inseparable. To recapitulate
Anderson's description: 'the idea of a sociological organism moving
calendrically through homogeneous empty time is a precise analogue of
the idea of the nation which is also conceived as a social community
moving steadily down (or up) history'.[18]
    The point about this mobilisation of history is that it is an exercise in
legitimation; it is not to be taken as a history lesson in the sense that it is an
accurate account of the past (although its authors clearly intend this to be
the case). We might characterise it as 'myth-history' in the sense that it sets

[16] Bill 1, an Act respecting the future of Quebec, preamble, Declaration of
Sovereignty, 1995.
[17] Anderson, *Imagined Communities*, 26.
[18] Ibid.

out to celebrate identity and associated values, and to describe and explain the world in which such identity and values are experienced. No amount (or at least not much) cold water can be poured over the 'facts' as presented in an attempt to wash them away with an accurate history. Just as there is no such thing as 'real' traditions as opposed to invented ones – all are invented, constructed, in Anderson's word, imagined – so tradition is an appeal to the present not the past. Karl Marx recognised this in his celebrated comment in 'The Eighteenth Brumaire':

> and just as when they seemed engaged in revolutionising themselves and things, in creating something that has never existed, precisely in such periods of revolutionary crisis, they anxiously conjure up the spirits of the past to their service and borrow from them names, battle cries and costumes in order to prevent the new scene of world history in this time-honoured disguise and borrowed language.[19]

The point Marx was making here is that inventing traditions is most often done precisely at the moment when change is being fostered, at the point at which it is necessary to mobilise the past as justification for going forward in a new direction. To present the future as a radical break with the past is difficult and dangerous, and while revolutionary regimes sometimes succeed in so doing, they frequently have to call up national, historic ghosts when it is necessary. After all, Stalin opted to mobilise a 'patriotic' war with all its historic richness against Hitler's regime in 1941. This, then, is the context in which the Scottish National Party, which steadfastly eschewed linking itself to an 'older' Scotland, has sought to make political capital out of the Oscar-winning movie.

NARRATING THE NATION

All in all, the 'past' is a powerful source of legitimacy for those who would change the present for a new future. Stuart Hall has pointed to the significance of 'discursive strategies' in the telling of national cultures.[20] The 'narrative' of the nation is told and retold through

---

[19] K. Marx, 'The Eighteenth Brumaire of Louis Bonaparte', in L. Feuer (ed.), *Marx and Engles: Basic Writings in Politics and Philosophy* (New York, 1959), 320.

[20] S. Hall, 'Introduction: Who Needs Identity?', in S. Hall and P. DuGay (eds), *Questions of Cultural Identity* (London, 1996).

national histories, literatures, the media and popular culture, which together provide a set of stories, images, landscapes, scenarios, historical events, national symbols and rituals. Through these stories national identity is presented as primordial, essential, unified and continuous. People of the late twentieth century are linked in a linear fashion with those of the distant past, even those, like fourteenth-century peasants in the case of the Hollywood movie *Braveheart*, with whom they manifestly would have little in common. To borrow the words of the English novelist, L. P. Hartley, the past is a foreign country. The national 'story' usually contains a foundation-myth, a story which locates the origin of the nation in mythic time, and which provides an alternative history or counter-narrative pre-dating ruptures or dispossessions. Becoming 'a nation again' is to evoke a future imaginable throughout the past. This nation is thought of as containing a pure, original people or folk.

Anthony Smith tries to capture this through his concept of 'ethnie' in which the myth of a common ancestry and shared historical memories are key elements. 'The sense of "whence we came" is central to the definition of "who we are".'[21] Similarly, actual history is often forgotten in favour of a foundational legend. Hence, the nineteenth-century liberation struggle in Greece claimed their legend of antiquity, as the founders of democracy who could not possibly be denied what they themselves had bequeathed to the rest of the world.[22] In like manner, claiming to be 'God's chosen people' is a common-enough feature of many ethnic/national groups for whom it cannot all be true (unless more than one God is imagined or he or she is promiscuous with favours). Hence, Jews, Muslims and denominations of Christians from Poles (Catholic) to Scots (presbyterian) to English (Protestant) are able to identify themselves in this favourable light, especially vis-à-vis 'Godless' nations, who may have superior force but not God on their side.

None of this is, of course, enough without a priesthood, religious or secular, which is able to read the appropriate runes, and to pronounce on the uniqueness of the nation. The intelligentsia provide the successors to the ecclesiastical priesthood. In Smith's words: 'Instead of being merely a chosen vessel of religious salvation and a passive recipient of divine ordinance, the "people" now become the source of salvation and the saints and sages of old become manifestations of the people's national genius.'[23]

---

[21] A. Smith, *National Identity* (London, 1991), 22.

[22] M. Herzfeld, *The Social Production of Indifference: Exploring the Symbolic Roots of Western Bureaucracy* (Oxford, 1992).

[23] Smith, *National Identity*, 64.

The role of the intelligentsia is to furnish 'maps' of the community, its history, destiny and place, as well as to furnish 'moralities' to inspire the public virtues expressing the national character.

The means of so doing was aided by the shift away from Latin to vernacular languages. English national identity, for example, was largely constructed by means of 'the book', linking Protestantism and the means of its dissemination through English.[24] Benedict Anderson shows how the development of 'print-languages' laid the basis for national consciousness in three ways: it created unified fields of communication and exchange which reached beyond and below the elite; print-capitalism gave a new fixity to language, manifested via official dictionaries, grammars and etymologies; and print-capitalism created languages of power such as 'standard English' and 'Hoch Deutsch', which were elevated to new politico-cultural eminence. This association of linguistic distinctiveness with national culture became so strong that language was often taken as the root, the expression of such culture, even when (as in the case of the Québécois) that language 'belongs' to another people. Similarly, where the vernacular language was absent (as in the case of the Scots, give or take debates about versions of 'English'), many scholars deemed this a considerable drawback for national self-determination.[25] Be that as it may, in Anderson's words: 'the convergence of capitalism and print technology on the fatal diversity of human language created the possibility of a new form of an imagined community, which in its basic morphology set the stage for the modern nation'.[26]

The 'capture' of history took its obvious expression in the founding of national museums in which the nation's 'heritage' could be shown to best advantage. The tale could best be told by constructing a narrative involving a golden age, a period in history when the nation was 'itself', and thence could be found again. The late nineteenth century was an important period for (re)constructing the national legends. In Ireland, for example, 'the vision of an ethnic golden age told modern Irish men and women what was "authentically theirs", and how to be "themselves" once again in a free Ireland'.[27] This was especially important in colonial situations in which people were culturally and ethnically treated as inferior. Finding one's culture was a key part of the national endeavour, not an optional extra.[28]

---

[24] L. Geenfield, *Nationalism: Five Roads to Modernity* (Harvard, 1992).
[25] Anderson, *Imagined Communities*, 90.
[26] Ibid., 46.
[27] Smith, *National Identity*, 67.
[28] F. Fanon, *The Wretched of the Earth* (London, 1967).

Where culture was missing, or at best, embryonic, it had to be 'made'. The Finns, for example, embraced the ballads and poems of the Kalevala, based as these were on Karelia, as their land of heroes, which was also part of the frontier of the nation in geo-political and cultural terms. If the region was the fount of the people's culture as well as a frontier zone, it had to be fought for, lest the culture disappear. Nor was Finland unique. As Neal Ascherson pointed out:

> We talk easily about the forging of a nation, but forgery has played a very real part in the foundation or revival of many nations. In Scotland, we should know that better than most. Ossian was a forgery, but the emotions about nations and history roused by James Macpherson's pastiche of genuine Gaelic myth cycles was real enough. Finland's national epic, the Kalevala, emerged rather later, but doesn't bear close inspection either. [29]

What this quest for a national culture did was to generate a search for, and a gathering together of, ethno-history. This took the form of setting up national galleries, museums and academies to capture and celebrate the nation. 'National' art was cultivated in the form of painting, sculpture, architecture, music and so on. If national art did not exist, then it was the role of artists to invent it, or at least discover or recover it from the fragments of the people's culture (hence, the interest in folk song and folk art). Many artists became in turn synonymous with national culture, as Smith points out, such as Chopin, Liszt, Dvorak, Bartok, Elgar, Verdi, Wagner, Grieg and Sibelius. He comments:

> It is the intellectuals – poets, musicians, painters, sculptors, novelists, historians and archeologists, playwrights, philologists, anthropologists and folklorists – who have proposed and elaborated the concepts and language of the nation and nationalism, and have, through their musings and research, given voice to wider aspirations that they have conveyed in appropriate images, myths and symbols. [30]

Hence, there is a strong, but by no means inevitable, association of a cultural renaissance with political developments. In those countries, like

[29] N. Ascherson, *Games With Shadows* (London, 1988), 61.
[30] Smith, *National Identity*, 93.

Scotland, where the association was more complex, many argued that its
national culture was 'deformed' and that this itself led to the failure to
pursue the political goal of independence.[31] Others argued that in this
regard Scotland was a deviant case (thereby reinforcing the dominant
thesis albeit obliquely), an exception which proved the general rule.
Having said that, the cultural renaissance of the 1930s and the 1970s
have both been linked to a political upsurge in nationalism, so that
Scottish exceptionalism need no longer apply.

MYTHOPOEIC AMBIVALENCE

We are now at the point in our argument at which we can explore once
more the key icons of Scottish history and culture. What we see is how
ambivalent they are, or rather the ways in which they can be mobilised
by quite different political-cultural viewpoints. Take William Wallace.
Graeme Morton describes him as 'a most efficacious patriot, one who
could be "remembered" by nationalists and unionists alike for their own
ends'.[32] Morton has argued that in the mid-nineteenth century a view
prevailed, echoed as we have seen by Ian Lang in the 1990s, that only
because Scotland won and retained her independence in 1314 was she
able to enter the Union of 1707 as an equal partner, with England, in the
British state. The National Association for the Vindication of Scottish
Rights, for example, which was founded in 1853, expressed a sense of
patriotism allowing it to proclaim admiration for its partner England.
Similarly, the erection of the monument in Edinburgh to Walter Scott,
which was begun in 1833, stressed the Scottish contribution to English
heritage. And perhaps more surprisingly (given Scott's political Tory-
ism) those who raised funds for the erection of monuments to the two
prime Scottish patriots William Wallace and Robert the Bruce did so by
stressing their contribution to the Union. The earl of Elgin, who claimed
descent from Bruce, took the chair at the inauguration in 1856 of the
movement to build the Wallace monument, and spoke in the following
terms:

> if the Scottish people have been able to form an intimate union
> and association with a people more wealthy and more

[31] C. Beveridge and R. Turnbull, *The Eclipse of Scottish Culture: Inferiorism and the Intellectuals* (Edinburgh, 1989).
[32] Morton, *Unionist Nationalism*, 188.

numerous than themselves, without sacrificing one jot of their neutral independence and liberty – these great results are due to the glorious struggle which was commenced on the plain of Stirling and consummated on that of Bannockburn . . . And, gentlemen, if time permitted, I would even undertake to show that it is the successful struggle carried on under Bruce and Wallace that it is that it is showing that the Union between Scotland and England has not only been honourable to the former but profitable to the latter . . . [With reference to the troubles in America and Ireland] I believe, therefore, that if the whole truth were to be told in this matter, we might show that England owes to Wallace and Bruce a debt of obligation only second to that which is due to them by Scotland.[33]

What we have here is a nice instance of how history can be mobilised for political purposes quite different from what we would expect today, for in the early twenty-first century Wallace and Bruce are icons of independence not Union (see, for example, the genre of heroic movies on the subjects). There is another twist to the Wallace/Bruce representation which speaks to the present, an embryonic class conflict, with Wallace the commoner and Bruce the aristocrat. The late Marinell Ash gave an interesting account of this construction, pointing out that popular histories often treated Wallace as the plain-speaking-forerunner of democracy and Bruce as the devious aristocrat, a piece of myth-history employed by the makers of the Hollywood movie *Braveheart* to give it added impetus to current political concerns.

The ambivalent play of Wallace by nationalists and by Unionists reveals the complexity of the iconography. Wallace does not 'belong' to any single political ideology. Similarly, we can find radical and conservative versions of Robert Burns: compare, as they say, 'be Britain still to Britain true, amang oursels united', with 'sic a parcel o' rogues in a nation'. Likewise, Jacobitism lends itself to both radical interpretations as well as the more conservative, aristocratic modes.[34] Nor is it simply a questions of people and events. The Scottish myth of egalitarianism – captured in the lad o'pairts, Jock Tamson's bairns and the democratic intellect – has a radical and a conservative take. The former stresses that social inequality is at odds with the Scottish mentalité, whereas the conservative places the emphasis upon equality of opportunity whereby

[33] Quoted in Morton, *Unionist Nationalism*, 177.
[34] M. G. H. Pittock, *The Myth of the Jacobite Clans* (Edinburgh, 1995).

everyone has the same chance of success, and achievement results from merit and hard work. Similarly, one can claim Walter Scott as both nationalist and Tory. The point of these instances is to remember that ambivalence and flexibility are built in to national iconographies, and are not the preserve of one or other ideology.

RENAN REVISITED AND BACK TO HISTORICAL ERROR

Let us now return to Renan's argument about historical error. The purpose of his essay was not to show that nationalists made especially bad historians, but to pinpoint the key issue of what we might call 'active forgetting'. Renan shows that one cannot define a nation by some set of key characteristics. Hence, he reviews and dismisses the usual suspects: race? – ethnographic considerations have played no part in constituting modern nations; languages? – but these are historical formations which tell us very little about the roots of those who speak them; religion? – there is plainly no state religion in any meaningful sense, even in the 1880s; geography? – 'but it is no more soil than it is race which makes a nation'; dynasty? – important though this was in state formation, a nation can exists without a dynastic principle; community of interest? – yes, but 'a *Zollverein* [customs union] is not a *patrie*'. What is left, then? Simply put, 'a nation is a soul, a spiritual principle'. By this Renan means something very similar to Ben Anderson's 'imagined community', that is, a community of the imagination (not, of course, imaginary). Renan develops this point:

> Two things, which in truth are but one, constitute this soul or spiritual principle. One lies in the past, one in the present. One is the possession in common of a rich legacy of memories; the other is present-day consent, the desire to live together.

In short, the past and the present coincide. Renan cites the Spartan song: 'we are what you were; we will be what you are'; the present connecting with the past, and thence to the future. That is what is captured in the descriptor by which this chapter is titled: 'tomorrow's ancestors'. In this construction, history is of central importance. Renan develops this point:

> A heroic past, great men, glory (by which I understand genuine glory), this is the social capital upon which one bases a national

idea. To have common glories in the past and to have a common will in the present; to have performed great deeds together, to wish to perform still more – these are the essential conditions for being a people.[35]

This vocabulary, which speaks of a heroic past, glory, the spiritual, is not one which is tailored to our early twenty-first-century age, but beneath the terms lies a very modern sense of the nation as being at the confluence of time and space, history and geography. The connection between late nineteenth-century and early twenty-first-century understandings of nationalism is captured by Benedict Anderson's interesting comment in the later editions of *Imagined Communities* (1996), which seeks to correct an earlier comment on Renan's 'need for forgetting'. The original comment by Renan was: 'tous citoyen français *doit avoir oublié* la Saint-Barthélémy, les massacres du Midi au XIIIe siècle'. Anderson accuses himself of 'peremptory syntax' in the 1983 edition by reminding himself that Renan did not say '*doit oublier*' but '*doit avoir oublié*' ('obliged to have forgotten'). That is, says Anderson, 'in effect, Renan's readers were being told to "have already forgotten" what Renan's own words assumed they naturally remembered!'[36] In other words, the state is reminding every French person of a series of antique slaughters which had become 'family history'. 'Having to "have already forgotten" tragedies of which one needs unceasingly to be 'reminded' turns out to be a characteristic device in the later construction of national genealogies', a new form of consciousness unique to modern times, a remembering/forgetting trope.[37]

Nations and forms of national consciousness always involve treating them as 'narratives', stories or accounts of a people which involves construction and interpretation, a refashioning of the persona and events of history. People are both historical 'objects' as well as contemporary 'subjects', who make their own narrative out of the fragments of the past. In this context, Scotland is not some strange and exotic abnormality in the story of nations. History tells us that we are much more normal than we have given ourselves credit for.

[35] Renan, 'What is a nation?'
[36] Anderson, *Imagined Communities*, 200.
[37] Ibid., 201.

Index

Sobieski Stuarts, 191, 199
Sociology, 9
Solemn League and Covenant, 121, 123, 142
state power, 91–3, 96, 97
Stevenson, Robert Louis, 143–4, 205
Stewart, Rev. Archibald, 133, 136
Stewart, Charles Edward, 193, 255
Stewart, James, 124
Stewarts, 31, 36, 52, 55, 59–60, 119, 123, 129, 141, 163, 172, 199, 218, 229
Stirling, 55–6, 58, 137, 211
Stone, Lawrence, 155, 157–8
Stone of Scone, 16, 26, 188, 203
Stuart, Gilbert, 2, 5

Tacitus, 151
Taitt, Alexander, 172
Tanner, Roland, 109
tartan, 191, 193–4, 199, 210–14
teutonism, 177, 179, 196, 257
three estates, 40
Tytler, Patrick, 42

Ulster, 8, 170, 185–9
Union, dynastic, 63, 104, 167, 219, 254, 256
Union, Political, 124–5, 128, 137, 173, 194, 202, 204–5, 207, 210, 225, 228–9, 259, 268
Unionism, 196, 251, 254, 257
United States, 145

Vickery, Amanda, 229
Victoria, 8, 197–8, 200, 202–3, 209 passim
volunteers, 220

Wales, 32, 51–3, 70
Walker, Patrick, 131
Wallace, William, 1, 75–6, 143, 226, 230, 238–9, 268–9
Wardlaw, Walter, 27
Wars of Independence, 7, 17, 25, 29, 32, 35, 38–9, 47, 60, 62, 71, 171, 175
Wars with England, 154
Watt, Donald, 12
Whiggism, 96, 109, 119, 129, 142, 171, 173, 205, 230, 231, 259
Wigtown Martyrs, 130–2, 134–5, 137
William I (the Lion), 21, 218
Williamson, Arthur, 118, 154
Wilson, Margaret, 131–2, 134, 136
Wodrow, Robert, 127–31, 135, 137–8, 144
women, 4, 8, 130, 132–4, 137, 205, 223, 225 passim
Wood, Wendy, 203
working-class, 226
Wormald, Jenny, 82
Wyntoun, Andrew of, 38–9, 47, 51, 59, 61, 65

Yeats, W. B., 200